PROGRESSIVE HOLLYWOOD

Published by The Disinformation Company Ltd.
163 Third Avenue, Suite 108
New York, NY 10003
Tel.: +1.212.691.1605
Fax: +1.212.691.1606
www.disinfo.com

Library of Congress Control Number: 2004114764

ISBN-13: 978-1-932857-10-8
ISBN-10: 1-932857-10-9

Cover Art: Brian Paisley
Design: Hedi El Kholti

All photos are by Ed Rampell unless otherwise noted. Photos on pages 65–68 are courtesy of the Academy of Motion Picture Arts and Sciences.

Printed in USA
10 9 8 7 6 5 4 3 2 1

Distributed in the USA and Canada by:
Consortium Book Sales and Distribution
1045 Westgate Drive, Suite 90
St Paul, MN 55114
Toll Free: +1.800.283.3572
Local: +1.651.221.9035
Fax: +1.651.221.0124
www.cbsd.com

Distributed in the United Kingdom and Eire by:
Turnaround Publisher Services Ltd.
Unit 3, Olympia Trading Estate
Coburg Road
London, N22 6TZ
Tel.: +44.(0)20.8829.3000
Fax: +44.(0)20.8881.5088
www.turnaround-uk.com

Attention colleges and universities, unions and other organizations: Quantity discounts are available on bulk purchases of this book for educational training purposes, fund-raising, or gift giving. Special books, booklets, or book excerpts can also be created to fit your specific needs. For information contact Marketing Department of The Disinformation Company Ltd.

PROGRESSIVE HOLLYWOOD

A People's Film History
of the United States

By Ed Rampell

Bobby Lees in interview with author.

DEDICATION

In less than a year, Progressive Hollywood lost three of its giants: Marlon Brando, Arthur Miller, and Bobby Lees:

Dedicated to **Marlon Brando**, America's angry angel, who not only gave us many of the screen's most moving moments, but played his greatest role off-screen, when he enabled an American Indian to provide us with Oscar's greatest political moment.

Dedicated to **Arthur Miller**, who when called before the House Un-American Activities Committee in 1956, refused to name names. Miller was cleared on appeal in 1958, and remained a voice of conscience throughout his life.

Dedicated to my friend **Bobby Lees**, the blacklistee, who made children of all ages laugh, and taught us all how to fight the good fight and still go on to live a happy, long life.

ACKNOWLEDGEMENTS

Even for an auteur, a film is a collective enterprise. And so it is for a book, and this movie history would not have been possible without the professional and personal support of a number of people, whom I'd like to recognize and thank here.

This film history evolved out of discussions with Italian journalist Beatrice Cassina. My literary agent, Diana Finch, provided invaluable guidance, insight and direction, combined with resoluteness, perseverance and patience, for which I am very grateful.

The savvy, generosity and youthful enthusiasm of the well-connected Ina Howard make her an indispensable force for the left's literary lions. Ina has much to offer the world of leftist letters, as a publicist, insider and advocate for writers and readers alike. *Mahalo nui loa!*

I am especially appreciative of the gang of five at Disinfo: publishers Gary Baddeley and Richard Metzger, who put their faith in me, gave me a shot and made me a "contender." My editor Jason Louv, who patiently chipped away at the marble to find the statue within. Marketing director Anne Sullivan, who promoted our book. Plus Ralph Bernardo and the rest of the Disinfonauts, for their work and help.

Film historian and author Dave Wagner read a portion of the manuscript and provided greatly appreciated feedback and wisdom, as well as encouragement along the way. My longtime Hunter College film school buddy, CUNY-TV program manager Brian Camp—who has the most encyclopedic cinematic mind of anyone I've ever met—likewise gave me advice, needed info and support. I'd also like to give a shout out to Luis Reyes, who played an indispensable role in launching my career as an author of movie history books.

I'd also like to express my gratitude to investigative reporter Greg Palast.

Carried within me always is the knowledge that I was fortunate enough to receive from my beloved Hunter College film professors. First and foremost my mentor, the Czech director Jiri Weiss, who also invited me to study at Richmond College and whom, alas, we lost in 2004 at age 90-something. I greatly value my ongoing relationship with my then-professor, now department head at Hunter, Joel Zuker. I'd also like to single out my other film professors, including Ken Roberts, Dick Tomkins and Emilie de Brigard. Without the enduring wisdom they instilled in me, the heart truly would have been a lonely Hunter.

The acknowledgements for this book would be incomplete without recognizing my early political mentors: Sammy Wohl and Nicky Licari, for whom my affection and gratitude for showing me the light remains undimmed. Collectively, they are truly the Salt of the Earth.

I am eternally grateful to Brian Paisley, that modern day Daumier, for creating the best cover for a pop project since *Sergeant Pepper's Lonely Hearts Club Band*. Brian's unflagging talent, patience, enthusiasm, innovativeness and good humor made this band less lonely and my heart fuller. Who would have thought that a byproduct of writing a book would be finding a new friend?

On a personal note, this book would not have been possible without the love, nurturing and support bestowed upon me by Alma and my parents that sustained me throughout the long literary march. I am also especially grateful to Mom and Dad for not having me until they bought a TV set and for teaching me to love the movies (which are, after all, better than real life, as Truffaut observed). Before I could read, I drove them nuts asking them to tell me the names of the movies displayed on theater marquees until, in exasperation, they ran out of patience and came up with the stock answer: "Three Blind Mice and a Rat Like You." For a few years, I thought this must be the most popular movie on Earth, until I finally and happily learned how to read. In any case, throughout the years, my parents generously and kindly encouraged my love and study of the movies. A film historian is, of course, a person with a mind filled up with totally useless information—unless he/she records it in tangible form. I hope that my folks will find this book to be worthwhile and worth the wait.

So you see, dear reader, a book is a collective undertaking. If you enjoy this film history, the credit is to be shared with all of the above. If not, it wasn't a case of too many cooks ruining the soup—you'll only have the master chef to blame. As I say whenever a movie's about to begin: "*Bon appetite.*"

TABLE OF CONTENTS

PREFACE

This is a book of celebrity journalism—but celebrity journalism with a difference. In our starstruck society, reporting on artists' offscreen activities usually stresses titillating private life and courtroom scandals, romances, peccadilloes, fashion and the like.

For instance, shortly before the 2004 Academy Awards ceremony, the *Los Angeles Times'* "Calendar" section ran a cover story about the then-13-year-old Keisha Castle-Hughes, a New Zealand Maori and the lead actress in *Whale Rider*. The cutesy article stressed the hairstyle, fashion and kid-like demeanor of the youngest female to ever be nominated for the Best Actress Oscar. While it mentions *Whale Rider*'s gender issues in passing, the story—by a writer who obviously hadn't been to New Zealand—never mentions the indigenous ethnic pride aspect of the movie. *Whale Rider* is about a girl who leads a tribal resurgence of Maori culture in a country where natives have become an oppressed minority and are outnumbered ten-to-one by the descendants of British settlers. Although readers would not have learned this from the *Times* piece, they would have found out scintillating tidbits such as what Castle-Hughes' favorite cartoon was and that she wipes her nose with her hand.

The Maori actress Rena Owen won numerous Best Actress awards at international filmfests for 1994's *Once Were Warriors*, appeared in two *Star Wars* episodes and is now planning to produce an epic about pre-colonial New Zealand based on the novel *Behind the Tattooed Face*, that would star Castle-Hughes. Owen told me: "*Whale Rider* has a universal theme of the preservation of culture." Owen described her countrywoman as "a very wise, intelligent young soul... I personally have a lot of expectation on her little shoulders," Owen said of Castle-Hughes.

And when the Dixie Chicks faced a press line during a December 2003 ACLU event at the Beverly Wilshire Hotel, a *People* magazine reporter asked questions like: "Will you shop for holiday gifts online or in stores?" As the reader will see, I preferred to ask the then-besieged Chicks and their manager about the First Amendment instead.

The point is that in our celebrity-obsessed culture, most reportage about people in the public eye emphasizes the trivial, tabloidy and salacious. In contrast, this book focuses on when actors, directors, producers and writers do something substantive, and what happens when they do. In particular, when talents take a stand on the issues of the day, off- and onscreen. Especially when they dissent from, and risk the wrath of, the powers-that-be in doing so. You are entering a gossip-free zone.

Since the silent screen, there have been progressive voices and visions in American cinema but, in general, I do not cover the handful of artists who single-handedly challenged the status quo as lone wolves. For example, worthy as they are, I don't detail the outstanding films of Stanley Kramer during the 1950s, or those that Oliver Stone produced during the Reagan era. Rather, in this people's film history of the United States, I zoom in on what I identify as the three key periods in American movies (and to a lesser extent TV) when left-leaning filmmakers formed a distinctive trend on- and offscreen. That is, when artists as a group influenced politics in the streets and on the screens, and found receptive mass audiences for their ideas and messages. Occasionally, I'll also mention artists who work in other mediums and are from other countries, where especially relevant.

Inevitably, in such a sweeping movie history book that covers several decades and periods of cinema, and literally hundreds of movies, I will leave out some readers' favorites and so on. In particular, the politics of 1930s and 1940s Hollywood movies and their aftermath have been exhaustively covered elsewhere, by participants and film historians alike. I apologize in advance for any oversights and welcome your additions and insights. Thanks for your understanding on this score.

Some may disagree with my categorization of certain films as "political," arguing that while movies such as the 1969 *Che!* may be about politics, they are not political pictures *per se*. I actually do think that this argument has some merit, but since this is a book primarily about cinema, and not politics or philosophy, I use the term "political" as shorthand.

To me, movies are our collective dreams, full of symbolism. My method of unraveling the inner meanings of films is, in part, drawn from Freud's *Interpretation of Dreams*, placed within a broader societal context. Ideas do not fall from the sky, but are created by humans in their interaction with each other and nature.

For instance, what do the following have in common: "My Favorite Martian," "I Dream of Jeannie," "Bewitched," "Mr. Ed," "My Mother the Car," "The Addams Family," "The Munsters," "Green Acres" and "The Beverly Hillbillies?" All were 1960s TV sitcoms involving different types of characters living with and near one another. The protagonists ranged from people of different social classes to supernatural creatures to extraterrestrials to talking animals or vehicles. As the civil rights movement swept America and posed the question of integration, commercial television generally forbid the airing of series that explicitly dealt with the issue of racial coexistence until (more or less) 1968's "Julia," starring African American actress Diahann Carroll.

Yet the aforementioned sitcoms were emanations of the collective unconscious that regularly dealt with the subject of assimilation in a metaphorical manner. They all attempted to answer the quintessential question that Rodney King would later pose in the aftermath of the L.A. riots: "Can't we all get along?" As in dreams, the superego (i.e., the exigencies of corporate-owned network TV, with advertisers, government agencies, lobbying groups, etc. that pressure programmers) may repress an idea of the id—but that doesn't mean it simply disappears. Rather, a compromise takes place, wherein the original idea is disguised through symbolism and expressed in a form that's more acceptable to the censorial superego. The use of humor in the sitcom format further made the deadly serious topics of race relations and integration more palatable to mass audiences. Viewers may not have been able to process a series about Martin Luther King, SNCC or Stokely Carmichael—but they could dream of Jeannies and other creatures or distinctive people cohabitating with human others.

I want to clarify the use of the term "Communist." When used with a capital "C," this generally refers to members of the Communist Party (particularly of the United States of America), and to this organization's political line. The CPUSA and other "official" Communist Parties usually supported the Soviet Union (and eventually other socialistic states) and, until his death, Joseph Stalin. In this book, former Communists elaborate on what they believed in and fought for in their own words. However, it should be noted that the Communist Party line is not automatically synonymous with Marxist and socialist philosophy and politics *per se*, and that within the left there have been different interpretations as to what communism, etc., are. Those to the left of the U.S.S.R., including little "c" communists such as the Trotskyists, as well as anarchists, pacifists and others in the left opposition, have differed with Moscow and CP policies over the years. However, as this is a film history and not a discourse on left-wing worldviews, this book will only touch on these issues sparingly and where relevant.

"Hollywood" refers to a geographic location, the entertainment industry, the creative community and a state of mind. In this book, I often use "Hollywood" in a very broad sense. So, in a book on "progressive Hollywood," I write about L.A. studio-based as well as independent filmmakers, who may operate outside of the majors' production and distribution system. This includes numerous documentarians and a few foreign cineastes whose work can be seen in the U.S. To the extent that "Hollywood" has become synonymous with television and movie production, I hope the reader will indulge me in my rather promiscuous use of the word.

Likewise, another word that is often used—but rarely defined—is "progressive." In this book, I shall try to define what "progressive" means in the early 21st century.

The most telling thing about the 2004 film *Team America: World Police* is that when the American left rises to resist the puppet government and support the peace movement (albeit as dupes of a diabolical Kim Jong II), who do Trey Parker and Matt Stone depict as leading the charge? No, not Ralph Nader, Howard Zinn, Noam Chomsky, Jesse Jackson, Gloria Steinem, Al Sharpton, Betty Friedan, Cornel West, Michael Eric Dyson or other leading left-leaning lights often associated with the antiwar movement and other causes. Rather, in *Team America* Michael Moore, Alec Baldwin, Sean Penn, Tim Robbins, Susan Sarandon, Helen Hunt, Janeane Garofalo and other actors provide the face of the left, and pick up the mantle of peace.

Progressive Hollywood traces the history, roots and legacy of film artists and their causes, from the Good War to the Vietnam War to the Iraq War, from the Great Depression to the Great Society to Bushworld. What is it about the creative personality that leads so many talented people to identify with the oppressed, the wretched of the Earth, *les misérables*? To fight for peace, the poor and dispossessed—even at great risk to their own individual safety and careers? I hope that *Progressive Hollywood* illumines why so many artists empathize with the downtrodden and support humanitarian causes.

FOREWORD

BY GREG PALAST

When OpEdNews.com asked me which journalists I appreciated, valued and respected, Ed Rampell was one of the five I named, right up there with Seymour Hersh and the *Nation*'s John Nichols. Who, you might say?

Rampell was a student revolutionary who majored in cinema at Hunter College on Park Avenue. When he graduated in the 1970s, Rampell was in a state of shock, asking: "Holy shit man, where's the revolution?" When he realized that he wasn't about to become the Sergei Eisenstein of another American Revolution, he resorted to an attractive "Plan B"—running away to Tahiti, Bora Bora, Pago Pago and other South Seas Islands. But during his search for paradise, Rampell encountered colonialism, militarism and nuclearism, and he emerged as one of Oceania's leading journalists. As a foreign correspondent, Rampell reported on indigenous rights and the nuclear free and independent Pacific movement for Radio Australia, Radio New Zealand, *Newsweek*, Reuters, *AP* and many other news outlets.

Rampell was the investigative reporter for an ABC News "20/20" segment that proved that three young men had been wrongly convicted of assassinating the president of Micronesia. Underneath the murderous skullduggery was a U.S. scheme to turn nuclear free Palau into a Club Med for hydrogen bombs. The framed activists, following Rampell's exposé, were exonerated. But Rampell was subsequently sued for libel after writing a related story for *Honolulu* magazine. At the risk of going to jail, Rampell refused to name his sources. Happily, the libel suit was deemed to have no merit and thrown out of court.

You'll find Rampell's work these days in the "alternative press," that is, the unbossed and unbought weeklies where real journalism finds political asylum in near anonymity.

That frustrating obscurity is about to end with this hot little book from the Disinformation Company Ltd. *Progressive Hollywood* is the book Ed was literally born to write. He tells me his mother went into labor watching Jacques Tati's *Monsieur Hulot's Holiday*. Of course, how would Ed know? But that's Hollywood for you. His dad called him Ed after the great Edward R. Murrow, the broadcaster who pants'd Joe McCarthy. That could also be apocryphal, but in Tinseltown, anything can happen.

Like Jimmy Stewart in that 1939 Frank Capra classic, Rampell is our journalistic *Mr. Smith Goes to Hollywood*, who fearlessly filibusters for freedom of speech. Boldly, he dares to remind us that a card-carrying member of the Communist Party wrote the original *Mr. Smith*, and the positive role Reds played during that era, which helped make it Hollywood's Golden Age. Herein you'll find one of the most comprehensive chronicles of the revolutionary films of the sizzling sixties. And like *Mr. Smith*, Rampell is a tribune of the people who are building a new, post-9/11 oppositional culture, which is leading and inspiring the resistance to the men who would be kings.

Greg Palast, author, *The Best Democracy Money Can Buy: The Truth About Corporate Cons, Globalization and High-Finance Fraudsters*

Michael Moore holds the Eleanor Roosevelt Freedom of Speech award given to him by the Southern California Americans for Democratic Action on March 20, 2003.

Center is "Acting President" Martin Sheen, who plays President Josiah "Jed" Bartlet on "The West Wing." To the left, is Bradley Whitford, who co-stars as Josh Lyman, wearing an "Artists United to Win Without War" T-shirt. Sheen declares: "Let my country awake!" at an antiwar rally in Hollywood on February 15, 2003.

Daniel Benzali, costar of the CIA series "The Agency," and actress Mira Sorvino backstage at the rally.

PROGRESSIVE HOLLYWOOD

TAKES TO THE STREETS

"All the world's a stage, and all the men and women merely players:
They have their exits and their entrances."

— William Shakespeare, *As You Like It*

George W. Bush ran for the presidency as "a uniter, not a divider." True to his word, during the build-up to war with Iraq, over dubious national insecurity assertions that were subsequently proven to be completely false, President Bush united much of the country and world against him and his pro-war policies. And nowhere in America was a community more united in opposing the war and Bush than Hollywood. Movie and TV talents were among the peace movement's first responders to Bush-Cheney-Rumsfeld-Powell-Rice-Wolfowitz-Perle's unholy war, and became the public face of the antiwar cause.

In the mad march towards murderous mayhem, the Democratic loyal opposition proved to be more loyal to the administration than against it. A form of mass hysteria—what pacifist presidential contender and Democratic Congressman Dennis Kucinich called "a virus"—infected the corridors of power. The leadership of the Democratic Party, along with too many of its representatives and a majority of its senators, cravenly caved in to the Bush-oisie's war fever. The news media failed to expose the "bogus-documents-and-sexed-up-dossiers-r-us" pathological lying of the Bush and Blair administrations. As of this writing, the imminent threats posed by Saddam's weapons of mass destruction and Baghdad's links to the September 11th terrorist attacks have proved to be as elusive and mythic as magic carpets.

This is the inside story of how another power center across the continent—Hollywood, America's cultural capital—filled a political and informational void and rose up to oppose the nation's governance center.

Hollywood progressives did so by taking to the streets, cleverly utilizing the electronic media and doing what Hollywood does best: producing entertaining, thought-provoking films. Left-coasters used their star power to fill a crucial vacuum in the national debate on war and peace, and sparked resistance to the attack on Iraq. In doing so, the Hollywood left made a comeback in the 21st century, standing on the shoulders of previous generations of filmdom's progressives: makers of the 1930s/40s movies about the Great Depression and the war against fascism, plus the social protest cinema of the 1960s and '70s counterculture classics. This is also the tale of how stars paid the price for speaking out, as the empire struck back and the right wing sought to punish dissenting talents.

On March 20, 2003, as the Bush regime plunged the country into war, Michael Moore made an impassioned address to the Southern California Americans for Democratic Action's 20th Annual Eleanor Roosevelt Awards Dinner, mere days before winning the Best Documentary Oscar for *Bowling for Columbine*. Presaging his "Shame on you, Mr. Bush!" Academy Awards acceptance speech, Moore told the Beverly Hilton crowd—which included Jane Fonda, Chicago 8 "co-conspirator" Tom Hayden, populist columnist Arianna Huffington (who'd soon run in California's gubernatorial recall race), Connie Rice (whose evil cousin Condoleezza was Bush's National Security Adviser), Stuart Whitman, and others—that the left's top priority was ousting Bush from office. "This country can't survive another four years of a Bush administration!" thundered the Eleanor Roosevelt Freedom of Speech award winner, as he brushed aside "Michael Moore for president!" chants.

Celebrities were literally on the front lines, as well as backstage, using their star power at mass demonstrations that shook Los Angeles. On February 15, 2003, celebrities lent their high recognition factor to the front row of a march down, appropriately, Hollywood Boulevard's Walk of Fame. Indeed, the vanguard of this procession of tens of thousands of antiwar Angelenos consisted of talents who merited their own Walk of Fame stars. As they gathered and prepared for the parade and rally, I covered the scene and interviewed the stars. Suddenly, Tyne Daly—co-star of the feminist-conceived, Emmy-winning '80s cop series "Cagney & Lacey" and the currently-running family drama "Judging Amy"—dashed in my direction, excitedly shouting "Ed! Ed!", throwing me for a loop. Of course, I recognized the actress. But how did Daly know who I was? My wonder ended as Daly approached us, and warmly greeted the star I was interviewing—Ed *Asner*, the longtime activist and labor leader, as well as former president of the Screen Actors Guild.

Wearing designer sunglasses, *Prizzi's Honor* Oscar winner Anjelica Huston—the daughter and granddaughter of Hollywood royalty and Jack Nicholson's ex-main squeeze, who'd grown up in Ireland during the McCarthy era—alternately clapped and waved a peace sign with her right hand. On Huston's right, "White House assistant" Donna Moss, played by Janel Moloney on NBC's "The West Wing" series (which was to win the Emmy for best drama series for the fourth year in a row on September 21, 2003), marched, sometimes raising a clenched fist. Beside her was a bespectacled Daniel Benzali, co-star of the then-CBS CIA series "The Agency." To the left of Huston strode Reverend Jim Lawson in his clerical collar, the civil rights peace veteran and Pastor Emeritus of L.A.'s Holman United Methodist Church. Lawson had studied Ghandhian nonviolence principles in India, been jailed for draft resisting during the Korean War, taught and struggled alongside Dr. Martin Luther King and, in September 2003, would take part in the coast-to-coast Immigrant Workers Freedom Ride.

Beside Lawson was the purple beret-wearing Tyne Daly, as well as the goateed David Clennon, who'd played a federal prosecutor in 1987's "Conspiracy: The Trial of the Chicago 8" and Joshua Nankin on "The Agency," and was, in real life, the target of a right-wing Internet campaign to have him fired from the CIA drama. (Clennon's crime? Allegedly comparing Bush's America to Nazi Germany.) Beside Clennon, clad in an "Artists United to Win Without War" white T-shirt, walked Bradley Whitford, who plays "West Wing" executive branch aide Josh Lyman. Nearby were "Malcolm in the Middle" star Jane Kaczmarek and Rob Reiner, the actor/director/child advocate who'd portrayed "Meathead" on the classic '70s comedy series "All in the Family," TV-land's most prominent Vietnam War era peacenik. Christine Lahti walked beside Mike Farrell, who'd co-starred in the sitcom "M*A*S*H." Nearby trekked "West Wing" left-winger Martin Sheen, the veteran activist who portrays Democratic President Josiah "Jed" Bartlet. Like Farrell, Jamie Cromwell—who co-stars in HBO's innovative "Six Feet Under" series—wore an "Artists United" T-shirt. A child rode piggyback on the shoulders of this vegan, who'd appeared opposite a talking pig in *Babe*. Beside Cromwell, the bearded Richard Schiff, who plays President Bartlet's "West Wing" conscience Toby Ziegler, marched wearing a backwards baseball cap. On Schiff's left, Alfre

Woodard occasionally—like Farrell—took a bullhorn and sloganeered against social service cuts caused by a bloated military budget.

The star-spangled phalanx stretched across Hollywood Boulevard, carrying a huge white banner that read, in big bold black letters, "NO WAR ON IRAQ!" and beneath this, in red, "¡NO A LA GUERRA EN IRAK!" In front of the crusading artists, parade marshals maintained logistical order and security and, significantly, in the very front, a large press corps photographed, videoed and audio taped the talents and tide of humanity they led. Behind and above the celebs waved a gigantic "No War Against Iraq!" yellow banner.

Using their own creativity and consciences, individual marchers carried a sea of homemade signs, that read: "Protest is Patriotic," "No Blood for Oil," "Axis of Racism, Bush-Cheney-Ashcroft," "Peace Salaam Shalom," "Money for Education Not for War," "No War," "Healthcare Not Warfare," "The War Leaves Every Child Behind" and "Not in My Name." A skull and bones accompanied the words "Bush Family Evil Empire, Blood & Oil"; in black letters "Stop" above a mushroom cloud; in white letters against a red octagonal background the words "Stop Bush"; "Bush" in red letters, with a swastika where the "S" should be. On several placards, a white dove soared against a blue background, above the words "Think Peace"; Malcolm X peered down from another picket sign; a white peace symbol adorned a placard reading "War is Not the Answer." Earth and Palestinian flags flew.

As the multitude moved from the Pantages Theatre—site of many Oscar ceremonies, and where the Martin Short/Jason Alexander production of Mel Brooks' antifascist *The Producers* would open months later—past the Egyptian, El Capitan and Graumann's Chinese movie palaces and the cement-enshrined footprints of the stars—the mood was downright festive. The artists and people were joyously united by a shared sense of empowerment. Demonstrators chanted: "What do we want?" "Peace!" "When do we want it?" "Now!" and: "We say healthcare, Bush says warfare!"

The dissidents had broken out of the isolation—the fortress of solitude—reinforced by a highly individualistic, competitive society and formed a unified mass. Not only was a sense of solidarity generated by the thousands thronging down Hollywood Boulevard, but by reports of other mass mobs around the globe, as millions collected to head the gathering gloom off at the pass. As Rob Reiner said to cheers during his speech: "I am so proud to be amongst all of these folks in Los Angeles, who are joining an effort that's happening all throughout the world today! In hundreds and hundreds of cities, people just like us are speaking with one voice today, to send a message to the Bush administration that this war is not wanted!" Individuals stopped feeling alone, lonely and vulnerable. They came and felt fully alive, with renewed confidence in themselves, drawn from the strength of their numbers. They had found something bigger and more important than mere "me, myself and I": a just cause that gave their lives and actions meaning. There was a sense of sheer delight in seeing the people awakened, as at no time since the 1970s anti-Vietnam War mobilizations. They truly were—in the immortal words of Jefferson Airplane—"Volunteers of America."

While the Hollywood Boulevard vanguard consisted of professional actors, the rear guard showcased some guerrilla street theatre talent. An unsmiling young woman with long auburn locks dressed as the Statue of Liberty, in a green toga, crown and chains stood in the middle of the street. With a forlorn demeanor, the would-be Lady Liberty held her hand high in a peace sign. A sea blue globe revealing a green/yellow Western Hemisphere rested on the head of a man with gray muttonchops. Straddling the globe, clad in a faux-ermine robe fringed with white fur, sat a puppet wearing a grinning George W. Bush mask, and a fake, bejeweled golden crown, his white gloved hands grasping the world. A bumper sticker across King George's royal chest said it all, that ever-popular standby: "No Blood For Oil."

Parading in the thousands past palms and Hollywood souvenir stores, the people were riding in the saddle. Optimism reigned supreme; the U.N. inspectors would be allowed to continue their search for alleged weapons of mass destruction, and would stave off armed conflict. It was unthinkable that the clearly outnumbered Bush administration would pursue its mad designs on Baghdad. The aroused citizenry at home and abroad would thwart war, just as longhaired students in the '60s, armed only with the flowers they placed in the barrels of the guns of soldiers defending the Pentagon, ended the war in Vietnam. Above all, what animated the rank and file and front and center stars alike was that they were fighting the good fight, for the loftiest of noble causes: Peace on Earth. Hollywood Boulevard had, momentarily, been transformed into Dr. King's "beloved community." The beloved felt invincible, unbeatable.

All together now, they proceeded towards the rally site, but before the throng turned south, a huge billboard came into view just past the El Capitan. Large gold letters against a red background proclaimed: "The Only Thing White is the House," as Chris Rock, in a suit and tie, waved

Martin Sheen of "The West Wing" and James Cromwell of "Six Feet Under" at an impromptu press conference on Hollywood Boulevard.

Hollywood left stalwart Ed Asner.

During a press conference at the March 15, 2003 antiwar rally in downtown L.A., Reverend Jesse Jackson declares: "If the U.S. kills people and occupies Iraq, that's a war crime. And those who execute it must face an international court of justice."

from a podium in front of the presidential seal. The gigantic billboard advertised Rock's then-upcoming movie, *Head of State*, about the first African American president. This perfectly set the stage for what was to follow at the march's destination: a speakers' platform erected in front of La Brea and Sunset Boulevard.

An overflowing multitude of marchers stretched out from the makeshift open air stage, flanked by public address system equipment, conga and snare drums, keyboards and paparazzi. A large backdrop declaring (in English on the left, and Spanish on the right) "NO WAR ON IRAQ" was connected to a poster for L.A.'s Pacifica radio station, KPFK, 90.7 FM, which broadcast the rally live. Suddenly, the mood became electric as Martin Sheen emerged onstage, with the cast of the Emmy award-winning "West Wing" drama, Whitford, Molone and Schiff. Whitford enthusiastically introduced Sheen as "the acting president of the United States!" Hugging Whitford, Sheen seized the mike and amidst cheers and cries of "Sheen for president," declared, "Peace be with you."

The devout Catholic—who began his activism with the '60s draft records-burning Berrigan brothers and United Farm Workers union organizer Cesar Chavez, and has been arrested for civil disobedience 64 times—launched into a sermon critiquing Bush. "By some demented logic, [Iraq's] men, women and children are collateral damage, as the dogs of war slouch towards Baghdad. Lord, make us instruments of your peace!" Despite conservatives' then-recent calls for impeaching the fictional liberal TV president by firing Sheen, who'd also co-starred in *Apocalypse Now* and *Gandhi*, "President Bartlet" concluded with his arms outstretched: "Let my country awake!"

Rob Reiner declared: "It's unconscionable that in less than [18 months], since 9/11, this president has taken the goodwill of the world and turned it on its ear. He's driven a wedge into NATO, destroying our relations with the international community, divided [Americans]. Well, we're not gonna let him get away with it, we're not gonna fight this war!" During the long march, the former Meathead told me: "It's important for everyone to stand up against war, not just actors and celebrities. I'm just a person, I have a voice like everyone else, and if we look around the world—especially today—we see millions standing up against an utterly misguided policy," Reiner insisted.

Proving, as Mayakovsky wrote, that there's "no gray hair in his soul," the *eminence grise* of American letters and the left, Gore Vidal—prompted, he said, by Hollywood Boulevard—delivered a history lesson to the crowd, explaining "how the hell we got into this mess, with prosperity, peacetime in the world and now we're threatening preemptively to bomb countries that have done us no harm." As a mike screeched, the quick-witted Vidal quipped, "The Bush family is everywhere," to the laughter and applause of the audience.

The novelist/screenwriter/actor and World War II veteran mused: "I can recall thinking when I got out of the army in 1946, 'Well, that's that. We won. And those who come after us will never need do this again.' Then came the two mad wars of imperial vanity, Korea and Vietnam. They were bitter for us; not to mention for the so-called enemy. Next, we were enrolled in a perpetual war against what seemed like 'the enemy of the month club.' Remember Qaddafi, Noriega, Bishop in Grenada, Bush Sr. standing tall in the Gulf somewhere? This long war has kept major revenues going to military procurements, secret police, while withholding money from us taxpayers with our petty concerns for life, liberty and the pursuit of happiness," Vidal argued.

"No matter how corrupt our system became over the last century we still held onto the Constitution and, above all, the Bill of Rights," Vidal continued. "I have been discouraged at times, like all of you, but I always felt that the Republic was upon such a firm foundation that no one could undermine it. I never once believed that I would ever see a day like this. We, the people, should be obliged to march against an arbitrary and secret government, preparing wars for us to fight in. Sensibly, they leave the fighting to us. During Vietnam, Bush fled to the Texas Air Force. Cheney, when asked why he had avoided service in Vietnam, replied [in Cheneyesque voice]: 'I had other priorities.' Well, so did 15 million of us, 60 years ago, other priorities many were unable to fulfill.

"How did human events bring us here today, and all across the country? We can certainly blame the oil and gas hustlers who have hijacked the government, from the presidency to Congress to, most ominously, the judiciary." The throng applauded Vidal. "It was Benjamin Franklin who saw our future most clearly back in 1787, when he was a delegate to the Constitutional Convention in Philadelphia. He prepared a text, so dark a statement that most school histories omit his key words. Franklin urged the Convention to accept the Constitution in spite of all its faults. It might, he said, 'provide good government in the short term and may be a blessing to the people it will administer. This is likely to be well administered for a course of years, and only end in despotism, as other forms have done before it, when the people have so become corrupted as to need despotic government, being incapable of any other.' Franklin's prophecy came true in December 2000, when the Supreme Court bulldozed its way through the Constitution in order to select as their president the loser in the presidential election," accused Vidal, as the crowd gave him an ovation.

"Despotism is now securely in the saddle. The old Republic is a shadow of itself. And we now stand in the glare of a nuclear world empire, with a government that sees as its true enemy we, the people, deprived of our electoral franchise." Thousands applauded Vidal. "War is the usual aim of despots, and war is what we're going to get, unless—with help from well-wishers in Old Europe, and from ourselves, awake at last—we can persuade this peculiar administration that they're acting entirely on their own and against all of our common history..."

The septuagenarian author, who ran for senator of California in 1982 and is a scion of an eminent political clan that includes Al Gore, looked out at the crowd. "President John Quincy Adams said in the 1820s on the subject of our fighting to liberate Greece from Turkey: 'The United States goes not abroad in search of monsters to destroy. If the United States took up all foreign affairs, she might become the dictatoress of the world, but she will no longer be the ruler of her own spirit.' So, let us regain our lost spirit, and should we be allowed in 2004 to hold a presidential election here in the homeland, we shall realize that the only regime change that need concern our regained spirit or soul, is in Washington." The crowd exploded into applause, cheers and cries of "bravo," "God bless you," "thank you" and "Gore for president," followed by spontaneous outbursts of "Impeach Bush!"

Backstage, David Clennon, who'd opposed the first Gulf War and U.S. policies in Latin America, summed up the demonstrators' hopefulness: "Maybe we can stop the war. After what I've seen here today, I think maybe we have a chance. He's determined—but we're determined too," Clennon said wistfully. After all, the governments of key allies such as Germany and France opposed going to war, as did the United Nations, and most importantly of all, an overwhelming majority of the world's people. The L.A. march was part of the biggest protest ever held in world history, with more than 10 million participants.

Exactly one month later, at another L.A. march and rally, the zeitgeist had significantly changed from optimism to grim determination, as it became obvious that, come hell or high water, Bush was indeed going to attack Iraq. Like a cliché in a bad *film noir*, the elements expressed the crowd's mood. On March 15, 2003, monsoon-like rains swept through a not-so-angelic City of the Angels. A Melvillean, damp, drizzly November of the soul gripped antiwar Ishmaels hovering on the brink of the abyss, as an Ahab-like Bush monomaniacally hunted Sadaam's great white whale. Yet, despite a storm worthy of Pago Pago's rainy season, the determined masses turned out again in their tens of thousands.

This time, the multitude snaked its way through downtown L.A., led by a covered truck bearing Reverend Jesse Jackson, as the media walked beside the vehicle during the downpour. The soul anthem "War! What is it good for? Absolutely nothing!" blared repeatedly from the mother ship's loudspeakers.[1] Accompanied by rappers, Jackson alternately swayed rhythmically to the music and waved the peace sign.

About half-way through the march, though Jackson wore a cast or brace on one leg, he still managed to do something Bush couldn't do: The civil rights and peace leader stopped the protest dead in its tracks. Wearing a baseball cap and yellow slicker over a black turtleneck, the man who had been with Dr. King when he was assassinated descended from the truck's protection. Bad leg and all, Jackson strode towards the front line, which had halted and went on to part like the Red Sea before Moses. The crowd roared, elated that Jesse was joining them.

En route, as if out of nowhere, a lone bespectacled man wearing a black poncho and hood burst out of the crowd in a wheelchair. In his right hand, the gray bearded man held an umbrella, while he made the peace sign with his left. The crowd went nuts again when they realized it was Ron Kovic, the marine who was paralyzed in Vietnam, became an antiwar organizer and was portrayed by Tom Cruise in Oliver Stone's 1989 *Born on the Fourth of July*. After the perils of guerrilla warfare in Indochina, a little rain was nothing to Kovic when it came to acting to prevent another grand American imperial tragedy that, as it turned out, would result in thousands more casualties.

Backstage, under a relatively dry tent for speakers and the accredited press near L.A.'s federal building, Jesse was treated like rock

---

1. Eerily, Edwin Starr, who'd originally performed the anti-Vietnam War anthem, died two weeks later. Although banned by the Clear Channel radio monopoly, the song and its sentiments live on—not only at protests but at rock concerts. Bruce Springsteen opened his performances during his March 2003 Australian tour with "War."

Ron Kovic—depicted by Tom Cruise in Oliver Stone's 1989 *Born on the Fourth of July.*

royalty. I asked the Reverend about his statement that President Bush was arrogant. "This is not a fight of the U.S. versus Iraq; it's Bush versus the world," Jackson responded. "And to close the world out and dismiss it as a 'focus group' is to express utter contempt for the world. The fact is that if the U.S. kills people and occupies Iraq, that's a war crime. And those who execute it must face an international court of justice," Jesse asserted.

While Jackson delivered his keynoter, an aide invited me to join a small press conference after Jesse completed his speech. While I waited under the tent and the rain pelted the canvas, I spied Matthew Modine and Mira Sorvino, surprisingly slimmer than the curvaceous hooker she'd won an Oscar for portraying in Woody Allen's *Mighty Aphrodite.*

Finally, Reverend Jackson appeared for the press conference, presciently telling a handful of reporters: "For the record, there's 22 million Iraqis. We can destroy them militarily. But then [after] the destruction is the occupation. America occupying an Islamic country—that's where the real battle begins; that's where the Third World War begins." Like many other opponents of the war, Jackson correctly predicted—unlike the Bushwhackers, who promised that our conquering heroes would be welcomed as liberators with flowers in the streets—the perils that would face an occupying force in Iraq. Jackson went on to say, "To us, if Iraq is destroyed, then Iran becomes another factor. But while we focus on Iran versus Iraq, al Qaeda remains an imminent threat. They are less checked and more of a threat than Iraq," he also presciently added.

Some months later, I was watching Fox "News" talk show host Bill O'Reilly—whose trademark is bullying guests he disagrees with—interview some Caucasian guest about Reverend Jackson, not one of O'Reilly's favorite people. Much to the delight of the right-wing O'Reilly, the interviewee insisted that Jackson had, by and large, lost his following. O'Reilly gleefully agreed that Jesse was washed up as a black leader. But it's a funny thing—I don't remember seeing either O'Reilly or his whitebread guest covering the March 15 L.A. rally. If O'Reilly had actually bothered to wear out some shoe leather on the streets and report—instead of pontificate—he would've seen the rock star treatment Jackson was accorded by the marchers. And unlike O'Reilly and company, Jackson was factually correct in his prognostications about WMDs, the occupation, *et al.*

The February 15 demonstrations around the world were reportedly the largest protests in human history. A reported 10 million-plus demonstrators participated in the antiwar outpourings. In contrast to corporate globalization, masses of people discovered international solidarity. America had seen nothing like these recurring rallies—in L.A., San Francisco, Washington, D.C., New York (where a Republican mayor unsuccessfully tried to ban a mass mobilization under the pretext of "national security"), etc.—since the Vietnam War. Bush had discovered his inner Nixon, and politically conscious Americans appropriately responded late '60s/early '70s-style, in the streets in the millions, with TV and movie stars playing leading roles.

What did these ten million demonstrators know that the so-called "experts" in the CIA, Pentagon and Bush White House didn't? According to the United Nations Special Commission's on-the-ground weapons inspectors, Washington's own chief weapons inspector David Kay, the Iraq Survey Group report, the Senate Intelligence Committee's July 9, 2004 report, Lord Butler's July 2004 report, Charles Duelfer's October 2004 report and other authoritative sources, the Bush administration's assertions regarding Iraq's alleged WMDs were completely wrong. And the protesters got it right—along with their celebrity spokesmen.

Why did artists play such prominent, vanguard roles in the antiwar movement and galvanize so much opposition to attacking Iraq? Which key creative community activists spearheaded entertainment industry opposition to the Iraq War and Bush? How did the Hollywood left organize celebrities and help generate antiwar resistance? What was their strategy? And what are progressive Hollywood's historic roots, traditions and legacies?

ACT 1

THE CRIMSON ERA

NEW DEAL AND POPULAR FRONT PICTURES

"It's really interesting, you always wondered, people in politically charged films—what were the politics of those actors who were in those films?... It's always exciting and inspiring to see that even in the conservative and controlled atmosphere of Hollywood, with the profit motive operating as powerfully as it does, that it is possible for films to break through and exhibit a kind of progressive, even radical spirit."

— Howard Zinn, in an interview with the author

THE WAY THEY WERE: BETTER RED THAN DEAD

"It is a way of life, an evil and malignant way of life. It reveals a condition akin to disease that spreads like an epidemic. And like an epidemic, a quarantine is necessary to keep it from infecting this nation."

— J. Edgar Hoover, in the documentary "Blacklist: Hollywood on Trial"

The "it," of course, was communism, and the F.B.I. director was terrified that Reds would use mass media to disseminate Marxist ideas and ideals to American audiences.

He wasn't the only reactionary who feared the power of radical ideals and the reach and persuasiveness of motion pictures. Congressman J. Parnell Thomas, Chairman of the House Un-American Activities Committee, which included Representative Richard Nixon, declared: "This committee under its mandate from the House of Representatives has the responsibility of exposing and spotlighting subversive elements wherever they may exist. It is only to be expected that such elements would strive desperately to gain entry to the motion picture industry. Simply because the industry offers such a tremendous weapon for education and propaganda," proclaimed HUAC's grand inquisitor.

Did Communist Party members and other left-wingers try to and actually succeed in putting political messages into movies, as right-wingers charged? Liberals have long dismissed this allegation as nothing more than Reds-under-the-beds mass hysteria and paranoia. Director Eddie Dmytryk, one of the Hollywood Ten, said it was crazy to believe that radical filmmakers could put ideas into moving pictures that studio chiefs—who controlled film content, final cut and the ultimate production as released—wouldn't understand, but proletarian moviegoers would.

The Hollywood Production Code was a form of movie industry self-censorship and the Hays Office greatly restricted explicitly political screen statements. Appendix III of the Code stated: "Nothing subversive of the fundamental law of the land and of duly constituted authority can be shown. Communistic propaganda, for example, is banned from the screen." Cinema did not have First Amendment protections and guarantees. And accentuating the escapist role of movies such as the MGM musicals, Metro-Goldwyn-Mayer mogul Samuel Goldwyn is famously supposed to have said: "If you want to send a message, use Western Union."

However, Communist Paul Jarrico said in the 1996 American Movie Classics documentary "Blacklist: Hollywood on Trial": "One of the recurrent conflicts within the Communist Party in Hollywood was whether we... as filmmakers could affect the content of... Hollywood films." Jarrico was Oscar-nominated for his script for the 1941 Ginger Rogers vehicle *Tom, Dick and Harry*, co-wrote 1944's pro-Soviet *Song of Russia* and produced 1954's *Salt of the Earth*.

During the 1947 HUAC hearings, actor Adolphe Menjou was asked: "Can you tell the committee whether or not there's been an effort... to inject Communist propaganda into pictures which would serve the Communist Party line?" Menjou, who appeared in more than 100 movies, including 1931's *The Front Page* and Clifford Odets' 1939 *Golden Boy*, replied: "I have seen things which I thought were against what I consider good Americanism... I've seen pictures I thought shouldn't have been made. This is a foul philosophy, this communistic thing. I would move to the state of Texas if it ever came here, because I think the Texans would kill them on sight." The dapper, cigarette wielding actor's testimony got lots of guffaws.

The charge of left-wing "infiltration" and influence in the film industry and movies during the 1930s and 1940s has long been a heated subject of debate. Now, at long last, the truth can be told. Yes, card-carrying members of the Communist Party of the United States of America and other leftists worked in considerable numbers in Hollywood. Yes, they did attempt to inject political and social messages into motion pictures. Yes, in a minority but substantial number of films, Communist and other left-leaning film-makers did indeed succeed in getting their ideas onto the silver screen.

Furthermore—and this may be the most important point—the movies, as well as the audiences of the 1930s and 1940s, were far better off because of it. Although it's rarely noted, the Golden Age of Hollywood coincided with its Crimson Era, when leftists had their greatest influence on filmdom. In *Radical Hollywood: The Untold Story Behind America's Favorite Movies*, Paul Buhle and Dave Wagner call the 1930s the "Red Decade." To properly assess the impact of the left on the period's pictures, it's essential to understand what Reds and other radicals believed in, and—to paraphrase Frank Capra's WWII documentary series—what they fought for. And how progressive artists translated and expressed their progressive visions onscreen.

The Great Depression and the struggle against fascism provided fertile subjects for artists. Mass unemployment, poverty and even starvation spread widely after the 1929 stock market crash. Fascism posed an alternative to the hard times and economic ruination of the Depression. This militaristic, dictatorial system based on slave labor and racism was imposed on the peoples of Italy, Germany, Japan, Spain and the many countries and territories the fascists eventually conquered and looted.

"It seemed to me and many people in my generation that the whole system had broken down and was not going to be fixed. That it needed a change," said CP member Ring Lardner, Jr., who won the Oscar for co-authoring 1942's *Woman of the Year* (the first of many pairings of Katharine Hepburn and Spencer Tracy) and co-wrote the 1944 anti-Nazi drama *Tomorrow the World!* based on the play co-written by Arnaud d'Usseau.

I spoke with blacklisted screenwriters Jean Butler Rouverol, Bobby Lees, Norma Barzman and Bernie Gordon at the "Reds and Blacklists in Hollywood: Political Struggles in the Movie Industry" exhibition at the Academy of Motion Picture Arts and Sciences in 2002. (You can see some of the photos from the exhibition on pages 65–68.)

According to former Communist screenwriter Bernard Gordon in *Hollywood Exile: Or How I Learned to Love the Blacklist*, "I felt that capitalism

Tender comrades: Blacklisted screenwriters Jean Butler Rouverol, Bobby Lees, Norma Barzman and Bernie Gordon at the Motion Picture Academy's Beverly Hills headquarters, reunited during the Academy's 2002 "Reds and Blacklists in Hollywood: Political Struggles in the Movie Industry" exhibit.

was a failed and brutal system that compounded poverty, caused shiploads of oranges to be dumped at sea rather than fed to the needy and sent marshals to evict tenants and scatter their few miserable belongings on the sidewalk. For the thinking people I knew, it appeared clear that capitalism had failed even to function as a viable system in a world plunged into economic chaos." Gordon wrote 1957's *Hellcats of the Navy*, the 1962 sci-fi pic *The Day of the Triffids* and 1963's *55 Days at Peking* with Charlton Heston, Ava Gardner and David Niven.[2]

Norma Barzman stated, "During the Roosevelt years, the CP was responsible for social security, unemployment insurance legislation... We got the teenage Latinos off for the Sleepy Lagoon murder [in L.A.]... We fought racism against the Japanese [and other minorities]... and from the time of the Spanish Civil War, fought fascism abroad and at home." Barzman wrote the 1946 Errol Flynn comedy *Never Say Goodbye* and the autobiography *The Red and the Blacklist: The Intimate Memoir of a Hollywood Expatriate*.

Actress/screenwriter Jean Butler Rouverol, who played W.C. Fields' daughter in 1934's *It's a Gift* and wrote the memoir *Refugees From*

---

2. At a New Year's Eve 2005 party in a country club in Tarzana, I asked Michael Reagan if he knew who had written *Hellcats*—the only movie that starred both Ronald Reagan and Nancy Davis. When the former president's son answered in the negative, I informed him that a blacklisted Communist had penned the script using a pseudonym. Reagan laughed, and expressed interest in having Gordon on the conservative talk show host's satellite radio program.

Hollywood, asserted: "The radicals were the only people who seemed to feel the sense that there was going to be terrible trouble from the fascists..." Like her late husband Hugo Butler, who wrote 1943's *Lassie Come Home*, Jean was a member of the CPUSA.

Robert "Bobby" Lees, who co-wrote Abbott and Costello comedies, joined the CP because: "During the 1930s, you couldn't avoid getting politically involved. I was concerned about the Spanish Civil War, Hitler, labor struggles during the Depression—including unionization of screenwriters... The Communist Party was a legal party."

"We were in the CPUSA because it opposed evils like racism, lynching and anti-unionism, and fought for workers, social security, unemployment insurance, health benefits, welfare, civil rights," stated screenwriter Bernard Gordon, author of *The Gordon File: A Screenwriter Recalls Twenty Years of F.B.I. Surveillance*. "The Party fought for political prisoners—Sacco and Vanzetti, Scottsboro Boys, Sleepy Lagoon. It fought fascism [and] was responsible... for creating the writers' and directors' guilds."

The Hollywood left also brought the war for social and economic justice home to Los Angeles. "We organized the guilds and unions—they have all these benefits we fought for—and went out on strike for the medical, pensions and what young people today take for granted," added Barzman, whose husband Ben co-wrote 1944's *Meet the People* with Lucille Ball and 1945's *Battle of Bataan*, starring John Wayne.

Victoria Riskin, who was the Writers Guild of America West's president in 2003, said: "The Guild was founded in the Depression, when many intellectuals felt the Marxist view of a more egalitarian society was a solution to the great suffering going on in the country... Those intellectuals, members in the early days, had a great influence on the founding of the Guild. It was a time when unions were just beginning to find their strength in a country ravaged by the excesses of greed."

Whereas fascists turned to the Axis powers, the Communists and much of the left turned to the U.S.S.R. for inspiration—and, perhaps, for too much guidance. "Socialism was the only answer we knew... Lincoln Steffens... who had visited the Soviet Union in 1919 wrote... 'I have seen the future and it works,'" Gordon noted in *Hollywood Exile*.

Song of Russia co-writer Richard Collins, whose grandparents starved to death during the Depression, said in "Blacklist: Hollywood on Trial": "The idealism brought into the Party was based on the feeling that we were going to get someplace. That the notion of decency was going to get someplace. That the notion of a fairer shake for people was going to get someplace."

Writer/director Abe Polonsky stated in the same documentary: "It was a great dream... that we could form a society where there would be no exploitation of anybody. And people would only do good things. And there wouldn't be very important people and very unimportant people. We'd be more or less equal. That was a utopian dream, of course," admitted Polonsky, who wrote 1947's *Body and Soul* and the 1948 *film noir* classic *Force of Evil*, which he also directed.

Howard Zinn observed, "This was a period, the 1930s and 1940s, when the Communist Party in the United States was at its height... of its membership, of its influence. They had powerful and respected figures in the entertainment world who, if not members of the CP, were certainly progressive and radical. Obviously Paul Robeson, and people like Frederic March and Florence Eldridge."

Ring Lardner, Jr. wrote in his autobiography *I'd Hate Myself in the Morning* that the Party had 200 members in the creative community. Norma Barzman estimated that 400 directors, writers and actors belonged to the CPUSA.

What kinds of pictures did Communist and other left-wing talents try to create?

"We were idealists... who wrote humanist films about real people and problems... progressive films way ahead of their time—feminist, anti-racist. Mostly well-made little 'B' films, such as Robert Rossen's [1937] *Marked Woman*, starring Bette Davis [and Humphrey Bogart] and John Howard Lawson's [1947] *Smash-Up*, starring Susan Hayward. We didn't try to get in any Communist propaganda," asserted Barzman.

Be that as it may, by 1935 Communist and other leftist literary lions had organized the League of American Writers. Dorothy Parker, Dashiell Hammett, Langston Hughes and John Howard Lawson—whom the press called the "leading Hollywood Red"—joined LAW. Donald Ogden Stewart, who would write the antifascist *A Woman's Face* and *Keeper of the Flame*, became League chairman in 1937. In 1939, LAW established in Hollywood the School for Writers. In addition to Lawson and Stewart, its instructors included Fred Rinaldo and Bobby Lees (a screenwriting team that scripted Robert Benchley and Abbott and Costello comedies), Robert Rossen (who'd eventually direct Abe Polonsky's 1947 *Body and Soul* and write and direct the 1949 Oscar winning Huey Long fictionalization *All the King's Men*),

Irwin Shaw (who'd co-write 1942's *Talk of the Town* and the novel that the 1976 miniseries *Rich Man, Poor Man* was based on) and Dore Schary (who'd produce 1947's pioneering look at anti-Semitism, *Crossfire*, directed by Edward Dmytryk and written by John Paxton and 1948's anti-prejudice *The Boy With Green Hair*, co-written by Ben Barzman).

Up to 300 students enrolled at the School for Writers. Playwright/ screenwriter Lawson specialized in teaching the history of American literature. According to *Radical Hollywood*, screenwriting classes and workshops were taught by teachers such as Paul Jarrico. These workshops "developed script originals for submission through Hollywood agencies." Other screenwriting courses were taught by Gordon Kahn (who'd co-write with Hugo Butler 1942's *Yank on the Burma Road*), Richard Collins and Gertrude Purcell (who'd co-write the 1945 WWII resistance drama *Paris Underground*). The School charged an $18 tuition fee, and its students included a young screenwriter named Carl Foreman, who became a Communist and started out writing Bowery Boys comedies before scripting classics such as 1952's *High Noon*.

A central concern at the School for Writers was: "How could writers in a commercial industry with inescapable managerial supervision survive without cynicism and perhaps even do (at least some) memorable work?" Buhle and Wagner wrote in *Radical Hollywood*. The League and the School were also involved in political activities, and provided a social nexus in Hollywood. In a town where it's not what you know, but who you know, it didn't hurt for newcomers to learn from established studio professionals, and it's arguable that the School helped the social and career advancements of up and coming talents.

THE POPULAR FRONT

"Your [i.e., a Communist's] training was that you didn't go to people and say: 'I believe in a Soviet America.' You went to them on the issue of the time, and you supported what was the left, and often the liberal position."

— Richard Collins, in "Blacklist: Hollywood on Trial"

Instead of expressing the Marxist, Moscow and/or Communist International line *per se*, leftist filmmakers, in particular screenwriters, promoted

Popular Front politics (which eventually wound up becoming the strategy of the Kremlin and ComIntern).

Of course, there was more to the Popular Front than this. In 1933 the German Communist Party (KPD) followed Stalin's ultra-left, sectarian line at the time and refused to form an alliance with the Social Democratic Party (SPD), which the KPD denounced as "social fascists." Without a united front of working class forces (which the by-then exiled Trotsky advocated), the Nazis won with a plurality—but not a majority—of the votes. According to Professor Zinn, "The Popular Front was prompted by the rise of Hitler and the recognition that there had not been a Popular Front in Germany against Hitler. That the left in Germany had been split, and had therefore made it easier for Hitler to rise to power and to take power."

In *Blacklisted: The Film Lover's Guide to the Hollywood Blacklist*, Paul Buhle and Dave Wagner, who are leading historians of Hollywood's Crimson Era and the subsequent backlash to it, defined the Popular Front as: "A shortened version of the 'Popular Front Against War and Fascism' declared at Communist International meetings in 1935, it served as a symbol and substance of a new approach toward noncommunists. Expectations of early revolution vanished in the dramatic change of tactics, and alliances with socialists (in the U.S., mostly with liberals) were urged, mainly but not only to combat the increasing danger of global fascism. The Popular Front allowed a relatively small CPUSA to enter the Democratic Party, the labor movement mainstream and the Roosevelt New Deal administration... [T]he Popular Front came to stand for an all-around aggressive liberalism-cum-radicalism with vigorous support of industrial unions and the causes of nonwhites, along with support for the Soviet Union."

Zinn added: "The Popular Front was a kind of coalition of left groups and left people, and it was a strategy of the Communist movement that realized the Communists themselves were a relatively small minority. But it was necessary for them to get together and join the people who were not Communists, but people who were left-leaning or socialist or who were progressive, who were liberal in some way in order to have a broad coalition... It was recognized that the Communist Party by itself was not strong enough to resist fascism or bring about any kind of policy changes. So the Popular Front was an attempt to create a left coalition in the U.S. and other countries," said the author of *A People's History of the United States: 1492–Present*.

During the Depression, the Popular Front also emerged in movie metaphors. In Errol Flynn swashbucklers such as 1935's *Captain Blood*, 1938's *The Adventures of Robin Hood* and 1940's *The Sea Hawk*, Flynn portrays a champion of liberty who battles dictators. In *Robin Hood*, he is the nobleman Sir Robin of Locksley who leads the peasants against the despotic Prince John (Claude Rains) and Sir Guy of Gisbourne (Basil Rathbone) and their henchman, the Sheriff of Nottingham (Melville Cooper), who clearly represent the reactionary wing of the ruling class. Robin Hood leads a peasant rebellion, but at the end, once the people's liberation army has stormed the tyrants' citadel, instead of seizing power for themselves, they turn political power over to King Richard the Lionheart (Ian Hunter), who leads the liberal wing of the elite. If Prince John and Sir Guy symbolize Hitler and Mussolini, Good King Richard represents FDR and the New Deal he will promulgate for his loyal—but obedient—servants (who still know their places, even after winning a violent revolution).

Robin Hood's co-writer Seton Miller sat on the board of what is now the Writers Guild of America in 1936 during its most left-wing period. Miller also co-wrote *The Sea Hawk*, with Howard Koch, who won an Oscar for co-writing *Casablanca*. Casey Robinson was an uncredited screen-writer for *Casablanca*—he also wrote *Captain Blood*. Koch also wrote the ultimate Popular Front pic, 1943's *Mission to Moscow*, which was direct-ed by Eastern European émigré Micahel Curtiz—who also helmed all of the above Flynn swashbucklers. (Flynn's last movie, by the way, was the 1959 pro-Castro *Cuban Rebel Girls*, filmed on location.)

CINEMA'S SALT OF THE EARTH

"You are the salt of the earth. But if the salt loses its saltiness, how can it be made salty again? It is no longer good for anything, except to be thrown out and trampled by men. You are the light for the whole world... The meek shall inherit the Earth."

— Jesus Christ, the Sermon on the Mount, *The Gospel According to Matthew*

The Popular Front had domestic and international components. At home, Communists and other radicals joined forces with liberals to support the New Deal social programs, such as the National Recovery Act and the Works

Progress Administration. Unemployment insurance, social security and other welfare state measures were enacted in order to alleviate the worst suffering wrought by the Depression. Unionization tripled during this period, the Congress of Industrial Organizations came into being and replaced the more conservative crafts-oriented American Federation of Labor at the helm of organized labor, as federal legislation ensured the right to organize.

Public works projects put millions to work—including artists, who extolled the virtues of the common man and woman in a variety of media, with and without government support. The Federal Theater Project presented proletarian dramas. FTP funded topical Living Newspaper productions and the Orson Welles-directed, all-black version of the so-called *Voodoo MacBeth*, which set Shakespeare's play in Haiti and imported actual Caribbean witchdoctors to perform in Harlem. FTP also featured a dramatization of Sinclair Lewis' *It Can't Happen Here*, about a fascist takeover of the U.S., although at the last minute, it pulled out of Welles' and Marc Blitzstein's pro-labor opera *The Cradle Will Rock*. Blue collar protagonists were featured in plays such as the Group Theater's *Waiting For Lefty*, Clifford Odets' searing story about cabbies that ended with actors urging the audience to chant "Strike!" Proletarian literature saw the rise of class struggle novels by John Steinbeck, John Dos Passos, Ernest Hemingway, F. Scott Fitzgerald and others. Painters created murals depicting brawny workers, and the Farm Security Administration photographers Dorothea Lange, Arthur Rothstein and Walker Evans immortalized Okies victimized by the Depression dustbowl. In music, Woody Guthrie rhapsodized about those same Okies, and Aaron Copland composed *Fanfare for the Common Man*.

Even if most of Tinseltown's output masqueraded as escapist fare to take the masses' minds off of hard times, Hollywood, too, was touched by this movement, and moment, and made movies about the dignity and worth of the ordinary people. "I remember films that seemed to have a class consciousness," recalled Zinn, who grew up during the Depression. "Jimmy Stewart, in *Mr. Smith Goes to Washington*... That struck me as an unusual film that managed to be both politically progressive and very well made. A film that stands up today, one of the great films of the era."

In *Smith*, Edward Arnold—who specialized in portraying *über*-moneybags onscreen—portrayed the evil capitalist Jim Taylor, who has Senator Paine (Claude Rains) in his hip pocket in Frank Capra's beloved populist picture. Although it's not widely known, the screenwriter of this 1939 anti-corruption classic was Sidney Buchman, who was a card-carrying member of the Communist Party when *Mr. Smith* was in theaters. The Red writer received an Oscar nomination for his script and won for 1941's *Here Comes Mr. Jordan* (remade by Warren Beatty in 1978 as *Heaven Can Wait*).

In a 1969 interview for the French film magazine *Positif*, Buchman told director Bertrand Tavernier: "Capra's great passion was Dickens... One day he came to see me in my room and we talked about *Smith*. I tried to show him what I meant to say, that it is necessary to maintain a vigilant attitude even when you think you are living in a democracy, that you should refuse to surrender even on the smallest things because their importance can be enormous. I ended by saying, 'There, that's my theme.' He looked at me and suddenly said: 'Go get fucked with your theme!' It was so sudden that I was dumbstruck. He tried to catch himself by saying that he didn't believe that an artist had to have political or social preoccupations, that he should content himself with entertaining the public, etc. I told him, 'How can you say that, you who claim to admire Dickens? The slightest line of Dickens has a precise social meaning... he tried to fight poverty, the exploitation of the poor.' He looked at me and said: 'Are you a Communist?' I answered him: 'Are you a Fascist?' And we left it at that."

Zinn went on to say: "There was a kind of class consciousness, even films made about miners in England or Wales... and what they had to go through and so on... [John Ford's 1941] *How Green Was My Valley*... [Ford's 1940] *The Grapes of Wrath* certainly stands out as one of the monumental films to come out of the New Deal." Screenwriter Nunnally Johnson expertly adapted John Steinbeck's novel about Oklahoma's uprooted Joad family, whose farmstead is repossessed by a faceless bank. The Okies embark on an odyssey to the supposed land of milk and honey in California.

The theme of the transcendental solidarity of man is set in the new realities of the Depression. The martyred labor organizer Preacher Casy (brilliantly played by the show-stealing John Carradine) represents the transfer of the sense of oneness formerly bestowed by religion to the union. As Casy explains to Tom Joad (a rarely if ever better Henry Fonda), a man doesn't have his own separate soul, but rather a piece of one big soul—which, given the class struggle of the times, could now be located in one big union. Universal unity was found in the working class sticking together through thick and thin in hard times.

In order to deceive potential reactionary opponents, and to enhance the film's realism, *Grapes* was shot in part outside of the studio sets and backlots. Since Twentieth Century Fox was afraid that the Texas and Oklahoma

Chambers of commerce would object to the filming of Steinbeck's pro-union novel, Fox announced that it was really making another story, entitled *Highway 66*. Gregg Toland's gritty black and white cinematography and location lensing bestowed a documentary-like sensibility on Johnson's adaptation of Steinbeck's book. (Johnson—who also received screen credit as *Grapes*' associate producer—was an independent leftist who had served in 1936 as the vice president of what is now the Writers Guild of America.)

In this way, the feature approximated the look and realism of New Deal documentaries by the left-leaning Frontier Films independent outfit and others. Pare Lorentz's *The Plow That Broke the Plains* was a Resettlement Administration-funded 1936 short documenting the effects of the Dustbowl and New Deal efforts to cope with the environmental disaster that led to the exodus of dislocated "Okies" and other farmers. Its world premiere took place not at Mann's Chinese Theater, but at FDR's White House. In *The River*, directed by Lorentz and shot by Paul Strand and Leo Hurwitz, the Tennessee Valley Administration program to produce electrification is documented. The 1938 short, about the Mississippi River, was financed by Roosevelt's Resettlement Administration; Lorentz's highly acclaimed narration was nominated for the Pulitzer Prize for Poetry in 1938. *The River* beat out Leni Riefenstahl's *Olympiad* to win 1938's Venice Film Festival in Mussolini's fascist Italy. Joris Ivens' 1940 rural electrification docudrama *Power and the Land*, which had been commissioned by the U.S. Department of Agriculture, plus the FSA's dustbowl photos, also influenced the look, sensibility and content of the cinematic adaptation of *The Grapes of Wrath*.

Critic Roger Ebert noted: "Even though the Joad farm is a studio set, Ford liked to shoot on location, and records a journey down Route 66 from the Dust Bowl through New Mexico and Arizona, past shabby gas stations and roadside diners." Locations far from Tinseltown's studio sets and backlots included: Sayre, Oklahoma (the courthouse); Gallup, Laguna Pueblo and Santa Rosa (the service station, diner, bridge and train sequences) in New Mexico; Arizona's Petrified Forest National Park; Lamont, California (at the Weedpatch Migrant Camp), as well as some L.A. locations, such as the Iverson Ranch in the San Fernando Valley.

During a strike of migrant fruit pickers, Casy is murdered by vigilantes; Tom kills Casy's murderer. Now a wanted man, Tom must leave the family. But he has come to a new consciousness, which he discusses with Ma Joad, movingly played as an Earth mother by Jane Darwell. Drawing on Steinbeck's novel, their dialogue is as close as any Hollywood movie of the New Deal and Popular Front pictures (with the exception of Chaplin's final speech in *The Great Dictator*) to the "magic words" that expressed America's aspirations during that era:

Tom Joad

I been thinking about us, too, about our people living like pigs and good rich land layin' fallow. Or maybe one guy with a million acres and a hundred thousand farmers starvin'. And I been wonderin' if all our folks got together and yelled...

Ma Joad

Tommy, they'd drag you out and cut you down just like they done to Casey.

Tom

They'd drag me any ways. Sooner or later they'll get me one way or another. Till then...

Ma

Tommy, you're not aimin' to kill nobody.

Tom

No, Ma, not that. That ain't it. Just, as long as I'm an outlaw anyways, maybe I can do something, just find out somethin', just scrounge around and maybe find out what it is that's wrong and see if they ain't somethin' that can be done about it. I ain't thought it out that clear, Ma. I can't. I don't know enough.

Ma

How am I gonna know about ya, Tommy? They could kill ya and I'd never know. They could hurt ya. How am I gonna know?

Tom

Maybe it's like Casey says. A fellow ain't got a soul of his own, just little piece of a big soul, the one big soul that belongs to everybody, then...

Ma

Then what, Tom?

Tom

I'll be all around in the dark—I'll be everywhere. Wherever you can look—wherever there's a fight, so hungry people can eat, I'll be there.

Wherever there's a cop beatin' up a guy, I'll be there. I'll be there in the way guys yell when they're mad. I'll be there in the way kids laugh when they're hungry and they know supper's ready, and when people are eatin' the stuff they raise and livin' in the houses they built—I'll be there, too.

Other Hollywood odes to farmers, factory workers and forgotten folks included 1935's *Black Fury*, about coal miners embroiled in a bitter, ill-conceived strike. Directed by Michael Curtiz, it starred Paul Muni as immigrant Joe Radek, J. Carrol Naish and Mae Marsh. In William Wellman's 1933's *Heroes for Sale*, Richard Barthelmess plays Tom, a WWI veteran who experiences drug addiction, unemployment, a strike, workers trying to destroy machinery and more. The same year, Wellman also directed the still moving *Wild Boys of the Road*, about dispossessed Depression youth forced to leave home and wander about the countryside (often in boxcars), searching for food, work and succor. The scene where a young vagabond's leg is severed by a train is an unforgettable symbol of hard times.

William Wyler's 1937 *Dead End*, with a script by Lillian Hellman, is a compelling look at slum life in Manhattan's Lower East Side. Reform-minded, unemployed architect Joel McCrea and his gal Sylvia Sydney compete with Humphrey Bogart as gangster Baby Face Martin for the hearts and minds of slum dwellers Huntz Hall, Leo B. Gorcey and the other Dead End Kids (who eventually morphed into the less threatening Bowery Boys). 1938's similarly-themed *Angels With Dirty Faces* was directed by Michael Curtiz and co-written by John Wexley. It starred Bogie, Jimmy Cagney, Pat O'Brien, Ann Sheridan and the Dead End Kids. According to Nancy Lynn Schwartz in *The Hollywood Writers' Wars*, along with John Howard Lawson, Wexley was the only screenwriter at Columbia who refused to contribute money to Harry Cohn's fund to stop the candidacy of the reformist Upton Sinclair, who was running for governor on the End Poverty in California platform. The studio moguls launched a false, defamatory media campaign to successfully defeat Sinclair, which Wexley and Lawson were fired for not "donating" to.

Dead End and *Angels* are crossover films that combine the down-and-out cycle with the gangster and prison genres. As *Radical Hollywood* explains at great length, movies about convicts and criminals served as subversive movie metaphors for Depression discontent, especially during the early, out-of-control years of the Depression, with a do-nothing, oblivious GOP president ensconced in the White House. 1932's *Hell's Highway*, co-written by Samuel Ornitz, is a bleak look at a prison riot and jailbreak, which sympathizes with the prisoners. Epitomizing and typifying this genre were 1931's *Little Caesar*, directed by Mervyn LeRoy, and *Public Enemy*. These hits thrust Edward G. Robinson and James Cagney into stardom, and were written, respectively, by Francis Faragoh and John Bright. According to *Radical Hollywood*, "Bright was, with Faragoh, the first important left-wing innovator in Hollywood." Bright was influenced by the Industrial Workers of the World and "intermittently a communist," Buhle and Wagner wrote.

Reds in various guises—Marxist intellectuals, labor agitators, Party members—appeared in numerous Depression pics. According to Peter Roffman and Jim Purdy in the superb film history *The Hollywood Social Problem Film: Madness, Despair and Politics From the Depression to the Fifties*, these films included: *Heroes for Sale*, 1933's Preston Sturges-written *The Power and the Glory* and adaptations of Elmer Rice's plays *Street Scene* (directed by King Vidor in 1931, starring Sylvia Sidney) and *Counsellor-at-Law* (directed by William Wyler in 1932, starring John Barrymore, Melvyn Douglas and Thelma Todd).

Aside from some Red references in *The Grapes of Wrath*, the most famous Marxist allusions are in Charlie Chaplin's 1936 masterpiece *Modern Times*. The most obvious reference is when Charlie's Little Tramp innocently walks down a city street and a construction truck drops its red flag. Charlie picks the flag up and waves it in an attempt to return the flag to its owners. At that moment a march of militant workers appears. Spotting the red flag-waving Charlie, the proletarians assume that he is their leader and, when the cops arrive, the Little Tramp is busted.

But on a deeper level, the brilliance of *Modern Times* lies in its critique of industrial society. As a factory worker, Charlie is spied on by a boss on a TV-like screen in the men's room, and ordered back to work. The speedup on the assembly line literally drives poor Charlie crazy. Missing his turn screwing a bolt, the Little Tramp jumps on the assembly line in an effort to keep up with the pace and do his job. Chaplin is literally swallowed up by the factory, as he descends into the bowels of the machinery, twisting and turning with the cogs and wheels. It is a visually stunning and hilariously funny scene, but also an ingenious visualization of Marx's critique of the alienation of labor in his 1844 *Economic and Philosophical Manuscripts*. Man becomes a mere extension of the machine and is estranged from the process of work, wherein the worker does not receive the fruits of his labor.

Before *Modern Times*, the politically conscious Chaplin helped King Vidor finance 1934's *Our Daily Bread*, an unusual Depression film featuring a cast of mainly nonprofessionals in a move that presaged Italian Neorealism. Even more notable is *Bread*'s theme and plot, which revolve around a collective farm that is upheld as a viable alternative to capitalism's hard times. The rhythmic, rapid cutting of the successful irrigation project in the picture's grand finale is reminiscent of Eisenstein's Soviet montage.

The collective approach to life returns in *Tender Comrade*, written and directed by Communists Dalton Trumbo and Edward Dmytryk. Ginger Rogers is a wartime defense plant worker who shares an apartment with three other proletarian gal pals in this homefront drama. The household is run democratically and collectively—as Ginger says: "Share and share alike, that's democracy." The theme of a cooperative is revisited in Trumbo's 1945 *Our Vines Have Tender Grapes*, a gentle, socialistic drama about Swedish immigrant farmers in Wisconsin which stars Edward G. Robinson, Margaret O'Brien and Agnes Moorehead.

1944's *Meet the People*, co-written by Party member Ben Barzman, is a celebration of the common man and woman that stars Dick Powell as a shipyard laborer-cum-playwright, Lucille Ball as a theater actress and Bert Lahr as the Commander. Powell balks when Broadway wants to turn his play into a musical, and like the Coen Brothers' 1991 satire *Barton Fink*, *People* comments on Clifford Odets-type proletarian playwrights who go Hollywood. The 1945 LeRoy-directed *The House I Live In*, starring Frank Sinatra and written by Albert Maltz, won a Best Short Oscar. In it, Old Blue Eyes sings the title song, which refers to America as a tolerant house we live in where all peoples of all religions, races and ethnicities are accepted.

ANTIFASCIST FILMS AT HOME

"Rosebud..."

— Orson Welles as Charles Foster Kane in 1940's *Citizen Kane*

Ever the insightful people's historian, Howard Zinn pointed out that Popular Front pictures concerned with the home front dealt with more than just labor and class issues *per se*. "As films against fascism, films were made that represented a defiance against, you might say, of fascism or repression at home. Paul Muni in [Mervyn LeRoy's 1932] *I Am a Fugitive From a Chain Gang*... films that represented the poor, the oppressed, the people who were put in jail... I remember a wonderful film with Cary Grant and Jean Arthur [George Stevens' *Talk of the Town*, co-written by Sidney

Buchman], which was really about, again, the system of justice. And how Cary Grant [as anarchist Leopold Dilg] was a fugitive from a crime that he didn't commit. And how the issue was raised. Ronald Colman was [law professor Michael Lightcap], who's been appointed to the Supreme Court. He has this moral decision to make about should he stick to the letter of the law and turn [Dilg] in." Lightcap evolves from a dispassionate ivory tower egghead to a crusader defending the rights of Dilg, who has been framed-up for arson that was actually committed by the industrialist Dilg was exposing, Andrew Holmes (played by Charles Dingle).

Other pictures that dealt with the theme of fascism at home included anti-lynch and anti-mob rule movies such as the 1936 films *Black Legion* and *Legion of Terror*. Both were inspired by a racist, anti-foreigner KKK-type group that actually existed in the 1930s called the Black Legion. Humphrey Bogart stars in the former as a factory worker who joins the hooded secret organization—like Bogie, this motion picture packs quite a punch. In *Legion of Terror*, the vigilantes send a mail bomb to a senator—a plot point that remained relevant in September 2004, when a number of state governors were mailed envelopes rigged to ignite when opened.

Spencer Tracy and Sylvia Sidney starred in MGM's 1936 *Fury*, the first Hollywood feature Fritz Lang directed after fleeing Nazi Germany the same day that Goebbels offered Lang the role as head of the Third Reich's film industry. In *Fury*, the district attorney states: "In the last 49 years, 4,176 human beings have been lynched... a lynching about every four days!" However, in Charles Higham and Joel Greenberg's *The Celluloid Muse: Hollywood Directors Speak*, Lang said: "Louis B. Mayer interfered only once on *Fury*, and for a very peculiar reason... I had a scene showing a group of Negroes... in the South listening on the radio to a... lynching trial. As the state attorney spoke about the high incidence of lynchings in the U.S. each year, I had the old Negro just nod his head silently without a word. Mayer had this scene, and others like it, removed because at that time I think even he was convinced that Negroes should be shown only as bootblacks, or carhops, or menials..."

Lang added that when a reporter asked MGM what was the press screening for the day, the reply was, "Oh, a lousy picture. Don't watch it, it is by that German son of a bitch, Lang." Although *Fury* turned out to be what Lang called "a tremendous success," he noted that he didn't direct at MGM again for 20 years. Lang had exchanged a *fuhrer* for a mogul. Lang, who had directed Hitler's favorite (pre-*Triumph of the Will*) film, *Metropolis*, also helmed (for United Artists!) 1937's *You Only Live Once*, produced by Walter Wanger, starring Henry Fonda and Sylvia Sidney. The story was suggested by the real life outlaws Bonnie and Clyde, and is also anti-lynching and anti-mob mentality.

In Mervyn LeRoy's 1937 *They Won't Forget*, Lana Turner had her first major role, as a character suggested by the real life Mary Phagan. Her ethnically-charged murder, allegedly by the Jewish Leo Franks (who was lynched), had triggered a crisis in the South. *The Ox-Bow Incident* was a 1943 Western allegory about mob rule, directed by William Wellman and starring Fonda.

In addition to the all-black *MacBeth*, 22-year-old Orson Welles directed Marc Blitzstein's *The Cradle Will Rock* for the Federal Theater Project—or at least tried to. The New Deal agency tried to shut down the production of the radical pro-labor opera, but on opening night in June 1937, Welles and company relocated to another Broadway theater at the last minute, and performed the play *sans* sets to a sold out audience. (This is movingly depicted in Tim Robbins' *Cradle Will Rock*.) Welles and John Houseman formed the famed Manhattan-based Mercury Theater, and its first stage production was a modern dress *Julius Caesar* set in then-contemporary fascist Italy. The Mercury Theater went on to rock radio, and was wooed by Tinseltown.

RKO made "Boy Wonder" Welles an offer he couldn't refuse: unprecedented creative control, including a closed set at RKO 281 and the coveted final cut (which subsequently eluded Welles, like most filmmakers). So the *wünderkind* went West to play with, as he put it, "the biggest electric train set a boy ever had!" in Hollywood. The result was 1941's *Citizen Kane*—which AFI voted the best American movie ever. Suggested by the life of media mogul William Randolph Hearst (the Rupert Murdoch of his day and Patty's grandfather), *Kane* may also be Hollywood's best look ever at a homegrown fascist. Welles shares credit with Herman Mankiewicz for *Kane*'s Academy Award-winning script. Gregg Toland was Oscar nominated for his deep focus camerawork that revolutionized cinematography. Welles was also nominated for Best Actor and Director, and the film received a Best Picture nomination.

Through flashbacks, *Citizen Kane* traces the life of John Foster Kane (portrayed by Welles and other members of the Mercury Theater, including Joseph Cotton and Agnes Moorehead). When sudden, inherited wealth is thrust on the boy as he is enjoying sleigh riding, he is ripped from hearth and home and leaves his father and mother to be "properly" educated at a fancy shmancy boarding school. As his middle name suggests, Kane becomes a foster child who yearns for his lost childhood and parents as he is raised by wealth. Mussolini-like, Kane becomes a force in journalism and moves rightward across the political spectrum. He ends up as the quintessential American right-winger, symbolizing wealth and power. He is surrounded by possessions—but all alone at his palatial mountaintop Xanadu, inspired by Hearst's San Simeon castle. This radical critique of crass materialism and acquisitiveness ends with the revelation that the last word on Kane's lips—"Rosebud"—referred to the sled he was playing on when his inheritance was announced.[3]

Other warnings against fascism at home were found in moving pictures like the Warner Brothers' 1939 *Confessions of a Nazi Spy*, featuring the Jewish actor Edward G. Robinson as an F.B.I. agent who busts the German *bund* in what is touted as Hollywood's first explicitly anti-Nazi movie. Capra's 1941 *Meet John Doe*, starring Gary Cooper, Barbara Stanwyck and that *über*-capitalist Edward Arnold, contains a warning against homespun fascism. In George Cukor's 1942 *Keeper of the Flame*, Christine (Katharine Hepburn) has murdered her husband, supposed war hero Robert Forrest, because he was secretly planning a fascist coup. Christine tells war correspondent Steven O'Malley (Spencer Tracy, but of course): "I saw the face of fascism in my own house. Hatred, arrogance, cruelty. I saw what German women were facing. I saw the enemy..." She goes on to say: "Of course they didn't call it fascism. They painted it red, white and blue and called it Americanism."

This sophisticated take on "native" fascism was written for the screen by Donald Ogden Stewart, a member of the famed Algonquin Roundtable who went on to chair both the influential Hollywood Anti-Nazi League and League of American Writers, and marry Lincoln Steffens' widow Ella Winter.

In *Native Land* the great Paul Robeson narrates and sings in what John Howard Lawson called "the first uncompromising treatment of racist terror in the South." The 1942 docudrama by Leo Hurwitz, Paul Strand and Ben Maddow is a pro-union statement against vigilante violence. *Native Land* was the last picture by the progressive Frontier Films group and for Robeson.

During America's run-up to WWII, left-coasters were also deeply involved in antifascist activities offscreen. Many stars and other film-

---

3. "Rosebud" was also reputedly Hearst's nickname for the private parts of his mistress, actress Marion Davies. Just another reason why Hearst's "yellow press" waged war against *Citizen Kane*, although its unflattering portrait of a megalomaniacal, militaristic capitalist didn't help.

makers participated in organizations such as the Hollywood Anti-Nazi League, which was founded in 1936. HANL's supporters included Eddie Cantor, Ernst Lubitsch, Frederic March, Dorothy Parker, Oscar Hammerstein, Philip Dunne and Dudley Nichols, among others.

In *Radical Hollywood*, Paul Buhle and Dave Wagner wrote: "Almost overnight, HANL fund-raising played a key role in the Hollywood social whirl. Director Mervyn LeRoy, producer Walter Wanger, studio czar Jack Warner, likewise F. Scott Fitzgerald (who, by this time, insisted that he had become a firm Marxist), and Chico Marx... listened to Judy Garland sing at a typical event that might have included other standard HANL performers such as Sophie Tucker, Dorothy Lamour, Ray Bolger, Benny Goodman, Fred MacMurray... the Ritz Brothers... and Martha Raye." HANL had a strong publicity arm and fundraising role, as celebrities' fame and fortune were parlayed into political capital used to fight the Nazis. When Hitler's favorite post-Fritz Lang director came to Hollywood, she was largely cold-shouldered (except by Walt Disney and Hal Roach), and HANL published ads in the trades declaring: "There is no room in Hollywood for Leni Riefenstahl."

Loyalist Spain was a particular *cause célèbre* for antifascist filmmakers. According to *Radical Hollywood*, HANL eventually "merged into the even more furiously active anti-Franco committees for the Spanish Republic." Lillian Hellman, Dorothy Parker, Langston Hughes, Ernest Hemingway and Errol Flynn went to the frontlines, and then reported back to the home front. Did the Republicans need ambulances in order to resist the *Generalissimo*'s Hitler and Mussolini-backed onslaught? Much as Judy Garland and Mickey Rooney would say onscreen, Hollywood's answer would be "Let's throw a party!" And the money would be raised, and the ambulances or whatever were dispatched forthwith to the besieged Spanish Republic.

THE PRE-WAR "PREMATURE" STRUGGLE AGAINST FASCISM ABROAD

"[I]n the name of democracy, let us all unite!"

— Charlie Chaplin as the Jewish barber in 1940's *The Great Dictator*

1937's *This Spanish Earth* is a documentary directed by Dutchman Joris Ivens and co-written by Lillian Hellman and Archibald Macleish. John Dos Passos and Ernest Hemingway (both of whom eventually wrote Spanish Civil War novels) narrated the film in English; Jean Renoir narrated it *en Français*.

The famous La Pasionaria appears in this pro-Republican film, arguably one of the most famous and best propaganda documentaries ever made.

Heart of Spain is a 1937 Frontier Films documentary depicting the Canadian doctor Norman Bethune, who joined the Loyalist cause against Franco's fascists. It was created by Herbert Kline, Geza Karpathi, Ben Maddow, Leo Hurwitz and Paul Strand.

China Strikes Back is another 1937 antifascist Frontier Films documentary. It was shot by Harry Dunham with a script by Ben Maddow (who went on to write the 1969 Gregory Peck thriller about Mao, *The Chairman*) and edited by Jay Leyda (Sergei Eisenstein's sole American student, author of *Kino: A History of the Russian and Soviet Film*). *China Strikes Back* portrays the Red Army and the Chinese struggle against Imperial Japan's militarism.

Perhaps the Hollywood feature—and screenwriter—that came the closest to injecting Communist *agitprop* into America's film culture was 1938's *Blockade*, written by John Howard Lawson. He was the first president of what is now the Writers Guild of America and reputedly the head of the Hollywood chapter of the CPUSA. Howard Zinn said Lawson "was considered the ringleader among the Hollywood Ten." According to "Blacklist: Hollywood on Trial," *Blockade* was the first U.S. feature film about the Spanish Civil War. In his book *Film: The Creative Process*, Lawson explained that *Blockade*'s producer, Walter Wanger, was an independent who released the movie through United Artists. As such, Wanger didn't have the capital available to studios and financed his pictures with bank loans. In order to compete with the majors, his productions often relied on "sensational" subject matter to attract audiences.

However, there was a limit to how far even Wanger—and Lawson—could go. In *Blockade* the "people's forces and their fascist enemies" could not be identified onscreen, Lawson wrote. Even though the country that aided the Spanish Republic most was the U.S.S.R., the boat that saves the blockaded antifascists from starvation couldn't be shown to be Soviet, either. Commercial contingencies also coerced Lawson into tacking a trite espionage plot onto the film, which starred Madeleine Carroll as a rich girl wooed by the Republican peasant Henry Fonda. ("Of course, Fonda himself was a progressive-minded guy all through his life," Zinn noted.)

Nevertheless, when the (unnamed) supply ship comes to the rescue of the anti-Franco forces in a rapid montage sequence, the rousing climax is reminiscent of Sergei Eisenstein's *Battleship Potemkin* masterpiece about the 1905 Russian Revolution. Indeed, Lawson noted that director William Dieterle "consciously followed Soviet examples" in this sequence.

The influence that revolutionary Soviet cinema exerted on the Hollywood left was profound. This was one of the rare happy occasions in the history of the arts that the political *avant garde* moved in synch with the artistic *avant garde*. The Bolsheviks acted as patrons to equally radical-minded filmmakers, including Eisenstein, V.I. Pudovkin, Aleksandr Dovzhenko and documentarian Dziga Vertov. During the 1920s, they created a cinematic Renaissance that rendered socialist concepts and passions onscreen, in both form and content.

Their classics include Eisenstein's *October* (aka *10 Days That Shook the World*), Pudovkin's *The Mother, Storm Over Asia* and *The End of St. Petersburg*, Dovzhenko's *Earth* and *Arsenal*, and Vertov's *Kino Pravda* and *The Man With the Movie Camera*. The films focus on the mass hero, exalting the common man and woman and their heroic struggles for social justice. And the leader of the Russian Revolution, Lenin, famously said: "For us, the cinema is the most important of the arts."

Blockade ends powerfully, with Fonda speaking directly to the audience, asking: "Where is the conscience of the world?" Wanger next set out to produce another "prematurely" antifascist film with a script by Lawson—this time, tackling Nazi Germany. Dieterle was set to direct again—until two days before production was to start. "The bank informed [Wanger] that he would never receive another loan if he proceeded," as Lawson wrote. Free speech definitely had its limits in Tinseltown, and *Blockade* was about as far left-field as Hollywood would venture into before WWII.

Orson Welles got around the censorship with a canny 1938 radio adaptation of socialist H.G. Wells' *The War of the Worlds*. The program about a Martian invasion of Grover's Mill, New Jersey and New York presented (and actually identified on the air) as a theatrical production and *faux* news broadcast, scared the bejesus out of its national audience—and not only because it was Halloween. With Japanese, German and Italian fascists invading countries right and left, the extraterrestrial invasion panicked Americans and struck a responsive chord in the collective psyche. Welles adapted Wells' story of intergalactic warfare to symbolize the impending global conflagration.

Donald Ogden Stewart also co-wrote MGM's 1941 anti-fascist flick *A Woman's Face*, starring Joan Crawford as a governess. Conrad Veidt plays her conniving lover, who pressures Crawford to kill the child she cares for in order to get an inheritance, but she kills Veidt instead after he reveals that he is a Nazi sympathizer. (Interestingly, Veidt, who was born in Potsdam, Germany, played the somnambulistic zombie-like murderer Cesare in the 1919 German Expressionistic classic horror film, *The Cabinet of Dr. Caligari*. Veidt went on to play Major Heinrich Strasser in 1942's *Casablanca*.)

There were other films that were "prematurely antifascist," as socially conscious Americans opposed to the brownshirts and black-shirts, were called prior to WWII. These premature antifascists were typified by Alvah Bessie, who fought in the Abraham Lincoln Brigade against the Hitler and Mussolini-backed Franco in Spain, and later wrote the WWII dramas *Northern Pursuit* and *Objective, Burma!* Both starred Errol Flynn and were directed by Raoul Walsh. Bessie received a Best Story Oscar nomination for *Objective, Burma!* 1940's *Three Faces West* was a rare pre-war antifascist film starring none other than John Wayne, in this drama about refugees who have fled the Nazis and relocated in America.

In *The Hollywood Social Problem Film* Roffman and Purdy report that director Frank Borzage made three movies set in Germany about people caught up in the emerging National Socialist maelstrom. The first, *Little Man, What Now?* was made in 1934 shortly after Hitler took power and starred Margaret Sullavan, Alan Hale and Mae Marsh. In 1938, Borzage made *Three Comrades*, which starred Sullavan, Robert Taylor, Robert Young, Franchot Tone, Guy Kibbee and Monty Woolley. According to Roffman and Purdy, F. Scott Fitzgerald's original script was politically eviscerated—Louis B. Mayer (a Jew!) privately screened (presumably, before its public release) *Three Comrades* for a Third Reich official, who demanded cuts. *Mortal Storm* was another anti-Nazi movie released in 1940, starring Sullavan, Jimmy Stewart and Robert Young. In the latter two pictures, protagonists flee Germany. Roffman and Purdy write in *The Hollywood Social Problem Film* that *Mortal Storm* is "important as the first Hollywood film to deal with the Jewish problem and the concentration camps..."

But of all the pre-war anti-Nazi movies, one American film towers above all the rest. "As far as fascism abroad, of course [the film] I think of is Chaplin in *The Great Dictator*," Professor Zinn said of the Little Tramp's masterpiece. In this 1940 satire on fascism, Charlie Chaplin plays a shell-shocked WWI veteran and Jewish barber, as well as Adenoid

Hynkel, the dictator of Tomania. Chaplin uses humor to mock and cut Hitler and Mussolini (Jack Oakie, as a scene-stealing Benzino Napaloni, dictator of Bacteria) down to size. After Hynkel *blitzkriegs* a neighboring country, the little Jewish barber is mistaken for the barbarian Hynkel at a Nuremburg-type mass rally. Believing that he is the great dictator, the fascists make the Jew speak at the microphone. In the guise of his character(s), Chaplin went on to deliver a hopeful and, given the fact that Washington was still neutral at the time, very daring speech, that expressed the quintessence of the Popular Front philosophy:

> I'm sorry but I don't want to be an emperor—that's not my business—I don't want to rule or conquer anyone. I should like to help everyone if possible, Jew, gentile, black man, white. We all want to help one another, human beings are like that.
>
> We all want to live by each other's happiness, not by each other's misery. We don't want to hate and despise one another. In this world there is room for everyone and the earth is rich and can provide for everyone.
>
> The way of life can be free and beautiful.
>
> But we have lost the way.
>
> Greed has poisoned men's souls—has barricaded the world with hate; has goose-stepped us into misery and bloodshed.
>
> We have developed speed but we have shut ourselves in: Machinery that gives abundance has left us in want. Our knowledge has made us cynical, our cleverness hard and unkind. We think too much and feel too little. More than machinery we need humanity; more than cleverness we need kindness and gentleness.
>
> Without these qualities, life will be violent and all will be lost.
>
> The airplane and the radio have brought us closer together. The very nature of these inventions cries out for the goodness in men, cries out for universal brotherhood for the unity of us all. Even now my voice is reaching millions throughout the world, millions of despairing men, women and little children, victims of a system that makes men torture and imprison innocent people. To those who can hear me I say "Do not despair."
>
> The misery that is now upon us is but the passing of greed, the bitterness of men who fear the way of human progress: the hate of men will pass and dictators die and the power they took from the people, will return to the people and so long as men die liberty will never perish...

Soldiers—don't give yourselves to brutes, men who despise you and enslave you—who regiment your lives, tell you what to do, what to think and what to feel, who drill you, diet you, treat you as cattle, as cannon fodder.

Don't give yourselves to these unnatural men, machine men, with machine minds and machine hearts. You are not machines. You are not cattle. You are men. You have the love of humanity in your hearts. You don't hate—only the unloved hate. Only the unloved and the unnatural. Soldiers—don't fight for slavery, fight for liberty.

In the seventeenth chapter of Saint Luke it is written "the kingdom of God is within man"—not one man, nor a group of men—but in all men—in you, the people.

You the people have the power, the power to create machines, the power to create happiness. You the people have the power to make life free and beautiful, to make this life a wonderful adventure. Then in the name of democracy let's use that power—let us all unite. Let us fight for a new world, a decent world that will give men a chance to work, that will give youth a future and old age a security. By the promise of these things, brutes have risen to power, but they lie. They do not fulfil their promise, they never will. Dictators free themselves but they enslave the people. Now let us fight to fulfil that promise. Let us fight to free the world, to do away with national barriers, do away with greed, with hate and intolerance. Let us fight for a world of reason, a world where science and progress will lead to all men's happiness.

Soldiers—in the name of democracy, let us all unite!

On December 7th, 1941, Americans finally united. This date, that would live in infamy, changed the U.S. and the motion picture industry forever, much as September 11th, 2001 later would. Shortly after the Japanese air raid on Pearl Harbor, the U.S. was at war with the original Axis of Evil—Japan, Germany and Italy. Neutral, isolationist America was now in the fray. The struggle against fascism became nothing less than a holy crusade to rescue and liberate the world from tyranny. The internal struggle of the U.S. working class against unemployment, poverty, the bosses, for unions and social benefits and programs, became externalized. The enemy was no longer at home, but was abroad, with names like Hitler, Mussolini and Tojo.

And the Russians were now our allies. The Big Three—Stalin, FDR and Churchill—became the public face of the Popular Front.

POP GOES THE FRONT

"The Hitler-Stalin pact, predicted by Trotsky alone after the Munich agreement, was broken, as he had also predicted, only by Hitler."

— Christopher Hitchens, *The Nation*

However, only five months earlier, this would have seemed impossible. The Soviets were desperate: their ultra-left sectarianism had divided the German left, inadvertently helping Hitler seize power. (The exiled Trotsky said at the time that if he had still led the Red Army, he would have mobilized the Soviet military on its western-most border as a signal to the German proletariat that if they arose, the U.S.S.R. would assist them.) The Popular Front failed in Spain. The Western democracies spurned Stalin's proposed collective security alliance against fascism.

Out of desperation, the Kremlin turned to Berlin, and on May 3, 1939, Stalin replaced his Jewish foreign minister, Maxim Litvinov, with Molotov, a non-Jew. On August 23, 1939, the foreign ministers of the Soviet Union and Nazi Germany, Molotov and von Ribbentrop, signed the Nazi-Soviet Non-Aggression Pact. The agreement stated that the signatories would not attack each other and defined spheres of interest. If Stalin had, as Trotsky charged, betrayed the revolution by slaughtering the left opposition, et al, he had now betrayed the anti-fascist cause. The agreement between fascists and Communists—previously mortal enemies—outraged world public opinion. A witty cartoon of the time put it well: The two dictators are doffing their caps and bowing to one another. Hitler says: "The scum of the earth, I believe?" Stalin replies: "The bloody assassin of the workers, I presume?"

Previously, the Soviet Union had provided more open assistance to the fight against fascism than any other nation-state. The democratic U.S. restricted arms sales to the Spanish Republic and American combatants from taking up arms as premature antifascists in Spain and Ethiopia, and members of the Abraham Lincoln Brigade eluded U.S. Neutrality Acts in order to fight for Spain. But the Soviets supplied the Republic and sent military advisers. Putting a good face on it, American and other Communists rationalized the Pact's betrayal by saying Stalin was buying time to build up the Soviet military and industrial capacity in order to prepare for Hitler's eventual invasion. Maybe so, but in reality, fascism's number one enemy was now not only neutralized, but

THE CRIMSON ERA: NEW DEAL AND POPULAR FRONT PICTURES

arguably acting in league with Hitler. The Pact must have made Lenin roll over in the Moscow mausoleum *ad nauseum*.

The Molotov-von Ribbentrop Pact included a secret protocol for the two dictatorships to partition Poland and part of Eastern Europe, with the Soviets receiving the Baltic Republics, Bessarabia and Finland. On September 1, Hitler invaded Poland, and the so-called "Red" Army followed suit on September 17. The U.S.S.R. attacked Finland in November 1939. This was far worse than the West's appeasement of Germany—this was military collaboration with the enemy. Unimpeded by a Soviet foe, Hitler proceeded to overrun Europe. The *Wehrmacht* entered Paris on June 14, 1940. A Stalinist agent assassinated Trotsky in Mexico on August 20, 1940. Stalin liquidated the world's leading proponent of world revolution in order to prove to the goosesteppers that he'd play ball.

Eisenstein's 1938 propaganda classic *Alexander Nevsky*—an allegorical warning to the Nazis, wherein 13th century Russians repel an Aryan invasion—was withdrawn from distribution. The Pact threw Hollywood Communists for a loop, too. Suddenly, the most ardent antifascists became pacifists and neutralists, as they followed the Party line. The putative Communists had more in common with American Firsters and other non-interventionists than they did with their former non-CP Popular Front allies. Indeed, during the Pact period, liberals were *de facto* to the left of Communists. During much of the Battle of Britain, the 20th century's first attempt at a socialist workers state was on the wrong side of history. The almost two years of the Nazi-Soviet Non-Aggression Pact were probably the low point of human civilization, as fascist and bureaucratic dictatorships invaded, conquered and held sway over most of Europe.

HOLLYWOOD REDS GO TO WAR

> "[T]he Party out-patrioted everyone else in Hollywood... the left's Hollywood moment had come."

— Paul Buhle and Dave Wagener, *Radical Hollywood*

Stalin's Pact maneuver/misadventure bought the Soviet Union less than two years. The Nazis launched Operation Barbarosa on June 22, 1941 and invaded the U.S.S.R. When Moscow zigged, the CPUSA zagged. Suddenly, the Hollywood Reds and their comrades around the world were back in the struggle against fascism. The pent-up antifascist ardor of individual members was now released and unleashed against an external enemy. The proletarian motion picture Prometheus was unbound, as CPers rejoined the Good Fight. Except, instead of being premature antifascists, the Communists were now sanctioned as part of a virtual holy crusade to rescue the planet from totalitarian barbarism, and make the world safe for democracy. And instead of being contrary to Washington's stance, by December 7, 1941 the CP was on the side of official U.S. foreign policy, as well as that of the studio system. Like the revolutionary Soviet filmmakers and Bolsheviks of the 1920s, it was another rare, happy confluence of radical artists backed with government and economic power and resources.

As Zinn pointed out, "Of course, the wartime films, it became easier to have antifascist films after the United States was in the war." In "Blacklist: Hollywood on Trial," screenwriter Richard Collins said: "The war period was the easiest period to be a Communist. Because the Communist Party was interested in doing everything possible to help the Soviet Union, which meant cooperating on every level." Later, in testimony to HUAC, Collins said Communists were useful "because they had a more international viewpoint [and]... were in a good position to help in many cases where there [were] assignments that had to do with our allies, Britain, China... Soviet Russia, the underground movements..."

Radical Hollywood declared: "The Party out-patrioted everyone else in Hollywood, from films to sales of war bonds and, above all, in mobilizing public support for the servicemen... So, in a real sense, the left's Hollywood moment had come. The politically shaded films on international themes that had been impossible to make as late as 1938-39 became barely possible in 1940, and sometimes wildly popular as well as widely admired by 1941-42. Left-wingers... rapidly enlisted in the war effort... Suddenly, a new generation of writers and directors took shape... finding ways to entertain and educate in the permissive atmosphere where Communists were, for the moment, anyway, both artistic and more than symbolic representatives of heroic Russia."

The narrator of "Blacklist: Hollywood on Trial," contemporary Hollywood liberal Alec Baldwin, commented, "Hollywood produced hundreds of patriotic war films... Left-wing writers were in demand. They could express the ideals the soldiers were fighting for." And many of the WWII pictures, including some classics, were written by Hollywood Reds and their so-called "fellow travelers," who were ready for their world historical close ups.

John Howard Lawson's premature antifascism of *Blockade* finally attained maturity with a trio of wartime flicks: 1943's *Action in the North Atlantic* and *Sahara* (which both starred Bogie, with Rex Ingram in a particularly dignified black role as an Allied African soldier in *Sahara*) and 1945's *Counter-Attack*, starring Paul Muni and Larry Parks. Dalton Trumbo wrote 1943's Victor Fleming-directed *A Guy Named Joe* and 1944's Mervyn LeRoy-directed *Thirty Seconds Over Tokyo*, both of which co-starred Spencer Tracy and Van Johnson. Trumbo also penned the Rosie the Riveter-like gals-on-the-home-front 1943 drama *Tender Comrade*, starring Ginger Rogers and directed by Eddie Dmytryk. Albert Maltz co-wrote the Oscar-winning 1942 documentary *Moscow Strikes Back*, narrated by Edward G. Robinson, as well as 1943's *Destination Tokyo* with Cary Grant and John Garfield, and 1945's *Pride of the Marines*, also starring Garfield, a well-known left-wing sympathizer. Another likeminded left-leaning actor, Gene Kelly (whose then-wife, Betsy Blair, was a fellow traveler, if not a Party member) starred in Ring Lardner Jr.'s 1943 *The Cross of Lorraine*. Lardner also co-wrote the 1944 anti-Hitler Youth drama *Tomorrow, the World!*

Lester Cole co-wrote 1943's *Night Plane From Chungking* and (with Alvah Bessie) *Objective, Burma!*, Cole co-wrote 1945's *Blood on the Sun*, starring Jimmy Cagney and Sylvia Sidney in one of the era's rare films that sympathetically portrayed Japanese antifascists. Marsha Hunt co-starred in Cole's 1944 *None Shall Escape*, about a Nazi war criminal. Herbert Biberman co-wrote 1944's *Action in Arabia* and *The Master Race*, which he also directed. Samuel Ornitz co-wrote the 1944 concentration camp-related drama *They Live in Fear* and 1945's Pacific Theater-set *China's Little Devils*, starring Harry Carey.

Ben Barzman wrote 1945's *Back to Bataan*, starring John Wayne and Anthony Quinn, directed by Dmytryk, who also helmed the 1943 Hitler Youth picture *Hitler's Children*. The productive Dmytryk directed 1942's *Counter-Espionage*, part of the Lone Wolf series, wherein the onetime jewel thief becomes involved in anti-Nazi espionage, and 1943's Asian Theater-set *Behind the Rising Sun*, which depicted torture. In Dmytryk's 1945 *Cornered* (co-written by John Wexley), an ex-POW and Canadian flyer played by Dick Powell goes down Argentine way to track down the ex-Nazis who murdered his wife, a member of the French resistance. The WWII actioner met *film noir* in *Cornered*, which was written by John Paxton and produced by Adrian Scott.

In 1943's *Watch on the Rhine*, co-written by Lillian Hellman and Dashiell Hammett, Bette Davis and Paul Lukas (who won an Oscar for this role as an underground leader) relocate from war-torn Europe to Washington, where they are pursued by Nazis right in the nation's capital. Hellman wrote *North Star*, one of five 1943 movies that extolled the virtues of our Soviet allies and took place (at least in part) in the U.S.S.R. Directed by Lewis Milestone with cinematography by James Wong Howe, the Russian guerrillas vs. invading Nazis drama starred Dana Andrews, Anne Baxter, Walter Huston, Walter Brennan and that professional Nazi, Erich von Stroheim, and featured music by Aaron Copland with lyrics by Ira Gershwin.

Guy Endore (who co-wrote the 1945 biopic of war correspondent Ernie Pyle, *Story of G.I. Joe*) co-wrote *Song of Russia* with Richard Collins, Paul Jarrico and others. It starred Robert Taylor as a conductor who goes to the U.S.S.R., weds a Russian, and is caught up in the Nazi invasion. In Lawson's *Action in the North Atlantic*, the film culminates as Bogie's merchant marine vessel arrives with its precious cargo of war supplies at Murmansk, where the Soviet comrades welcome their *Americanski tovariches*. *Mission to Moscow* is arguably the most notorious of all of Hollywood's Popular Front pictures—although it is far from being the best. Walter Huston plays U.S. Ambassador Joseph Davies in this story about his diplomatic assignment to and travels throughout the U.S.S.R. Oscar Homolka plays Maxim Litvinov and Manart Kippen impersonates Uncle Joe Stalin, our pipe-smoking, benign, wise ally in this propaganda movie written by Howard Koch and directed by Michael Curtiz (*sans* his usual panache). In addition, there were other U.S. features about the Soviet Union, such as the B-picture *Three Russian Girls*, but most are now forgotten.

Of course, Communists weren't the only ones cranking out propaganda pictures about the Good War. Zinn also correctly pointed out, "One of the things that interests me is that some good films, films with a progressive or radical message, were not made by radicals." The historian cited John Ford as an example, and recalled some other WWII-era antifascist flicks. "There was the Spanish Civil War film with Gary Cooper and Ingrid Bergman [1943's *For Whom the Bell Tolls*, Sam Wood's version of Hemingway's novel]... *The Seventh Cross* [directed by Fred Zinnemann in 1944, starring Spencer Tracy] was about seven people being hunted down by the Nazis [in 1936]. They were seven people who had escaped from [concentration] camps. They erected seven crosses and promised that every one of those people would be found and hanged by this cross. Very exciting," Zinn remembered. (The next project for *Cross'* screenwriter, Helen Deutsch, was the Elizabeth Taylor and Mickey Rooney horse racing favorite *National Velvet.*)

Fritz Lang got his revenge on the men who would have dragooned him into helming the Reich's film industry. His anti-lynch mob movie metaphors morphed into explicit anti-Nazi propaganda with 1941's *Man Hunt*, about an almost assassination of Hitler, starring Walter Pidgeon, George Sanders and John Carradine, and written by Dudley Nichols. *Radical Hollywood* considers Lang's 1943 *Hangmen Also Die* (an ironic title for a director obsessed with lynching) to be one of the best resistance dramas. It is the fictionalized story of the assassination of Nazi *Reichsprotector* Reinhard Heydrich by the Czech underground, and is considered to be the most successful Hollywood project playwright Bertolt Brecht was involved with (as co-writer). John Wexley wrote *Hangmen's* script.

Communist, other leftist and patriotic talents were part of a national effort that the government formally played a role in. Only 11 days after the sneak attack on Pearl Harbor, FDR appointed Lowell Mellett, the then-director of Government Reports, as the Coordinator of Government Films, in order to officially mobilize Hollywood for the war effort. The Office of War Information was created in June 1942, with CBS News' Elmer Davis as its director. Mellett's film office became the Bureau of Motion Pictures. As actors such as Clark Gable, Jimmy Stewart and Tyrone Power joined the armed services, directors like John Ford, John Huston and Frank Capra volunteered for duty with their cameras.

Major Capra was ordered by Army Chief of Staff George C. Marshall to make a series of motivational documentaries that would explain to the fighting men exactly what they were fighting for. The seven-part *Why We Fight* series proved to be so successful that in addition to the troops, the docs were screened for war production plants and the general public, too. Carl Foreman co-wrote *Know Your Enemy: Japan* with its director, Capra; John Huston narrated the documentary.

Like many Reds and other filmmakers, Jean Butler Rouverol "discovered the joys of patriotism" during the war. But this seemed to be nothing compared to a joint victory with our Soviet ally. In "Blacklist: Hollywood on Trial," Rouverol went on to say: "We really had enormous optimism about the future. Essentially you believed you were fighting for a better world... The Russians were our allies."

As World War II ended, Red and two-time Oscar winner Ring Lardner, Jr. experienced "a growing good feeling... [A]n Allied victory... had been won by the two great powers... one democratic, one Communist, who... work[ed] together for shared ideals..."

In *Blacklist*, Lardner added, "The defeat of fascism seemed to be the defeat of unreason and prejudice. One felt that the whole nationalist idea had been exposed, the myth of the Aryan race, superiority. That this could lead to greater racial understanding." The Hollywood left had every reason to feel hopeful. In addition to winning the war, the filmmakers had secured hard-earned gains in the studio firmament and were in well-paid positions of influence.

Dalton Trumbo was reportedly the highest paid screenwriter working in Hollywood. "By 1946, Trumbo's salary was $3,000 a week or $75,000 a script... Nowhere else in the world, except possibly in the Kremlin, had there been... Communists with a higher standard of living," Lardner wrote in his autobiography, *I'd Hate Myself in the Morning*. MGM paid Lardner and a co-writer $100,00 for 1942's *Woman of the Year*. Bobby Lees said that he was earning $1500 a week writing comedies like *Abbott and Costello Meet Frankenstein*.

The Hollywood Reds and radicals had power, prestige, persuasiveness and talent. A war galvanized them into action, and their gifted support for the war effort threw them into the mainstream and the spotlight. Their noble crusade paid off, their side—including our Soviet allies—were triumphant, and now they were going to bring the war home. In John Huston's 1948 *Key Largo*, based on Maxwell Anderson's play and adapted by Richard Brooks, Bogie plays a veteran tired of fighting. But aboard a boat in Florida, he encounters gangster Edward G. Robinson, and Bogart realizes that he must continue the fight. And so, with their enemies abroad vanquished, like before the war, the left-coasters trained their sights on social injustice back on the home front.

The repatriated G.I.s and the problems they faced were dealt with head-on in classics such as William Wyler's 1946 *The Best Years of Our Lives*, written by Robert E. Sherwood. Stanley Kramer's 1950 *The Men*, which introduced Marlon Brando to the screen, was written by Carl Foreman. Both films squarely dealt with disabilities, and the new maturity also allowed movies to also depict mental illness, as in 1948's *Snake Pit*, starring Olivia de Havilland and directed by the Ukrainian Anatole Litvak, who had also directed part of Capra's *Why We Fight* docs, including 1943's *The Battle of Russia*.

In addition to Dmytryk's 1947 *Crossfire* (produced by Adrian Scott, based on Brooks' novel and scripted by John Paxton, starring Roberts Ryan, Mitchum and Young), ex-Communist Elia Kazan's 1947 *Gentlemen's Agreement*, starring Gregory Peck and John Garfield, took on anti-Semitism. Racism was tackled in movies like Kramer's 1949 *Home of the Brave*, scripted by Foreman and co-starring Jeff Corey and Peter Moss, Kazan's 1949 *Pinky*, written by Philip Dunne and Dudley Nichols, co-starring Jeanne Crain, Ethel Waters and Ethel Barrymore and 1949's *Intruder in the Dust*, with Ben Maddow adapting the William Faulkner novel, co-starring Juano Hernandez and Will Geer.

Radical Hollywood postulates that *film noir*, with its obsession with greed, was a metaphorical expression of disillusionment with the capitalist system that reached its apotheosis in postwar America. Buhle and Wagner point out that Communists played key roles in launching the cynical genre. Dashiell Hammett's novels pioneered *film noir*, spawning 1931 and 1941 versions of *The Maltese Falcon*, 1935 and 1942's *The Glass Key*, and *The Thin Man* films from 1934 to 1947. Back in 1942, Albert Maltz had co-written the script for *This Gun for Hire*, co-starring Veronica Lake and Alan Ladd, based on a novel by Graham Greene. (Maltz's next project was the 1942 doc *Moscow Strikes Back*.) Abraham Polonsky's 1948 *Force of Evil* was an obvious Marxist critique of capitalism. And so on.

The Hollywood left's postwar talkies did not fall on deaf ears—indeed, they spoke to a receptive audience. In *Projections of War: Hollywood, American Culture and World War II*, Thomas Doherty asserts: "Far from having a mesmerized gaze or a goosestepped soul, the average American moviegoer circa 1945 had acquired a more alert, attuned and skeptical eye than the circa 1941 model. Graduating from the four-year curriculum in motion picture technique and propagandistic persuasion was the first generation of moving-image spectators as accustomed to education as entertainment, as prepared for critical engagement as for cultural diversion. Axis cinema, endowed elsewhere with an almost hypnotic power of persuasion, could rightly be marked as crudely obvious and transparently deceptive to the discerning American whose Hollywood-trained vision was sharp enough to spot the con. 'You are up to his tricks,' Warner Bros.' *Divide and Conquer* assures. 'You can see through his technique...' [T]he *Hollywood Reporter* bragged: 'Military authorities and OWI men are convinced that American films are the most important means of disintoxicating people in areas formerly occupied by the enemy from Axis propraganda and re-educating them to the knowledge of the free world and free people from which they have been cut off.'"

As Lenin had said: "To us, cinema is the most important of the arts." Indeed. Postwar, open-minded audiences, which had just triumphed over fascism, were predisposed to social message movies. The Hollywood Reds and leftists were armed with movie cameras—and dangerous.

They had to be stopped, by any means necessary. As Lardner pointed out in his autobiography: "The movies had seemed to be coming down from the clouds, at least until Congress began looking our way."

THE EMPIRE STRIKES BACK

"Are you now or have you ever been a member of the Communist Party?"

— House Un-American Activities Committee

If the Second World War had brought respectability and mass audiences to cinema's socialists and radicals, the Cold War would prove to be their undoing. The entertainment industry was hit particularly hard by this postwar backlash.

"Almost no one had anticipated how quickly the tide would turn to rightist reaction," Lardner wrote in *I'd Hate Myself in the Morning.* "One of the first acts of the Republicans who took control of Congress in 1946 (for the first time in 20 years) was to convert a temporary [HUAC], which had been investigating fascist sympathizers during the war, into a permanent [committee] concentrating on the... left," Lardner noted with alarm.

"They came at the worst possible time," Dmytryk groused in "Blacklist: Hollywood on Trial." "My career was flying away... I was at the top. Everything was going great and then all of a sudden you got these subpoenas."

When the Cold War between the Soviet Union and United States heated up, HUAC congressmen charged that there was "subversive influence in motion pictures" and that Communists had infiltrated the motion picture industry, much as Joe McCarthy would allege about the State Department and Army in the Senate. By 1947, Congress subpoenaed the Hollywood Ten to appear before the House on Un-American Activities Committee. The suspected Communists included screenwriters Lardner, John Howard Lawson, Dalton Trumbo, Albert Maltz, Alvah Bessie, Lester

Cole, Samuel Ornitz, screenwriter/producer Adrian Scott, directors Edward Dmytryk and Herbert Biberman.

The F.B.I., HUAC and studio chiefs collaborated to crush Tinseltown's "Red Menace." Gerald Horne's well-researched *Class Struggle in Holly-wood: 1930–1950* documents that for movie moguls the Red Scare was, at least in part, a smokescreen for studio union busting. As WWII wound down, craft workers in the Conference of Studio Unions clashed with movie industry employers in 1945 and 1946 strikes, part of the upsurge of labor activities as the wartime victory seemed inevitable. (During WWII, most U.S. unions abided by a no-strike pledge endorsed by the CP.) As Horne observed: "Accusations of communism were not just designed to drive out practicing Reds with ties to Moscow... [T]hese bombardments were also intended to damage militant non-Communist labor, which suffered fatal collateral damage."

Commenting on the essential role Communists played in building moviedom's unions and guilds Norma Barzman, asserted: "That's why the studios hated us and went along with the blacklist." Indeed, during the HUAC hearings, Walt Disney (one of the few Hollywood talents who would meet with Leni Riefenstahl during her visit to L.A.) grew animated as Uncle Walt exclaimed: "And the thing I resent the most is that they're able to get into these unions and take them over..."

Blacklist historian Nat Segaloff added that the stated threat of mono-lithic "communism wasn't the greatest worry" for moguls who had economic motives to fire highly paid talent, breaking contracts under the pretext of national security. And although it's often claimed that celebri-ties endorse causes for free publicity, obscure politicians "can always get headlines by attacking Hollywood," Segaloff acidly observed.

In October, 1947, when HUAC asked witnesses questions such as: "Are you now or have you ever been a member of the Communist Party?", the Hollywood Ten invoked the First Amendment, asserting Congress had no right to compel Americans to testify about political affiliations. In May 1947, stars such as Katharine Hepburn and Henry Wallace, who had been FDR's veep during his third term, participated in the *Hollywood Fights Back* program. On November 24, 1947, the Hollywood Ten were cited for contempt of Congress, while the Motion Picture Association held a secretive financiers' and producers' powwow at Manhattan's Waldorf Astoria. The following day, MPA President Eric Johnston announced: "We will not re-employ any of the Ten until such time as he is acquitted, or has purged himself of contempt, and declared under oath that he is not a Communist."

The defeat of Henry Wallace and the Progressive Party in the 1948 presidential race was another huge blow against Hollywood progressives. By 1950, the Hollywood Ten lost their appeals and began serving prison sentences, and HUAC had launched a new wave of hearings. (Ironically, once behind bars, Lardner ran into the grand inquisitor again at the Federal Correctional Institution in Danbury, CT, where the corrupt Congressman Parnell Thomas was also serving time.) How did the Hollywood blacklist work? In essence, individuals who were subpoenaed or otherwise named had to denounce not only whatever left-wing ties they themselves had (from CP membership to having supported anti-Franco forces back in the 1930s during the Spanish Civil War). Very importantly, cooperative witnesses also had to name the names of others who'd also had leftist links. Those who had recanted, purged themselves and informed on others were generally "rehabilitated" and allowed to return to work.

Hollywood had been divided between friendly witnesses who cooperated with the committee, and "unfriendlies" who defied it. Left-leaning celebrities were in the Hollywood Independent Citizens Committee of the Arts, Sciences and the Professions, including Frank Sinatra, Lena Horne, Dore Schary, Olivia de Havilland, Linus Pauling and lyricist Yip Harburg, who'd penned the words for that Depression ode, "Brother, Can You Spare a Dime?" as well as for 1939's "The Wizard of Oz" and "Song of Russia." On the right, the Motion Picture Alliance for the Preservation of American Ideals included Disney, Director Sam Wood, Gary Cooper and King Vidor.

However, screenwriter Robert Lees—blacklisted in 1951 for refusing to name names—recounted: "After the Ten were imprisoned, and the anti-Communist McCarran and Smith Acts were passed, the Fifth Amendment against self-incrimination became the defense. The government couldn't jail and fine you for contempt of Congress, but the punishment came from the studios, who fired you."

Dave Wagner, co-author of *Blacklisted: The Film Lover's Guide to the Hollywood Blacklist*, said 40 ex-Reds became "friendly" witnesses. (This doesn't include conservatives such as Walt Disney, Adolphe Menjou and Robert Taylor, who gleefully testified against La-La-Land leftists.) Segaloff estimated that 435 entertainment industry employees were blacklisted. Wagner added that in various other industries, 8-10,000 Americans were blacklisted nationwide.

Studio agitprop ballyhooing a 1949 anticommunist B-pic about a veteran tricked by commies, narrated by L.A. City Councilman Lloyd Davies.

In response to the anticommunist witch-hunts, Hollywood talents formed the Committee for the First Amendment, which went to Washington in October 1947. The Tinseltowners included: actress Marsha Hunt (first in line), who was not a Party member but was eventually blacklisted for refusing to name names; actor Sterling Hayden (in middle on left); above Hayden, Lauren Bacall; to her right Danny Kaye; above Bacall on the left is Humphrey Bogart.

As they await imprisonment, members of the Hollywood Ten participate in a protest against the anti-communist inquisition.

In Tinseltown, the postwar labor militancy and Reds-under-the-beds hysteria incited political passions across the spectrum, from Left to Right. Above is one such vigilance group, the Citizens Committee.

An anticommunist zealot protests the 1951 biblical epic "David and Bathsheba," foreshadowing the fanaticism of the contemporary "Christian" Right. Civil libertarian Philip Dunne was a member of the Committee for the First Amendment, Gregory Peck was a noted liberal and Darryl Zanuck produced some social problem movies, such as 1947's "Gentleman's Agreement" (starring Peck) about anti-Semitism and 1949's "Pinky," about racism, both directed by ex-CPer Elia Kazan, who eventually named names to HUAC.

Scenes from the class struggle in Tinseltown: Relatives of members of the militant Conference of Studio Unions picket a movie studio in 1946.

One of the Cold War publications, such as "Red Channels," which named suspected "subversives" and urged their blacklisting—today, several websites continue in this dubious tradition.

RED CHANNELS

"Do not make me crawl through the mud like an informer."

— Actor Larry Parks to HUAC, 1951

Besides HUAC, there was another way to smear members of the entertainment industry. *Red Channels: The Report of Communist Influence in Radio and Television,* was a paperback brochure published in 1950 by former F.B.I. agents and businesspeople, who called themselves American Business Consultants, Inc. "They published a newsletter called *Counterattack,*" Segaloff stated. "Red Channels had... an alphabetical index of names... listing organizations they'd [allegedly] supported, contributions made, petitions signed, [political] appearances made. I don't know where anybody could've gotten this information, if it wasn't leaked by the F.B.I.... The second part was an alphabetical index of organizations, from the Abolish Peonage Committee to the Theatre Workshop, cross-referenced with the names of groups that Red Channels felt were Communist or front organizations... Red Channels was mailed free of charge to everybody who hired [talent] in radio and television. It was one way of vetting people," explained Segaloff.

The blacklist scholar went on to say: "Before hiring, every network had someone who'd either have a contact with the government, for checking F.B.I. files, or to whom you'd go to clear your name if there was a question. Often this meant being represented by lawyer Martin Gang who, for a fee, would... test your employability and your willingness to name names... If you were named in front of HUAC, one of its investigators, William Wheeler, would meet with Gang... Gang listened to your *mea culpa* and announced you'd become patriotic again."

Segaloff cited others who could clear names: the American Legion, projectionists' union head Roy Brewer and B'Nai B'rith's Anti-Defamation League. "One of the most notorious groups was... set up by then-Screen Actors Guild President Ronald Reagan, before whom you could admit you were a dupe and make an effort to show what a good American you were... As Reagan said, the most important thing was to show you were honestly repentant," Segaloff added. According to Victor Navasky, author of *Naming Names*: "Ronald Reagan was president of the SAG and enforced the blacklist. He also was an F.B.I. informant with his own special code name: T-10."

"Commies" were denounced as Stalinist stooges and agents, helping Moscow spread totalitarianism and world domination, and subverting movies. In postwar USA, Tinseltown was especially reviled for a handful of wartime pro-Soviet films, such as *Mission to Moscow*, made at the behest of the Roosevelt administration when Russia was our WWII ally. The screenwriter of 1939's beloved *Mr. Smith Goes to Washington*, Sidney Buchman, was cited for contempt of Congress in 1953.

Blacklist historian Dave Wagner commented, "They were called 'swimming pool Communists'—but only 40 people cracked under that kind of pressure, and refused to cave in so they could continue to work? That suggests to me something deeper was going on there... commitment." Unfriendly witnesses such as Lillian Hellman and Paul Robeson defied the committee. "I am not willing, now or in the future... to hurt innocent people... in order to save myself... I cannot and will not cut my conscience to fit this year's fashions," Hellman boldly testified in 1952.

When a 1956 HUAC subcommittee asked Robeson "Are you now a member of the Communist Party?", the singer/actor replied: "As far as I know it is a legal party like the Republican Party and Democratic Party. Do you mean a party of people who have sacrificed for my people, and for all Americans and workers, that they can live in dignity? Do you mean that party?... Would you like to come to the ballot box when I vote and take out the ballot and see?"

Wagner described the Hollywood left's social milieu as "a magic circle" and "beloved community" that "charmed everybody who came into it... When the moment of crisis came... they stood on the right side."

KING RAT

"I could have had class. I could have been a contender. I could have been somebody, instead of a bum, which is what I am, let's face it."

— Marlon Brando, *On the Waterfront*, directed by Elia Kazan

Elia Kazan, who had left the Party before he relocated to Hollywood, was not a member of this charmed circle. Kazan was born in Turkey in 1909, and emigrated to America soon after. He joined the Group Theatre in 1932 and the CPUSA in 1934; after a falling out, Kazan quit the Party in 1936. He worked in documentaries, and directed his first Hollywood feature, *A Tree Grows in Brooklyn*, in 1945. His Broadway and Hollywood productions were noted for nitty-gritty realism, Stanislavsky's Method Acting and liberal themes. As previously noted, Kazan's films included 1947's Best Picture, *Gentlemen's Agreement*, and 1949's *Pinky*.

During the witch-hunts, HUAC subpoenaed the ex-Communist. On January 14, 1952, Kazan confessed to having been a member, but refused to name others—and was asked by a committee member if he "knew the risks of contempt?"

Pressure was brought to bear on Kazan by studio chiefs and others, and his movie career appeared jeopardized. It's alleged in Navasky's *Naming Names* that Kazan went to Washington with producer Spyros Skouras and met with J. Edgar Hoover. After voluntarily asking HUAC to reopen his case, on April 10, 1952, Kazan informed on eight former Group Theatre comrades, including playwright Clifford Odets and around seven CP functionaries. He denounced the Party for "taking its orders from the Kremlin and acting as a Russian agency in this country," and for trying to takeover the Group Theatre. When Kazan resisted this purported power grab, he was "invited to go through a typical Communist scene of crawling and apologizing and admitting the error of my ways." Sickened by the Party's "habitual violation of... democracy," Kazan left in disgust.

On April 12, 1952, Kazan went on to publish an ad in the *New York Times* rationalizing his treachery by stressing lofty principles. He condemned "a dangerous and alien conspiracy" that had given him "a taste of the police state," and implored: "Liberals must speak out [for] free speech, a free press... above all, individual rights."

With his informing, compounded by the ad, "Kazan emerged in the folklore of the left as the quintessential informer" and "ultimate betrayer," Navasky wrote in *Naming Names*. In *A Life*, Kazan described his HUAC testimony as "a degradation ordeal" that was "humiliating," and caused "anger." Yet, although Stalin was half a world away, America's Communists were on the ropes and neither had any power over him, Kazan's highfalutin' HUAC statement and his *Times* ad did not contain a single word criticizing the Congressional grand inquisitors— even though Kazan "bitterly resented" them, as he safely admitted 36 years later.

Kazan also rationalized his informing by claiming that he did not act out of careerist and money interests, but out of conscience. He justified naming people who "were already known, it's not as if I were turning them over to the police... It was a token act to me," the *über*-squealer is quoted as saying in Navasky's book.

But blacklistees begged to differ. "He was a Broadway director, Broadway did not have a blacklist, and he could have made lots of money in the theatre," insisted Lees. "I knew the Brombergs and Carnovskys [whom Kazan named] from the Actors' Lab. Bromberg died of a heart attack after being summoned by HUAC... The committee included southern rednecks... Kazan could say, 'I'm disillusioned with the Communists and U.S.S.R.,' which is perfectly permissible, but to say: 'I hate them, but I love you,' embracing HUAC, and giving cachet to them... He knew how lousy they were... Taking out the big *Times* ad, for my money, ended Kazan," Lees adamantly asserted.

"Kazan said it really didn't matter that he'd named names, because everybody he'd named had been named by somebody else," noted Wagner, who co-wrote *Hide in Plain Sight: The Hollywood Blacklistees in Film and Television, 1950–2000*. "There was one guy Kazan named nobody else [except for Clifford Odets] ever named: Tony Kraber, an actor... He became an executive producer at CBS, and when Kazan outed him, he lost his job. So, when Kazan says he didn't do anybody any harm, it's not true." In *A Life*, Kazan wrote about an anxiety dream he had about Kraber—although it probably wasn't as nerve wracking as the nightmares Kraber may have experienced, courtesy of Kazan.

"There's no doubt he was motivated by the fact he was offered big salaries and positions to continue his work as a Hollywood director... he did not want to give up that career for refusing to name names," insisted Bernard Gordon. "Kazan... crawled before the committee... [which] wasn't interested in getting names... What they wanted was to get [prestigious] people like Kazan... cooperating with them and, in effect, validating them, and saying, 'Yes, you have a right to ask these questions.' Although they were against the Constitution and freedom of speech... where you don't have to tell Congress or the police... what your political or union affiliations are. It was strictly a stunt to get headlines," declared Gordon.

King Rat's betrayal epitomized for many the horrors of the McCarthy era. The wounds inflicted by McCarthy, HUAC, Kazan and the Hollywood blacklist remain open more than half a century later, as we'll see.

CAN WE TALK?

"There you have the smoking gun. As HUAC... set out to prove: the Party was endeavoring to insert Red propaganda into films."

— Bernard Gordon, *The Gordon File: A Screenwriter Recalls Twenty Years of F.B.I. Surveillance*

In the immortal words of that great existentialist philosopher Joan Rivers: "Can we talk?" Now that the Cold War is over and the Berlin Wall has come down, perhaps we can objectively assess the Communist Party, USA and its offbeat Hollywood branch. Many charges were hurled at moviedom's Reds, including the accusation, as Lardner noted in *I'd Hate Myself in the Morning*, of "a link between Hollywood and Soviet spying and sabotage..."

Now the truth can be told! One of the Beverly Hills Bolsheviks was indeed a secret agent! In "Blacklist: Hollywood on Trial," Abe Polonsky confesses that yes, he was a spy and that he did engage in underground activities. However, this was during WWII as a member of the American forerunner to the CIA, the Office of Strategic Services—and he was on the Allies' side. Polonsky's left-wing background was valuable, because he was able to relate with the European resistance fights, many of whom were Communists.

Deprived of their livelihoods and facing persecution at home, many Red talents went into exile. But did they go to Mother Russia? Only a handful of artists who were themselves of Eastern European background returned to their homelands, such as Brecht, who went to the German Democratic Republic, aka East Germany. None of the North American born and raised blacklistees moved to the Soviet bloc countries, although some visited but did not remain there, like the Barzmans, who ended up in France. After Hugo Butler was subpoenaed in 1951, he and Jean went into exile in Mexico, where the Trumbos also moved. Bernie Gordon relocated to Spain, Carl Foreman to England. Bobby Lees skeedaddled not to Tblisi but to Tucson. And so on.

Let's be honest about it and put the redbaiting aside. A realistic reappraisal is that the American Communists were neither angels nor devils. They had no horns or halos. They did both good and bad. In a sense, the CPUSA was like an abusive loved one who does some harm, but also nurtures and loves the abused. To be sure, when it came to foreign policy, the CP generally followed the Moscow line. But was this always automatically bad? Sometimes, as during WWII, Capitol Hill and the Kremlin were allied in the grand struggle against Hitler and Mussolini. During the Nazi-Soviet Pact period, Washington's policy was better than Moscow's, but during the Spanish Civil War days, Stalin arguably did more to fight fascism than FDR did.

Having said that, CPers were ignorant of or turned a blind eye and deaf ear to the Moscow show trials, famine in the Ukraine, the Gulag archipelago of Soviet labor and prison camps, the liquidation of Lenin's central committee culminating with the assassination of Trotsky and so on. The Molotov-von Ribbentrop Pact was the most egregious example of Stalin's poor leadership. Buying time (precious little, as it turned out) through a non-aggression agreement was one thing—dubious, but perhaps understandable in terms of *realpolitik* and the West's (including America's) lack of resolve to fight Hitler. But to connive to secretly carve up parts of Eastern Europe with Berlin was inexcusable. How could a workers' state do such a thing? How could a socialist society invade countries in collaboration with fascists? How could Jews, who were in disproportionately large numbers in the Hollywood branch of the CPUSA, go along with this?

On the film front, at around the same time that the prohibitive 1934 Production Code was imposed on American cinema, Stalin virtually banned the *avant garde* Soviet cinema with its emphasis on montage, and dictated so-called "socialist realism" (which wasn't socialist and wasn't realistic) in the arts. How could Hollywood's creative comrades tolerate this, plus the tirades directed against Albert Maltz when he dared differ with the official Party line on the role of the arts?

The reason is likely that on the home front, the CP was in the vanguard of fighting for positive social change, such as welfare state reforms like unemployment insurance and social security, unionization, and struggling against racism and other societal evils. A strong case could be made that during this time in history, the Party did more to help the down and out, the common people, the working class, than any other political organization in America did.

So like an abusive parent, spouse, lover, *et al*, the Communist Party should not be vilified or beatified. Like the Soviet Union itself, it had both its negative and positive points.

THE CRIMSON ERA: NEW DEAL AND POPULAR FRONT PICTURES

And did the left-wing filmmakers inject the Moscow line and Marxism into movies? The most offensive thing about *Mission to Moscow* wasn't its extolling of the virtues of a wartime ally, but its screed against Trotsky and the left opposition, and defense of the police state-like show trials. To the extent that the ComIntern line did make it onto the screen, if at all, it was to espouse the Popular Front, especially when it became Washington's own official policy to win the war.

HUAC asked former Writers Guild President Emmett Lavery, who'd written the two Eddie Dmytryk-directed 1943 pictures *Hitler's Children* and *Behind the Rising Sun*, if Marxist ideas had been put onto the screen. Lavery, a liberal Catholic, replied that the studio moguls were "as alert as this committee to not allow Marxist doctrines in pictures."

1948's *Abbott and Costello Meet Frankenstein*, written by CP members Fred Rinaldo and Bobby Lees, provides an illuminating look at the extent that Reds were able to inject politics into scripts. In this scene, a rude customer picking up a large box (secretly containing Frankenstein) argues with Lou Costello as Wilbur:

Customer

If that's the way you handle baggage, I'm gonna have the insurance agent there to inspect them before I accept delivery.

Wilbur

Well, then it's gonna cost you overtime, because I'm a union man. And I work only 16 hours a day.

Customer

A union man only works eight hours a day.

Wilbur

I belong to two unions!

The dialogue may have been pro-organized labor, but it was hardly revolutionary. And as for Bernie Gordon's confession that opened this section, what was the choice piece of subversion that this then-Communist screenwriter was trying to slip past producers and sneak into a movie in 1948? As his screenwriting career got underway with an assignment at Columbia Pictures, Gordon recalls in *The Gordon File*:

"Despite our new status, we did not forget our social obligations and the fact that the Party kept urging us to do whatever we could, as writers, to work in roles for black actors. So, to make our tiny contribution, when we wrote in a taxi driver, we specified that he be black. It might mean only a day's work for a bit player, but work was work... [The producer] automatically crossed out the word 'black' and... explained that it was not permitted because it would only cause trouble in the South, where theaters would refuse to play the film. There you have the smoking gun. As the HUAC... set out to prove: The Party was endeavoring to insert Red propaganda into films."

Ironically enough, the period movie that most expressed Marxist philosophy wasn't by a Party member. Chaplin's *Modern Times* incorporated Marx's concept of man and the alienation of the labor process into a radical filmic critique of capitalism more than any Hollywood Red did. Although Chaplin campaigned during the war to open a second front in order to aid the besieged Soviets, he did not belong to the CP. The role of non-Communist independent leftists in filmdom also has to be factored into the equation. Like Chaplin (whose 1957 *A King in New York* was that rare film that dared ridicule HUAC), Orson Welles and John Huston largely sat out the McCarthy era overseas. And many non-CPers like actresses Marsha Hunt and Lee Grant were blackballed by the cinematic Spanish Inquisition.

In any case, McCarthyism left the Hollywood left in tatters. Jailed, blacklisted, exiled, using pseudonyms or fronts, Khrushchev's revelations of Stalin's crimes and his own invasion of Hungary finished off what remained of the CPUSA in Hollywood. The Party was over.

It would take another war to revive progressive Hollywood.

ACT 2

THE WHOLE WORLD WAS WATCHING

POWER TO THE PEOPLE PICTURES

COUNTERCULTURE CLASSICS

*"Being indicted for a conspiracy to cross state lines for the pur-
pose of inciting a riot at the Chicago Convention was like winning
the Academy Award of protest."*

— Jerry Rubin (played by Barry Miller), in "Conspiracy:
The Trial of the Chicago 8"

The recipe for the '60s/'70s power to the people pictures consisted of
these obligatory ingredients: two teaspoons of snazzy opening credits; one
cup of pop song(s) by trendy musicians such as Crosby, Stills, Nash and
Young, Grateful Dead or Pink Floyd; one pound of young, attractive, longhaired lovers; minced artsy film techniques, including zooms, flash
forwards, moving camera shots and montage sequences; dollops of nudity; one tablespoon of violent confrontations between protesters and "The
Man"; a twist of Afros; a *soupçon* of psychedelics; one teaspoon of Volk-
swagen minibuses; a pinch of sexplicit sex; plus dashes of Elliott Gould,
Candice Bergen, Bruce Dern, Bud Cort and the Fondas. Cook on a high
flame, bring to a boil in a large cinematic skillet and sprinkle liberally
with marijuana, tear gas, inter-generational angst, alienation, rebellious-
ness and topical politics.

Who was the audience for these radical reels? The fact that millions
of mostly young people participated in antiwar and other protest marches did not escape the attention of Tinseltown executives and filmmakers
as a new, emerging target market to tap into—and cash in on—by putting
their concerns onscreen.

Roger Corman was a prolific creator and pioneer of so-called "youth
exploitation" flicks, which were often shot on a shoestring budget in a

matter of days for AIP and Corman's own companies. Corman told me: "During the '60s and '70s I was a young producer/director and I was aware of the fact that the major studios were using middle-aged and older stars as the leads in their pictures. Yet at the same time, the audience was primarily teen-aged and in their twenties. And I felt I related to the youth market and that the youth market was much bigger than the major studios realized. So I concentrated on making films for that market," said Corman, who is currently president of the production and distribution company New Concorde Pictures.

Corman went on to say: "The youth market in the '60s and '70s, but particularly in the '60s was more rebellious than today. Today youth seems to be more conformist. I, at the same time, was liberal in my political beliefs, so my beliefs went along to a certain extent with what the beliefs of the youth market were. So pictures that I did such as *Wild Angels*, the first of the motorcycle films, and *The Trip*, which was about an LSD experience, and other films I did, which were somewhat rebellion-oriented were exemplars of the counterculture... I also did some car racing pictures, *The Wild Racers* [1970], did a picture [called] *Rock All Night* [1957 plus 1979's *Rock 'n' Roll High School*] about rock and roll, subject matter that would interest the youth."

Sometimes, when major studios did venture into youth market movies, the established powers-that-be deemed the final products to be too outré and even outright subversive. As a result they deliberately failed to properly promote and distribute them. The films, which captured the *zeitgeist* and which were suitably released, included the era's most profitable picture and a Cannes Film Festival Palme d'Or winner. As the demonstrators at the 1968 Democratic Convention in Chicago chanted, it seemed as if the whole world really was watching.

Experiencing a retrospective of the antiestablishment movies of what film historian Peter Biskind called "the Sex-Drugs-and-Rock 'n' Roll Generation" decades after they were shot is a revelation. The genre ranges widely, from naïvete to cynicism—with insight, and occasionally even wisdom, found somewhere in-between. Viewed as a group, these movies' raw passions—from the sexual to the political—retain their power to move, and even shock, today's audiences. Unfortunately, a third of a century anon, many of the issues that preoccupied these counterculture classics are still with us, and remain major bones of contention. Gender roles, race relations and, arguably most apropos for our age of preemptive strikes and imperial ambitions, the antiwar theme, retain their relevancy and potency. Perhaps most disturbing of all, the peoples' power pictures' prescient peek at militant direct action presage the terrorism besetting our own anxious age.

The postwar generation experienced economic growth and an unprecedented middle class, with young people gaining disposable incomes. These and other factors—anthropologist Margaret Mead pointed out that baby boomers were the first generation to grow up with the bomb, pill and tube (not to mention Dr. Spock's "permissive" child rearing philosophy)—helped spawn the youth rebellion of the 1960s. The entertainment industry lost no time in flattering the flower power generation that they epitomized hip and *chic*, the coolest kids in the history of cool, catering to (and exploiting and manufacturing) their wallets, fashions, music, movies and more that appealed to their sensibilities, dollars and cents. The technique and content of foreign films, such as Costa-Gavras' *Z*, Gillo Pontecorvo's *The Battle of Algiers*, Jean-Luc Godard's *Breathless*, Luis Buñuel's *Belle de Jour*, etc., also sharply impacted American moviemakers and moviegoers.

Whereas the '30s/'40s social protest films were preoccupied with the class struggle and crusade against fascism, their '60s/'70s counterparts focused on cultural matters. Instead of rich against poor, it was more often than not the straights, squares and jocks against the hippies, Yippies and freaks, the old versus the young, the sexually uptight pitted against the liberated. "One generation got old / One generation got soul / This generation got no destination to hold," as Jefferson Airplane sang in "Volunteers."

This generational component is a marked departure from the Depression and WWII era flicks, and to some extent was an outgrowth of the Marlon Brando/Montgomery Clift/James Dean rebels-without-causes 1950s sensibility and syndrome. In addition, some of the more rebellious aesthetics not only took on the military industrial complex, but the entertainment industry itself, challenging norms of filmmaking (dictums such as: "Never shoot into the sun! It creates flares that shatter the suspension of disbelief!"), and the studio system itself. The counterculture classics are documents from the ground zero of the "culture war" that is still being fought today.

When referred to as "radical," this is shorthand for the fact that these films dealt with radical subject matter—even if their treatment of left-leaning content was not necessarily progressive, let alone revolutionary. Where relevant, other movies—including some influential, inspirational foreign films—are also considered. In terms of politics *per se*, the power to the people pictures were most notably preoccupied with antiwar sentiments, ethnic issues and minority rights. That being the case, this book zooms in on those films that were the era's most explicitly politically engaged.

Mike Nichols' deftly directed and well-acted *The Graduate* struck a responsive chord and was a critical and box office hit, proving that the theme of youthful rebellion could attract large audiences. The 1967 film brilliantly and wittily explored the cultural discontent of a student after he graduates from college. Benjamin Braddock (an ill-at-ease Dustin Hoffman) is faced with a big future in the "plastics" of the hypocritical society of the generation of his parents—and of his older mistress, Mrs. Robinson (Anne Bancroft). There's a funny scene at the Berkeley board-inghouse Benjamin moves into when he's pursuing the new subject of his affections, Elaine (Katharine Ross), Mrs. Robinson's daughter. His errat-ic behavior prompts Benjamin's nervous busybody landlord (Norman Fell, who went on to play another landlord in the 1970s sitcom "Three's Company") to question whether or not Benjamin's one of them "outside agitators." This section focuses on the period's movies about "outside agi-tators" and other motion picture *provocateurs*.

STUDENT POWER PICTURES

"You're crazy... It's too late for these answers. Twenty years too late!... I feel like Lafayette in the court of Louis XVI... You'll drive them crazy, Dr. Vandenburg. They'll burn down your school. You're turning them into full scale revolutionaries!"

— Elliott Gould, *Getting Straight*

If... was the era's first major feature about student protesters violently clashing with authorities—and the best. British director Lindsay Anderson was a self-described "anarchist," and few films captured the anarchic spir-it of the times as fully as *If...*, inspired by anarchist Jean Vigo's 1933 *Zero for Conduct* (photographed by Boris Kaufman, Dziga Vertov's brother), about unruly children at a French boarding school. Anderson also looked back in anger at his own childhood; *If...* was the culmination of the British "angry young man" cycle, pitting youthful idealists against the powers-that-be in Tony Richardson's 1962 *The Loneliness of the Long Distance Runner*,

Anderson's 1963 *This Sporting Life*, etc. Only this time, the nonconformists are armed and dangerous, the rebels evolving into full-on revolutionaries.

In *If...* Anderson drew upon his memories of attending Cheltenham College, a stiff upper lip British "public" school (in America, a "private" school) for the Empire's sons. Lensed largely on location at Cheltenham, in the Neorealist tradition, actual students appear onscreen. *If...* introduced Malcolm McDowell to the movies in this tale of adolescent revolt and repression—sexual and otherwise, including a gay sub-theme. *If...* alternates between reality and fantasy, accentuated by transitions between black and white and color. In a Brechtian—and Godardian—way, it's divided into chapters by titles.

Cheltenham is a microcosm of Western society, with its pillars of church, state, military and tradition. Mick Travis (McDowell) leads a small band of rebels in resisting authority, embodied by whips (student prefects collaborating with the adult administration), the headmaster, chaplain and soldiers. In the final section, entitled "Crusaders," Mick leads an insurrection during a school ceremony, furiously firing at establishment representatives from a rooftop—one of the great '60s movie moments.

With its pull-no-punches story and lines like "Violence and revolution are the only pure acts," Anderson and screenwriters David Sherwin and John Howlett captured the slogans, dreams, yearnings and actions of revolutionary students at Berkeley, Columbia, the Sorbonne, etc. *If...* emerged shortly after the apocalyptic year of 1968, when the Tet Offensive, Chinese Red Guards, the Prague Spring, Columbia University strike, Black Power-saluting athletes at Mexico's Olympics and protests at Chicago's Democratic Convention shook the global established order. More than any other 1969 film, *If...* distilled New Left ideas and was a clarion call to revolution. In capturing the temper of the times, *If...* swept Cannes (itself swept up by France's '68 student-worker strike), winning the festival's Palme d'Or award, much as Michael Moore's *Fahrenheit 9/11* did 35 years later. It also triggered the cycle of student unrest pictures.

Not all student power pictures took place on campus. The 1926-born Haskell Wexler directed, wrote and photographed 1969's innovative *Medium Cool*. "I was involved in a lot of radical things... a member of practically every organization [including the CPUSA] on the Attorney General's list... [I]nformation I got under the Freedom of Information Act showed that the F.B.I. and [HUAC] had spoken to my eighth grade teacher," Wexler told David Talbot and Barbara Zheutlin in the 1978 book *Creative*

Difference: Profiles of Hollywood Dissidents. The five-time Oscar nominated Chicagoan lensed many left-wing documentaries and top studio features, including 1967's *In the Heat of the Night,* 1968's stylish *The Thomas Crown Affair* and 1975's *One Flew Over the Cuckoo's Nest.* Wexler won Best Cinematography Oscars for 1966's *Who's Afraid of Virginia Woolf?* and 1976's *Bound for Glory.* When accepting the statuette for *Woolf,* Haskell proclaimed to the Academy, "I hope we can use our art for love and peace."

Medium Cool deals with the journalist's role in society, a personal story and protests at the Democratic Party's Chicago '68 Convention. Windy City cameraman John Cassellis (Robert Forster) develops relationships with hillbillies who've relocated to Chicago—assembly line worker Eileen (Verna Bloom) and her son Harold (non-actor Harold Blankenship).

As what a federal commission called "a police riot" sweeps Chicago, Eileen walks the streets, searching for Harold. This is where fact meets fiction, as a fictional character is filmed amidst a very real—and violent—news event, with feature filmmaking intersecting *cinema verite,* you-are-there documentary. Demonstrators make peace signs or clenched fists, carry black and red flags and signs that declare "Bring the GIs Home." They chant "Hell no, we won't go!", "Peace now!" and "Join us!" Tanks and police arrive, greeted by shouts of "Fuck you, pigs!" Teargas is fired; all hell breaks loose. The demonstrators' famous chant "The whole world is watching!" is ultimately heard.

Reality overtook fantasy in the greatest show on Earth as the Chicago police department went berserk in front of live TV and movie cameras, and Wexler wanted to put this reality onscreen. As one of the cameramen, Wexler recalled in the 2001 documentary *Look Out Haskell, It's Real!: The Making of "Medium Cool"*: "Filming in the riots was like any kind of filming I've ever done... I was watching a good movie until I got teargassed. It makes you think you're going to die. Because you can't breathe... and your skin burns like hell."

Wexler directed his sole feature by falling through the studio system's cracks. A Paramount executive asked Wexler if he wanted to direct an adaptation of a New York-set novel. Wexler asked if he could change the script, and entirely rewrote and structured it around the upcoming Chicago convention. When he finally screened it for Paramount's suits, "They didn't know how to deal with the film, because most Hollywood films didn't have anything practical to do with... the immediate real world," Wexler said. Wexler had to fight to get the film released, and claims that Paramount "effectively sabotaged" its distribution.[4]

In 1970, five features depicted campus unrest. *Getting Straight* was directed by Richard Rush (who directed Jack Nicholson in 1967's *Hell's Angels on Wheels* and wrote 1990's CIA picture *Air America*), with cinematography by Hungarian DP Laszlo Kovacs, who had shot *Easy Rider*. Elliott Gould and Candice Bergen play the ambivalent Harry Bailey and Jan, whose tempestuous affair is organically set against the backdrop of a university in turmoil. Ironically, Harry's nemesis is portrayed by blacklisted actor Jeff Corey, who seeks to blacklist Harry.

Harry is a caustic character with a handlebar mustache and—supposedly—all the answers. He's a movement veteran, from Selma's Freedom Riders to Berkeley's Free Speech Movement to the Sorbonne of 1968's *le rouge Mai*, and is around 30, when one could no longer be trusted. After six years, he's returned to a university to earn his masters in English so he can teach. Almost a decade younger than him, Jan—who conducts experiments in the college lab—is likewise conflicted. She marches on picket lines, is sexually active, yet yearns for marital stability and suburbia. Ultimately, the duo's swept away by the revolution that engulfs the campus, as pupils battle police during Harry's orals.

Getting Straight has much sharp dialogue about Vietnam, Black Power, sexual liberation and student rights. In a face-off between Harry and the university president, Dr. Vandenburg argues, "Do you think people should be allowed to decide for themselves whether a law is just? Why, that's anarchy! This nation was founded on law and order." Harry replies: "Bullshit! This nation was born out of disorder and founded on freedom and the will of the people." Vandenburg says, "Give them what they want today, and what will they ask for tomorrow?" "I don't know. Maybe a 40-hour week... the vote for women. What difference does it make? Will you let go? Let go! Stop trying to hold back the hand of the clock. It'll tear your arms out!" Harry pleads.

The Strawberry Statement was based on the 1968 Columbia University student strike, which—with student takeovers at the Sorbonne and Berkeley, and shootings at Kent and Jackson States—epitomized '60s/'70s campus unrest. The Stuart Hagmann-directed, Irwin Winkler-produced adaptation of a journal by one of Columbia's protesters, James

---

4. Director Stephen Marshall and Rosario Dawson were busted in Manhattan while shooting the *Medium Cool* homage *This Revolution* during 2004's Republican National Convention.

Simon Kunen (who has a bit part as strike chairman), won a Cannes Jury Prize. Bruce Davison depicts Kunen's alter ego, Simon James; Kim Darby plays his lover, Linda. The soundtrack includes Crosby, Stills, Nash and Young songs—David Crosby told me CSN&Y music appeared in several antiwar movies because the group was pro-peace.

The title was suggested by Columbia President Grayson Kirk's cavalier comment: "whether students vote 'yes' or 'no' on an issue is like telling me they like strawberries." This Queen Marie-Antoinette-like, "let-them-eat-cake" statement summed up the generation gap and autocratic attitude of "the establishment" and "The Man." A disclaimer states Columbia wouldn't allow filming on campus, and the movie is set at fictionalized Western University in San Francisco.

The Strawberry Statement is about a young man's youthful identity crisis and his coming of age, set against the backdrop of student unrest. Simon is a longish-haired, idealistic student who crews the school's rowing team. A strike opposes the administration's complicity in war research and scheme to turn a college-owned park into an ROTC building. Simon joins the university occupation to resist the Vietnam War—and cruise sexually liberated movement chicks, meeting Linda.

At the occupied gym, the police and National Guard burst in on the students, singing John Lennon's "Give Peace a Chance." The "pigs" spray them with teargas and viciously club and drag the students—including Simon and Linda—across the gym floor, outside the building and downstairs. A huge American flag hanging above a stage is symbolically ripped; the carnage is glimpsed through one of Old Glory's white stripes. In a freeze frame outside the gym, the athletic Simon tries to rescue Linda from being brutalized, leaping into the air.

R.P.M. ("Revolutions Per Minute") is produced and directed by Hollywood's message movie master Stanley Kramer, and written by *Love Story*'s Erich Segal. Anthony Quinn stars as renowned liberal Professor F.W.J. "Paco" Perez, who espouses tolerance of activists. Students occupying a university building demand a new college president—either Che (dead), Eldridge Cleaver (exiled) or Paco. The board of trustees appoints Paco president.

He proceeds to contend with students continuing their occupation. Ultimately, in this clash between liberalism and radicalism, Paco calls in the police to evict the students by force. A disastrous confrontation erupts and gets out of control, engulfing not only the activists and police, but townspeople and centrist student bystanders. Ultimately,

Kathleen Cleaver, executive producer of the International Black Panther Party Film Festival and former Panther Communications Secretary, in 2003 at the Armand Hammer Museum at UCLA, interviewed by the author.

everyone turns against Paco, including his lover (Ann-Margret), her faith in Paco—and liberalism—shattered. It is much like LBJ after 68's New Hampshire primary.

Italian director Michelangelo Antonioni's 1970 big budget MGM picture *Zabriskie Point* is named after a site located in Death Valley, the lowest, driest, hottest place in North America, and is one of the era's most astonishing films. Antonioni co-wrote (with Sam Shepard and three others), and in keeping with Italy's Neorealist tradition cast non-actors Mark Frechette, Daria Halprin and Black Power revolutionary Kathleen Cleaver.

After police teargas student occupiers and shoot a black pupil at a California university, longish-haired dropout Mark apparently shoots a policeman, and goes on the lam by hijacking a small plane. Flying over the Mojave Desert, he buzzes the car of anthropology student Daria, driving to her realtor employer's (Rod Taylor) posh real estate development in Arizona. Mark lands and romances Daria. They participate in a steamy orgy set to a Jerry Garcia guitar solo with other hippie couples at Zabriskie Point. Eventually, pleading innocence, Mark decides to turn himself in. But upon landing his plane at L.A.'s airport, police gun him down. Hearing the news on her car radio, Daria arrives at Arizona, where—seemingly willed by Daria—her boss' materialistic home blows up in a slow motion montage.

Kathleen Cleaver told me, "You have to understand, *Zabriskie Point* did not really have much of a script. It was an idea of Antonioni's, who wanted to do something. Antonioni does not speak English. He came to California with his ideas, but he had to interact with other people. Some of his ideas were completely strange. Like I think he wanted to actually film an ongoing gun battle with police," said Kathleen, then married to Black Panther Party Minister of Information and *Soul On Ice* author Eldridge Cleaver.

Cleaver got involved with *Zabriskie* through an antiwar activist who cast the Bay Area sequences. "I don't remember if there were any auditions; we got the script and I think they asked me if I'd do this part... I was a fan of Antonioni's. I was very impressed with his filmmaking," said Cleaver.

Zabriskie opens with activists meeting in a California classroom, debating how confrontational their tactics should be. Cleaver portrays the black student union president. The ex-Panther Communications Secretary told me the scene's dialogue combined improvised and written words, except for Frechette's entirely scripted lines.

Cleaver added, "This scene was portrayed as... a meeting of the black students' union, and it's loosely based on what was going on at San Francisco State. There was a student strike in process, or being discussed. All the black people cast in that scene are members of the Black Panther Party. And all the white people in that scene are antiwar activists, with the exception of [Frechette]... All of the participants are students... So it's a very improv-type scene... It was a one day shoot," recalled Cleaver, currently a senior lecturer at Yale and Emory University School of Law, and executive producer of the International Black Panther Party Film Festival.

In that remarkable cinematic year of 1970, Jon Voight starred as *The Revolutionary*, about young European terrorists. Hollywood's student protest sub-genre reached its apotheosis with one of TV's finest moments, Jeremy Kagan's 1975 "Katherine." The made-for-TV movie has a great rock score by Jefferson Airplane, Beach Boys, etc., and documentary feel, using news footage with images of Che, Castro, King, RFK, etc. (which ABC objected to), to introduce each turbulent year depicted onscreen. Sissy Spacek plays a character loosely suggested by Diana Oughton, one of three Weathermen believed killed in the March 6, 1970 explosion in a Manhattan townhouse. Flashbacks are intercut with a disguised Katherine en route to carrying out a "propaganda of the deed" bombing mission in San Francisco.

Along the way, we see what radicalized Katherine, daughter of loving but misunderstanding upper middle class parents played by Art Carney and Jane Wyatt. As a Peace Corps-type volunteer in South America, she encounters social injustice, and dedicates her life to fighting it. Back home, she works for civil rights in the south, and meets Bob (Henry Winkler). They become lovers and SDS organizers and are caught up in protests at the

Democratic Party convention, and CSN&Y's *Chicago* play. (In 1987 Kagan directed a superb companion piece to "Katherine," called "Conspiracy: The Trial of the Chicago 8," for HBO.) Katherine and Bob advocate armed struggle, go underground and join the Weathermen. Katherine leads a detachment of helmet-clad, bat-wielding Weatherwomen in breaking into a high school to "liberate" students. Katherine is clubbed and busted; she jumps bail. For the last time, Katherine is seen on the streets of San Francisco, apparently trailed by an undercover agent, as she prepares to set off an explosion. The bomb prematurely explodes, killing Katherine.

Kagan brought radical politics to a mass TV audience. Initially, the network was timid about releasing such a political hot potato and delayed its airing, Talbot and Zheutlin contend in *Creative Differences*. But the real life Patty Hearst-Symbionese Liberation Army kidnapping and brouhaha made "Katherine" a commercially viable project, and it was rescheduled; broadcast opposite "Kojak," it got deservedly good ratings.

GIVE PEACE A CHANCE PICTURES

"I said shrink, 'I wanna kill! I wanna kill! I want to see blood and gore and guts and veins in my teeth. Eat dead, burnt bodies. I mean kill.' And I started jumping up and down yelling 'Kill! Kill! Kill!'"

— Arlo Guthrie at a draft induction center, "Alice's Restaurant"

One of the three most electrifying moments in Academy Awards politics was when the antiwar *Hearts and Minds* won 1975's Best Documentary Oscar. While accepting his gold statuette at the podium, producer Bert Schneider read a telegram from the Provisional Revolutionary Government of Vietnam on live television.

The war in Indochina was certainly the single cause that united more people in opposition to the U.S. government than any other '60s/'70s issue. It directly affected white as well as black and other minority males of draft age, whereas civil rights, Black Power and racism indirectly affected Caucasians. Women's Liberation likewise affected females across the board, but as momentous as they were, issues of gender inequality weren't as life-or-death as getting shipped out to 'Nam. And even though women were exempt from the draft and lottery, it was their lovers, husbands, friends, brothers fighting and dying waist deep in the big muddy.

Singer Helen Reddy, whose feminist anthem "I Am Woman" is in Shola Lynch's *Chisholm '72—Unbought & Unbossed*, being screened at 2004's Los Angeles Film Festival.

Minus those coveted college deferments (or sweetheart deals landing privileged sons in the Champagne Unit of the Texas National Guard), white members of SDS or of the working class could be drafted along with their brethren in the Black Panthers, Young Lords, American Indian Movement and America's ghettos, *barrios* and reservations. Proletarians and minorities stood greater chances of becoming Southeast Asian cannon fodder, but the war in Vietnam, Cambodia and Laos was the common denominator for those protesting the powers that be. You didn't have to drop acid or experience segregation firsthand in order to angrily chant: "Hey, hey, LBJ, how many kids did you kill today?"

In the documentary *Chisholm '72—Unbought & Unbossed*, screened at 2004's Los Angeles Film Festival, a segment about the war shows how it affected the Democratic Party's primary race and national convention in 1972. Animosity towards the Indochina war animated the candidacy of Brooklyn Congresswoman Shirley Chisholm, the first African-American woman to seriously run for president, who advocated immediate withdrawal from the Southeast Asian quagmire. Chisholm understood interconnections between the war and plight of minorities at home, and that, as Martin Luther King put it, LBJ's "war on poverty" was being lost in the rice paddies of Vietnam. Johnson's—and later, Nixon's—war was, arguably, America's greatest injustice and unifier of the youth movement (at home and abroad).

Almost 30 years after the Vietnam War ended, Michael Moore explained to *Entertainment Weekly* the animus underlying his anti-Iraq

War *Fahrenheit 9/11*: "Nine guys died from my high school. That war, of all the political events of my lifetime, had the most profound impact. And I carry it with me to this day. That our government would actually sacrifice the lives of 58,000 of our people for nothing immediately makes you suspect [something] when the government says it's time to go to war again." Thus, the Vietnam War formed the subtext and backdrop for many of the '60s/'70s radical pictures—and, occasionally, it took center stage.

Indochina is at the heart of director Arthur Penn's 1969 *Alice's Restaurant*, based on Arlo Guthrie's song "The Alice's Restaurant Massacree," a droll account of how Arlo beat the draft. Longhaired Arlo plays himself, and a recurring theme throughout the film is gentle Arlo's anxiety over getting sent to Vietnam. After artistic differences lead to his being thrown out of a midwestern college, Arlo loses his precious student deferment.

Arlo visits his dying father, folksinger Woody Guthrie, in New York, and a middle-aged hip couple Alice (Pat Quinn) and Ray Brock (James Broderick) in Massachusetts, where they've opened the eponymous restaurant and bought a church to turn into a hippie commune. There, Arlo romances Asian Mari-chan (Tina Chen), and sees a maimed black Vietnam vet with a hook, instead of a hand. The Brocks throw a 1967 Thanksgiving feast. Afterwards, Arlo throws out tons of garbage in his VW minibus but, the dump closed, Arlo tosses the trash elsewhere. He is busted for littering, and then summoned to the induction center. "Flunking" his urine test, Arlo asks men at urinals, "Anybody got any to spare?" Arlo tells a psychiatrist he wants to kill women and children; the Army figures he's officer material. But Arlo's prior conviction renders him ineligible for the draft. He tells a sergeant: "You wanna know if I'm moral enough to join the Army, burn women, kids, houses, children and villages after being a litterbug!"

Vietnam is at the forefront of *Getting Straight*. Professor Willhunt threatens Harry with losing his student deferment in a classroom clash. Harry's stoner buddy Nick (Robert Lyons) does lose his student deferment—and his mind—in the process. He drives into the ghetto and chases after a black woman with numerous children, shouting, "I want to marry you!"—in order to retrieve a deferment. He unsuccessfully tries to flee to Canada, seeks a religious deferment dressed like a Buddhist and pretends he's gay.

The war's polarization, which divided up families, is expressed in "Katherine" when Thornton (Carney) discusses burning draft cards with Bob (Winkler). Thornton asks, "You don't feel any sense of duty to serve your country?" "Sure I do," Bob replies. "That's why I'm not going to

Vietnam." Carney repeats the official line, "We're fighting there to protect the people of South Vietnam from invasion." Bob retorts, "Wrong. We are the invaders there. And if you think we can win by supporting a corrupt government, you have to think again."

Jane Fonda epitomized Hollywood's political commitment. She starred with Donald Sutherland in 1972's *F.T.A.* (*Free The Army* or *Fuck The Army*), an agitprop documentary of the radical revue these antiwar agitators performed near military bases. In Hal Ashby's 1978 *Coming Home*, Fonda plays Sally Hyde, whose Marine husband Captain Bob Hyde (Bruce Dern) ships out to 'Nam. She volunteers for the military hospital, and is shocked by substandard conditions there. One wheelchair-bound vet, Luke Martin (Jon Voight), went to high school with Sally. The paralyzed ex-athlete is embittered over being maimed in Vietnam and the hospital treatment he and his comrades receive. He and Sally fall in love. After one of Luke's comrades kills himself, he decides to protest the war. Luke chains himself and his wheelchair to the Marine base's gates, as Steppenwolf's "Born to Be Wild" plays. Bob returns home; the F.B.I. informs him of Sally and Luke's affair. Unable to cope with the war and Sally's infidelity, he drowns himself. Luke continues his activism, speaking to youth at a school, saving another generation from becoming cannon fodder. Fonda, Voight and blacklisted screenwriter Waldo Salt won Oscars.

The '60s/'70s Hollywood feature that most vividly and prominently depicts American war crimes in Indochina is 1978's *Apocalypse Now*. A river patrol boat carries Captain Benjamin Willard (Martin Sheen) to Cambodia so Willard can "terminate" renegade Special Forces Colonel Kurtz (Marlon Brando) "with extreme prejudice." The Green Beret has recruited his own rogue ragtag army of Montagnard tribesmen in a Cambodian jungle outpost to fight a ferocious freelance war of such savagery against the communists that even the U.S. military considers Kurtz to be too outré.

The boat requires the assistance of gung-ho Colonel Kilgore's (Robert Duvall) Air Cavalry to pass a river shallow. For this reason, and so that champion surfer Lance B. Johnson (Sam Bottoms) can surf there, Kilgore sics choppers blaring Wagner's "Ride of the Valkyries" on the Vietnamese village at the mouth of a river. The ominous air strike is probably the most chilling battle scene in the Vietnam features. Kilgore delivers the immortal line "I love the smell of napalm in the morning."

Up river, the patrol boat encounters a "gook" boat, which the crew searches, finding fruits, rice, etc., but no weapons. When a Vietnamese girl makes a sudden move to a basket, the Yankees open fire, massacring the "slopeheads." Jay "Chef" Hicks (Fredric Forrest) discovers what's inside the basket: a puppy. Chief Phillips (Albert Hall) sees that the girl's still alive, and wants to bring her aboard the patrol boat to take her to some "friendlies" for assistance. Willard objects, as this will distract from his mission; he cold-bloodedly shoots her.

Kurtz's own demise is horrific—and carried out on the orders of the Americans' high command. "The horror! The horror! The horror!" Kurtz mumbles when Willard machetes him (the harrowing scene is intercut with the Montagnards sacrificing a water buffalo, also using machetes).

Director Francis Ford Coppola and screenwriter John Milius' updating of Joseph Conrad's 1902 novel *Heart of Darkness* is one of the best adaptations of literature in Hollywood history. They cannily re-set Conrad's Belgian Congo—with its 19th century colonial atrocities—in Indochina, along with Conrad's theme of how the imperial quest for empire and treasure in the Third World causes Westerners to lose their civilized selves, and find hearts of darkness. *Apocalypse Now* is, along with *Reds*, one of the greatest achievements of the period's progressive pictures, made possible by the genre's power and successes for more than a decade.

Not all '60s/'70s antiwar films were set in the here and now, or explicitly dealt with Vietnam, a very controversial subject. Setting the films long ago and far away, peacenik picture makers could elude censors and shoot movie metaphors of the Indochina inferno. In 1974, Stanley Kramer produced/directed the made-for-TV "The Court-Martial of Lt. William Calley," but four years earlier, a Wild West cavalry movie beat Kramer to the punch, using allegory to powerfully depict 1968's My Lai massacre. *Soldier Blue* is directed by Ralph Nelson, who also explored race relations in 1970's *...tick ...tick ...tick*. Indigenous activist/folksinger Buffy Sainte-Marie performs the theme song of the film, which focuses on Cresta (Candice Bergen), who had been abducted by Cheyenne, and cavalryman Honus Gent (Peter Strauss), sole white survivors of an Indian ambush of a cavalry detachment.

With great difficulty, they cross the wilderness, finally arriving at the fort, where Cresta clashes with pith helmet-wearing Colonel Iverson (John Anderson), who has a Custer-like goatee. The genocidal colonel rallies the troops to raid a Cheyenne settlement, denouncing "the dark abominations of these godless barbarians." When Cresta learns of cavalry plans to attack the tribe, she returns to the teepees to warn them. When the bluecoats arrive, Spotted Wolf rides towards them holding American and white flags, but Iverson orders his troops to open fire.

Pounded by artillery, teepees are blown to smithereens. Beheadings, dismemberment, rape and general chaos wipe out the Indians. Cavalry-men's horses trample Spotted Wolf's fallen American flag. After Spotted Wolf shoots Iverson off his horse, the colonel orders: "Raze the village! Burn this pestilence!" A shot of dead bodies seems deliberately suggestive of Ronald Haeberle's famous My Lai massacre photo. Indeed, *Soldier Blue* is not merely a commentary on one of the worst genocidal attacks on Indi-ans—the November 29, 1864 Sand Creek Massacre —but one of filmdom's most powerful condemnations of U.S. war crimes in Vietnam. Estimates vary that from 150 to 500 Native Americans were butchered at Sand Creek. 504 men, women, children and babies were slaughtered at My Lai.

Another 1970 Western used the redskins vs. whitey clash of civiliza-tions as a metaphor for Vietnam. In stark contrast to Errol Flynn's heroic Custer in Raoul Walsh's 1941 *They Died With Their Boots On*, Richard Mulligan's General George Armstrong Custer in Arthur Penn's *Little Big Man* is portrayed as a homicidal maniac who gets his at Little Big Horn, the 7th Cavalry's Dien Bien Phu.

Tony Richardson's 1968 *The Charge of the Light Brigade* deconstructs Flynn's swashbuckler film of the same name. It has become *de rigeur* for "postmodern" scholars to "deconstruct" tropes and conventions in the lit-erary canon created and propagated by "dead white men." Perhaps one of the first literati to be so debunked was Lord Alfred Tennyson, a poet lau-reate of British imperialism. In his 19th century poem "The Charge of the Light Brigade," Tennyson canonized cavalrymen charging cannons during the 1853–1856 Crimean War:

> "Cannon to right of them,
> Cannon to left of them,
> Cannon in front of them
> Volley'd and thunder'd;
> Storm'd at with shot and shell,
> Boldly they rode and well,
> Into the jaws of Death,
> Into the mouth of hell
> Rode the six hundred."

Tennyson's poem extols the notion that war is a noble endeavor fought by gallant gentlemen, as did the original 1936 Michael Curtiz-directed actioner about courage in the face of insurmountable odds, with Flynn and David Niven fighting nationalists in India and Russian expansionists. War is a heroic enterprise fought for the empire. As Captain Nolan (David Hemmings) replies when asked if war is terrible: "It is the stuff we're all hoping for. Soldiers do... Those that are waiting to use their talents."

Tony Richardson's *The Charge of the Light Brigade*, co-starring Vanessa Redgrave and written by Charles Wood, has a decidedly different take. The film depicts military racism, snobbery, blundering, cowardice and cruelty. An officer defends whipping soldiers, insisting: "They will not fight unless they are flogged to it... Would you ask they fight like fiends of hell for money or ideas? That would be unchristian."

Christian pacifists opposing militarism begin to protest, and Lord Cardigan (Trevor Howard) and horseback soldiers break them up. A speaker, with Bible in hand, says: "...Peace my brethren." Someone shouts, "Go back to Russia!", a reference updating the Russian vs. British Crimean War to the Cold War.

The troops are dispatched to Sebastapol, where the British high command squabbles over how to carry out the campaign, bungling and missing opportunities. Nolan realizes the folly of his earlier gung-ho attitude and comments on "the ridiculous supposition that war is akin to civilization. War is destruction." Nevertheless, exasperated with the leadership's botching of the operation, he leads a desperate, doomed charge of the Light Brigade right into Russian artillery (captured from the inept British). The horsemen are ignobly slaughtered. Finally taking action, Cardigan rides over Nolan's corpse. Afterwards, just as the officers argued over who was in command, they debate who's to blame for the Light Brigade's loss. Rather than being a paean to glory, the film reveals that the cavalrymen are merely cannon fodder for queen and country.

This is the viewpoint of another British pacifist picture, Richard Attenborough's 1969 *Oh! What a Lovely War*. World War I stands in for Vietnam in this 2 hour, 19 minute star-studded surreal satire using period songs, such as *Over There*. The film opens with Europe's grand Pooh-Bahs—John Gielgud as Count Leopold, Jack Hawkins as Emperor Franz Joseph, Ralph Richardson as Britain's Foreign Secretary Sir Edward Grey, etc.—bungling their way into global conflagration. Grey observes: "The lamps are going out all over Europe. We shall not see them lit again in our lifetime."

Cheering crowds, parades and a military band celebrate war's onset with much "patriotic" fervor at an English seaside resort. *Lovely* follows members of the Smith family, as they go off to a war portrayed as senseless mass murder. In a memorable recurring image, a huge scoreboard tallies battlefield casualties and ground gained, with 607,000 lost in the Somme versus zero gains. Field Marshal Sir John French (Laurence Olivier) explains trench warfare's policy of attrition.

Highlights include spontaneous Christmas Eve fraternization of enemy soldiers, who leave their trenches to celebrate together in no man's land. And if America had Jane Fonda, Britain had Vanessa Redgrave, who ran for Parliament on a Trotskyist ticket. Scene-stealing Vanessa the Red plays protester Sylvia Pankhurst, the British socialist suffragette who traveled to the U.S.S.R. and was convicted of sedition. Amidst peace banners, antiwar suffragettes hold a rally, and Pankhurst reads an antiwar letter by George Bernard Shaw. Hecklers try to shout her down, crying, "pacifists is traitors!" "Who tells you this?" Pankhurst asks. "The newspapers who refuse to publish the pacifists' letters. Who distort the facts about our so-called 'victories'... The sons of Europe are being sacrificed on the barbed wire because you misguided masses are crying out for it. War cannot be won. No one can win a war. Is it your wish that the war goes on and on?" Onlookers and soldiers sing "Rule Britannia." *Lovely* ends with a huge aerial shot of a field of crosses, marking the endless dead.

World War II was also a Vietnam stand-in for antiwar period pics, such as Mike Nichols' 1970 big budget, star-studded adaptation of Joseph Heller's cult classic about the absurdity of war, *Catch-22*. Alan Arkin starred as Yossarian, the bombardier so desperate to save his own life and get out of flying bombing missions that he feigns insanity. However, according to military regulations, if any serviceman tries to get out of warfare, it only proves he's sane. Meanwhile, the brass keeps raising the number of missions bombers must fly before flyers no longer have to go into combat.

In 1972, George Roy Hill adapted *Slaughterhouse-Five*, based on the novel by another of the counterculture's favorite authors, Kurt Vonnegut. Unlike Vietnam, WWII was a "Good War," the last war when America was unambiguously the good guy. We were attacked at Pearl Harbor, and fighting the good fight for democracy to save the world from fascism. But *Slaughterhouse* depicts the firebombing of Dresden, which killed innumerable German civilians. The film implies: If this is what America did when it was the good guy, what's Washington doing in 'Nam?

M*A*S*H was another 1970 movie metaphor of Vietnam, but by setting the conflict in Korea during the 1950s, Robert Altman and screenwriter Ring Lardner, Jr., of Hollywood Ten fame, were able to slip another one past censors and comment on Indochina in the 1960s. However, audiences weren't fooled: they knew exactly what the warfare between Americans and Asians referred to. As Mike Farrell—who co-starred in the 1972-83 TV sitcom spun off of the movie—admitted in an interview with the author, "Of course we were talking about Vietnam, and of course we were talking about Korea... [antiwar sentiment] was universal within the company. Some probably were less active than others. But Alan [Alda] was probably most noted for his support of the women's rights movement and the Equal Rights Amendment—although he was very actively involved in protesting the Vietnam War. He was, and continues to be, a very intelligent, very deeply thoughtful, very dedicated man who takes lots of heat for being a, quote, "liberal." Harry Morgan [Captain Sherman Potter]—although... less active —Jamie Farr [Klinger], Bill Christopher [Father Mulcahy], Loretta Swit [Hotlips Houlihan], originally Larry Linville [Major Frank Burns], Gary Burghoff [Radar] and ultimately David Ogden Stiers [Major Charles Winchester] were all, I think, of a like mind about the message of *M*A*S*H*. Which was really that war hurts, and that we should guard ourselves and guard our principles as a nation, rather carefully, rather than simply give in to the bellicosity and jingoism thrust upon us by so-called leaders," Farrell stated.

Just as *Soldier Blue*'s massacre raised the level of screen violence, *M*A*S*H*'s blood-soaked operating room scenes set a new standard in motion picture squeamishness. The new realism in both films reflected Vietnam's violence, which was increasingly being brought home into American living rooms in living color.

FLOWER POWER PICTURES

The alienation and reaction of young people to Vietnam and other perceived American ills, such as rampant materialism, wasn't only political—it was cultural, too. Indeed, countercultural. The hippies' mantra of peace and love was a direct response to the war, U.S. militarism and violence in general. Youth yearned to be free of a responsibility and conformity that seemed to stifle spontaneity and individualism. The young longed to be instinctually liberated of civilization and its discontents, of the constraints of the industrial nightmare's nine to five

drudgery. The counterculture's response to the older generation mani-
fested itself in many ways: outrageous fashions, hairstyles, lifestyles,
music; sexuality beyond the heterosexual monogamous norm; a desire to
return to nature. Drugs were ballyhooed to expand consciousness—or for
helping to cope with unpleasant, disturbing reality by altering percep-
tions of it. As youth thronged to Haight Ashbury, the East Village, be-ins,
love-ins, the Fillmores, etc., "hip" marketers and merchandisers sensed
gold in them thar hippie hills. The freaks turned on, dropped out—and
tuned in to Flower Power Pictures. And of course Hollywood—Old and
New—reflected, cashed in on and generated the counterculture.

Ever-mindful of the youth market, Roger Corman helped launch
countercultural flicks. "I wanted [1966's] *The Wild Angels* to represent as
accurately as it could what the Hell's Angels were doing," the indie producer says. "Chuck Griffith, the writer, and I went to a number of parties
with the Hell's Angels and listened to them, talked with them, drank and
smoked and so forth with them, and learned some of their thinking and
stories of what they had done. And the whole picture was based on stories they told us of things they had done. We wanted to represent exactly
what they were like and they used a lot of Nazi symbolism in their uni-
forms, posters and things like that. So we reproduced that in the film."

In 1967 Corman also directed "*The Trip*, based upon an LSD trip and
written by Jack Nicholson, and starring Peter Fonda, Bruce Dern and
Dennis Hopper, names that were really strongly associated with the counterculture. It was an antiestablishment film and also was, in some
respects, anti the war, but also anti-racist, anti the excesses of the capitalist system. Much of what the counterculture stood for was in the film,
as well as accepting a more liberal political agenda and sexual agenda…
It was more dealing with a lifestyle," states Corman.

AIP also set the stage for counterculture movies with 1968's *Wild in
the Streets* satire about 14-year-olds getting the vote, hippies taking over
the White House and interning anyone over 30 (pushing to its ultimate
logical conclusion the slogan "Don't trust anyone over 30").

No film about the counterculture captured the *zeitgeist* like 1969's
Easy Rider. Its stars were biker-flick graduates—Peter Fonda from Corman's
Wild Angels, Jack Nicholson from 1967's *Hell's Angels on Wheels*, Dennis
Hopper from 1968's *The Glory Stompers*. Hopper directed *Easy Rider*,
which he co-wrote with Fonda and Terry Southern. Fonda produced, Bert
Schneider executive produced and Nicholson and Karen Black co-starred.

In 1940's *The Grapes of Wrath* Henry Fonda's Okies drove West in their jalopy, searching for the American dream. Although Steppenwolf's "Born to Be Wild" replaced "Red River Valley," *Easy Rider* is about an American odyssey, '60s style. After a profitable drug deal, Captain America (Fonda) and Billy (Hopper) drive East on cool motorcycles to fulfill the American Dream circa 1969: retirement in Florida.

Captain America wears a leather jacket with Old Glory sewn on its back, and drives a high handlebar hog emblazoned with the Stars and Stripes. Billy wears a buckskin jacket and cowboy hat. In the ultimate road movie, the bikers visit a sincere hippie commune that impresses Captain America. En route to Florida, the longhairs encounter hostile squares and good ol' boys. Busted in the South for parading without a license, they meet George Hanson (Nicholson), a loveable local ACLU lawyer incarcerated for public intoxication. Upon getting out of jail, George dons a football helmet and joins the bikers.

After rednecks taunt them at a greasy-spoon, the trio camp out. George says: "You know, this used to be a helluva good country. I can't understand what's gone wrong with it." Billy snorts: "Man, everybody got chicken... They're scared, man." "Oh, they're not scared of you," George replies. "They're scared of what you represent to 'em." Billy says, "Hey man. All we represent to them, man, is somebody needs a haircut." George insists, "Oh no. What you represent to them is freedom." Billy asks, "What the hell's wrong with freedom, man? That's what it's all about."

George explains: "But talkin' about it and bein' it—that's two different things. I mean, it's real hard to be free when you are bought and sold in the marketplace. Course, don't ever tell anybody that they're not free, 'cause then they're gonna get real busy killin' and maimin' to prove to you that they are. Oh yeah, they're gonna talk to you... about individual freedom, but they see a free individual, it's gonna scare 'em... it makes 'em dangerous."

The dialogue is prophetic: rednecks attack the trio at their campsite, and just as Preacher Casy is killed in *Grapes*, George is clubbed to death. Later, in Louisiana, other rednecks gun the bikers down. *Easy Rider* became one of the most profitable movies ever made. Costing around $500,000, the low budgeter earned more than $50 million, proving the counterculture and movies about it could be boffo box office.

Nicholson plays pianist-turned-oil rigger Robert Eroica Dupea in 1970's *Five Easy Pieces*, directed by Bob Rafelson, executive produced by Schneider, co-starring Karen Black. Dupea, a misfit, attempts to order a meal his way in a roadside diner that has a "no substitutions" policy in a scene emblematic of the bureaucratic establishment versus nonconformity. After much haggling with the by-the-book waitress, Dupea orders, then adds: "Now all you have to do is hold the chicken, bring me the toast, give me a check for the chicken salad sandwich and you haven't broken any rules." The waitress spitefully asks, "You want me to *hold* the chicken, huh?" Dupea retorts, "I want you to hold it between your knees." The server tells Dupea to look at the "No Substitutions" sign and orders him to leave. Dupea asks, "You see this sign?" and knocks the glasses and menus off the table, striking a blow against the impersonal system.

The generation gap was at the heart of Flower Power pictures. In "Katherine," when the young revolutionary couple visit her bourgeois parents, her mother refuses to allow the lovers to sleep together. They also argue over politics. Later Katherine (Spacek) sneaks into her boyfriend's room. (Unbeknownst to her parents, she's already pregnant.) After Katherine's gone underground and become a Weatherman, her father comments, "I wanted to help her but I didn't know how. I felt impotent."

In *Soldier Blue*, Cresta (Bergen) sasses gray-haired Iverson. The colonel responds: "When I see young people today behaving like that... I can't help but wonder what this damn country's coming to." Although set in the Old West, this refers to the 1960s—not 1860s—generation gap.

Susan Sarandon's first political feature was 1969's *Joe*, directed by John Avildsen. In a premonition of the culture wars, Peter Boyle played Joe, prototype for the angry white male. In this hard-hitting story, the disgruntled factory worker grumbles about how the kids have taken over American culture. Advertising executive Bill Compton (Dennis Patrick) inadvertently kills the junkie boyfriend of his daughter Melissa (Sarandon).

Their antipathy to the counterculture unites the blue collar and white collar men, who search for Melissa in the East Village. Along the way they participate in what Joe hilariously calls a hippie drugs and sex "orgee." But when the freaks steal their belongings, Joe and Bill track them down to an upstate counterculture commune, where they embark on a shooting spree. Egged on by Joe, Bill opens fire on a young woman—who turns out to be his daughter. In the age of the generation gap, adults are devouring their children.

In *Getting Straight*, Harry (Gould) spars with middle-aged academic Wade (William Bramley, Officer Krupke in 1961's *West Side Story*), who grouses: "Every time one of these kids with long hair blows his nose it makes page one... If the kids would only stop trying to run the schools themselves and mind their own business and keep out of left-wing politics... Lovely they are. Twelve year old girls on LSD... when they get to be 16, you see them *on television in living color* in Chicago, rioting at the convention." Harry responds, "[T]hose kids are protesting a bunch of maniacs... sending them off to drop napalm on... ordinary people, like you and Alice and the kids. Merely defecating in the lobby of the... Hilton hotel seems to be a pretty tame gesture. I'd call it fantastic restraint."

Later, when he farewells freshmen he's given orientation to, Harry quips, "Now remember, anybody over 30 is the enemy, so be careful when you cheat on college boards, okay?"

THE FILM FIRE NEXT TIME: BLACK POWER PICTURES

"What we got now is a colony. But what we want to create is a new nation."

— Lawrence Cook, *The Spook Who Sat by the Door*

Movies closely mirrored the civil rights movement as the '60s opened. 1961's *Paris Blues*—directed and written by blacklistees Martin Ritt and Walter Bernstein—featured Paul Newman and Sidney Poitier as expatriate jazz musicians who romance Joanne Woodward and Diahann Carroll in the City of Lights. The latter reminds Poitier that these Americans in Paris must return home eventually to fight for their people's rights.

Poitier, Ruby Dee and the Younger family yearn to better themselves by moving out of the ghetto into a white middle class neighborhood in 1961's *A Raisin in the Sun*, based on Lorraine Hansberry's play. Although at one point the characters play-act a return-to-Africa nationalist fantasy, *Raisin* is essentially an assimilationist, pro-integration drama.

In 1962, the Stanford and Oxford-educated Roger Corman directed "*The Intruder*, which was Bill Shatner's first picture," Corman says in an interview. "It dealt with racial integration of American schools in the South... Shatner played the part of a rabble-rouser who went to a small Southern town to prevent the integration of schools... The film was obviously for civil rights, it was from a book by Charles Beaumont, who wrote the screenplay, but we chose to tell a pro-civil rights story from the standpoint of an anti-civil rights person... It got wonderful reviews. All of these films went to major film festivals. *The Wild Angels* and *The Intruder* went to the Venice festival, and *The Trip* went to Cannes... So they were recognized as comments on American society probably more in Europe than in the U.S.," Corman asserted.

Ossie Davis wrote and starred in 1963's *Gone Are the Days!*, a spoof of Southern paternalism and stereotypes. Alan Alda plays Charlie Cotchipee, liberal son of a bigoted patriarch. When he quotes his fellow Southerner Thomas Jefferson's dictum that "all men are created equal," a good ol' boy socks Charlie.

James Whitmore played real life Caucasian author John Howard Griffin, who dyed his skin to experience life as an African American in the still-segregated South in 1964's *Black Like Me*, a stinging rebuke of racism. The hot potato of interracial marriage was depicted in 1964's *One Potato, Two Potato*, and returned to the screen in Stanley Kramer's 1967 *Guess Who's Coming to Dinner?* starring Poitier, Katherine Hepburn and Spencer Tracy, in his last role as a liberal who must live up to his "we shall overcome" ideals. Melvin Van Peebles' 1967 France-set *The Story of a Three Day Pass* recounted a love affair between an African American G.I. and a French woman.

According to Donald Bogle in *Toms, Coons, Mulattoes, Mammies & Bucks*, Ivan Dixon played a railroad worker whose "independence from his white bosses marks him as a target for their racism" in 1964's *Nothing But a Man*. Bogle writes that Dixon's "Duff was a fitting precursor to the militant spirits about to burst on the scene"—and screen. As SNCC changed its "N" from "Nonviolent" and the organization became known as the Student National Coordinating Committee, and even more radical groups like the Panthers emerged, challenging pacifism with militancy and integration with nationalism, the movies also felt the coming changes. Adherents of Mahatma Gandhi and Martin Luther King were pitted against followers of Stokely Carmichael, H. Rap Brown and Huey P. Newton, white radicals against black nationalists.

In 1970's *The Strawberry Statement*, former Panther Minister of Justice H. Rap Brown (who changed his name to Jamil Abdullah Al-Amin and is currently serving a life sentence for shooting a sheriff's deputy and wounding another in 2000 in Georgia) is seen in a clip saying: "Violence is as American as cherry pie." Just as 1970 was the year when at least five student unrest features were released, 1970 was the turning point for black militancy on screen. Student power pictures were full of debates about nonviolence versus revolution, solidarity versus separatism.

Zabriskie Point's opening encapsulates the clash over nonviolence versus militancy. During the classroom meeting Kathleen Cleaver argues in favor of the kind of militancy Panthers were noted for. A black student declares: "There's one way to talk to a man—and that's in his own language. If the man's language is guns, we talk to him with guns..."

The white revolutionary Mark (Frechette) asks, "Are you willing to die?" The African-American pupil responds: "Black people are dying already in this country. Black people have earned this leadership in blood." Mark responds, "I'm willing to die." Tired of blabbing and—as Stokely put it—ready for revolution, Marks walks out of the talkfest.

When Mark and Daria (Daria Halprin) are driving near Zabriskie Point, the radio reports that a white guy shot a policeman. Mark laughs: "Ooh. White man takes up arms with the blacks? Just like old John Brown."

In 1970's *Getting Straight*, Ellis (Max Julien) takes a more strident tone and position than his Caucasian comrades at a student meeting. "You don't ask for what's yours. When we get a Black Studies department on this campus we'll tell them who's gonna teach..."

Ellis tries to convince Harry (Elliott Gould)—who's studying for his orals—to attend a meeting regarding the Black Studies department. When he declines, Ellis says, "Hey man... I don't want to marry your sister." Harry good-naturedly jokes, "You, marry my sister? Ellis, I will arrange it for you, man. With the analyst, the astrologist and the two neurotic kids... You can be husband number four she wipes out." Ellis laughs amidst more banter alluding to black penis size.

Nevertheless, Harry attends the meeting, and says: "Ellis, will you stop hating so much, man? You'll get so caught up in it you'll never get anything important done." Ellis responds, "Don't tell a black man what's important or what's not important. You walk around in a black skin before you do that." The implications are clear: white middle and upper class grievances aren't as serious as blacks', who are more oppressed because they grew up in poverty under American apartheid in the South and ghettoes in the North.

In 1975's "Katherine," a fire department inspector declares that the Children's Place, where Bob (Winkler) and Katherine (Spacek) teach black pupils, violates safety codes and the inspector harasses the free school. Then, African-American militants are angered by Bob's mocking of an older black man as an Uncle Tom, and they no longer want any white teachers. The Caucasian instructors are told: "You've got to liberate yourself. You are the enemy." A female black teacher asserts, "Right now hate is the strongest weapon we got... Besides, you can't love a system you're trying to destroy. If you do, then you really are the enemy." Katherine muses, "My white skin has given me a lot of privileges in this society."

The leftward-veering screen image of Poitier reflected the offscreen Stokely vs. King, the-fire-next-time vs. we-shall-overcome dynamics. In 1967's *In the Heat of the Night*, Poitier is Philadelphia police officer Virgil Tibbs, confronted by bigotry while trying to solve a murder down South. When a prominent Southerner slaps Tibbs because of his disrespectful questioning, Tibbs slaps the white man right back on his face. As the sequel's title suggests, Poitier insists on his honorific—and respect—in 1970's *They Call Me Mister Tibbs!*

From the black Irish to black Americans, Carol Reed's 1947 *Odd Man Out* IRA classic was adapted to a black militant milieu in Philadelphia in 1969's *The Lost Man*. Poitier uses the activist group as a diversion in order to pull a heist. When John Kane (Poitier) returns home to a small Southern town to attend his sister's funeral in 1971's *Brother John*, he's suspected of being an outside agitator from the North on a mission to incite black folks. Instead, the mystical movie reveals that Kane is the messiah—and he's black! (Guess who's second coming to dinner?) That same year, Poitier reprised his role as Lieutenant Virgil Tibbs in *The Organization*, as he cooperates with a band of black radicals to stop drug trafficking in the community.

1970's *The Liberation of L.B. Jones* crossed racial melodrama with soap opera. It pitted the black bourgeoisie personified by middle aged Roscoe Lee Browne (as the title character) against the young, militant man of action epitomized by Yaphet Kotto. By 1970, the latter type of character began to become preeminent over the black bourgie persona, as black nationalism and separatism vied with integration and assimilation, and militancy confronted nonviolence offscreen.

In Melvin Van Peebles' 1970 *Watermelon Man*, Godfrey Cambridge is bigoted Caucasian businessman Jeff Gerber in whiteface. One morning, the insurance salesman wakes up, and to he and his wife Althea's (Estelle Parsons) horror, the racist has turned black. When Gerber loses Althea and his job, and experiences one indignity after another in racist America, he undergoes a psychological transformation. On the receiving end of racism, Gerber joins a black nationalist organization, and trains with blacks using broom handles—instead of guns—to prepare for combat with whitey.

The tide of militancy culminated in a trenchant genre of Black Power pictures. According to James Robert Parish and George H. Hill in *Black Action Films*, 1968's *Up Tight!* "was the first Hollywood feature to deal with contemporary black revolutionaries." Blacklisted director Jules Dassin returned to America, and with co-stars Dee and Julian Mayfield, rewrote Liam O'Flaherty's novel about betrayal in the Irish Republican Army, which John Ford had made as 1935's *The Informer*. The IRA was again transmogrified into an underground black militant group and the story was set in Cleveland's ghetto during the tumultuous days after Dr. King's assassination.

In Marlon Brando's 1994 CNN interview with Larry King, he cited 1969's *Burn!* as the most interesting film he'd acted in. Among the best Black Power pictures, *Burn!* is agitprop disguised as an adventure movie, posing as a swashbuckler but, in reality, a revolutionary follow-up to Gillo Pontecorvo's 1965 *Battle of Algiers*. The first film Pontecorvo helmed after his classic account of urban guerrilla warfare against French colonialism, *Burn!* critiques neocolonialism's inner workings. The screenplay is by Franco Solinas, who co-wrote Pontecorvo's 1959 *Kapo* and *Algiers* and 1973's *State of Siege* with Costa-Gavras.

Brando plays Sir William Walker, a 19th century soldier of fortune and secret agent for the British crown (or the highest bidder). Walker (the name of an actual American mercenary involved in covert actions in 19th Central America) is dispatched to a Portuguese colony to foment an uprising. Like Haiti, the island has a revolutionary heritage, and derives its name—Queimada, Portuguese for "burn"—from a slave revolt that resulted in the burning of the isle. When Brando arrives at Queimada, Jose Delores (Evaristo Marquez), a black man of the masses, offers to carry Walker's bags from the docks. The *agent provocateur* lures the spirited but uneducated black into leading an armed rebellion of peasants against the Portuguese colonialists. Walker trains, arms and funds the revolutionaries.

However, Walker is out to get Queimada's Lisbon-bound sugar for London. Walker explains neocolonialism at a meeting of "half-caste" and other upper echelon non-Portuguese, non-black men. He compares slavery to marriage and the free market to prostitution, pointing out that husbands pay for wives' food, shelter and sex, while men only pay prostitutes for sex. Likening wage earners to hookers, Walker asserts that free enterprise is more profitable for owners than plantation slavery.

Delores' peasant army overthrows the Portuguese, and he wants the former slaves to seize power, but the national bourgeoisie led by *mestizo* Teddy Sanchez (Renato Salvatori) claims the presidency. This leads to a tense standoff between the two factions—sugar sales plummet, the economy faces disaster. Receiving guarantees from Sanchez, Delores finally agrees to disarm. Mission accomplished, Walker prepares to set sail. Delores surprises Walker at the docks, offering once again to carry his bags—but as a friend, not as a servant. When Delores asks the British agent what his next port-of-call is, Walker replies "Indochina."

But all is not smooth sailing for Queimada, where the revolutionary aspirations of the black masses remain unfulfilled. Over time, Delores rearms his followers and launches another guerrilla war, so that he who swings the cane can control the fruit of his labor. Life hasn't been too kind for Walker, either; emissaries find him fighting in a bar. They offer Walker a way out of the hard times he has fallen on by leading a counterinsurgency campaign against Delores' ragtag army.

Under Walker's guidance, the armed forces—with many black recruits—eventually crush the poorly armed guerrillas. When Walker encounters his old comrade-in-arms, he's increasingly enraged by Delores' refusal to crawl or accept favors. Walker tries debating Delores, but the rebel's reply is scathing silence. Although the Englishman is the captor and Delores the captive, the revolutionary wins the debates, even though sentenced to death.

Mission accomplished, Walker returns to the wharf to leave the country. But before boarding a ship, somebody asks if he can carry the Englishman's bags. Walker smiles, believing Delores has somehow not been hanged. But it's another freedom fighter who has taken Jose's place, and stabs Walker. The revolution continues—it is permanent, unstoppable.[5]

---

5. The night I wrote the above, Brando died. The next day, July 2, 2004, Reverend Jesse Jackson appeared on CNN to discuss the 40th anniversary of the Civil Rights Act, prefacing his remarks by remembering Brando for marching in the South and making such a contribution to the movement for racial equality. Kathleen Cleaver told me that when Brando attended the funeral of "Little Bobby" Hutton—a 17-year-old killed in a shootout with Oakland police (Eldridge Cleaver was wounded) two days after King's assassination in April 1968—the star's presence helped attract attention to the Panthers. Cleaver said Brando was carrying the script for *Burn!* with him during his visit, as the method actor prepared for his role.

In Lindsay Anderson's 1973 *O Lucky Man!*, starring Malcolm McDowell, British imperialists meet with a Third World dictator for a presentation about foreign investment and labor conditions in the fictionalized African nation of Zinagara. British actor Arthur Lowe, in blackface, plays African strongman Dr. Munda. His economist narrates an audiovisual account of Zingara's free export zone, offering foreign investors excellent labor conditions: peon wages, the illegality of strikes, no income tax. Sir James Burgess (Ralph Richardson) asks if there's the "threat of insurrection?" Germanic Colonel Steiger shows another film, about a counterinsurgency campaign against rebels. The essence of the transaction is that Dr. Munda and Colonel Steiger want to grant Burgess the rights to construct resorts along Zinagara's coasts, in exchange for napalm which the African dictator will deploy against insurgents.

Oppression, police brutality and black self-defense are at the heart of 1971's *Sweet Sweetback's Baadasssss Song*. A title at the beginning states that it is "dedicated to all the Brothers and Sisters who have had enough of The Man," and the credits reveal that it stars "The Black Community," with a cast of non-actors. The Panthers' newspaper devoted an entire issue to *Sweetback*, which Huey Newton called "the first truly revolutionary black movie." Melvin Van Peebles, *Sweetback*'s star and auteur, printed "Free Huey" on the back of his debut album, *Brer Soul*, and wrote the novel and screenplay for 1995's *Panther*, directed by his son Mario Van Peebles, who also plays Stokely Carmichael.

The low budget indie was a box office smash and, along with *Shaft*, released shortly afterwards, launched the "Blaxploitation" genre. *Sweetback*'s power is a combination of its anti-police theme, raw sexuality and cinematic style. Sweetback has a handlebar mustache, resembles Panther Chairman Bobby Seale and performs live sex acts in a bordello. He accompanies two white vice squad cops to HQ for questioning. En route, the plainclothesmen arrest a young black man and viciously beat him at a deserted locale.

Sweetback defends the brutalized youth, thrashing the cops with his handcuffs. The movie is essentially a long chase, "the parable of a modern black fugitive/runaway slave told in the raw, liberating language of a poet-warrior," Darius James writes in *That's Blaxploitation!: Roots of the Baadasssss'Tude*. Throughout the movie, Sweetback eludes and offs a number of pigs, and is protected and hidden by the community. There's lots of location shooting in the ghetto, bestowing street cred on a film highlighting the lumpenized masses, not the black bourgeoisie.

After a young man is shot by the police, a black biker dispatched to rescue Sweetback can only take one rider. Sweetback tells the biker to take the wounded man instead. They exchange Black Power salutes as the biker rides off.

Sheriffs release bloodhounds when Sweetback nears the border, but bloody dogs are later seen dead in the river. Sweetback crosses the Rio Grande to freedom in Mexico. A title appears on screen: "Watch out. A badass nigger is coming to town to collect some dues."

Sweetback took advantage of the Production Code's collapse, and the movie's explicit sex caused it to be "Rated X by an all white jury," as Van Peebles noted. In the context of the times, in *Sweetback* and *Shaft*, black males were depicted as potent, sexual men, whereas most previous movies had emasculated African American men. Even if Poitier played more dignified parts than Eddie Rochester, Stepin Fetchit and Mantan Moreland's usual servant roles, he was usually desexualized. When Poitier appeared opposite white women, they were nuns, as in his 1963 Oscar-winning *Lilies of the Field*, or blind, as in 1965's *A Patch of Blue*. Even when Poitier marries a Caucasian woman in *Guess Who's Coming to Dinner?*, he's reduced to a quick kiss—glimpsed in a cab's rear mirror. This doesn't mean black male sexuality was completely ignored—indeed, it was considered such a threat that in 1915's *The Birth of a Nation* it inspired the creation of the Ku Klux Klan, which rode to the rescue of blonde Lillian Gish's virginity.

At a panel on Blaxploitation during 2004's L.A. Film Festival, Mario Van Peebles stated that black men did not have facial hair onscreen prior to his father's film. By asserting black masculinity, *Sweetback* made a liberating political statement.

According to Sam Greenlee, author of *The Spook Who Sat By the Door*, *Battle of Algiers*' Pontecorvo expressed interest in directing *Spook*, but Greenlee preferred for an African American to helm the 1973 feature. Ivan Dixon (*Hogan's Heroes*' Sergeant Kinchloe) directed *Spook*, Greenlee co-wrote the script and has an associate producer credit. The music is by Herbie Hancock and, Greenlee says, financing came from the black community. Greenlee adds that except for a few surreptitiously shot exteriors, *Spook* was actually shot in Gary, Indiana, with the cooperation of Richard Hatcher, one of the first post-Reconstruction black mayors of a major U.S. city.

Korean War veteran Dan Freeman (Lawrence Cook) becomes the first black CIA agent, as the agency uses tokenism to avoid discrimination charges. After serving faithfully for five years in a token position, Freeman leaves the CIA and returns to Chicago to head a social work foundation. But this is a cover: Freeman puts his CIA training to use, recruiting and training an underground resistance army, the Black Freedom Fighters of North America, to wage guerrilla war against whitey. Banks are robbed to payroll the revolution. Molotov cocktails fly, snipers shoot and bombs explode, as a *Battle of Algiers*-type insurgency erupts. *Spook* ends as the revolt spreads to eight major urban centers—once again, the revolution is permanent.

Spook has sharp ideas and dialogue. The sophisticated movie raises the question of spontaneity vs. organized resistance, as police brutality triggers urban riots. Class struggle versus race war, Marxism versus nationalism, and the roles of movies and news media are also touched upon. When National Guardsmen occupy the ghetto, Freeman asks a policeman what white people call blacks like them—with degrees and a badge—in private? "Niggers," Dawson states.

Spook is one of the most remarkable films of this era and in the entire history of American political cinema. Along with *Sweetback* and *Brothers*, it is among the most politically conscious of the '60s/'70s Black Power pictures. This probably accounts for Melvin Donalson's comment in *Black Directors in Hollywood* that *Spook* "failed at the box office, though some have suggested that it was intentionally pulled before it could find an audience."

Director/co-writer Perry Henzell's 1973 *The Harder They Come* combines Neorealist elements with a cast of nonprofessionals and actual locations (this was Jamaica's first homegrown feature), along with artsy techniques, including jump cuts and flashbacks, and a great score. The title track, and songs such as "Rivers of Babylon" and "You Can Get It If You Really Want," introduced reggae to Americans. Reggae singer Jimmy Cliff stars as the rural youth Ivan O. Martin, a contemporary Ivanhoe based on the legendary gangsta Rhygin, a Jamaican Jesse James. Ivan moves to the bright lights, where he's taken advantage of by city slickers.

Ivan crosses a record producer, who wants to pay the aspiring musician very little for the rights to his potential hit song. Ivan turns to dealing marijuana, but soon clashes with the ganja kingpin. Bushwhacked by police, Ivan kills them, flees and becomes a Jamaican folk hero noted for eluding and taunting the fuzz. However, he's eventually wounded.

The fugitive attains a heightened awareness. The wounded Rasta gangsta attempts to escape to Cuba, which has free healthcare, and become "a revolutionary for Ras." Ivan's dream almost comes true, as he swims with his one good arm towards a Cuba-bound ship, unsuccessfully reaching for a rope dangling from it. Almost drowning, Ivan washes up on the beach, where soldiers shoot him to death.

Max Julien, who played revolutionaries in *Up Tight!* and *Getting Straight*, starred in the 1973 Blaxploitation classic *The Mack* and 1974's *Thomasine and Bushrod*, which Julien wrote and co-produced. Gordon Parks, Jr. directed the audacious *Thomasine*, a sort of *Bonnie and Clyde* set in 1911 Texas. Like Bernie Casey in 1972's *Boxcar Bertha*, by traveling back in time Julien and Casey engaged in shootouts with honkies as violent as any Panthers vs. pigs battle.

As the genre wound down, 1977's *Brothers* was a last gasp of the era's politicized Black Consciousness films, and one of the best—if largely forgotten—of the Black Power pictures. (*Brothers* was largely overshadowed at the time by Blaxploitation fare such as the Fred Williamson directed/produced *Mister Mean.*) *Brothers* fictionalizes the life story of *Soledad Brother* author, San Quentin inmate and Panther Field Marshal George Jackson (Bernie Casey) and the Afro-coifed Communist Party member Professor Angela Davis (Vonetta McGee). Richard Collins, who co-wrote 1943's *Song of Russia,* has his one movie acting credit in *Brothers.*

Casey's character, David Thomas, is arrested for armed robbery and comes under the tutelage of his Black Consciousness cellmate Walter Nance, played by *Superfly*'s Ron O'Neal. They collaborate on an underground newspaper for inmates; Caucasian guards beat Nance to death. David, who is innocent, goes on trial for murdering a guard. Seventeen-year-old Jonathan Jackson's alter ego, Joshua Thomas (Owen Pace), dies in a desperate attempt to free his older brother, based on the August 7, 1970 Marin County Civic Center shootout, wherein a judge and two other inmates also died.

McGee—whose radical professor character is named Paula Jones!—is emotionally involved with David and suspected of supplying Joshua's weapons. Paula goes underground as public enemy number one— although she's innocent and ultimately acquitted. David dies in a bold prison escape attempt.

By the late '70s, politically conscious Black Power pictures were largely spent and superseded by Blaxploitation pix. Whereas lumpenized characters such as prostitutes did indeed appear in militant movies like

Actors Antonio Fargas (1972's *Across 110th Street*), Mario Van Peebles (1995's *Panther*, 2004's *Badasssss!*) speaking in mike, and Lawrence-Hilton Jacobs (1974's *Claudine*; 1975's *Cooley High* and *Welcome Back, Kotter*), at the 2004 L.A. Film Festival's Blaxploitation panel.

Sweetback and *Spook*, they were subservient to and subsumed by the radical politics in each. *Sweetback*'s anti-police brutality theme and *Spook*'s urban guerrilla plot took precedence over these films' hooker subplots and characters. Powered in part by their hard-hitting anti-The Man diatribes, Black Power pictures helped garner audiences for moving pictures featuring African American actors and subjects.

But once Black Power pictures created and established a viable viewership, Blaxploitation (often controlled by white studios and filmmakers primarily profit-motivated by high returns from low budget, low quality product) proceeded to strip-mine African American-themed movies of their politics. More and more, hos, pimps, drug dealers and other criminals took center stage, as revolutionaries increasingly disappeared. The civil rights and nationalist ideals of integration and egalitarianism were simplistically rendered and even caricatured.

Hence, in American International's 1973 *Black Caesar*, linebacker-turned-actor Fred "The Hammer" Williamson's notion of equal opportunity is for blacks to be able to become gangsters, too. With their monsters in blackface, AIP's 1972 *Blacula*, Exclusive International's 1973 *Blackenstein* and Dimension's 1976 *Dr. Black, Mr. Hyde* integrated horror movies. Just as today's porn industry exploits successful mainstream movies by making XXX versions playing off of their titles and plots, Blaxploitation threw the word "black" in front of a studio title, such as 1974's *Black Godfather*, in order to make a dollar.

Sam Greenlee, author of *The Spook Who Sat By the Door*, interviewed by the author at the 2004 Los Angeles Film Festival.

Most Blaxploitation pix accepted the framework of the power and wealth relations of capitalism—their individual characters generally just wanted their share of the pie, loot and booty. The machismo and bling-bling obsession of thug culture and many gangsta rap CDs and music videos appear to be direct outgrowths and continuations of Blaxploitation's iconography. At their worst, Blaxploitation presented '60s/'70s updated Amos and Andy stereotypes in modern minstrel shows.

Robert Downey, Sr. was aware of this problem in his 1969 *Putney Swope*. The title character is the token black executive of a Madison Avenue advertising firm who's accidentally elected its head. Putney (Arnold Johnson) places militants in charge of the company, renames it "Truth and Soul, Inc." and hires a white housekeeper. Regarding new commercials, Swope's acolytes declare, "Putney says it gotta have soul." Swope and the new regime reverse the power structure—but are themselves exploitative, corrupt pigs. The film is a satire of narrow nationalism, and makes the point that it doesn't matter whether blacks or whites control hierarchies—top/down relationships are inherently unjust and have to be changed, instead of just the boss being changed. In a sense, Downey, Sr. predicted the dilemma Blaxploitation would eventually find itself in (as well as future hip-hop artists and recording executives), as any form of exploitation is innately unfair. Pigs come in all colors.

In 2004, the L.A. Film Festival presented an Elvis Mitchell-moderated panel on Blaxploitation, with directors Michael Campus (1973's *The Mack*; 1974's *The Education of Sonny Carson*), Joel Freeman (*Shaft*), Jack

Hill (Pam Grier's discoverer and helmer of 1973's *Coffy* and 1974's *Foxy Brown*) and actors Lawrence-Hilton Jacobs (1974's *Claudine*; 1975's *Cooley High* and *Welcome Back, Kotter*), Antonio Fargas (1972's *Across 110th Street*) and Mario Van Peebles (1995's *Panther*, 2004's *Badasssss!*). Every panelist said they despised the word "Blaxploitation." During the panel discussion, Van Peebles stated that Blaxploitation "had the body, but not the mind" of the Black Consciousness films. In an interview, *Spook* author Sam Greenlee (who attended the panel discussion) said that the genre died and "people stopped going to see these movies because they were no longer political."

But the spirit persists. In 2004, Mario Van Peebles directed a documentary for the First Amendment Project of Robert Redford's Sundance Channel, which looks at free speech issues. *Poetic License* examines attempts to strip New Ark-based Amiri Baraka of his post as New Jersey's Poet Laureate due to an allegedly anti-Semetic verse in a post-9/11 poem. (Baraka recited *Who Blew Up America* during 2003's Pan-African Film Festival, when the author of the 1966 film *Dutchman*, about interracial love and violence, won PAFF's lifetime achievement award.)

ARMED CINEMATIC STRUGGLE: TINSELTOWN'S TERRORISTS

"It is hungry people who make revolution. Poor people."

— Hector Elias as the guerrilla Juan, "Katherine"

Coming hard on the heels of the Cuban Revolution, numerous national liberation struggles shook the Third World during the '60s, stretching from Algeria to Indochina to Bolivia. There, in the heart of South America, Che Guevara sought to spread what the far left envisioned as world revolution. "Create one, two, many Vietnams!" was their slogan, as national liberation movements confronted—often successfully—"imperialism" and its "running dogs." Some New Left extremists in America tried to enlist in the unfolding showdown between the metropoles and colonies/underdeveloped nations, and "bring the war home." The tension between those who wanted to "overcome" and "give peace a chance" and a minority who believed, as Mao put it, that "political power grew out of the barrel of a gun," was reflected in student protest, Black Power and other freedom fighter films of the period.

The undisputed greatest one of them all was Gillo Pontecorvo's 1965 *Battle of Algiers*, a Best Foreign Film Oscar Nominee. *Cineaste* writes that it "is frequently cited by critics and filmmakers as one of the seminal works of the sixties, both for its form and its orientation." The Jewish Pontecorvo served in the *maquis*—the anti-Mussolini underground resistance—and is an ex-Italian Communist Party member, who co-scripted *Battle* with Franco Salinas (and, it could be said, with the Algerian masses). National Liberation Front leader Saadi Yacef reportedly wrote the treatment on the backs of envelopes in prison, and eventually produced the gripping drama. With relentless realism, Pontecorvo masterfully depicts the Algerians' bitter anticolonial struggle against France. *Battle*'s gritty, grainy black-and-white photography and Neorealist use of many non-actors (Yacef plays himself) and locations, including Algiers' bazaar, led many viewers to erroneously assume that this was a documentary, prompting distributors to add a disclaimer: "Not one foot of newsreel or documentary film has been used."

Battle follows an anti-French underground cell. Its depiction of urban guerrilla warfare inspired Panthers to screen it as part of BPP cadre training. In one scene that could be ripped out of headlines about Baghdad or Jerusalem, an Arab woman leaves a package at a bar, blowing up numerous French civilians. The human rights abuses of French paratroopers is also especially relevant, given the current Abu Ghraib, Navy SEAL, etc. abuses. Today, this potent story of a hit-and-run campaign against an occupying Western army remains so timely that *Battle* was re-released in 2004, as the Iraqi insurgency mounted resistance using similar terrorist tactics.

In "Katherine," the fictionalized biopic of a member of the Weather Underground, Sissy Spacek's do-gooder Katherine Alman goes to the mountains to meet with South American guerrillas. Their leader Juan (Hector Elias) asks the Peace Corps-type volunteer to raise money for guns. She refuses, saying she'll fundraise for food, but not "bloodshed." Reflecting the liberalism versus radicalism debate taking place on- and offscreen, Juan retorts: "That's nothing. You only delay the revolution by such things. You dilute the anger of the people and keep them from rising up to kill their oppressors. It is hungry people who make revolution. Poor people." Privileged Katherine, who's argued for teaching and reading about malnutrition, asks, "Do you really think the people want a revolution?" The guerrilla replies: "If you were really one of the people, if you were poor, you would not ask..."

The theme of nonviolent versus violent tactics is revisited later on in "Katherine," with what's probably the only fiction film depiction *per se* of the SDS' split. At a turbulent student meeting, Bob (Henry Winkler) pro-claims: "I'm talking about the Cambodian violence... the My Lai massacre... the killing of blacks. It's about time we meet some of this vio-lence with violence of our own!" Another activist replies that this is "totally counterproductive. It shows you don't want to do the hard work of changing people's minds."

Bob advocates "armed struggle," and army jacket-clad Jessica (Nira Birab), who looks like Weatherwoman Bernardine Dohrn, shouts, "Split or fight!" (J. Edgar Hoover called Dohrn "the most dangerous woman in Amer-ica" and "*la Pasionara* of the Lunatic Left" and put her on the F.B.I.'s Ten Most Wanted list). Most activists walk out, and Jessica harangues: "This is... not a tea party. Our greatest weakness has been our belief in our weak-ness... We've got to stand up in the face of the enemy and risk our own lives. We will show them what you do is fight back. We support all those who take up the gun against imperialism. We too must take up the gun. You don't need a weatherman to know which way the wind blows, 'cause it's clearly in the air. We will forecast the end of the system in blood! [Jessica waves her fist.] We are the Weathermen! Seize the day!" Other extremists pick up the chant.

In *Zabriskie Point*, Mark and Daria debate militancy. "...[Y]ou have to choose one side or another," Mark asserts. "There's a thousand sides—not just heroes and villains..." Daria responds. "...[I]f you don't see them as villains you can't get rid of them," Mark replies. "You think if we can get rid of them we'll have a whole new scene?" Daria asks. "Why not? Can you think of any other way that we can go about it?" Mark insists.

After police kill Mark, hippie-dippy Daria experiences an epiphany. The *bourgeois* home where businessmen wrangle over the Sunny Dunes suburban development explodes in an orgy of Eisenstein-like montage, while Daria watches. As rock music pulsates, close-ups of clothes, glass tables, Wonder Bread and other consumer society accoutrements fly in the air—as do a newspaper, *Look* magazine and TV set, as Antonioni cri-tiques American media. Afterwards, Daria tranquilly drives away, and *Zabriskie Point* returns to nature, as the sun sets on the Arizona desert.

Mark Frechette's bizarre real-life story was stranger than his charac-ter's. Discovered by the filmmakers, *Zabriskie* briefly thrust Frechette, a commune member, into the limelight. Apprehended during a politically-motivated bank robbery in Boston, he died behind bars in 1975, due to an apparent bench-pressing accident. His *Zabriskie* co-star Daria Halprin married Dennis Hopper.

Not all Tinseltown terrorist tales were set in America. Otto Preminger's 1975 *Rosebud* stars Peter O'Toole as a secret agent posing as *Newsweek* correspondent Lawrence Martin (suggesting O'Toole's other British imperialist agent, *Lawrence of Arabia*). *Rosebud* is notable for its prescient depiction of Islamic fundamentalist terrorists.

Young wealthy Western women aboard a yacht in a Mediterranean port are boatjacked by Arab terrorists, as *Exodus'* director focuses on the Palestinian liberation movement. O'Toole infiltrates the inner sanctum of the terrorists, led by English Islamo-phile Edward Sloat (Richard Attenborough). The true believer doesn't want negotiations with Israel—he wants to annihilate it. Inhabiting a cave (he's literally underground) and eerily sounding like bin Laden, Sloat proclaims: "This is the beginning of *jihad*. A holy war. And I have been chosen to regain all of Arabia for the faithful."

Sloat denounces secular socialists and his prophetic demands are: "No deals. [Israelis] will have no peace until we have... [a]ll of Arabia, including Palestine, united under the flag of Islam. A Muslim holy land, where we can live in peace... I seek the restoration of the faith—all of Arabia united, following the laws of Mohammed." The difference between Sloat and Osama is that al Qaeda has moved beyond pan-Arabism to pan-Islamicism, from North Africa to the Philippines.

Joan Baez sings "Rejoice in the Sun" in 1971's *Silent Running*, ostensibly a sci-fi flick. But like 1973's Charlton Heston overpopulation thriller *Soylent Green*, *Silent Running* is a message movie about an eco-terrorist. Along with Hitchcock's 1963 *The Birds*, *Silent Running* is among the first ecology films.

After an earthly ecocide, botanist Lowell (Bruce Dern) cares for a garden inside a biodome aboard a spacecraft soaring through space, as a way to preserve nature. He clashes with three environmentally insensitive shipmates, arguing: "There's no more beauty... and imagination... nobody cares... there's not going to be any trees." When the order comes from Earth to "nuclear destruct all... forests," Lowell takes direct action to defend his ship's sylvan glade. Arguably becoming moviedom's first Earth Liberation Front or Earth First member (although taking their "eco-terrorism" to its extreme), Lowell kills his fellow astronauts. Aided by two robots, Lowell alters the spaceship's course towards Saturn's rings. When earthlings track Lowell down in deep space he fires a capsule that separates the biodome forest from the rest of the craft, which explodes. But the robots are seen tending the garden, which floats away into space, saved.

BOLSHIE BIOPICS BY BLACKLISTEES

"I can see... the clear blue sky above the wall, and sunlight every-where. Life is beautiful. Let the future generations cleanse it of all evil, oppression and violence, and enjoy it to the full."

— Richard Burton as Leon Trotsky, *The Assassination of Trotsky*

With the end of Hollywood's blacklist, two things were—to use Marxist terminology—historically inevitable. Many blacklistees would return to filmmaking and Tinseltown would turn to renowned revolutionaries with high brand-name recognition factors to lure politicized ticket buyers. It was natural that these movies would draw upon blackballed left-wingers. Although most of these pictures weren't particularly successful or influential, they are examples of how the Old Left returned onscreen and played roles in movies aimed at New Left consumption. And while they're not all strictly biopics *per se* telling life stories of actual personages, since they use the name (or honorific) of real revolutionaries in their titles and depict these world historical personalities (if sometimes ahistorically and badly), "biopic" is used broadly.

The first of these Bolshie biopics by blacklistees was undoubtedly the best. Not only in terms of screen aesthetics, but because it played a major role in breaking the Hollywood blacklist. When *The Brave One* won a Best Screenplay Oscar in 1957, screenwriter "Robert Rich" failed to pick up his golden statuette—because Rich was really the pseudonym of the Hollywood Ten's Dalton Trumbo, living in exile in Mexico. In the 1940s, Trumbo had been Hollywood's highest paid screenwriter, and the one-time Communist was imprisoned for refusing to be a friendly witness when he testified before HUAC.

Kirk Douglas' greatest role was offscreen, when he insisted on giving blacklisted Trumbo screen credit, for the first time in about a dozen years, for 1960's *Spartacus*. The Stanley Kubrick-directed epic was based on Howard Fast's novel, which he'd written behind bars for also refusing to testify during the McCarthy era. Thus, a movie about a slave revolt is credited with breaking the blacklist. This gladiator-turned-rebel is an enduring leftist icon; Rosa Luxemburg and Karl Liebnicht named Germany's revolutionary party, the Spartacus League, after him, and an American Trotskyist Party still bears the ex-slave's name. A Soviet ballet, too, was named after Spartacus.

Although Douglas got that coveted screen credit for Trumbo, final cut eluded the executive producer/star. A gay bath scene featuring Tony Curtis and Laurence Olivier ended up on the cutting room floor (until restored in a 1991 re-release). More tellingly, according to Duncan Cooper in *Cineaste*, Universal forced the filmmakers to blunt and diminish the scope and strength of Spartacus' revolt. Apparently, the studio found the notion that a slave revolt had come within a hair's breadth of overthrowing the mighty Roman Empire too threatening to tell.

Nevertheless, the ex-slaves' fighting spirit and nobility shines through, as Douglas delivers the performance of a lifetime in his signature role. The ending of the three-hour plus CinemaScope epic is one of the most memorable evocations of human solidarity ever put on celluloid. After the Roman legions finally crush the rebels, they are given a choice: turn over Spartacus to be nailed on a cross, or they will all be crucified. When Douglas starts to turn himself in and save his fellow freedom fighters, his comrades rise, declaring: "I'm Spartacus!" (This scene was wittily trivialized in a soft drink commercial that played during the 2005 Oscar ceremony.)

In the end of the movie, which was based on a novel and a script by men imprisoned for refusing to cooperate with blacklisters and McCarthyites—the ex-slaves literally refuse to name names. The Romans crucify the rebels, but their moving martyrdom is arguably the most stirring screenic expression of the people sticking together since *Potemkin*. Their solidarity is simply incomprehensible in a dog-eat-dog capitalist society. Trumbo, of course, had written the dialogue "Share and share alike; that's democracy," for Ginger Rogers in the wartime morale booster *Tender Comrades*, and understood socialism means togetherness and unity.

Spartacus not only helped break the blacklist, but was the first in the '60s/'70s mini-trend of biopics written by ex-Reds and blacklistees finally returning to the big screen under their own names. It could also be argued that *Spartacus* marked the return of progressive Hollywood, and launched the power to the people pictures that soon followed.

At the height of the Great Proletarian Cultural Revolution, Conrad Yama played Mao Tse-Tung in the 1969 Cold War thriller *The Chairman*. Renowned Hollywood liberal Gregory Peck stars as Nobel Prize-winning scientist John Hathaway. At the U.S. embassy in London, Lieutenant General Shelby (Arthur Hill) asks Hathaway—who opposes U.S. policy—to undertake a mission to Peking. The pro-peace scientist refuses, but at the president's request travels to the People's Republic of China, then nearly inaccessible for Westerners. A transmitter has been implanted in Hathaway's skull so he can communicate with his London handlers—but unbeknownst to him, it includes an explosive device that can be detonated by Shelby to blow up Chairman Mao (with Hathaway). This story about a human bomb (with eerie echoes to our age of suicide bombers) is, however, a bomb, with little Mao in this trite Hollywood espionage actioner in redface.

However, it is interesting to note that *The Chairman*'s screenwriter, blacklistee Ben Maddow, wrote the 1937 Old Left documentaries *Heart of Spain*, featuring Dr. Norman Bethune (who went to China and trained medics for the Red Army), *China Strikes Back* (with the actual Mao) and the Paul Strand-Leo Hurwitz 1942 docudrama *Native Land*, narrated by Paul Robeson. Maddow adapted William Faulkner's *Intruder in the Dust* in 1949, Jean Genet's play *The Balcony* in 1962 and Stanley Kramer's 1969 *The Secret of Santa Vittoria*, and was an uncredited contributor to the script for Kramer's 1953 Brando biker pic *The Wild One*. When he wrote *The Chairman*, Maddow was "back from the blacklist after giving names privately," as Buhle and Wagner note in *Radical Hollywood*.

Ernesto "Che" Guevara is the *campesinos'* knight in shining armor, the handsome, forever young people's champion who never lived long enough to become blemished. Although he could have discarded his fatigues for a banker's suit, and the asthmatic could have chosen a bureaucrat's comfortable air con office instead of steamy jungles (where he fought in the end minus asthma medicine), the heroic Argentine guerrilla remained true to his creed of world revolution.

However, action director Richard Fleischer's 1969 *Che!* is among the most derided political movies ever. Blacklisted screenwriter Michael Wilson "described this film as his greatest professional disappointment," according to Buhle and Wagner in *Blacklisted: The Film Lover's Guide to the Hollywood Blacklist*. Leonard Maltin rates *Che!* "BOMB," adding: "[Y]ou haven't lived until you've seen [Jack] Palance play Fidel Castro." According to film historian Luis Reyes, author of *Hispanics In Hollywood: A Film and Television Encyclopedia*, Puerto Rico doubles for Cuba and the Fox Ranch (now Malibu State Creek Park) for Bolivia.

Nevertheless, *Che!* is an interesting feature with a pseudo-documentary style. Buhle and Wagner call the movie's Che "a nutty romantic with a gangster's ruthless streak." Omar Sharif's Guevara is indeed a fanatic, enforcing discipline by executing guerrillas lax in their duties or suspected of treason during Cuba's revolution. Once the *barbudos* seize power, Che presides over mass executions of political prisoners. When Khrushchev and Kennedy avert atomic war by defusing the Cuban Missile Crisis, Guevara urges Castro to seize the Soviet nukes for a nuclear showdown with the Yankees.

Sharif's Che becomes disenchanted with U.S.S.R. bureaucrats, and disputes over guerrilla warfare and Moscow vs. world revolution are portrayed. Che slips into Bolivia, contiguous with five South American countries, to spread the revolution. But unable to generate indigenous support, Bolivia's Green Beret/CIA-trained Second Ranger Battalion hunt the guerrillas down, wounding and capturing Che. Imprisoned at a remote village, an old goat-herder rebukes his would-be liberator. Che tells the peasant he's come to free him. "To free me from what?... Ever since you came to these mountains with your guns and your fighting, my goats give no milk." The *campesino* tells Che he wants to be free of *him*.

To avoid a trial attracting worldwide publicity Che is executed. But *Che!* doesn't show what really happened to Guevara. In *Politics and Film* Isaksson and Furhammar observe that in Hollywood's version, "the CIA was not involved..." But a June 3, 1975 declassified document notes, "When Che Guevara was executed... one CIA official was present—a Cuban-American operative named Félix Rodríguez... After the execution, Rodríguez took Che's Rolex watch, *often proudly showing it to reporters...*" Che was buried in a secret grave after his hands were amputated for fingerprint verification. Thirty years later, Che's burial site was found, his corpse exhumed and finally laid to rest in Cuba amidst much popular outpouring.

Sharif depicts the 39-year-old Argentine as fearless in the face of death. *Che!* ends as the actuality of protest and revolution sweep the globe, inspired by Che.

In *Blacklisted*, Buhle and Wagner insist: "A sympathetic screenplay was eviscerated by producer Sy Bartlett in a cold-blooded act of cinemacide. If [it were]... shot as Wilson wrote it, the film would have shown Che's development unsentimentally, with a clear-eyed hardness... A great screenwriter's last film, now difficult to find, richly deserving its obscurity. (Happily, the original screenplay has survived.)"

Blacklistee Abe Polonsky wrote and directed 1969's *Tell Them Willie Boy is Here*, one of the best and most sympathetic of the era's cycle of pro-Indian pictures. Robert Blake stars as a real-life Native American suspected of murdering his lover's father and girlfriend (Katharine Ross), too. (*Willie Boy* is in an eerie premonition of Blake's future murder trial for purportedly killing his wife.) Robert Redford portrays the deputy sheriff who hunted Willie down in the turn-of-the-century manhunt in California, as the U.S. president visits.

The story packs the punch of Polonsky's 1940s, pre-blacklist *Body and Soul* and *Force of Evil*, and was among the most aesthetically and politically successful returns to the American screen of the banished artists. Along with Ring Lardner's *M*A*S*H*, *Willie Boy* pointedly raises the "what if?" question—what if these dissident talents hadn't been cut down in their prime and allowed to continue developing their art and vision? How much richer would we as a nation and film culture have been?

James Earl Jones delivered a K.O. of a performance—possibly the best in all Black Power pictures—in 1970's *The Great White Hope*, directed by Martin Ritt, who had been blacklisted during what Lillian Hellman called "scoundrel time." Howard Sackler adapted his play, a Broadway sensation. Ray vividly portrays boxer Jack Jefferson (based on Jack Johnson, the first black heavyweight champion), and his struggles with racism.

As Muhammad Ali noted at the time, the story closely reflected his own life, in that Jefferson's biggest battle was outside of the ring. However, Ali was stripped of his title because the Black Muslim protested the war in Vietnam—he provocatively declared "No Vietcong ever called me 'nigger'"—and refused to be drafted. Unlike Ali, Jefferson transgressed against whitey by romancing a Caucasian woman (Jane Alexander). And in general—like Ali—the "uppity" champ just didn't "know his place." Jefferson throws the fight to a white boxer, so whitey will get off his back and get the heavyweight title back. But first, Jefferson pummels his Caucasian opponent, blood pouring over his eyes.

Two of the era's other Tinseltown Bolshie biopics are set in Latin America. Like Che, Leon Trotsky was an advocate of international revolution, a hope that was in the air during a period of Third World liberation movements, New Left insurgency in the West, Cultural Revolution in China and aspirations for "socialism with a human face" in Prague. In 1972, the joke among Trotskyists was that Joseph Losey's *The Assassination of Trotsky* was the second assassination of the Russian revolutionary. Even though Trotsky was portrayed by a first rate actor—Richard Burton—this is lousy Losey, a blacklisted ex-CPer who relocated to Britain during the McCarthy period. Franco Solinas contributed to the screenplay. As in *The Chairman*, the emphasis again is not on the leftist leader depicted or his beliefs, but on a plot of intrigue that surrounds him.

A montage opens the feature, with historical photos of Trotsky during his life and revolutionary career. Aside from some dialogue, this is the sole exposition regarding Trotsky. If you're searching for definitions of "permanent revolution," don't rent this movie—contact the Spartacists or SWP. This is, as the title suggests, not so much a biopic about Lenin's comrade, but rather mainly about Trotsky's final days as a political refugee near Mexico City, when Stalinist NKVD agent Frank Jackson (French action star Alain Delon) liquidated the apostle of world revolution.

The action opens in Mexico City on May Day, 1940 with a workers' march. At a bullfight, Jackson enjoys the bloodshed. Throughout the film, he suffers from psychological problems that appear to stem from being dispatched by Stalin to eliminate his archenemy during the 1939-1941 Hitler-Stalin Pact. The Nazis invaded France in May 1940; fascism and Stalinism ruled most of Europe. No longer content with having expelled the Red Army's ex-commander from the U.S.S.R. in 1929, Stalin struck out against his left opposition to prove to Berlin that he was a reliable ally.

Jackson is the lover of Gita Samuels (Romy Schneider), a Trotskyist aide. Through her, the spy infiltrates the old Bolshevik's inner circle in Mexico. There, Trotsky dictates his thoughts, writes, ruminates and survives an armed May 1940 attack on his compound. But on August 20, 1940 Jackson worms his way into Trotsky's inner sanctum, and as the Russian Revolution's co-leader tries to help Jackson with an article he's writing, Stalin's henchman pierces Trotsky's skull with an ice pick.

The blood-drenched 61-year-old revolutionary struggles with Jackson, preventing him from escaping. Trotsky dies the following day.[6]

A highlight in this stodgy film is when Burton recites what's regarded as Trotsky's testament in one of the English language's most mellifluous, glorious voices: "I can see the bright green strip of grass beneath the wall, and the clear blue sky above the wall, and sunlight everywhere. Life is beautiful.[7] Let the future generations cleanse it of all evil, oppression and violence, and enjoy it to the full."

---

6. The assassination is humorously revisited in 1966's *Morgan! A Suitable Case for Treatment*, wherein David Warner plays a bonkers British Bolshevik, who reenacts Trotsky's assassination using an ice pick to smash an eggshell. The droll *Morgan!* was directed by Czech-born Karel Reisz —who was married to Gene Kelly's ex-wife, Hollywood leftist Betsy Blair—and co-starred the real life Trotskyist Vanessa Redgrave. It ends with Morgan committed to an insane asylum—where the Bolshie Brit unabashedly plants flowers in the shape of a hammer and sickle in the sanitarium's garden.

The last of the Bolshie biopic trio set in Latin America also takes place largely in Mexico. The most recent example of a pre-September 11 attack on the soil of an actual state took place March 1916 at Columbus, New Mexico. This raid by Mexican revolutionaries is the highlight of 1972's *Pancho Villa*, and the movie's appropriate tagline is: "The only man to invade the USA!"

Telly Savalas, of "Kojak" fame, plays sombrero-wearing Pancho with *mucho* panache, as an *hombre* gutsy enough to raid the American town and its garrison. TV's "Rifleman," Chuck Connors, plays General "Black-jack" Pershing, Clint Walker co-stars as Pancho's arms-savvy *gringo amigo* Scotty and Anne Francis plays Clint's ex-wife, Flo.

What is most revelatory about *Pancho Villa* is that its producer is Bernard Gordon, the ex-Red screenwriter who escaped the blacklist. In Spain, the screenwriter joined forces with Phillip Yordan, and became a producer and studio chief at what Gordon called "a Hollywood *in extremis*." By shooting overseas at less costly locations and studios, they originated "runaway productions," and providing refuge from blacklisted talents, ironically freer in Franco's fascist Spain than in democratic America. (Yordan also employed blacklistee Ben Maddow of *The Chairman*.)

In Gordon's *Hollywood Exile: Or, How I Learned to Love the Blacklist*, the former Communist writes, "Pancho Villa… had actually invaded the United States… the one and only foreign invasion of the United States. This historical curiosity has been ignored, at least by Americans, but it seemed a promising idea." Gordon goes on to call this Spaghetti Western "the first production I might call my own." The story was originated by one of Gordon's blacklisted comrades, Bob Williams, and scripted by Gordon's City College classmate, blacklistee and probable Party member Julian Zimet.

U.S. Army officers look buffoonish in this film made during the Vietnam War. Gordon writes that Connors "play[ed] the insanely spit-and-polish general who was being driven mad by the slippery, unpredictable Mexican." Pershing humorously winds up in a full body cast after a head-on collision with Villa's train, although Pancho escapes—as he did in real life.

Like *Che!*, *Pancho Villa* reflects the Third World, anti-imperialist movements of the time. Of the quartet of biopics about revolutionaries, *Pancho* arguably had the most subversive script—and the most leftist input.[8]

---

7. Some believe the title of Roberto Benigni's 1998 Oscar winner *Life is Beautiful* is derived from Trotsky's testament.

FULL FRONTAL ASSAULT: SEXUAL REVOLUTION REELS

"Marriage is a bourgeois trait."

— Henry Winkler, "Katherine"

In Gordon Parks' autobiographical 1969 *The Learning Tree*, as a twister sweeps Kansas, young Newt (Kyle Johnson) runs for cover in a wooden house. Inside, an older girl seduces the virgin, as cyclone symbolizes sex.

Sexuality was at the forefront of the '60s/'70s rebellion, which launched a full frontal assault against America's mores and values. The "do it!" youth culture regarded American sexual morality as hypocritical, repressive and puritanical. It was Woodstock versus Comstockery. Filmmakers led the charge, defeating the stringent Production Code which censored movies. American cineastes were joined at the barricades by European comrades, as foreign films such as 1968's Danish *I Am Curious (Yellow)* stormed the Bastille of pulchritude. By the late '60s, movies received free expression legal protections. A new rating system allowed nudity and sensuality to be legally shown onscreen in pictures rated "R" or "X" (such as John Schlesinger's *Midnight Cowboy*), as long as theaters restricted admission of minors. The liberating effect of the Production Code's overthrow—enforced for 30-plus years—cannot be overestimated.

Getting naked and doing it onscreen was a big part of period pictures. Stars were expected to let it all hang out. Jane Fonda performed an outer space striptease and sexual antics in her then-husband Roger Vadim's 1968 *Barbarella* (Fonda took lots of heat for this when she became an activist, but people forget *Barbarella* was an intergalactic revolutionary.) Ken Russell's 1969 *Women in Love* and Stanley Kubrick's 1971 *A Clockwork Orange* broke ground with full frontal nudity of British stars Oliver Reed and Alan Bates in a homoerotic wrestling scene in the former, and Malcolm McDowell as the droogie Alex in the latter. In Michael Wadleigh's 1970 *Woodstock*, the peace and love generation returned to nature *au*

---

8. Gordon also co-wrote the 1969 historical epic *Krakatoa, East of Java*, about the 1883 volcanic eruption and ensuing tidal wave that killed 36,000 Indonesians. Gordon's *Krakatoa* is a McCarthyite movie metaphor: The volcanic explosion and tsunami are unconscious projections of General Suharto's 1965 U.S.-backed coup that overthrew the nationalist Sukarno and massacred hundreds of thousands of Indonesian Communists in the ultimate blacklist.

natural amidst three days of music and mud. In the *New Yorker*, critic Pauline Kael breathlessly wrote that 1972's *Last Tango in Paris* "must be the most powerfully erotic movie ever made, and it may turn out to be the most liberating movie ever made... The movie breakthrough has finally come... Bertolucci and Brando have altered the face of an art form."

Come, indeed. Orgasmo-mania hit the screens, and full-on hardcore porn in the Earth-shattering year of 1972—*Deep Throat* starring Linda Lovelace, *The Devil in Miss Jones* starring Georgina Spelvin and *Behind the Green Door* starring the not-so-all-American-girl Marilyn Chambers—openly did theaters from Dallas to Peoria. While porn pushed envelopes and boundaries, the New Hollywood's nude Hollywood features were arguably more subversive. Whereas porn reduced sex to mere mechanical acts, movies such as Jane Fonda's Oscar-winning turn in 1971's *Klute* as a troubled call girl, or Jack Nicholson, Art Garfunkel, Candice Bergen and Ann-Margret in Mike Nichols' 1971 *Carnal Knowledge* revealed the complexity of sexuality. While porn was purely physical, Luis Buñuel's chilling 1967 *Belle de Jour* combined the physical with the psychological, sensuality with sensibility.

The linking of sexual liberation to the movement may seem naïve, but some power to the people pictures do make this connection. When I asked Jack Nicholson about the politics of his feature film directorial debut, 1971's antiwar *Drive, He Said*, Nicholson—who also co-wrote *Drive*—said it incorporated the philosophy of Wilhelm Reich, the German Communist psychoanalyst who tried to merge Marx and Freud. Nicholson went on to say that Karen Black's orgasm was banned in Britain (she plays the repressed wife of campus basketball coach Bruce Dern who has a more satisfying affair with a countercultural athlete).

In Warren Beatty's 1981 *Reds* scenes of the Russian Revolution are intercut with images of journalists John Reed (Beatty) and Louise Bryant (Diane Keaton) overcoming their estrangement from one another. They rapturously make love in between marching in St. Petersburg's streets and singing "The Internationale." The point is that the revolution will set you free—in and out of bed. The apotheosis of this commingling of political and sexual liberation is in Dusan Makavejev's 1971 *WR: Mysteries of the Organism*.

In *The Strawberry Statement*, student occupiers impressed by Simon's (Davison) bloody lip (caused by police, he falsely claims) include a buxom blonde who summons Simon to a Xerox room covered with Che posters. Stripping off her shirt, the beauty asks: "Did you know that Lenin liked women with big breasts?" The people's groupie gives Simon head, humorously intercut with the Xerox machine reaching a sort of climax.

Reproductive control over one's own body appeared onscreen. In "Katherine," following the 1968 Chicago demonstrations, Spacek dedicates her life solely to radical politics, has an abortion and declares: "First you make the world a better place for children, and then you have children."

Conventional monogamous relationships were subverted in many radical pictures. The Weathermen shared sexual partners, and in "Katherine," Bob (Winkler) tells Katherine, "Marriage is a bourgeois trait." He splits for Canada, leaving Katherine behind. As 1969's *Bob & Carol & Ted & Alice* philosophized, infidelity was a small step for man, but a giant step for mankind (and womankind). Robert Culp, Natalie Wood, Elliott Gould and Dyan Cannon swap partners and have a foursome, as Dionne Warwick sings Burt Bacharach's "What the World Needs Now is Love." In 1970's *Diary of a Mad Housewife*, Tina Balser (Carrie Snodgrass) cheats on her husband Jonathan (Richard Benjamin) with George Prager (Frank Langella).

The tedium of monogamy is also a theme of 1971's *Carnal Knowledge*. College roommates Sandy (Garfunkel) and especially Jonathan (Nicholson) have numerous partners. So does Beatty in Hal Ashby's 1975 *Shampoo* as randy haircutter George Roundy, who beds several women the day Nixon's elected—and ends up (like Nixon's America) empty, alone and fucked. In *Women In Love* Rupert Birken (Bates) yearns for what author D.H. Lawrence called "separateness-in-union," defying the tyranny monogamy imposes, longing for a more expansive, less exclusive type of relationship—perhaps one allowing for bisexuality. And in movies like William Friedkin's 1970 *The Boys in the Band,* homosexuality started being overtly presented, and increasingly positively.

Interracial sex was a hot topic onscreen, just as it was incendiary offscreen. In 1970's *Getting Straight*, Harry (Elliott Gould) fights with girlfriend Jan (Bergen) and later wakes up in bed with a black woman. She asks Harry "what do you think of James Baldwin... Did you ever make it with a black chick before?... You're pretty good but a little inhibited." Unlike the covered breasts of Jan (his girlfriend, played by Candice Bergen) and the other white woman Harry beds onscreen, Luan's nipples are glimpsed.

When a foxy student in Harry's class asks for a reading suggestion, he recommends the Marquis de Sade. When a sex ed film is screened in Jan's science class, he repeats that Reichian mantra: "Sexual repression breeds violence... Look at Vietnam and Korea..." When he insists over her objections that they rendezvous later to have sex, Jan relents, "Come at 7:30... It's the least I can do to avoid WWIII." During a meeting of activists, Herbert (John Rubinstein) asserts, "We should demand an end to the separation of the sexes in the dorms." Like Vietnam, sexual liberation was an important part of the student power movement—call it sexual self-determination.

The women's movement challenged and changed gender roles. In *Carnal Knowledge*, Bobbie (Ann-Margret) complains to the controlling, manipulative male chauvinist pig Jonathan (Nicholson): "You wouldn't even let me canvas for Kennedy." In Sidney Lumet's hilarious 1976 media send-up *Network*, TV executive Diana Christensen (Faye Dunaway) has quickies with Max Schumacher (William Holden), with Diana in the superior position. For Diana, it's slam-bam-thank-you-man.

Today, Hollywood and indie filmmakers have inherited the hard-earned sexual rights '60s/'70s cinema stalwarts struggled for, with much blood, sweat, tears and cum. Yet few contemporary moviemakers use these rights. Nudity is often hidden beneath the covers in sex scenes. The MPAA wields the "NC-17" rating like a kiss of death, slapping it on films that sexually transgress. Good old fashioned American Puritanism masquerades as political correctness. When even uttering the word "pregnant" on "I Love Lucy" or in an Otto Preminger film was *tabu*, the '60s/'70s devil-may-care smashing of censorship was considered liberating—not exploitative. The open sexuality of this period's pictures serves as a reminder and lesson for today's more inhibited *cineastes* and audiences.

FREE FILM FORM

"They came out looking like somebody hit them on the head. They literally didn't know what to think. They knew they were in the presence of a kind of film they hadn't seen before. It threatened them."

— Haskell Wexler, on screening *Medium Cool* for Paramount executives

As part of their struggle to change the world, '60s/'70s progressive filmmakers also sought to seize the means of production, change the studio system, the way audiences saw films and the very form of conventional, narrative movies. A number of pictures dealt with movies, moviemaking and the news media, such as Dennis Hopper's 1971 *The Last Movie* and 1976's *Network*, and challenged how they were produced. The so-called

"Easy Riders" and "Raging Bulls" of the New Hollywood wanted to control the studios and stamp their creative sensibility and politics on cinema.

The 1969 movie *Medium Cool*'s form is as avant garde as its content. Wexler combines his documentary and feature film backgrounds to create a "cin-thesis." By placing his actors on Chicago's streets during a police riot and in the convention hall, Wexler merges nonfiction and narrative filmmaking, cinema verite and studio movies. With the help of Studs Terkel, the director eschews sets and backlots for real locations, including Chicago's ghetto. The cast and crew travel to the tent shantytown of the 1968 Poor People's Campaign's "Resurrection City" near Washington's mall and reflecting pool, which Dr. King initiated shortly before his assassination. (A clenched fist-waving Jesse Jackson is briefly glimpsed.) *Medium Cool* is a forerunner of so-called "reality TV." As Talbot and Zheutlin note in *Creative Differences*, *Medium Cool*'s "documentary footage of the Convention hall hysteria and police violence in Grant Park gave the film a political immediacy which no other Hollywood picture of the period carried."

Wexler started out shooting labor docs funded by unions, such as 1946's *Deadline for Action*, focusing on postwar national CIO strikes. As a cameraman he lensed nonfiction films about Vietnam, disarmament, Kurds, Zapatistas and Hawaiians. He's also directed several documentaries, including 1965's *The Bus*, about the 1963 March on Washington, 1976's *Underground*, about the Weathermen, (co-directed by Emile de Antonio and Mary Lampson) and 1999's *Bus Riders' Union*, about L.A. straphangers who assert that mass transit is a civil right.

As a cameraman, he's shot studio fare such as 1968's *The Thomas Crown Affair* and 1996's Halle Berry thriller *The Rich Man's Wife*. Wexler has also lensed numerous features with political themes—Gore Vidal's 1964 *The Best Man*, about a nominating convention, the 1976 Woody Guthrie biopic *Bound for Glory*, 1978's antiwar *Coming Home* and John Sayles' 1987 depiction of a violent strike in *Matewan*, as well as Sayles' 2004 *Silver City* and Ken Loach's 2000 *Bread and Roses*, starring Adrien Brody as an organizer of L.A.'s "Justice for Janitors" unionization campaign. Wexler was the DP for Michael Moore's only feature, *Canadian Bacon*, a satire about Washington declaring war on Ottawa. As an interviewee, Wexler outspokenly denounces Bush's Iraq invasion in the 2004 documentary *Declarations of War*.

In Paul Cronin's 2001 *Look Out Haskell, It's Real!: The Making of Medium Cool*, which includes interviews with former Chicago 8 attorney

Leonard Weinglass, Bernardine Dohrn, Studs Terkel and cast and crew members, Wexler states: "I think of documentary as being narrative. It's just a different kind of fiction. That whole idea... thought... and discussion of what's real, what's cinema verite, what's truth... In working in documentaries I realized I could get deeper into the true reality of the scene by arranging... organizing things, by playing with what you might call 'reality'... I was trying to utilize what I learned from documentary filmmaking and integrate that into theatrical or fiction filmmaking."

When bewildered Paramount execs saw *Medium Cool,* "They came out looking like somebody hit them on the head. They literally didn't know what to think. They knew they were in the presence of a kind of film they hadn't seen before. It threatened them," Wexler recalled in *Creative Differences.*

As much as being a rumination on antiestablishment politics, *Medium Cool* pondered cinematic aesthetics plus news media sensibility and responsibility—years before Sidney Lumet's 1976 *Network*, James Brooks' 1987 *Broadcast News* and Michael Moore's *Fahrenheit 9/11* raised similar questions. Although Wexler denies it in *Look Out,* some believe the title refers to the medium-is-the-message media high guru Marshall McLuhan, who defined television as a "cool medium."

John Cassellis (Forster) is a detached TV news cameraman with a professional veneer of objectivity. As *Medium Cool* opens, John and his soundman Gus (Peter Bonerz) coolly record a car crash. Throughout the film, John becomes more personally involved. When he finds out the station allowed the F.B.I. to review his footage, John freaks out at this betrayal of journalistic ethics. "What am I—a fink?" John asks. (The feds took Wexler's passport away and F.B.I. agents tailed him during the McCarthy era.) As Chicago burns during the 1968 convention, *Medium Cool* closes as it began—with an auto crash. This time, John is one of the corpses recorded by a cameraman who then aims his camera directly at the audience. The shooter is Wexler himself, who says in *Look Out:* "I wanted to make something that felt more personal to me. And that's why I made a film about a cameraman. I am that news cameraman." Wexler appears to be asking formal questions similar to those posed 60 years earlier by *Kino Pravda* ("Film Truth") documentary pioneer Dziga Vertov in the Soviet classic *The Man With the Movie Camera. Medium Cool's* point seems to be that one has to get involved.

Media savvy Wexler tells *Look Out:* "The whole idea of theatre and of showing and of presenting ideas in dramatic theatrical ways was something the antiwar movement knew very well. With Abbie Hoffman and the theatricality of the actions that were taken to get the attention of the media. The people in the streets were more aware of the importance of theatre than the police and National Guard. Everyone's putting on a show for somebody. Probably in our culture for television. Otherwise you're ignored. If you're not on television, you don't exist."

Wexler criticized *The Thomas Crown Affair* for being "a hyped-up picture replete with vacuity" that's "about absolutely nothing," and yearned to inject reality into his feature directorial debut. In addition to incorporating references to real life 1968 events, such as Bobby Kennedy's assassination (although the kitchen where Wexler shot this scene is not where RFK was carried after Sirhan Sirhan shot him in L.A.'s Ambassador Hotel), like postwar Italians, Wexler turned to Neorealism. He cast Harold Blankenship, an Appalachian boy he found in Chicago's ghetto, to play Eileen's son. The West Virginia non-actor is depicted taking his first real-life shower onscreen at John's apartment. Enhancing the realism, Verna Bloom adds that as she ran through the riotous streets as Eileen, she reacted to what she saw going on around her without any direction. "It was so unreal to be... in the street in a major city in the United States of America and having these tanks come at you... I was playing a part in a make believe story in a real situation."

The teargassing of Wexler and his producer is seen onscreen, shot by crew members without sound. Ironically, the accompanying quote, "Look out Haskell, it's real!" was added afterwards.

Inspired by the French New Wave's *gauchiste*, Jean-Luc Godard and others, forsaking the cumbersome gear of studio pictures, and even of some network news outfits, Wexler uses technology to enable him to capture reality. *Medium*'s assistant cameraman Andrew Davis says Wexler used "very fluid small film crews... His technique was putting actors in real situations and using that backdrop, without having a director stage people. We spent a lot of time just trying to be a part of the fabric of what the kids in the streets were doing... Haskell was forcing himself to use his documentary roots to create this movie." During the entire riot, *Medium Cool* used only three cameras.

In a noteworthy scene set in the ghetto, John is confronted by African Americans angry over how they are depicted in the news: "You are the exploiters... the ones who distort and ridicule and emasculate us... You don't know the people. You don't show the people... Why do you always got to wait till somebody gets killed, man? 'Cause somebody is gonna get killed!" the black nationalist asserts.

The Spook Who Sat by the Door similarly criticizes Tinseltown's derogatory treatment of African Americans. At a meeting of black nationalists, militants act out a "plantation movie" with happy darkies but no chains or whips. A bearded, dark-skinned activist plays a "faithful retainer," who greets Colonel Beauregard (a light-skinned revolutionary) exclaiming "Lawdy, lawdy, lawdy!" as his ex-master returns from the war, which the South has lost. Nevertheless, the now ex-slave pledges eternal fealty to his ex-master, despite the Yankee carpetbaggers forcing massa to mortgage the big house, which means George can't be paid. The colonel tells "George" he's free and can leave the plantation now. The ex-slave asks if freedom is bad, and declares he wouldn't know what to do with money, anyway.

Freeman (Lawrence Cook), the underground leader and a comrade scat "Dixie." The militants laugh. This is arguably the best and most explicit critique of Hollywood's "history written with lightning" (as Woodrow Wilson reportedly said at a White House screening of *Birth of a Nation*), films such as *Birth* and *Gone With the Wind*. "You have just played out the American dream. And now, we are going to turn it into a nightmare," Freeman states.

If... found a poetic aesthetic that perfectly expressed its anarchistic content. In addition to many dreamlike sequences, the modestly budgeted feature's innovative use of black and white and color was much commented on. The alternating from color to black and white may have a disruptive effect, like the Brechtian alienation technique, which serves to remind audiences that they are observing a work of art—not real life. By throwing them out of their trance-like suspension of disbelief, viewers should use reason, not just emotions, to assess the work.

In a deeper sense, the switching from black and white to color simulates the transition from a dream state to a waking state of consciousness. This ambiguity between reality and fantasy underlies the very title of *If...* This technique is used to great effect in scenes such as the café sequence, where Mick (McDowell) wrestles with and then makes love to the Girl (Christine Noonan), followed by their soaring through the countryside on a motorcycle. The Girl stands on the seat, her hair flying freely in living color.

Flash forwards—the opposite of a flashback, whereby action is glimpsed before it occurs in the story's narrative arc—are seen in movies such as 1969's *Easy Rider*. An exploding bike is briefly shown before the film's violent ending. *Medium Cool* has a sound flash forward—a news report of the final car crash is heard before it happens. Other artsy effects—some imported from France's New Wave and other overseas cinematic sources—were used. With zooms (in and out), multiple exposures, freeze frames, color processing, split screen, etc., radical substance was accompanied by avant-garde style, as the vocabulary of the film narrative was expanded along with its subject matter. Even cartoons loosened up, with Ralph Bakshi's 1972 *Fritz the Cat* expanding the form and sensibility of a medium previously aimed mainly at children.

Perhaps the era's greatest experiment in film form by a Hollywood studio movie was 1968's *Head*, an exuberantly psychedelic picture. Written by Jack Nicholson and director Bob Rafelson, with contributions by the Monkees, who starred, and executive produced by Bert Schneider (whose father was the head of Columbia Pictures), *Head* set out to shatter all cinematic conventions. In a series of vignettes, the Monkees mock various stock film genres—sci-fi, French Foreign Legion, Western, war movies, etc.

The film's irreverent shape matches its antiestablishment politics. At a stadium concert, the Monkees demand "Give me a W—A—R," and the fans dutifully assemble to form the letters as they're called out. The film cuts between the concert and combat scenes; black and white shots of Vietnamese are glimpsed via intercutting and superimposing. As the Monkees croon "What you have seen you must believe if you can," the infamous footage of a South Vietnamese soldier shooting a Viet Cong suspect screens. This was not the stuff that the Monkees' TV show— which Schneider and Rafelson co-created and made a fortune on—was made of. Teenyboppers were bewildered. Peter Rafelson (Bob's son) told me in a phone conversation that *Head*'s purpose was "to destroy the Monkees." According to Peter Biskind's *Easy Riders, Raging Bulls*, the film lost so much money that Bert's older brother, Stanley, later (unsuccessfully) begged his prodigal brother not to let Rafelson direct 1970's *Five Easy Pieces*.

Head has one of Hollywood's most subversive endings. As credits roll, a filmstrip flutters, breaks, then burns. The famous Lady Liberty-like Columbia Pictures logo appears; a woman laughs. The point is that New Hollywood was out to destroy the studio system.

Even Tinseltown's most sacred cow, the hallowed Academy Awards ceremony, televised annually to many millions on live TV, came under frontal attack during this tumultuous period. George C. Scott refused his Oscar for 1970s anti-militarist *Patton* on the grounds that actors shouldn't compete against one another. But the greatest moment in Oscar's political history came on March 27, 1973, when Marlon Brando was awarded his second Best Actor Academy Award for *The Godfather*, that critique of corporate America in the guise of a Mafioso movie.

"When I was nominated... it seemed absurd to go to the Awards ceremony," Brando wrote in his autobiography, *Brando: Songs My Mother Taught Me.* "Celebrating an industry that had systematically misrepresented and maligned American Indians for six decades, while at the moment 200 Indians were under siege at Wounded Knee, was ludicrous. Still, if I did win an Oscar, I realized it could provide the first opportunity in history for an American Indian to speak to 60 million people—a little payback for years of defamation by Hollywood."

That "payback" was delivered by 26-year-old Sacheen Little Feather. Born Maria Louise Cruz in a reservation near Tucson, she participated in the Native American occupation of Alcatraz. Arriving just 15 minutes before the end of the Academy Awards ceremony, when Liv Ullmann announced Brando won his second Oscar, Sacheen sashayed to the stage in a traditional Indian buckskin dress and turquoise jewelry, her hair braided. She motioned to Roger "James Bond" Moore not to give her the gold statuette. Refused permission to read Brando's 15-minute explanation, she instead said:

"I'm Apache and I am the president of the National Native American Affirmative Image Committee. I'm representing Marlon Brando this evening and he has asked me to tell you, in a very long speech which I cannot share with you presently because of time but I will be glad to share with the press afterward, that he very regretfully cannot accept this very generous award. And the reasons for this are the treatment of American Indians today by the film industry and in television reruns. I beg at this time that I have not intruded upon this evening and that we will, in the future, in our hearts and our understanding meet with love and generosity. Thank you on behalf of Marlon Brando."

Sacheen then read aloud the ending of Brando's written statement: "I would have been here myself tonight but I thought I could do more good at Wounded Knee." This referred to the then-ongoing siege and face-off between authorities and American Indian Movement militants at South Dakota's Pine Ridge Reservation, site of an 1890 slaughter of many Native Americans.

Reaction to the stunning snubbing of the Academy for its denigration of America's aboriginal peoples was divided. Many derided Brando for trespassing on Tinseltown's sacrosanct, self-congratulatory backslapping event. Oscar presenters and members of Hollywood's establishment were in high dudgeon: Rock Hudson stated, "Often to be eloquent is to be quiet." Co-presenting the Best Actress statuette, Raquel Welch said of the nominees, "I hope they haven't got a cause." Spaghetti Western and *Rawhide* star Clint Eastwood—future Republican mayor of Carmel, CA— asked if the Best Picture Oscar should be awarded "on behalf of all the cowboys shot in John Ford westerns over the years." As Peter Manso relates in *Brando*, in the Dorothy Chandler Pavilion's parking lot, racists mobbed Sacheen and then the Cadillac she was riding in, "shouting mock Indian war whoops. 'Where's your tomahawk?'" a heckler yelled.

However, not everyone reacted this way. Manso adds that as Sacheen left the Oscar ceremony, "Outside the stage door a group of blacks and Chicanos cheered, 'Right on, girl! Right on, you really spoke it.'" The televised awards ceremony speech electrified Indian occupiers at Wounded Knee, raising morale. Manso quotes AIM's Dennis Banks: "Suddenly, with just this three minute statement from Brando, people all over the world would be watching. It was the biggest exposure we'd had for the month we'd been under siege in out bunkers. At that moment it was like the war was over. Total euphoria. People ran outside into the snow to fire off their rifles, yelling. We just couldn't believe it."

Brando later said that he didn't have the right to gratify his ego by accepting the Oscar, when he could instead provide oppressed Indians a forum to air their grievances worldwide. Sacheen's refusal of Brando's Oscar remains unforgotten. Irene Bedard—voice of *Pocahontas* in Disney's 1995 animated feature co-starring Russell Means, and female lead of the first Indian-directed and written feature, 1998's *Smoke Signals*— told the *Gallup Independent* in 2003 she "credits the freedom to play Native American roles to Sacheen Little Feather..."

WORKING CLASS HEROES

"As soon as you're born they make you feel small
By giving you no time instead of it all
Till the pain is so big you feel nothing at all
A working class hero is something to be."

— John Lennon, "Working Class Hero"

Unlike the '30s/'40s progressive pictures that rhapsodized proletarian protagonists, the New Left emphasized students, lumpenized minorities and Third World revolutionaries. Nevertheless, power to the people pictures had their share of working class heroes.

In 1970, Sean Connery played a labor leader in *The Molly Maguires*—a real life 1870s underground organization that used terroristic methods to fight for Irish miners' rights in Pennsylvania's coal mines. The film co-starred Richard Harris and Samantha Eggar, was directed and written by blacklistees Martin Ritt and Walter Bernstein and was lensed by James Wong Howe. Unfortunately, the big budget Paramount movie, pitting Pinkertons against the militant miners' secret society, failed to catch fire. In *Blacklisted*, Buhle and Wagner comment, "Ritt... made the film that his generational cohorts had talked of making since the days of radical Depression theater."

Ritt and Bernstein next teamed up for 1976's drama about the Hollywood blacklist, *The Front*, wherein Woody Allen plays Howard Prince, a cross between a *schnook* and a working class hero. The film opens with black and white 1950s period footage, starting with Senator Joe McCarthy's marriage as Frank Sinatra croons "Young At Heart," with the lyrics: "Fairy tales can come true..." Prince is a cashier at a bar who fronts for blacklisted screenwriters unable to use their own names on scripts.

Zero Mostel plays entertainer Hecky Brown, who—like himself, Herschel Bernardi and others who made this movie—was denied work during the McCarthy era. Like other real-life blacklistees such as Phillip Loeb, Hecky commits suicide. When Prince is ensnared by a Red Channels-type clearinghouse due to the scheme to beat the blacklist, he is subpoenaed to appear before a HUAC executive session, where he can save himself by becoming a friendly witness. But when he testifies, Prince tells HUAC: "Fellas, I don't recognize the right of this Committee to ask me these kind of questions. And furthermore, you can all go fuck yourselves."

According to Buhle and Wagner in *Hide In Plain Sight*, in *The Front* Lloyd Gough—who, along with his wife, Karen Morley, was blacklisted—portrays a character based on Abraham Polonsky, who makes a point of telling Prince that he is indeed a Communist. This is a rare Red role in and departure from most movies about the Hollywood blacklist, which usually feature noncommunist characters as victims. In Sydney Pollack's 1973 *The Way We Were*, Barbra Streisand's feisty Katie Morosky (same initials as Karl Marx's) is a working class Brooklyn Jew and card carrying CPer. However, it is her husband Hubbell Gardner (Robert Redford) who plays the screenwriter during the Hollywood blacklist segment (much of which ended up on the cutting room floor).

Martin Scorsese's 1972 *Boxcar Bertha*, produced by Roger Corman, is based on the memoirs of real life labor hero Bertha Thompson (Barbara Hershey). David Carradine plays union organizer Big Bill Shelly, whose name Corman says refers to the Wobbly firebrand Big Bill Haywood. After being convicted of sedition for calling a strike during WWI, Haywood fled to the U.S.S.R. (his ashes are buried next to John Reed).

In *Boxcar*, Big Bill tries to organize railroad workers. Bernie Casey plays Bertha and Bill's friend, Von Morton, who takes no guff from whitey and even shoots a few unionbusting rednecks. At the end Big Bill is crucified, Christ-like, on the outside of a train, which moves down the track with Bertha running after Bill.

"*Boxcar Bertha* was a follow-up to [1970's] *Bloody Mama*, the picture starring Shelley Winters about the Ma Barker gang," Corman says. "*Bloody Mama* did extremely well... Both of those films were very populist in nature. In each case they talked about the dispossessed of the 1930s and particularly rural 1930s America, at a time when farms were failing and farmers and small townspeople particularly were feeling the brunt of the Depression. Starting with *Bloody Mama* then going to *Boxcar Bertha*, and then to *Big Bad Mama*, all three pictures were very strong populist pictures... dealing with the ravages of the Depression in rural America."

The master of low budget movies went on to say, "The labor politics of *Boxcar Bertha* were played both through Bertha herself, and her companion Big Bill Shelly, a labor organizer. Bertha was the daughter of a crop duster killed [in a test plane accident], and together with Shelly did embark on a partial life of crime, and, from Bertha's standpoint, an attempt to help organize railroad workers in particular, and simply the dispossessed. It really told the story of the dispossessed, just as *Bloody Mama* and [1974's] *Big Bad Mama* did... I think of the three as a trilogy. They were all the story of the dispossessed in the South in the 1930s. And they were all told through the guise of rural crime, with a woman in the leading role... Yes. That's exactly what we were doing"—using the crime genre to comment on the American economic and political system, Corman states.

Corman helped launch the careers of New Hollywood directors like Scorsese, Francis Ford Coppola and Jonathan Demme, who directed 1976's *Fighting Mad*. "This is another film—that was more ecologically-oriented, talking about the environment. I'd say yes, Peter Fonda in that film—all of these films represent a liberal, antiestablishment point of view." The film pits Fonda as a defender of the land and its people against rapacious developers. Scenes of farmers being thrown off of their home-steads are ripped right out of Henry Fonda's *The Grapes of Wrath*.

In 1976, David Carradine starred in Hal Ashby's *Bound for Glory*, the beautiful Woody Guthrie biopic with sumptuous cinematography by Haskell Wexler. Carradine plays Arlo's dad as the Okie who escapes the dustbowl and finds fame in radioland—but uses his guitar to fight against the ruling class. (Guthrie said of his guitar, "this machine kills fascists.")

Terrence Malick's 1978 *Days of Heaven*, starring Richard Gere, Brooke Adams and Sam Shepard deals with migrant workers harvesting wheat in Texas. The big budget movie was produced by Bert Schneider, flopped at the box office, and was the next to last picture produced by Huey Newton's Hollywood pal. Michael Cimino's much-maligned, big bud-get 1980 *Heaven's Gate* was a class struggle epic set in the Old West, pitting sodbusters against gunslingers. Leonard Maltin reviewed it as "dealing, more or less, with the conflict between immigrant settlers of 19th century Wyoming and ruthless American empire-builders who want them eliminated." But the class conflict story got lost amidst the buzz about Cimino going way over budget, which started a new trend in entertainment reporting. Both Malick and Cimino's films were noted for their heavenly cinematography by, respectively, Oscar-winning Néstor Almendros and Vilmos Zsigmond.

As the '70s ended, two of the peoples power pictures' best offerings graced the silver screen. The audience and the Academy liked, really liked! Sally Field as *Norma Rae*, the real life spirited Southern factory worker who reaches a new level of consciousness under the tutelage of New York labor organizer Reuben Warshawsky (Ron Leibman). In this 1979 biopic Norma Rae spearheads a unionization drive in her noisy tex-tile plant, and in an unforgettable scene, stands atop a table holding a sign that reads, simply, "union." This ranks as one of blacklistee Ritt's finest films, and surely is his best working class hero movie.

Warren Beatty has long been one of Hollywood's most politically con-scious filmmakers, and as the Reagan-Thatcher era ascended, 1981's *Reds* is in many ways the swan song and culmination of the power to the people pictures. Beatty directed, co-wrote, co-produced and starred as John Reed, the American left-wing journalist who wrote *Ten Days That*

Shook the World, the classic book about the Russian Revolution. The all-star cast includes Diane Keaton as Reed's wife, radical writer Louise Bryant; Jack Nicholson as playwright Eugene O'Neill and Maureen Stapleton as anarchist Emma Goldman. The 3 hour, 20 minute, big budget film has the epic sweep of the October Revolution itself, as comrade Reed is consumed by the cause. *Reds* is also a great love story. Like Lillian Gish in D.W. Griffith's 1920 *Way Down East*, Bryant crosses ice floes as she struggles to be reunited with her man.

Beatty won a well-deserved Best Director Oscar, Stapleton scored one for Best Supporting Actress, while Vittorio Storaro won for Best Cinematography. A decade and a half of the counterculture classics made it possible for this lavish production about American dissidents to be filmed. Although there would certainly be other progressive pictures here and there throughout the '80s, '90s and early 2000s (notably by Oliver Stone, Spike Lee and John Sayles), before the 2002 rebirth of progressive Hollywood as a movement, power to the people pictures as a trend and genre seem to have ended—albeit brilliantly—with *Reds*. The flow of Hollywood's progressive content ebbed, and was down—if not completely out.

STAR JAWS: THERMIDOR, THE SEQUEL

"Hello darkness my old friend, I've come to talk to you again."

— Simon and Garfunkel, "The Sounds of Silence," in *The Graduate*

What happened to the power to the people pictures? What caused the demise of progressive Hollywood's second great era?

These movies—like the New Left—were, to some extent, victims of their own successes. American radicals brought the war home, and by marching in the streets and on college campuses, hastened the increasingly unpopular war's grand finale. The flowers hippies placed in the barrels of the guns of soldiers during the 1967 march on the Pentagon clogged their rifles. For the radical movement, political power instead grew out of the barrel of a camera lens. Eighteen-year-olds got the vote and, powered by the biggest youth vote in American electoral history, a peace candidate actually won the Democratic nomination. The Yippies' incantations finally worked, and the Pentagon was, at long last, levitated. On April 30, 1975, the world was turned upside down. America's longest war was over, in a cataclysmic defeat for U.S. imperialism and foreign policy. Vietnam was liberated. And with the ending of the war—and the draft—the central motivating factors for the antiwar and youth movement also came to an end.

On the civil rights front, minorities also made striking strides. If King's dream of the Beloved Community still hadn't come true, there were certainly undeniable gains. Jim Crow's back was broken, the American apartheid system was toppled. Blacks could attend school with, order sandwiches at the same lunch counter as, and vote like whitey. Integration paid off—affirmative action and other social programs promised a way out of the ghetto. Black candidates were elected to office. Rabblerouser Stokely Carmichael had called ghetto rebellions the stuff that dreams are made of, and the riots in the streets had showed the Man that black folks meant business. There was a newfound black-is-beautiful ethnic pride and awareness. Even if there was still a long way to go, look how far blacks had come in a relatively short time. With these victories, the future looked bright, and much of the anger and initial impetus for the Black Consciousness cause dissipated —and, along with it, the related films.

But there was a dark side—along with the victories came defeats. With King—as well as numerous Panther COINTELPRO victims—dead, imprisoned or in exile, the civil rights movement ebbed, militancy peaked and Black Power politics receded onscreen. The empire prepared to strike back in Central America and Afghanistan. As for the Sexual Revolution, on- and offscreen, AIDS and other plagues caused counterrevolution. As Biskind stresses in *Easy Riders, Raging Bulls*, drugs also helped level the Babylon that New Hollywood had built.

A combination of these successes and failures led to the ebbing of an essential ingredient of the counterculture classics—good discerning audiences. A right-wing actor rode on a white horse into the White House, and conspired to undo the Russian Revolution Beatty had celebrated in *Reds* by bringing down the "evil empire." Reaganism rescinded news media's equal time doctrine, and a correlative seemed to beset the movie industry.

With the catalysts gone that had stimulated audience demand for quirky, character-driven and politically charged movies, New Hollywood's indie spirit was increasingly superceded by mindless blockbusters with comic book mentalities, such as *Jaws* and *Star Wars*. The studio system re-entrenched itself—with a vengeance—and the bottom line and week-end box office take (and reporting on them) replaced meaning and politics onscreen. The Reagan Revolution and the blockbuster "Star Jaws" phenomena joined forces, threatening to extinguish films of consciousness and conscience.

It was back to business as usual. Hippies cut their hair; blacks conked their Afros. In the face of the Thermidorian thaw, where would *Getting Straight*'s Jan and Harry Bailey or *The Graduate*'s Benjamin Braddock and Elaine Robinson go? "Hello darkness my old friend, I've come to talk to you again" indeed, as dreams of world revolution and the Age of Aquarius ebbed, and Reaganism flowed—led by a former Tinseltown actor, no less. Counterrevolution trumped counterculture.

It would, again, take yet another war to rekindle the flame of progressive Hollywood.

ACT 3

===

THE RETURN OF
PROGRESSIVE HOLLYWOOD

"Cry 'Havoc,' and let slip the dogs of war."

— William Shakespeare, *Julius Caesar*

"WE WERE THE ONES": THE ORGANIZERS

"Here I was suddenly in a place where people were... paying me to say the things I would have said on any street corner—and did. God, it was a wonderful boost both to my career and me as a person, just to have the opportunity to be there and talk about war."

— Mike Farrell on being cast in "M*A*S*H," in an interview with the author

If the war against fascism had been the *raison d'être* for the '30s/'40s Hollywood left, and Vietnam had been the *cause célèbre* for '60s/'70s dissident filmmakers, it took the Iraq War to revitalize a dormant progressive Hollywood—in the streets and, most importantly, on the screen.

Physically, Mike Farrell and Robert Greenwald form an odd couple. The former was born in 1939 in St. Paul, Minnesota, is 6 foot 3, has longish white hair and towers over the balding Greenwald, who was born in 1945 into a pro-union, antifascist New York family. But politically and spiritually, the two are in synch—both express their beliefs in their film/TV projects and are pulled together by shared convictions. "There was a tremendous fringe benefit to being associated with the [cause], and that was to begin to develop a deeper relationship with a man I've come to regard so hugely," gushed Farrell. "This has begun a friendship that I treasure, and am thrilled to be able to look forward to [for] a long time."

The death of Greenwald's father in 2001, and the September 11th tragedy, compelled him to become more active. He produced a video and held a fundraiser for Peaceful Tomorrows, a group of families who'd lost relatives on 9/11. Encouraged by Tom Hayden, Steven Spielberg, the Streisand Foundation's Marge Tabankin and environmental activist Earl Katz, Greenwald took "the most active lead" starting in 2002, which included co-launching RDV Books, a progressive publishing company.

Yet even before 9/11, Greenwald's *oeuvre* had always evinced a humanitarian tinge, and he specialized in topical made-for-TV-movies inspired by real events. Greenwald directed 1984's "The Burning Bed," proving Charlie's Angel Farrah Fawcett could act (she was Emmy-nominated for depicting a real life battered wife who set her husband on fire). Greenwald went on to executive produce 1990's anti-bomb "Hiroshima: Out of the Ashes"; 2002's "Redeemer," starring Matthew Modine in a drama about a former Black Panther set up by an F.B.I. COINTELPRO sting operation and serving a life sentence; 2002's *Unprecedented*, a hard-hitting documentary featuring BBC investigative reporter Greg Palast, about the Republicans' alleged theft of 2000's presidential election; and 2003's "The Crooked E: The Unshredded Truth About Enron." Greenwald produced and directed the theatrically released *Steal This Movie*, the Abbie Hoffman biopic co-starring Vincent D'Onofrio and Janeane Garofalo. Pictures of Hoffman, John Lennon and Che Guevara decorate the Robert Greenwald Productions office in Culver City. As we'll see, Greenwald went on to produce and direct a series of anti-Bush, anti-Iraq War documentaries that have helped lay the foundation for the current renewal of progressive Hollywood productions.

On September 7, 2003, the American Civil Liberties Union of Southern California held its 40th Annual Garden Party. ACLU/SC Executive Director Ramona Ripston proclaimed: "Robert uses the power of the medium to ask hard questions about, and shed light upon, the issues of our day. He dedicates himself to community activism, to issues like affordable housing and gang rehabilitation. In all his work, Robert shows the way to combining professional success with active citizenship, helping the socially conscious of Hollywood appeal to the conscience of America."

Steve Rohde, a noted L.A. attorney who practices constitutional law and is a former American Civil Liberties Union of Southern California president, introduced Farrell at the ACLU-SC's September 7, 2003 Garden Party awards ceremony. "For more than 20 years, Mike traveled on peace and human rights missions, going at a moment's notice. A special group receives his personal and tireless support, the men and women on death row, [including former Black Panther and alleged cop killer] Mumia Abu-Jamal. In each and every case, Mike has been there personally to plead for their lives. He takes the death penalty personally. He's devoted thousands of hours flying to implore anyone who would listen, from governors to ordinary folks, to save the lives of individuals from state-sanctioned murder. In some cases, Mike succeeded, and he would admit [that] all too often, he did not. But Mike has succeeded in changing the entire debate on the death penalty in this country, in forcing America to re-think its use of this abominable form of punishment... capital punishment [will be] abolished in America... due, in large part, to Mike Farrell," Rohde asserted.

Mike Farrell's political coming of age, from a working class youth to military grunt to out-of-work actor to one of Hollywood's most committed activists, is a remarkable tale. "I was raised to believe [that] this is a country with certain fundamental principles... [that it is] of, by and for the people, and that's what we ought to be [articulating]," Farrell said in an interview at the San Fernando Valley office of his company, Farrell/Minoff Productions. "My parents weren't particularly politically involved. My father was a laborer, a working man, a union man. They were both Democrats and believed that the Democratic Party [was] the party of the people, the working person, and that the Republican Party was the party of the wealthy, the corporations, etc. They didn't talk about politics, they weren't really involved in political organizations. My dad was trying to keep food on the table and a roof over our heads [as a carpenter at Hollywood Studios]. And my mother was a homemaker."

Like his TV alter ego, "M*A*S*H's" Captain B.J. Hunnicut, Farrell was in the armed services. "I joined the marine corps out of high school—Hollywood High—went through MCRD [Marine Corps Recruit Depot] in San Diego, served as a grunt in the Marines and was, I suppose, as politically naïve as 17, 18-year-olds were in those days. Bought into all the stuff about going and fighting communism, and being a warrior for the U.S., and god and country, and all that stuff... One isn't drafted into the Marines. It's a voluntary service... There was a draft in effect, and if I hadn't gone to college—which I had no plans to do—I would've been drafted. So I joined the Marines. I was in Okinawa with the Third Marines. I wasn't fighting. It was before Vietnam, in the late '50s.

"I got out of the service and was more concerned, frankly, with sort of figuring out how to make a living, how to get a start as an actor, than I was involved in politics. I got married quite young," Farrell related. He went on to attend UCLA and study acting in blacklisted actor Jeff Corey's workshop, as the cataclysmic events of the '60s impacted Farrell's evolving awareness of politics, as well as that of the role of media.

"By the time I was old enough to vote, the candidacy of John Kennedy caught my attention, because he was—as I was—an Irish Catholic. He was lace curtain Irish, while my family was shanty Irish," said Farrell. "Nonetheless, he was a figure that was inspiring to me. I followed his campaign to some degree, I voted for him and was thrilled to do so. I was delighted when he was elected. I was not particularly aware of what was going on internationally at the time.

"I was, like most people," Farrell went on to say, "staggered when he was murdered. I was particularly struck by the fact that I was a 24-year-old ex-marine, and I was told that the man who killed him was a 24-year-old ex-marine. And then I watched, with the rest of America, as... Jack Ruby killed Lee Harvey Oswald in front of a couple of dozen Dallas police, and found it very hard to comprehend. I was stunned by the fact... staggered and emotionally shattered and terribly confused and frustrated by the sham of the investigation."

News disinformation likewise troubled the young Farrell, who "was also very disturbed by what I saw as a... campaign on the part of the media to pat us on the head and tell us everything is fine. By converting or flipping their presentation of the character analysis of Lyndon Johnson, completely, from a hick, sort of an embarrassment that he had been portrayed as by the media during the time he was Kennedy's vice president to, suddenly, a statesman. A man of great vision who had all of the tools to do what was necessary to bring this country right. And I found myself thinking, 'Jesus, we're being spoon-fed a kind of *it's okay, don't think too hard, don't worry, everything's under control.*' I understand that from a paternalistic perspective, but I don't understand it from a media that has, it seems to me, the obligation of being objective, discerning and investigating the facts, and presenting objectively. So, that began to sort of steer me away from a kind of willingness to rely on generalized media pronouncements."

The liquidation of JFK and the subsequent cover-up moved Farrell "to the point that I started reading books about the Kennedy assassination and, later, in the '60s, I helped found and run an organization kind of ineptly called the Kennedy Assassination Truth Committee. And I, along with lots of other people, looked into the evidence, got a copy of the 26 volumes of the Warren Commission Report, and I lectured on this topic, and got one of the early copies of the Zapruder film and showed it. We did lots of public interest, public education work in the hope of trying to generate support for a new public investigation of the assassination. Because it continues to be my belief that we were never told the truth about who killed John Kennedy and why." (Farrell portrayed JFK in a televised 1984 one man show.)

Farrell's JFK activism "obviously... bled into the Vietnam War. Opposition to the war was, seemed to me, automatic and appropriate. I was involved with an organization that worked with people out of prisons and mental institutions—it was a halfway house... I went into prisons with the organization for the first time, and saw the conditions of people in prisons... That gave me my first personal experience of being inside a prison, as an ambassador if you will, from this organization, to tell people that they had an option when they came out to go to a place that sort of wasn't back in the jungle. It began to sensitize me to the prison system and the incredible ugliness of it and the unfairness of the system, and the biases built into the system.

"So from that to the Vietnam War to the black revolution to the brown revolution to the gay revolution to the women's rights movement, I just kind of got involved in things and supported lots of different organizations and worked in support of their goals... I voted for [Black Panther Minister of Information] Eldridge Cleaver [on the Peace and Freedom Party ticket] in 1968 because I was so angry at Hubert Humphrey for not having the courage to stand up against Lyndon Johnson."

The aspiring actor had mixed feelings about the militant Panthers. "I certainly was involved with lots of people in trying to put pressure on the authorities about the Fred Hampton murder. I was not a fan, frankly, of Huey Newton and some of these guys... I met some of them. I did take a truckload of food down to the Panthers in L.A. when they were under siege by the L.A. police and feared being attacked, and subsequently were. So, I know my name and photograph were on LAPD lists, and I was involved as a plaintiff in a lawsuit against the LAPD about this kind of surveillance and wiretapping and who knows what else," Farrell said.

Over the years, before and after fame came to him, Farrell stumped for a number of Democratic candidates. "In '72 I worked very hard for George McGovern, I spoke as a surrogate for him in a number of situations. In '76 I was in the snows of New Hampshire, campaigning for Fred Harris, whose candidacy didn't last very long, but [is] a wonderful guy. Over time I campaigned for Tom Harken in Iowa, and when he campaigned for president in the '80s."

The actor "was certainly involved on the grass roots level. And I was involved as an individual, rather than as a member of any organization... I helped get Russell Means out of jail, supported the American Indian Movement. I put up the bail actually for Russell after the Wounded Knee siege. I worked with Caesar Chavez and the farm workers," stated Farrell.

Until he got his big break on TV, Farrell was "just another guy, an actor trying to get a job. I was not somebody anybody paid any particular attention to. I was a guy who carried signs, and one of the individuals at demonstrations. Then, when I got a few jobs and I had a couple of television series and people began to know a little bit more about who I was, I got involved in some other things on a slightly different level. But nothing really... meaningful in terms of my—ultimately, nobody gave a shit about what I said or did until I got involved with 'M*A*S*H,' I think."

Before stardom hit, Farrell "didn't travel in the kinds of circles that would have qualified as progressive Hollywood. I went to some meetings, and I was part of demonstrations and stuff. But because I didn't matter, from a lot of people's perspectives, and I wasn't in those sort of social circles, my presence was really not particularly noted. I only knew [producer] Bert Schneider slightly. And I was not part of the drug scene, so I didn't get involved with the people who were."

Nevertheless, the struggling actor was "clearly aware of what Jane and a lot of these folks did... I admired Jane Fonda greatly, and continue to to this day. I thought she was quite extraordinarily courageous and took a tremendous amount of heat. I remember writing an editorial in defense of her when somebody was attacking her from Sacramento. I didn't know Tom Hayden until he came out here and he and Jane got married, and I only met him casually a few times," Farrell recalled.

"I saluted Jane for what she did in *Coming Home*, she and Jon Voight, and for the films that were done at the time... and I thought she was very classy in the way in which she did it. I remember when she got the Academy Award for *Klute*, I think it was, she made a statement to the effect that—there was lots of concern, because Brando had done the Sacheen Little Feather thing maybe the year before or something. There was some concern when Jane was nominated that she would make some sort of statement that some people would deem inappropriate. And I remember she got up there and said something to the effect of: 'You know there are things I could say, but I don't think this is the appropriate place, and I just want to thank you'—and went on very graciously. I thought, man, this is a classy lady, this is somebody who understands the way in which we need to communicate. Even though she has done some things that have offended and frightened and been used by the other side against her and to tarnish her. She's a woman I really admire," Farrell stated.

Farrell's most prominent role came in a sitcom based, appropriately, on a feature written by Ring Lardner, Jr., one of the Hollywood Ten, 1970's antiwar *M*A*S*H*—which used the Korean War to criticize war in general, and the Vietnam War in particular. From 1975 to 1983, Farrell co-starred as Captain B.J. Hunnicut, a Korean War surgeon in the 4077th Mobile Army Surgical Hospital. Farrell replaced Trapper John McIntyre (played by Wayne Rogers—now a Wall Street analyst and cable TV commentator) as Captain Hawkeye Pierce (Alan Alda)'s tent-mate and iconoclastic co-conspirator in breaking Army rules and regulations.

Like Rob Reiner as "Meathead," conservative Archie Bunker's counter-culture foil on another politicized '70s sitcom, "All in the Family," B.J.'s irreverent persona and antiwar politics were ideally suited to the left-leaning actor portraying him. "Here I was suddenly in a place where people were... paying me to say the things I would have said on any street corner—and did. God, it was a wonderful boost both to my career and me as a person, just to have the opportunity to be there and talk about war. And no—of course we were talking about Vietnam, and of course we were talking about Korea. But of course, we were also talking about the military mindset and dogmatic authoritarianism, and the fact that war does not happen only by the sound of trumpets and flags waving. It happens by people's limbs being torn apart and blood being shed and lives being lost, and we have to keep that in the forefront of our minds, before we enter into these things," Farrell said.

Appearing in one of the most popular TV sitcoms ever changed the striving actor's life. "[F]or me it was just a godsend. I was an actor under contract to Universal Studios, having done a television series and a movie or two there. I was involved with things like the Daniel Ellsberg defense big event we had in L.A. I was just struggling along as an actor, trying to make a living. And this opportunity came my way. And I was thrilled that it did."

"M*A*S*H" raised Farrell's recognition factor, and his opportunities for engagement with humanitarian causes. Farrell "was approached by a refugee aid organization, Concerned America, that asked me to take a look at a film... describing the plight of children in Asia... As a result of seeing that film, I started to do some work for them to help their work... Ultimately, my work with that organization took me on an around-the-world trip looking at refugee situations, particularly... to the Thai-Cambodian border area, where the people [had] been victimized by... the Pol Pot slaughter... and the Vietnamese army that came in to throw out the Khmer Rouge. As is the case, one thing leads to another, you know?"

The next movement Farrell became involved in remains at the core of his social concerns. "[A] minister came to visit me on the ["M*A*S*H"] set and asked me to take a look at death row in Tennessee with him, and I went down there. He knew that I was opposed to the death penalty, and wanted some help." Farrell's Catholic faith played a role in his continuing anti-capital punishment commitment, as well as his antiwar stance. "I thought killing people was wrong. That's what I was taught as a child. 'Thou shalt not kill.' I felt that didn't just mean me, it meant sort of everybody. The idea that the state killed, was a kind of tilt for me. I just thought, it sorta doesn't make sense. There's gotta be better ways to go about... having a criminal justice system."

Opposing capital punishment became the signature cause of Farrell, who says his "affiliation with the abolitionist movement in the country has grown to the point that it has taken up a tremendous amount of my time and energy. I've been involved in countless numbers of cases around the country... [and] have taken that upon myself, because I think the death penalty is a true shame in this country, and an embarrassment, and I think we are doing ourselves great harm." According to ACLU's Rohde, "In 1994, Mike was elected president of Death Penalty Focus; his leadership proved so effective he was continually re-elected."

During the Reagan and Iran-contra years, Farrell's attention was also focused on Washington's policies south of the border. "The next place I went for this refugee aid organization was to Central America, to the camps on the Salvadoran-Honduran border, Guatemalan-Honduran border and then down into Nicaragua. And it was an education, to see the impact of the U.S. government's support of the Salvadoran and Guatemalan governments, their opposition to the Nicaraguan [Sandinista] government. The way in which the U.S. authorities and U.S. power really controlled Honduras... After I got involved with the human rights movement as a result of some of these trips on behalf of refugees, then I went with a human rights delegation to El Salvador, two years running, in the 1980s. First time in Central America was in 1982, second time '83, third time '84, fourth time '85, then again in '89. In '86 I was in Chile and Paraguay... Back to Salvador in '89."

A year after leaving "M*A*S*H," Farrell wed Shelley Fabares (his second wife), who'd co-starred in "The Donna Reed Show," and appeared opposite Fabian and Tab Hunter in 1964's Hawaii-lensed *Ride the Wild Surf* and Elvis in 1967's *Clambake*. (Erin Farrell, Mike's daughter from his first marriage, has worked for Jesse Jackson and Greenpeace.) The year Mikhail Gorbachev became the U.S.S.R.'s leader, Farrell's activism branched out beyond the Western Hemisphere. "In '85 I went to the Soviet Union with a peace delegation. In '88 I went to the Middle East. In '90 I went back to the Middle East. And then again in '92 and '93. I went to Czechoslovakia with an election monitoring organization. '92 I went to Bosnia. And Somalia with the U.N. in '95. I went to Rwanda..."

Like Audrey Hepburn and Angelina Jolie before and after him, Farrell was a Goodwill Ambassador for the United Nations High Commissioner for Refugees. (Asked if he still holds the position, Farrell replied: "I guess so, although they haven't contacted me for a while, so I don't know.") The actor "was a supporter, obviously, of Amnesty International and the ACLU. I have subsequently become over time—as Human Rights Watch developed from Americas Watch, which I first ran into in Salvador in '83 and now it's Human Rights Watch, globally—now I'm co-chair of Human Rights [Watch's California Committee South]. That's a relationship that's developed over the last two decades."

Farrell describes his political awakening and activism as "a tremendously impacting ongoing educational process. As I became more and more aware, I became more and more outspoken and I don't want to say 'radicalized'—because I don't think I fit the description of a radical, although in some people's eyes I do—but I was certainly energized by what I saw."

Farrell brought that energy to helping to revive the antiwar movement. The dynamic duo of Greenwald and Farrell are largely behind progressive Hollywood's struggle to prevent war in Iraq, and have not gone unnoticed by Hollywood progressives (and probably not by the White House). Both received ACLU/SC Garden Party awards for their activism. Introducing Greenwald at the event, Ramona Ripston noted: "Recently, as our country moved down a path toward war, he joined with Mike Farrell and others in the entertainment world to form Artists United to Win Without War, understanding that sometimes dissent is the truest form of patriotism." Steve Rohde observed, "Mike became a national leader in the movement to prevent the Bush administration from launching pre-emptive war against Iraq."

During the summer of 2002, Greenwald and Farrell e-mailed and phoned one another about the impending Iraq attack. "We were expressing our concern about the fact that while this was building up in late summer, early fall, we didn't see any organized opposition," Farrell remembered. "We kept saying, 'Certainly, somebody's going to stand up. Somebody's certainly going to lead an opposition to this war.' And we began to recognize that the media was creating a kind of megaphone effect for the White House, and that nobody could break through."

Greenwald went on to say, "Five hundred television stations, and all the radio stations that they own, and all the newspapers that the television and radio stations own. Throughout that period of time, in our free and democratic media, we were hearing one message: 'War, terrorism, war, weapons of mass destruction, war.' There literally was not another voice in the media at that time."

Farrell added, "I was very alarmed, as was Robert, at the lack of any contrary voice to the administration's ratcheting up the war drums, and I was particularly alarmed and we had a great discussion about the fact that the media was acting as a megaphone for the administration, because—well, 'because' is a whole other question. But certainly, there was no responsible voice on the other side."

The November 2002 Congressional elections neared, and politicians who didn't support Bush's hell-bent drive towards war risked being branded as "unpatriotic."[9] On October 11, 2002, the U.S. Congress authorized Bush to use military force in Iraq. 126 Democratic members of the House opposed the resolution, but 81 Democrats joined Republicans in voting to cede the legislative branch's constitutional war-making powers to the executive branch. In the Senate, where Vermont Senator Jim Jeffords' 2001 defection from the GOP to become an Independent had placed the leadership in Democratic hands, 29 Democrats voted in favor of the authorization—including then-Senate Majority Leader Tom Daschle—while only 21 opposed it.

---

9. TV political ads by his Republican opponent, who had not served in Vietnam, compared Georgia's Senator Max Cleland—who had lost three limbs fighting in Vietnam—to Osama Bin Laden; Cleland lost his re-election race.

Among those members of the "opposition party" voting for the resolution were Democrats who'd later run for the presidency, with the albatross of this vote tied around their necks: House Democratic Leader Dick Gephardt (who helped draft the resolution), Senator Joe Lieberman, and the two senators who'd go on to become the Democratic Party's standard bearers, John Edwards and the supposedly "dovish" John Kerry. (Months later, the chickens seemed to have come home to roost. Untainted by this "yes" vote, the stridently antiwar presidential candidate and Vermont Governor Howard Dean broke out of the pack to frontrunner status among the Democratic hopefuls—in and out of Hollywood.) Minnesota Senator Paul Wellstone, widely regarded as the Senate's conscience, tragically died about two weeks after voting against the resolution.

"SPARKPLUGS": ARTISTS UNITED TO WIN WITHOUT WAR

The dogs of war were being loosed. Cravenly behaving as if Bush had won a landslide election in 2000, the Democratic leadership abdicated its war power authority to an unelected president who had actually lost the popular vote. The gauntlet had been thrown down—and somebody in the public eye had to pick up the challenge.

Farrell remembered, "Robert and I kept saying, 'Why is there nobody speaking up? Why are we not seeing the organization of a counter thrust to the administration's position?' And ultimately, I began to explore it. Contacted some people. I frankly said to Robert, 'The only person I see, the only voice I hear is Scott Ritter's. And I'm not convinced that Scott is somebody we should trust. I don't know his motives. And I've heard some things about him that trouble me. So, let me reach out and do some checking.' I did, and the people with whom I checked were people that had been involved in the peace movement for years who knew Scott who said what you ought to do is meet him."

Greenwald and Farrell acted. "So three people came out from the East," Farrell said. The three wise men from the East were "Scott Ritter, Erik Gustafson [Executive Director] of EPIC [the Education for Peace in Iraq Center], a group of Gulf War veterans against this new [war] and [Notre Dame peace studies professor] David Cortwright who was one of the founders of SANE, Safe Action on Nuclear Energy. Robert and I put together this event at the home of Stanley Sheinbaum, sort of the basis of a lot of progressive activity. And we invited everybody we could think of, saying

Bonnie Franklin, Mike Farrell and Cindy Asner at a 2004 *soirée* at the Brentwood home of Betty and Stanley Sheinbaum.

just come and hear what is going on here. David, Eric and then Scott spoke, and it was riveting. They were quite extraordinary, and Scott in particular was very impressive."

On October 2, 2002, Warren Beatty, Annette Bening, Tom Hayden, former Senator Gary Hart and around 50 others attended the progressive powwow in Brentwood. Farrell recounted, "I got up at the end and said, 'You know, it was not our intention to form another organization. The last thing we want to do is start an organization. But we hope that something will happen as a result of this.' Then, the next day, it was [laughs] very clear to Robert and me that we were the ones. It was just simply going to have to happen. So we sat down and drafted a mission statement of Artists United to Win Without War. David Cortwright had at the time begun discussions with people in Washington about a Win Without War coalition. We said ours would be an affiliate of that. Win Without War would be the sort of core organization. There'd be Artists United, Musicians United, there'd be whomever, and it began to grow just from that meeting," Farrell recalled.

As for the role of the outspoken former U.N. Weapons Inspector, Farrell stated, "Ritter was not the sparkplug, no. If anyone was, Robert and I certainly were on this end, David Cortwright on the other end. Robert and I drafted the mission statement, and once we got it to where we wanted it to be, we circulated it." According to Greenwald, "Mike and I got together and had this idea we could reach out and maybe we could get four or five actors. Really, that was our hope. Four or five actors, who'd come forth and say: 'Yup, it's not fun right now; the times are tough, it's unpleasant, but we're gonna take a stand,'" Greenwald said.

Farrell stated, "Robert's view was, he said, 'if we can get some very high profile names, that'll be great and it'll get the media attention. But if we can't get them, and sometimes it's just a huge pain in the butt to get through the assistants and go through all that process, let's get some sort of television names, people whose faces and names will be recognized by the public. And if we can get half a dozen, a dozen of them, we'll have something that—the whole purpose of which was to break through this media curtain we saw having been established. The media was not allowing any contrary opinions to be voiced. We wanted to raise the level of the dialogue on the issue."

Using computers and phones, the dynamic duo set about "getting a bunch of people whose names and faces are known to the world," Farrell stated. "And getting them to make a declaration in opposition to the war, and holding a press conference, and beginning this organized opposition to Bush's war in Iraq."

The organizers were stunned by Hollywood's response. Farrell recollected: "So we circulated this thing and had suddenly over 100 people saying, 'Absolutely! We've just been waiting for somebody to stand up and speak out. And we're willing to join up.' Then, of course, it was really just a question of scheduling the media, because the media were all over us." Greenwald recalled, "Well, six, eight weeks later, to our amazement, to my eternal pride and joy in this community, we had over 100 actors. One after another they said: 'Count us in.'"

Around the same time, acting independently, Sean Penn published a $56,000 open letter to Bush in the *Washington Post*, urging the president to slow his rush to war. Two months after the Democratic leadership caved in to Bush, and about five weeks after Republicans took control of both houses of Congress, progressive Hollywood acted and rose to the occasion.

Two dozen actors held a widely covered December 10 press conference at Hollywood's trendy Les Deux Cafes to read an antiwar declaration. Participants included Martin Sheen, Mimi Kennedy (who played a counterculture mom named after Abbie Hoffman on ABC's "Dharma & Greg" sitcom), Ed Begley, Jr., Hector Elizondo, Wendie Malick, David Clennon, Will Farrell, Robert Greenwald, Lebanese actor Tony Shaloub (who'd go on to win the Best Actor in a Comedy Emmy on September 21, 2003), etc. The prescient declaration was forwarded to President Bush, and on December 15, 2002 was published as a full-page ad in the *New York Times*. In bold letters, the declaration began:

KEEP AMERICA SAFE

Artists Say Win Without War
   War talk in Washington is alarming and unnecessary.
   We are patriotic Americans who share the belief that Saddam Hussein cannot be allowed to possess weapons of mass destruction.

We support rigorous United Nations weapons inspections to assure Iraq's effective disarmament.

However, a preemptive military invasion of Iraq will harm American national interests. Such a war will increase human suffering, arouse animosity toward our country, increase the likelihood of terrorist attacks, damage the economy, and undermine our moral authority in the world. It will make us less, not more, secure.

We reject the doctrine—a reversal of long-held American tradition— that our country, alone, has the right to launch first-strike attacks.

The valid U.S. and U.N. objective of disarming Saddam Hussein can be achieved through legal diplomatic means. There is no need for war. Let us instead devote our resources to improving the security and well-being of people here at home and around the world.

Signed,

Artists United to Win Without War

Looking back in anger, contrary to all of the Bush administration's "experts" and *idiot savant* pro-war pundits, the actors' manifesto uncannily and accurately predicted the way things would turn out in Iraq. In retrospect, it is indeed a quite modest and reasonable statement.

Co-chairs Greenwald and Farrell jointly founded Artists United to Win Without War. Kathryn McArdle, a left-leaning film and TV production executive for 15 years, was appointed executive director of the structurally loose committee created to oppose invading Iraq. AUWWW worked with the Win Without War coalition of 15 groups, including the National Association for the Advancement of Colored People, the National Organization of Women, the National Council of Churches and MoveOn.org. Thus the Hollywood left forged a close alliance with left-leaning organizations, a coalition of the anti-killing that played an essential role in mobilizing the antiwar movement.

Although most of those who signed the declaration are actors, authors Studs Terkel (*The Good War*) and Howard Zinn (*A People's History of the United States*) also put their John Hancocks on the document, as did these noncelebs: former U.S. ambassador to Iraq Edward Peck; Steve Robinson, Sergeant U.S. Army (Retired), of the National Gulf War Resource Center; Ambassador Jonathan Dean; U.S. Representative to NATO-Warsaw Pact deputy director of the Center for Defense Information and Retired Rear Admiral Eugene Carroll.

"THEY WENT FORTH": OUTFOXING THE COMPLICIT NEWS MEDIA

"[O]n a personal level, there was a lot to lose. 'Terrorists,' 'traitors,' 'scum,' 'I know where you live and I'm coming to get you'—those were a few of the nicer things that were thrown at Artists United when we were organizing and trying to stop the insanity in the move towards war. The threats were organized, they clearly started at a certain point when we started to become effective."

— Robert Greenwald, in an interview with the author

Greenwald, Farrell and their *celeb-istas* hit upon the same game plan John Lennon (who had starred in Richard Lester's 1967 antiwar movie *How I Won the War*) and Yoko Ono had articulated and used to oppose the Indochina War. In 1969, when John and Yoko got married, they realized that no matter what he did and where he went, the Beatle and his bride would be big news. So the canny singers decided to use this coverage to benefit the antiwar cause, as "advertisers for peace." After their wedding, the newlyweds held a "bed-in" for peace in Amsterdam, where they used the media to spread their pacifist messages. Lennon said at the time in a documentary:

"Yoko and I are quite willing to be the world's clowns, if by doing this we do some good. For reasons known only to themselves, people print what I say. And I'm saying 'peace.' We are not pointing the finger at anybody. There are no good guys and bad guys. The struggle is in the mind. We must bury our own monsters and stop condemning people. We are all Christ and Hitler. We want Christ to win. We're trying to make Christ's message contemporary. What would he have done if he had advertisements, records, films, TV and newspapers! Christ made miracles to tell his message. Well, the miracle today is communications, so let's use it."

John and Yoko also took out a number of billboards (this was before Clear Channel owned much of the open air advertising space near the Great White Way) in prominent places, such as Times Square, declaring: "War is over if you want it." They recorded a number of movement songs, such as the antiwar anthem "Give Peace a Chance." And in the Beatles' "The Ballad of John and Yoko," Lennon sang: "Drove from Paris to the Amsterdam Hilton / Talking in our beds for a week / The newspapers said / Say what're you doing in bed / I said we're only trying to get us some peace."[10]

Artists United, in turn, made Christ—and Lennon's—message "contemporary," updating it for the 21st century's brave new media world of "all Iraq, all the time" radio and cable TV. AUWWW's sly strategy made an end run around the media's blackout of alternative voices (in some cases, appearances by pro-war talking heads outnumbered antiwar guests by 100 to 1). Artists United exploited the news media's—and the public's—insatiable obsession with celebrity and fame, and talk radio and cable TV's ceaseless demand for content to feed the maw of their voracious 24/7 news cycles. "The actors did press conferences," Greenwald stated. "['Six Feet Under' co-star] Jamie Cromwell did an amazing amount of work. They went on TV shows. Now, I want to be clear," insisted Greenwald. "We would have preferred it if the media interviewed the Nobel Prize winners, scientists, experts, journalists and professors. But that was not the case. They did not have that option, and it wasn't going to happen. So we called upon these actors, and they went forth."

"I was on 'Hannity and Colmes,' Bill O'Reilly's show, and this show and that show, you name it, the networks as well as the cable shows," Farrell said. "What we tried to do was be responsible and say, 'Yes, I'll come on the show if you'll also have Lawrence Korb, former Assistant Secretary of Defense, or Joe Wilson, a former ambassador to Iraq, or [former Congressman] Tom Andrews, who became the chair of the Win Without War coalition.' So, we just said, 'Yeah, you want to play celebrity games, we'll do that. But how about if we bring with us someone who can speak to this issue, like a former ambassador or former CIA person...' It was very successful. We got Joe Wilson involved [and] Admiral Carroll, before he passed away," stated Farrell.

---

10. During the lead-up to the Iraqi War, Ono rented a billboard in London's Piccadilly Circus that read: "Imagine all the people living life in peace," a lyric from "Imagine." Yoko had also placed full-page antiwar ads in newspapers around the world stating: "Imagine Peace... Spring 2003." On September 15, 2003, Lennon's 70-year-old widow did a strip-in, performance art event for peace. The show took place at a Parisian theatre, where Yoko asked members of the audience to come onstage, cut off pieces of her clothing and then send them to people they love. John and Yoko's son, Sean Lennon, was the first to wield scissors during the "Cut Piece" peace protest. At the end, Ono stood on the stage wearing only her bra and panties, once again, garnering publicity for the cause she and her late husband had first embraced in the 1960s.

Greenwald ridiculed the notion that actors shouldn't use their star-power for causes, calling it "the softball of all time." The producer explained that AUWWW preferred for the electronic and print press to interview Hayden, Zinn, Noam Chomsky, Norman Solomon (the Institute for Public Accuracy's Executive Director, who accompanied Sean Penn to Baghdad in December 2002), and other lions of the left. However, the reality was that the ratings and sales conscious media wasn't interviewing out-and-out activists—but would put actors on the air. Since this was who the cable news and talk shows would book for appearances, AUWWW provided these programs with the guests they would take.

"Media saying that celebrities shouldn't use their fame reminds me of the kid who shoots his parents and then begs for mercy from the judge because he's an orphan. They create the situation and then they have the audacity to attack us for it!" groused Greenwald. He added that AUWWW lobbied bookers to have political experts, such as Maine's ex-congress-man, Tom Andrews, Win Without War's chairman, accompany celebrities onto programs.

"I defy anyone to be more knowledgeable than Farrell, Janeane or James Cromwell," Greenwald challenged. "We provide briefings. Getting them together is tough because of schedules. It's more effective to send material. Solomon's book *Target Iraq*, Zinn's *Terrorism and War*. We urge people to hear Ritter's tapes. Certainly in the group I'm working with, the amount of time and attention many have given to educating themselves surpasses [that of] the talk show hosts, who focus on anger, bombast and talking louder. We want to be out there. I don't want to just leave it to hate radio and television," maintained Greenwald, who'd utilize this experience well in his 2004 documentary *Outfoxed.*

What was the upshot of progressive Hollywood's information offensive, which filled the void created by the Democrats' and news media's compliance with and complicity in Bush's anti-Iraq jihad? "Over three months, these 100 actors reached over 100 million people with a message which they otherwise would not have gotten," Greenwald claimed. Artists United also ran commercials featuring Sheen as part of its February 26 "Virtual March on Washington" with MoveOn.org, and as a result, Congressional offices were flooded with antiwar faxes, calls and e-mails.

However, the actors' antiwar activism came at a price. "Now remember, they didn't have a lot to gain, except if you think being an active citizen in a democracy is being something to gain, but on a personal level, there was a lot to lose," Greenwald pointed out. "'Terrorists,' 'traitors,' 'scum,' 'I know where you live and I'm coming to get you'—those were a few of the nicer things that were thrown at Artists United when we were organizing and trying to stop the insanity in the move towards war. The threats were organized, they clearly started at a certain point when we started to become effective."

Those contending that the artists merely sought free publicity should consider that they didn't receive compensation for their appearances on news—as opposed to entertainment—programs (indeed, Greenwald insisted that many paid for their traveling expenses out of their own pockets). "They don't pay," Farrell asserted. "That's a news show. News shows don't pay. The 'Johnny Carson,' 'Jay Leno' things traditionally have to pay [union] scale rate for an actor to come on and promote his or her television show or movie. But I stopped doing those shows years ago because they were about nothing. I said, 'If you want to talk about something, I'm happy to come on. But I don't want to just come on and blab about my career. That's really pretty boring. I really haven't done those shows for a long time. When this came up, and it was an issue worth discussing, I said, 'Absolutely, let's go!' and we did," said the actor.

Instead of getting star treatment from friendly entertainment reporters trading access for P.R. fluff, the United Artists had to steel themselves to face hostile interviewers. Their course diverged sharply from Arnold Schwarzenegger's crafty—and arguably cowardly—strategy of parlaying celebrityhood into media coverage from mostly nonpolitical TV/radio outlets, while strictly denying access to political reporters more likely to ask hard-hitting questions.

The antiwar actors bravely faced off against unfriendly questioners. Instead of professional flattery and adulation, actors found it was more often like hand-to-hand combat with hostile, agenda-driven interviewers. "They fought with the nutcases on Fox [News Channel]. They did the radio shows, with the worst and [most] abusive call-in listeners, [as were] some of the hosts," observed Greenwald.

Farrell added: "And when those actors—Martin Sheen, Janeane Garofalo and Susan Sarandon—were invited to go on television and talk about their opposition to this war, and talk about the inhumanity and insanity of Bush administration policies, they were derided in most cases for being actors."

Interviewed as California's recall election loomed, Farrell asked: "Do actors have a right to be involved in politics? I wonder today, when we

THE RETURN OF PROGRESSIVE HOLLYWOOD

[saw] the machine gun-carrying candidate for our governor's race, if the people who so derided those actors for being involved in politics recognize the hypocrisy of the position they now espouse in supporting this man. It's sort of an astonishing thing, and what it does is lay it bare, the utter mendacity that is associated with those people, who care not about the validity, the honesty, really the integrity of their position, as long as they think it can draw blood at the moment," Farrell said.

Despite attempts at intimidating activist actors, Greenwald asserted, "Throughout this period of time—I'm not going to say it was easy, because it wasn't always easy—not one of the 100 actors buckled, not one of the 100 actors ran for cover. And in this case, they really stayed united, throughout that time. Working with this really extraordinary group was so satisfying." But the winter of their discontent was to haunt many of the outspoken celebrities. In stark contrast to the charge that antiwar actors benefited from free P.R., their stances cost the thespians dearly.

"SHARP ELBOWS"

The ACLU-SC's 2003 Garden Party took place on a sunny September day, and drew hundreds to the posh Brentwood home (across from O.J. Simpson's former estate) of liberal stalwarts Betty Sheinbaum (the daughter and niece, respectively, of Harry and Jack Warner, the founders of Warner Brothers) and her husband Stanley. The party was emceed by Ed Asner, and attended by *Boondocks* cartoonist and fellow ACLU award winner Aaron McGruder, "The Practice" co-star Camryn Manheim, "All in the Family" and "Maude" producer Norman Lear, director Reg Hudlin, Joan Sekler and Richard Perez (co-directors of *Unprecedented*, which Greenwald had executive produced), William Schallert (who played the father on the '60s sitcom "The Patty Duke Show"), Hector Elizondo and then-independent gubernatorial candidate Arianna Huffington. Barbra Streisand was among the fundraiser's sponsors.

Clearly moved by Rohde's introduction of him, wearing a DPF (Death Penalty Focus) cap, T-shirt and jeans, Farrell seemed to fight back tears as he took the podium. But this didn't stop him from attacking "the Bush administration's ugliness, the brutality of its war in Iraq and the postwar situation." Farrell praised his comrade Greenwald, and urged people in and out of public life to "stand up for issues and associations, such as the ACLU, that hold high the values we know provide the fundament for this great nation." He went on to quote a novel by lawyer Baine Kerr: "'In cynical times, right and wrong can be hard to sort out. Goodness and truth can seem beyond our reach. But we have the option, the obligation, to put cynicism aside and exercise the public virtues. To find truth, oppose wrong, protect innocence, promote good and do right.'"

In Greenwald's acceptance speech, the producer *kibitzed*: "Mike had to say nice things about me because I cast him in the one role he was born to play: Enron head Ken Lay. It was a breathtaking performance, reached from inside himself and giving us all that Kenny Boy should be." The producer cited Stanley and Betty Sheinbaum and Norman Lear as politically engaged role models who inspired him, and criticized the war fever and fear that gripped post-9/11 America.

"I'm working on a documentary right now called *Uncovered*," Greenwald continued. "I had the privilege of interviewing Ambassador Joe Wilson, thanks to Norman and Lynn Lear. Ambassador Wilson is a real hero, who spilled the beans on the lies [that] Iraq was trying to buy uranium from Niger. And because of his spilling the beans, they came after Joe and his wife [outing her as an alleged CIA agent]. I said: 'How did you handle it? What did you do?' Wilson said: 'You need sharp elbows.'"

"As we go forward, we're going to see more and more efforts to try to keep us quiet," Greenwald cautioned. "The ACLU has done an amazing job over the years to allow us to keep talking. We all know how hard the regime change is going to be. Everyone here is working for it." More applause broke out. "Let's not wait, and count on the candidates to do the heavy lifting with the sharp elbows. Every single social change has come from the grass roots. Whether it was the war or women's movement or civil rights, it starts with the grass roots. There's an enormous amount we can do. And if our elbows are sharper and we are tougher, we will create the candidates we need, rather than waiting for them to come to us. There's an amazing number of really extraordinary people and groups right now. I've been fortunate to work with some of them. From the Office of the Americas to Military Families Speak Out, mothers and fathers whose children have gone to war. Some of them have been killed." Greenwald lowered his voice; choked up, he continued: "Can you imagine as a parent losing your child to this war? These parents, and they're really amazing, are continuing to work to try to stop this madness... We have to help them.

"I hope everyone here is signed on for MoveOn.org. The amazing work [Norman Lear's] People for the American Way are doing. Kim Spencer and

LinkTV—progressive television in 20 million homes. Don Hazen and Alter-Net. Peaceful Tomorrows. Going postering with [L.A. guerrilla artist] Robbie Conal. There's 1,000 options, they've given us lots of targets; there are many places where a sharp, well-placed elbow can have a really good effect. It feels *very* good to score with an elbow to a weak spot. I want us to all get out there with our elbows flying and let's kick some ass!" The rallied troops roared, psyched to continue fighting the good fight against King George, as election 2004 neared.

In July 2003, AUWWW changed both its name—to simply Artists United—and focus. In June 2004, Farrell said: "Robert and I decided we wanted to take the same energy and move people, move it into areas of social importance. One of the ways is to try to use those whose names will gain attention, to associate themselves with certain things. Whether it be the needs of labor or political candidate or movement. MoveOn.org has done a terrific job of putting things out there. Robert's movie *Uncovered* has had a tremendous impact. Many of our people are supportive, working behind the scenes, are up front in a lot of these different campaigns, candidacies and efforts. We're just simply trying to maintain contact with those folks and say, 'Can you help us with this? Are you willing to go there? Are you willing to sign this?'"

According to Executive Director Kathryn McArdle, "We will continue to offer a mainstream, patriotic and positive voice for progressive issues, and encourage public debate, engage opinion makers and activate concerned citizens. As we brought greater media attention to the threat of war through celebrity appearances on television, radio and in print and at rallies, we'll do the same for urgently needed social justice, environmental and educational issues, events and organizations. Working with the ACLU, in September 2003, Artists United launched a print campaign in defense of freedom of speech, and is providing Physicians for Social Responsibility with artists for a year-long campaign on the environment and Hispanic communities."

McArdle added: "Artists United will continue to draw on the unique abilities of our community to produce plays, radio and television productions, and help provide talent for like opportunities. We'll continue to use the media to raise the profile of issues pertinent to the well being of people here and abroad in order to advocate the values that have made America the beacon of hope." AU's postwar productions included an evening of peace, poetry and music at San Francisco's Castro Theatre, starring Janeane Garofalo, Hector Elizondo, Mimi Kennedy and Mike Farrell, plus a reading of John

Hersey's *Hiroshima* for Pacifica Radio Network at the Feminist Majority in Beverly Hills. The radio drama starred Tyne Daly, Ruby Dee, Roscoe Lee Browne, Tony Plana, Jeanne Sakata and John Valentine, and aired August 8, 2003—the anniversary of Hiroshima's nuking. As part of the Fourth Freedom Forum that started the Win Without War movement, Artists United has a 501c3 nonprofit tax status, and can't advocate for any particular candidate—although it can advocate for progressive candidates in general.

PRIMARY COLORS

Bush had thrown down the gauntlet and said, "You are either with us or against us," and the Hollywood left resoundingly replied: "We're against you!" Although progressive Hollywood had arguably contributed to slowing down Bush's rush to war, the fact is that on March 20, 2003, the U.S. attacked Iraq. The Left Coast was down, but not out, as it sought to bring the war against Bush home, by mobilizing to oust the cowboy president from the saddle in November 2004. The entertainment industry's crusade for regime change in Washington was gearing up. In the tried and true tradition of moviedom, the 2004 presidential campaign would be the Hollywood progressives' sequel to the 2002-2003 peace movement. As former Senator Carol Moseley Braun and the men-who-would-be-president fought it out, activist actors, antiwar writers, dissident directors and populist producers sought—off- and onscreen—to influence the outcome of a race for the White House, and the hearts and minds and souls of the nation.

During a Southern California campaign swing, Democratic presidential contender Representative Dennis Kucinich—who'd voted on the House floor against authorizing Bush's use of force in Iraq—spoke at a Laurel Canyon fundraiser on September 21, 2003, the International Day of Peace. If Paul Wellstone had represented—as he'd said—the "democratic wing of the Democratic Party," then Kucinich arguably represents the "love wing" of the Democratic Party. He was introduced by Ed Begley, Jr. (wearing a T-shirt depicting a Hitler Youth-like Aryan lad in front of a "News Channel" flag, with the words "Fair and Balanced O'Reilly" printed on the shirt) and, after Kucinich spoke, James Cromwell made additional comments.[11] Fresh from attending the 75th birthday of Dr. King's

---

11. Ironically, both actors not only share a passion for progressive politics and Kucinich's candidacy, but on "Six Feet Under" they each wooed Ruth Fisher, portrayed by Frances Conroy.

Mimi Kennedy of "Dharma and Greg" at a 2003 Winter Solstice campaign
rally for presidential candidate Representative Dennis Kucinich.

onetime adviser Reverend Jim Lawson, Mimi Kennedy schmoozed with
Kucinich, who was also endorsed by Willie Nelson.

When I asked the Democratic presidential aspirant what role progressive artists could play in the 2004 election, the visionary Congressman told
200 Angelenos, and thousands of listeners via a conference call to 1,100
Kucinich-for-president fundraising parties around the nation:

"You have not campaigned in Iowa until you've campaigned with Ed
Asner. This community has the ability to help shift the dialogue nationally. Because this is part of what we know as cultural creatives, people
who help to shape the direction of the culture. They're artists, actors,
writers, people who help to create the awareness of this country, the
direction America can go in. So I value the connection I have with this
community, which reaches out and connects with the rest of the world. It
helps to create the metaphor for this world in so many ways. All of those
who have a vision of a better world, will have the opportunity through this
campaign to feel part of it and connect with it, and see their own life's
work be recognized in a way that connects their aspirations to the world,
in a way their art connects them to the world," stated Kucinich.

Asner, Cromwell, Kennedy, Elliott Gould, ice cream magnate Ben
Cohen, musician Ani DiFranco and *Nickel and Dimed* author Barbara
Ehrenreich signed a September 24 letter endorsing Kucinich. The pro-
nouncement declared: "We want Democrats to stand up against the Bush
administration's war in Iraq, and the continuing occupation which is so
costly in lives and resources. We want a Party that stands up for genuine

Presidential candidate Howard Dean works the crowd at a September 30, 2004 fundraiser in L.A.'s landmark Union Station.

universal health coverage and for expanded educational opportunities and environmental cleanup paid for by cuts in the bloated Pentagon budget. Our country's military spending now rivals that of all other countries in the world combined."

During the Winter Solstice, the Kucinich campaign held a fundraiser at a posh Malibu beach house on Zuma Beach. Vegan cuisine was served at the New Age-tinged event, which was attended by Lindsay Wagner, who starred as "The Bionic Woman" from 1976 to 1978, as well as Mary McDonnell, who'd co-starred in 1990's *Dances With Wolves*. Mimi Kennedy introduced the surprisingly smooth, polished and well-spoken candidate. On September 29, Norman Lear threw a $2,000 per plate fundraiser in L.A. for the tenth Democrat to enter the fray, retired General Wesley Clark, who criticized Bush's war and occupation.

Surprisingly, the antiwar Farrell said: "I've been supporting John Kerry since the beginning... I've already given him some money, and appeared at a couple of events where I've been asked to come... I will continue to support him. I've known him for over 30 years, I knew him before he was a U.S. senator, I admired greatly what he did during the whole Iran-Contra debacle, and the terrible things that were happening in Central America. I think he's a much stronger, much more decent, much more honest and much more honorable man than certainly the Bush administration would have you believe."

And seven months after his rousing address at the antiwar demonstration in Hollywood, "Acting President" Martin Sheen made much the same speech at a September 30 fundraiser at L.A.'s landmark Union Station for former Vermont Governor Howard Dean. Underscoring the continuity of peace activism and the Dean candidacy, Sheen concluded his introduction to the Democratic antiwar whistle-stopper with the exact words he'd used at the February 15 rally: "Let my country awake!" Rob Reiner, who'd likewise marched and orated during the February protest, also endorsed Dean at the mobbed Union Station fundraiser.

State Senator Sheila Kuehl, costar of *The Many Loves of Dobie Gillis* sitcom and California's first openly gay legislator (Courtesy of Shelia Kuehl).

Ironically, another TV star joined Meathead and the "West Wing"-er onstage: Sheila Kuehl, who'd played boy crazy Zelda on the popular 1959-63 sitcom "The Many Loves of Dobie Gillis" (which, among other things, co-starred Bob Denver in pre-Gilligan days as TV's very first beatnik, Maynard G. Krebs). When some erroneously assert that only Hollywood right-wingers run for office, Kuehl is being left out of the picture. Being outed as a lesbian in the 1960s put the kibosh on Kuehl's acting career, and she ended up in politics, becoming California's first openly gay legislator, and the first woman named Speaker pro Tempore of the Assembly. The popular Kuehl is now a state senator for District 23 in L.A. Senator Sheila pushes for universal healthcare legislation and according to Governor Dean, was the first officeholder to endorse his candidacy for president.

Thus Dr. Dean, inheritor of the antiwar mantle, took the stage flanked by actors who'd starred in television series of the '50s, '60s, '70s, and the new millennium. Shortly before his arrival at the train station, Dean was a guest on "The Tonight Show," strumming a guitar in a shot-on-location skit (wherein Reiner tossed a few bucks into the candidate/troubadour's guitar case, underscoring the fact that September 30 closed the fundraising quarter), and appearing in-studio with Jay Leno. Dean charged up 500-plus contributors at Union Station with his stump speech about "taking America back" from Bush. During the fundraiser, as he pressed the flesh, I asked the presidential hopeful which entertainers and artists supported his candidacy, and the governor answered that there were so many, he'd lost count. I went on to ask the then-Democratic frontrunner,

"What is the role of Hollywood progressives in election 2004?" Proving that the doctor was indeed in, the man-who-would-be-nominee responded with the canny instincts of a politician who has his eyes firmly planted on the prize and the big picture. Dean pithily shot back a reply that summed up the persuasive power and impact of big and little screen stars on America's political and cultural galaxies:

"The bigger, the better!"

THE POLITICAL EDUCATION OF PROGRESSIVE HOLLYWOOD

"Teach your children well."

— Crosby, Stills, Nash and Young

A common knock against celebrities who speak out is that they are ill-informed "Malibu airheads" who spout off half-cocked about the issues of the day. The book jacket of James Hirsen's *Tales From the Left Coast: True Stories of Hollywood Stars and Their Outrageous Politics* contends "lots of stars try to use their status to mess with public policy. Never mind that Hollywood celebs often have no more training or expertise in the stuff they're promoting than the average John or Jane Q." Hirsen writes that during the lead-up to the war in Iraq, Artists United to Win Without War "Co-chairs Mike Farrell and Robert Greenwald hit the radio and TV talk-show circuit and filled the airwaves with their harebrained attempts at geopolitics." The signers of AUWWW's December 15, 2002 antiwar ad in the *New York Times* are dubbed "100 Hollywood Half-Wits" in a subhead and referred to as "the haughty hundred" in the back.

Hirsen's diatribe (which is published by Crown Forum, the same right-wing imprint that published Ann Coulter's *Treason: Liberal Treachery From the Cold War to the War on Terrorism* includes a section called "How a Political Issue Becomes a Hollywood One." It purports, with an accompanying diagram, to reveal how left-coasters embrace and advocate causes. Although the Washington-based Eleanor Clift was never brought up by a single one of the numerous artists actually interviewed—nor seen at any of the many events actually covered—for this book, for some reason Hirsen (who never misses an opportunity to bash an opponent) mentions the *Newsweek* contributing editor and McLaughlin Group panelist in this section.

In connection to the animated feature *Team America*, Hirsen repeated his airhead allegations from October 11, 2004 on—where else?—Fox News. What reactionary hitman Hirsen never mentioned in this section of his book or on Fox is the political education of Hollywood's progressives, and how they become informed about the movements they publicly support. The school for celebrities is, in fact, quite extensive.

PATRIOTIC HALL AND ARIANNA OF ARC: SHADOW CONVENTIONEERS VS. LAPD

Although it took place prior to 9/11, the Shadow Convention was an excellent example of Hollywood progressives cooperating with liberal politicians and activists in order to raise consciousness—and more than a little hell. The Shadow Convention took place at Patriotic Hall, a county facility in downtown L.A. about two blocks south of Staples Center, where the 2000 Democratic National Convention was held. The idea behind the Shadow Convention was to offer an alternative vision to that being espoused by the Gore/Lieberman campaign (not to mention the Bush/Cheney ticket). The brainchild of socialite and lapsed right-winger Arianna Huffington, the Shadow Convention dealt with issues the two parties were neglecting, from class inequities to poverty to race to the drug war to corporate sway in the political process, and the like. Panel discussions, speeches, etc., were open to members of the public. This gathering of dissidents—which attracted leading lights of the left and thousands of participants—didn't escape the notice of the powers-that-be.

I covered the Shadow Convention and the Democratic National Convention as part of the L.A. chapter of the Independent Media Center. Amy Goodman and the "Democracy Now" team were stationed a few feet from where we'd meet with the revived *L.A. Free Press*.

A "Rapid Response Panel" was scheduled at 7:00 p.m. on August 14 to immediately respond to speeches at the Democratic Convention as they aired. However, it was delayed, as I and a few other members of the media and the public who'd already been admitted to Patriotic Hall's auditorium were ordered out. In the lobby, hundreds of Shadow Conventioneers, mystified as to what was going on, waited for the scheduled event wherein novelist Gore Vidal, author Christopher Hitchens, citizen watchdog Norm Ornstein, educator Jonathan Kozol and actor Michael McKean would reply to the Clintons' speeches, to be aired live on twin screens inside the auditorium.

At 7:30 p.m., Shadow Convention organizer Arianna Huffington stood on a table in the lobby to announce that blocked admission to the auditorium, plus audio technical problems, were due to an alleged "bomb scare" at Patriotic Hall, however, sounding like Joan of Arc, Arianna declared: "One way or another, we'll do our program." She also criticized the police.

Shortly afterwards, I noticed the actress/model Lauren Hutton at the front of the crowd, right outside the doors to the auditorium. Somebody mentioned police had locked people out of the fourth floor of Patriotic Hall as part of the purported bomb brouhaha. Finally, by 7:45 p.m., the (approximately) 500 people moved out to the street and the media van directly in front of Patriotic Hall on Figueroa Street. I tried to leave at an empty side exit, as the front doors were mobbed, but was told by the Sheriff's deputies that I couldn't, so I had to follow the large numbers of people slowly moving outside. This struck me as rather odd, as we were supposed to be evacuating due to a possible bomb, and it occurred to me that during a real bomb threat, authorities would want people out and away from the area ASAP.

In any case, the overflowing, peaceful crowd spilled out from the sidewalk and into the actual street and, undeterred, the Rapid Response Panel prepared to hold its event from the van. But first, the technicians announced they had no mike, so this reporter volunteered his microphone and the event proceeded. The panelists were positioned in such a way that they could not see just a short way up Figueroa from them, as they faced south. Michael McKean, who was emceeing, took the mike and joked: "Loretta Sanchez, put your top on!" (McKean, co-star of the comedies *This is Spinal Tap* and *A Mighty Wind*, was making light of the Democrats' then-disavowal of Congresswoman Sanchez's ultimately cancelled Playboy-sponsored fundraiser.)

Then Gore Vidal—America's venerable man of letters, long a conscience of the nation—spoke. As demonstrators fought LAPD a few blocks north (unbeknownst to the crowd at Patriotic Hall at the moment), Vidal presciently said: "This reminds me of Chicago in 1968. A merry time, and yes, William F. Buckley was there." At this point, since I was on the street beside the van, with an unobstructed view of what was happening a few feet up the street, I interrupted Vidal to warn that riot police were nearby and seemed ready to move in. By about 7:50 p.m., around 40 officers (apparently from the L.A. County Sheriff's Department) in riot gear were deploying in a menacing manner just north of the van.

Christopher Hitchens took the mike, and made remarks which Ornstein later called "rabblerousing." The then-radical writer questioned the credibility of the so-called bomb scare. Hitchens pointed out that if there really was a chance of an actual bombing incident just two blocks or so away from where the Leader of the Free World was speaking, intelligence and law enforcement would have shut down the area and completely evacuated it.

Sirens sounded and, ominously, by 7:55 p.m., the 40 riot gear-clad Sheriff's deputies were reinforced and joined by about 60 or more LAPD officers. They deployed down 18th Street, the small side street perpendicular to Figueroa and directly facing Patriotic Hall's main entrance, where the crowd and van were located. Simultaneously, LAPD squad cars massed just south of the Hall on Figueroa, and the vehicles were parked perpendicular to the street, as those armed officers blocked the other end of Figueroa. As if this wasn't enough, a police chopper burst overhead. I cried out: "The gang's all here!"

The Shadow Conventioneers were completely surrounded—on three sides by police and, above, by a helicopter. But at the van, Arianna—who is becoming something of a *La Pasionaria* for the movement—and Vidal, Hitchens, Kozol, Ornstein and McKean stood tall. And the masses of people on the sidewalk and street did not budge. The speakers and the assembly stood together-and, as the old song goes, they were not moved.

One thing that was eerie was that the authorities did not once, at any point, use their bullhorns, etc., to order the crowd to disperse, as is usual standard operating procedure. For example, a few blocks north, following the Rage Against the Machine concert, LAPD repeatedly ordered demonstrators to disperse for 20 minutes via loudspeaker equipment before charging. This did not happen at Patriotic Hall, where there was absolutely no provocation of authorities (although there were brave, but not provocative, words from Hitchens and company) by a completely peaceful crowd. Yet this tranquil assemblage, which came to hear political commentary, found itself completely surrounded and confronted by what Jack London called the iron heel of the state.

The impasse ended at 8:00 p.m., as it was announced that the all clear was given to Patriotic Hall by the authorities, and throngs of people re-entered the auditorium for the better-late-than-never Rapid Responsers. Arianna of Arc told the crowd: "You don't look dangerous to me!" By 8:10 p.m., the mysteriously blacked-out media system was up and running, and President Clinton was being heard. Applause went on as the sound was restored, but boos resounded through the auditorium as the Shadow Conventioneers realized who the sound was emitting from.

Ironically, as LAPD cavalry charged and pepper gassed demonstrators right outside Staples Center, Clinton recited the alleged human rights record of the U.S. government, and went on to laud U.S. armed forces. Given the ordeal the Shadow Conventioneers had just gone through, it was a bit too much. When it was time for the Rapid Response team to rapidly respond, Hitchens—with his trademark acidic wit—excoriated Clinton. "When you look at that bloated face of a rapist, war criminal and psychopathic liar, one can't eat enough to vomit enough. I'm still smarting from Arianna's remark that we 'don't look dangerous.' We better start looking dangerous. How long are you willing to be treated like this? Everyone here is outvoted by one foreign campaign contributor who can't even vote. You're treated like a serf!" thundered one of America's then-leading leftist journalists.

Needless to add, no "bomb" was ever found. The massive police presence at Patriotic Hall seemed designed to menace, threaten and intimidate the alternative assembly gathered there. Their only possible infraction of the law might have been blocking some traffic—not to do civil disobedience, but only because their assembly-place had been co-opted and they had been forced out into the overcrowded sidewalk and street. But given the peaceful nature of the throng, a mere handful of non-riot gear clad officers would have sufficed in order to enforce any possible traffic problem. The police overkill was an excessive use of force. But given the fact that Vidal used to talk about socialism on Johnny Carson's show, Arianna's then-new book was called *How to Overthrow the Government* and Hitchens' (also then-new) book about Clinton was titled *Nobody Left to Lie To*, perhaps this massive show of force was not a total shock.

Due to the unexpected "technical difficulties," the Hall's generators only had 45 minutes worth of power left for the Rapid Response session, and that night's Shadow Cabaret was rescheduled for Tuesday night. But the power of the people was shown when Arianna, Vidal, Hitchens and hundreds of nonviolent dissidents refused to be cowed by the armed might of LAPD and company. The anti-colonial American Revolutionaries depicted in a mural on the outside of Patriotic Hall would have been proud. Although the subsequent election of the then-police chief, Bernard Parks to the L.A. City Council and his 2005 campaign for mayor may have disturbed the 1776ers.

During the DNC, Staples Center was turned into a veritable fortress, and a high fence divided the Democratic Party from the masses, as Vice President Al Gore was anointed. Along with my Indymedia comrades Jackie Carpenter and Art Pinero, I walked up to the fortifications and tall fence, shook my fist, and declared: "Mr. Gore-bachev: Tear down this wall!"

CONSCIOUSNESS RAISING 101

Marge Tabankin heads the nonprofit consulting firm Margery Tabankin & Associates, which manages philanthropic foundations for Steven Spielberg, Barbra Streisand and DKNY's Donna Karan, and she is also a political consultant to Rhino Records' Richard Foos. Tabankin is the former director of the Hollywood Women's Political Committee and was director of VISTA during the Carter administration. "It's important to know that many different groups hold regular salons and educationals with leading public policy experts in those fields in Hollywood on a regular basis," she insisted.

Tabankin, who is a politically well-connected insider in Hollywood's left-leaning circles, cites numerous examples of what could be called the entertainment industry's school of higher consciousness learning. These salons, soirées, educationals, et al, take place in a variety of venues, from posh Bel Air homes to Beverly Hills restaurants to West Hollywood highrises to exclusive hotels to Malibu beach houses. The topics likewise stretch across the progressive spectrum.

"On South Africa, there's been lots of salons in people's homes, learning about the issues facing that country," Tabankin said. "Albie Sachs, who was the person who wrote the constitution for South Africa, who was [Black Consciousness activist Steve] Biko's lawyer, and had his arm blown off—he came and talked about what it was like to do a reconciliation situation there. Not live through vengeance, but live through moving forward. Whether it's Kate Michaelman, who used to be at NARAL [the National Abortion Rights Action League and] Pro-Choice America, Gloria Feldt at Planned Parenthood, Bobby Kennedy [Jr., president of the Waterkeeper Alliance, senior attorney for the Natural Resources Defense Council (NRDC), co-author of *The Riverkeepers*] on the environment... A lot of people learn about a lot of issues by going to these private salons that are held... [former U.N. Weapons Inspector] Scott Ritter came and did an event. Lots of celebrities came and met with him. He actually came

Marge Tabankin of Margery Tabankin & Associates, which manages philanthropic foundations for Steven Spielberg, Barbra Streisand, DKNY's Donna Karan, is also a political consultant to Rhino Records' Richard Foos.

several times. And different celebrities—and industry people—were at different gatherings. I remember Dr. Michael Oppenheimer, on global warming, came out at one point. He's now at Princeton; he was at Environmental Defense. Recently we had Bobby Kennedy talking about the Bush administration's rollback on all the environmental laws. Human Rights Watch just had a group of some of the most amazing people from different countries in conflict around the world that spoke to groups of individuals. So that it goes on at a fairly regular basis—since the Hollywood Policy Center and the Hollywood Women's Political Committee closed out—it's now done under lots of different organizations," said Tabankin, who manages Spielberg's Righteous Persons Foundation.

Many talents open their homes to educational events. "Laurie David [wife of "Curb Your Enthusiasm" star Larry David] has lots of them at her home. Mike [Farrell] and Shelley Fabares have had some at their home. Barbra did one at her home for Madeleine Albright to talk about world politics. [Streisand] lives out-of-town, so it's hard for people to get there. It's usually people who live on the West side of town [who hold the L.A. informational gatherings]. Robert Greenwald holds some at his house. Marilyn and Alan Bergman often hold things at their house," stated Tabankin.

Tom Hayden, who appeared in and was depicted by Brian Benben in Jeremy Kagan's 1987 HBO movie "Conspiracy: The Trial of the Chicago 8," has also hosted educational gatherings—at his home and on the road.

Since his relationship with Jane Fonda, the co-author of SDS' Port Huron Statement, former defendant and California state senator has been an influential member of the Hollywood left.

Tabankin said, "They had a very pivotal role, because he clearly was the most significant adviser to Jane. But more than that. They put millions of dollars up to organize Hollywood in this group called Network... and got that celebrity caravan to go... buses all throughout California, performing and talking to citizens. Alfre Woodard, Sarah Jessica Parker, Rob Lowe—a lot of young Hollywood at the time... Jane had events—she'd have Bishop Tutu at her home. She'd have lots of Hollywood invited to hear them and seeing what it was to be an activist. Tom was the inspiration behind a lot of that, and then Jane clearly picked it up. Jane was very much her own person, and really has strong beliefs, in fact sometimes I think she gets short-shrifted, but it's just because of Tom. But I think it was a way for her to get exposed, and then she did. She learns, and eats it all up, and studies whatever she's interested in."

Many left-coasters regard Hayden as an inspiration, even as a mentor—including the Newark-raised Tabankin. "When Newark was in total turmoil... I first met Tom Hayden. When he came to Newark as an organizer, I was 15 years old. And I went to listen to him speak. He was there during what was called the Newark Community Union Project for SDS. And it had a profound, life changing affect on me. That people could actually go do what he was doing with their lives, as opposed to being a teacher, a doctor, whatever. I mean, it was just the first adult I'd ever seen so passionate about making a difference, in where he was living and working. And it really put into my mind the notion of what an organizer could be. It was later, after I went to the University of Wisconsin in Madison... It was a very radical time... I was [in SDS] and was very involved, I went to the Alinsky Training Institute, the Industrial Areas Foundation—Saul [Alinksy] was still alive—where I learned how to be a community organizer. It was really that role model that Tom set for me that I never got out of my eyes. It was always in my head," Tabankin related.

Hayden continues to write, be politically active and hold soirées at his book-packed Brentwood home. On February 22, 2004 the Public Citizen and anti-globalization organizer Lori Wallach spoke there about her new book *Whose Trade Organization?: The Comprehensive Guide to the WTO*. Comedienne Paula Poundstone and author Gioconda Belli were among those in the Haydens' packed living room.

Tabankin considers the charge that Hollywood personalities who take public stands on issues are not up to speed on the causes they champion to be a bum rap. "Whether it's human rights or the death penalty or the environment or reproductive choice, these celebrities are exposed to some of the smartest minds in the country. And that's really just a taking-off point, for those who become more interested where they can go and read more and build relationships that are long-lasting... I can tell you that people like Ted Danson on the environment, Mike Farrell on the death penalty and human rights, Barbra Streisand on global warming, women's rights—these people are voracious readers. They happen to be actors or directors or singers, whatever, for their jobs, but just like anybody else they're smart people, they're really well informed," Tabankin added.

The director of the Streisand Foundation said, "On a Sunday morning, I will get a call from Barbra, she will have already finished the *New York Times*, she'll be bitching about some stupid article that she felt was way off the mark. She'll start telling me what she thinks of it. She'll be quoting from an article in the *Nation*, she will have seen something either from the *Guardian* or the *Economist* online that she wants to talk about—I mean, she's really well informed. You know, she really keeps up," Tabankin asserted.

THE SHEINBAUMS

While researching this book, I covered a number of progressive Hollywood's educationals. A mainstay of these consciousness-raising gatherings is the home of Betty and Stanley Sheinbaum. Stanley has been an academic, economist, president of the police commission that fired LAPD's Daryl Gates, a Mid-East peace negotiator, SoCal ACLU chapter president and also appeared in Warren Beatty's 1998 *Bulworth*. Betty is an accomplished painter and a child of Tinseltown royalty. She's the daughter of mogul Harry Warner and niece of Jack Warner. The Warners fled Poland because of antisemitism, started a Pennsylvania nickelodeon in 1903, and "felt very lucky to live in America," says Betty Sheinbaum, Harry Warner's daughter.

The Warner Bros. released many of the most progressive and anti-fascist movies during the New Deal and WWII. Harry's granddaughter, Cass Warner, head of the pithily-named Warner Sisters Productions and author of *Hollywood Be Thy Name: The Warner Brothers Story*, says her favorite Depression-era movie is Warners' 1932 *I Am a Fugitive From a Chain Gang*, about bleak prison conditions and injustices. Warners' gangster flicks, including Robinson's 1930 *Little Caesar* and Jimmy Cagney's 1931 *Public Enemy* (scripted by screenwriters Francis Faragoh and John Bright, identified as "left-wingers" in Paul Buhle and Dave Wagner's *Radical Hollywood*), reflected the grim social conditions Americans faced under President Herbert Hoover. Even WB musicals, such as *Gold Diggers of 1933* (with its wish-fulfillment "We're in the Money" song) mirrored desperate Depression realities. The Warner Bros. also released Hollywood's first explicitly anti-Hitler feature, 1939's "prematurely anti-fascist" *Confessions of a Nazi Spy*, starring Edward G. Robinson.

The Warners' liberal legacy lives on in the generous support the Sheinbaums lend left-leaning causes, candidates and groups. The couple often donates their posh Brentwood home (across from O.J.'s former estate) for functions benefiting liberal Democrats and organizations. Presenters get the use of a lovely home and grounds (including a spacious, shady front yard and a backyard with a lovely view) free of charge, with their main cost being the catering for the events, which are often packed. These happenings are extremely educational in nature, as leaders from the arts, politics and culture discourse on matters of the moment. The Sheinbaum venue is a beloved, much-sought-after and indispensable element in the consciousness raising of the creative community. As Mike Farrell said, the Sheinbaums' salon is "the basis of a lot of progressive activity."

Speakers at Sheinbaum gatherings have included: Senators Paul Wellstone and Russ Feingold, Representative Dennis Kucinich, Norman Mailer, Arab scholar Edward Said, speakers from Human Rights Watch, etc. The audiences are star-studded, with notables such as Beatty, Annette Bening, James Cromwell, John Saxon, Bonnie Franklin, Norman Lear, Aaron McGruder and Arianna Huffington attending.

In August 2003, Southern California Americans for Democratic Action held a book party there for Jim Hightower and his *Thieves in High Places: They've Stolen Our Country—And It's Time to Take It Back*. The overflowing crowd stretched out of the Sheinbaums' living room, into row after row of lawn chairs in the backyard, as Hightower regaled listeners with his populist take on plutocrats, "kleptocrats" and "the Super-Duper Empire of King George the W."[12]

---

12. When the Texan denounced Bush as a heavy-handed tyrant, I whispered to Cass Warner: "Who does Bush think he is? A studio mogul?" Harry's granddaughter mischievously retorted: "You'll never work in this town again!"

At another Sheinbaum shindig organized by Greenwald in early 2004, Stanley Greenberg discussed and signed his book *The Two Americas: Our Current Political Deadlock and How to Break It.* Greenberg was a member of Clinton's 1992 "war room" and is married to Congresswoman Rosa DeLauro (D-Conn). The pollster/strategist outlined a strategy as to how the Democrats could retake the White House.

With incisive analysis, Greenberg dissected data of the contemporary "political parity" between "red Republican" and "blue Democratic states." He argued that "America is divided" by "a historic political deadlock" between "the two big political parties" that has lasted for the last 50 years. The "current pathologies" of "the 49% nation" exist because it's the "first time since the 1880s" that there's been "three consecutive presidential elections... [and] three consecutive congressional elections where neither party gets 50% of the vote; first election since 1876 where the popular vote winner loses the presidency."

In his tome, Greenberg painstakingly breaks down the statistics, rendering numbers accessible with colorful voting bloc names, such as "white, married and educated Republican partisans" called "Privileged Men," who earn $50,000-plus. The "F-You Boys" are "white men, without college degrees, many blue collar... being squeezed... by college-educated voters, increasing minorities and immigrants and... radical changes in gender roles." They "think... Bush is their guy, speaking to them man to man." "Democratic loyalists" include "super-educated women with postgraduate degrees" and "Secular Warriors," committed "to self-expression, autonomy and freedom... [with] a tolerance for lifestyle choices, including homosexuality and gay unions."

Greenberg proselytized that to return to "one America," Democrats need winning strategies in 2004 that transcend today's quagmire politics. *The Two Americas* calls for "a bold politics," which includes tax reform (such as closing corporate loopholes), universal health insurance coverage and a foreign policy that doesn't unnecessarily piss the rest of the world off. Actors, producers and directors listened raptly in the Sheinbaums' living room and then, led by the insightful Arianna, peppered Greenberg with questions.

Of course, the Sheinbaums' salon played a decisive and key role in the creative community's opposition to the invasion of Iraq. Former UNSCOM Weapons Inspector Scott Ritter, the Education for Peace in Iraq Center's Executive Director Erik Gustafson and Notre Dame Peace Studies Professor David Cortwright presented a forum on October 2, 2002, at the Brentwood home. The audience of Hollywood heavy hitters included Warren Beatty, Annette Bening, Tom Hayden, as well as former Senator Gary Hart and 50 others. Greenwald and Farrell organized this educational at the Sheinbaums', which led to the formation of Artists United to Win Without War, the spearhead of Hollywood's peace movement.

Betty said, "Dad always felt films were for education, as well as for fun. He got theatre and opera talent, and felt film was a great medium to distribute this kind of entertainment. Dad was also interested in the constitution, and there was a whole series of films about civil rights, the Ten Amendments, he constantly was trying to have films express this outlook. He was a serious man—he loved entertainment, don't misunderstand me—but he particularly felt he wanted to educate. Dad was primarily interested in a different aspect [of movies]. Although he was the businessman in the family and had to make the studio a viable corporation, he was not only interested in making money. It wasn't the days of the blockbuster, it was the days of subjects about people and what was going on—the Depression, people in trouble," recalls Sheinbaum.

In 2003, the Warner Bros.' antifascist films and activities were highlighted in the USC exhibit "Warners' War: Politics, Pop Culture & Propaganda in Wartime Hollywood." The Fisher Museum show included Warners-related stills, letters, Senate testimony and other memorabilia, cartoons and shorts.

Domestically, the Warners supported Roosevelt's New Deal in the 1930s, while they challenged Nazism on the foreign front. As the USC exhibit stated, "Despite the fact that Hollywood's film empire had been built largely by Jews, there was little overt acknowledgement of the atrocities committed against Jews in Hollywood. The exception was Warner Bros.," which cut ties with Germany after Hitler rose to power.

In 1939's docudrama *Sons of Liberty*, which was continuously screened at USC's exhibit, Claude Rains depicts a Jewish patriot who helped saved America's Revolution, with a key scene in a synagogue, wearing a tri-corner hat—and *talis*. According to the exhibition, in-your-face pictures such as *Confessions of a Nazi Spy* prompted a Senate investigation of La-La Land's pro-war propaganda in isolationist, neutral America as well as a Production Code ban on anti-Nazi pictures, and "inspired Hitler to put Jack Warner on his hit list." A disturbing anti-Semitic flyer displayed at USC proclaimed: "BOYCOTT THE MOVIES! Buy

Employ Vote Gentile. Hollywood is the Sodom and Gomorrah where International Jewry controls Vice—Dope—Gambling. Young gentile girls are raped by Jewish producers... The Jewish Hollywood Anti-Nazi League Controls Communism in the Motion Picture Industry."

Once Pearl Harbor was bombed, "premature antifascists" joined the war effort. Warner Bros.' White House correspondence is in the USC show, including a telegram Harry and Jack sent FDR asserting that "Any sacrifice you may desire of us or our company please call on us." According to exhibit notes, "Jack Warner was even commissioned as a lieutenant colonel in the Army Air Forces to set up the First Motion Picture Unit. The unit made training films for the military as well as PR pictures for the public, starring such servicemen as Ronald Reagan and Jimmy Stewart." The studio pumped out hundreds of morale boosters and WWII movies, such as *Yankee Doodle Dandy* and *Casablanca*. As one cartoon (screened on a gallery TV) showed, even Porky Pig became patriotic.

After the U.S. joined the war effort, the Senate investigation of anti-Nazi sentiment in Hollywood was dropped. Ironically, USC's show displays a letter by Spanish Civil War veteran/screenwriter Alvah Bessie (Oscar-nominated for Warner's 1945 *Objective Burma!*) congratulating Colonel Warner on *Mission to Moscow*. Although, as the exhibit notes, Jack claimed FDR "personally asked him to make what would become Warner Bros.' most infamous film," this ode to America's wartime Soviet ally was "Exhibit A" for those alleging Communist infiltration in Hollywood. By 1947, Congress was investigating "subversive" influence in the movies—but this time, the House Un-American Activities Committee aimed at purported Communist propaganda. Bessie became one of the Hollywood Ten, talents accused of being Reds and cited for contempt of Congress and jailed. (Warner Bros.' role during the Hollywood blacklist was not as exemplary as its New Deal/WWII stances—but that's another story.)

HOLLYWOOD GOES TO WAR—AGAIN: 527S

If preventing the war in Iraq had been uppermost in progressive Hollywood's collective mind in late 2002 and early the following year, by the end of 2003 the focus had changed to how to re-defeat Bush. Educationals honed in like proverbial laser beams on how to win back the White House. During World War II, Tinseltown joined the war effort, from shooting morale boosters such as *Guadalcanal Diary*, to Jimmy Stewart,

Tyrone Power, Clark Gable and other stars enlisting in the military, to starlets dancing with G.I.s at the Hollywood Canteen. With the zeal of Frank Capra's *Why We Fight* documentaries, by 2003 the entertainment industry went to war again—this time, against the Bush administration.

"We're up against the end of democracy as we know it," warned Ilene Proctor, a publicist who attended a December 2, 2003 strategy session at the Beverly Hilton on how to beat Bush presented by America Coming Together and the Media Fund, and co-hosted by the indefatigable Greenwald. The invitation-only powwow attended by 300-ish Hollywood liberals was preceded by a press conference, where Media Fund President Harold Ickes, ACT President Ellen Malcolm, ACT CEO Steve Rosenthal and event hostess Laurie David (wife of "Seinfeld" creator Larry David) spoke to reporters.

Malcolm, who had been president of the feminist fundraiser Emily's List, called ACT "a political action committee... to turn [voters] out" in 17 battleground states. "There's a tremendous energy and enthusiasm from people who want to know what can be done in the 2004 elections... We're talking about a strategy... Republicans now are moving the country really to a radical agenda, and trying to turn back the clock... In the last election, 60% of eligible adults did not vote. Politics wasn't talking to them," observed Malcolm, who expressed hopes to "re-ignite our democracy... and bring those people back into the political process."

She said ACT and the Media Fund sought to raise "$190 million; we've raised upwards of $40 million." This organizing/fundraising drive bears the mark of Soros: According to Tabankin, anti-Bush billionaire philanthropist George Soros "gave $10 million to ACT."

Ickes said, "Our purpose is to raise money to produce and run TV and radio commercials starting next year to talk about the Democratic message and the importance of Democrats winning across the country."

Referring to a nonprofit tax designation for political organizations, Malcolm said, "The Media Fund is a 527. Both organizations are raising money from a whole host of members across the country. We're reporting all our expenses and contributions to the appropriate legal authority, the Internal Revenue Service of the Federal Election Commission."

On a point of contention, Ickes denied using a "loophole" and argued that "There's been some misconception, started by others, that we are evading the McCain-Feingold law... pending before the U.S. Supreme Court [the 527s subsequently won]... Our lawyers... advised us on structuring these organizations. They're permitted to raise contributions from

"M*A*S*H" costar and Artists United co-founder Mike Farrell speaks at the March 20, 2003 Southern California Americans for Democratic Action's 20th Annual Eleanor Roosevelt Awards Dinner.

individuals, unions and corporations... We're operating in very strict compliance with the law. Any rumors to the contrary are completely erroneous," the Washington lobbyist asserted.

ACT CEO Steve Rosenthal added that, running unopposed in primaries, Bush "will raise... $600 million... Until there are changes in the campaign finance laws... we have to make sure there's a message out there."[13]

After the press conference, David, Malcolm, Ickes and Rosenthal moved to a larger Hilton venue to present the strategy session, which was closed to the press. Attendees reportedly included Donna Mills, Rob Reiner, Julia-Louis Dreyfus, Earl Katz, Christine Lahti, Mike Farrell and Larry David. Ed Asner called it "a fantastic event, packed to the gills... the panel's presentation... showed various graphics... showing the narrow edge in target states—how they were lost or won, and can be retained or regained without great effort. How important it is to get out the vote... It was beautifully planned and demonstrated... It also showed very promising recent polling showing where generically any Democrat stood against Bush... There was no hyperbole—it was straight facts as to how the plan was to progress, with appropriate funding... to supplement the Democratic candidate... They

---

13. According to Chuck Lewis, Executive Director of the Center for Public Integrity, "Under the McCain-Feingold law, you can't run an ad in a primary inside 30 days... Theoretically, an issue ad that affects campaigns—these broad ads about issues, but they don't say 'vote for' or 'vote against'... are [called] '527'—that's an IRS tax code [designation]... They can be very negative or positive, and are clearly political, [and] cannot now run if they're paid for by a labor union or a company."

filled the audience with great hope as to potentially winning. They had envelopes to contribute—I have mine and plan to," Asner said.

Co-host Greenwald called the primary season parley "One of the best organizing meetings I've ever been to... They talked about a very organized plan—no matter who the candidate is—to work to raise... money, and work very hard to get major turnout... in '04 by a long running sustained organizing campaign... [the] plan got a standing ovation." Publicist Proctor dubbed the meeting "sensational," and added, "Ickes spoke about electronic voter fraud."

Predictably, the right-wing media badmouthed the strategy seminar as a "hate Bush" bash—and, in the process, inadvertently ballyhooed the parley. According to November 30th's Drudge Report, "Laurie David... sent out invites to the... meeting at the Hilton with the bold heading: 'Hate Bush 12/2—Event.'" The online item moved NeoCons into overdrive drivel. Fox's Bill O'Reilly opened "The Factor's" December 1 "Talking Points" attacking the confab. In the so-called "No Spin Zone," O'Reilly went on to debate *Nation* editor Katrina vanden Heuvel, and threatened to shut her microphone off when she started making sense.

Rush "News Junkie" Limbaugh derided the gathering of "Left Coast Hollywood Kooks." Greenwald battled Media Research Center President Brent Bozell and co-anchor Robert "Agent Outer" Novak on CNN's "Crossfire." Across from the Hilton on Wilshire Blvd., about 35 noisy pro-Bushies waved American flags and "I [heart] W." placards, as the meeting took place.

But at the earlier news conference, David insisted the "piece that ran in the Drudge Report was completely inaccurate in its characterization of this meeting, and was total misrepresentation... I never, ever used the words 'Hate Bush.' This is a result of what happens with the Internet. I [e-mailed] the invitation... to a small group of friends and colleagues. They sent it out to other people, who sent it out to other[s]... Someone, somewhere—apparently not even from L.A.—decided to tag it 'Hate Bush,' and it was picked up by the Drudge Report." (Drudge printed some of David's comments on December 3.)

Media Fund President Harold Ickes asserted: "We do not hate George Bush. We do not like his policies. We hope to find gainful employment for him in another line of work in 2005," Clinton's ex-Deputy Chief of Staff magnanimously offered. Asner stated, "This was a terrible misnomer, the right wing kept branding it that. There was no 'hate Bush' going on there. It was strictly a cold-blooded evening designed to win for Democrats, with no strong polemics against Bush or the Republicans... I was uplifted by its objectivity and lack of rancor, and enormous preparedness."

Mrs. Larry David couldn't curb her enthusiasm as Laurie thanked Internet *yenta* Matt Drudge for "helping turn a small gathering of political activists into a very large gathering of political activists. Now, that's grass roots networking." Malcolm added, "We've already moved the event from one [Hilton] room to a larger room. We've gotten so much response we're... turning people away." Greenwald observed, "As soon as the right wing started attacking, everyone wanted to be there."

Besides alleged contempt for their beloved commander-in-chief, what got NeoCons' panties in such a knot? Right-wing performance anxiety over Democrats harnessing Hollywood liberals for 2004's campaigns.

Asner, who was campaigning for Representative Dennis Kucinich at the time, said that Hollywood progressives "should get in and participate, not sit back on their haunches." Greenwald urged activist artists to "work our asses off in every way we can to help defeat Bush and elect Democrats nationwide. All the skills people have will be available to defeating this radical right-wing takeover of our country."

MR. SMITH GOES TO BEVERLY HILLS AND WEST HOLLYWOOD

Since 1998, TV and feature directors' agent Paul Alan Smith has hosted periodic speaker soirées for entertainment industry workers (from assistants to company heads), featuring provocative proponents of various causes who discuss "what makes our democracy healthier and stronger," as Smith put it. They have included FAIR's Jeff Cohen, Howard Zinn, Representative Barbara Lee, *artiste provocateur* Robbie Conal and John Stauber, Executive Director of the Center for Media and Democracy and co-author of *Banana Republicans*. Dinners had been at Smith's home until 9/11, when—after Smith was called "un-American"—the soirées went on hiatus, returning a year later at a Beverly Hills restaurant Malcolm X's daughter recommended. Smith said he pays for the dinners and expenses of out-of-town lecturers, without declaring them tax write-offs.

In 2004, Smith moved the speaker soirées to his new spacious 16th story pad in West Hollywood, with its commanding views stretching to the Pacific Ocean and a high power telescope for scoping out the heavenly bodies. The apartment is filled with the agent provocateur's eclectic art collection, which ranges from Conal's political iconography to ethnic

U.S. Representative Barbara Lee, the only member of Congress to vote against the September 15, 2001 resolution authorizing President Bush to use "all appropriate and necessary force," at a 2004 *soirée* presented by agent Paul Alan Smith.

imagery. A repeat visitor to Cuba, Smith displays a black and white photo of a young Fidel Castro *sans* beard strolling through Central Park in the 1950s. An original photo of Che Guevara by Cuban photographer Alberto Korda also hangs on his walls.

In February 2003, 150 diners attended a talk by Institute for Public Accuracy journalist Norman Solomon, who discussed his trip to Baghdad with Sean Penn and signed copies of *Target Iraq*. March 2003 speakers include pro-civil rights attorney Constance Rice, who was joined by L.A. anti-gang activists. Connie's evil cousin is Bush's National Security Advisor, Condoleezza Rice.

Smith has represented Matt Damon, Ben Affleck and historian Howard Zinn in a project to televise Zinn's *A People's History of the United States*. For two years running, he has emceed the National Lawyers Guild's annual fundraiser dinner in L.A. Smith has been labeled a "socialist" and "communist" because he's criticized capitalism. "I'm a Hollywood agent, please! Who are we kidding?" he laughs.

In any case, Smith's speaker series brings thought-provoking ideas to members of the Hollywood community, from the rank-and-file to stars to moguls. At the John Stauber-catered event in July 2004, Smith criticized some Hollywood politicos for an "elitism" that stressed star power, and ignored the gaffers, gofers, assistants, secretaries and others who have the motion picture and TV industry's behind-the-scenes less glamorous—albeit still essential—jobs. And Smith's salon makes him an essential player in the political education of Hollywood.

Amber Tamblyn sounds like Joan of Arc as she speaks passionately at *Pulp Fiction* producer Lawrence Bender's home.

Julia Ormond, star of 1995's *Sabrina* and 2004's Suffragette drama "Iron Jawed Angels," at the Rock the Vote consciousness raiser.

Attorney Gloria Allred at producer Lawrence Bender's home.

MIND BENDER: ROCK THE VOTE

"We [celebrities] need to do it [be politically active], and recognize our power. The greatest force behind that [persuading youth] is the celebrity."

— Amber Tamblyn, at Rock the Vote, February 4, 2004

The actress starring in CBS' "Joan of Arcadia," as a teenager whom God talks to, is herself becoming a modern day Joan of Arc. In a stirring speech, Amber Tamblyn announced she'd make a political fashion statement as a presenter on live TV at the February 8 Grammy Awards. (Indeed, Tamblyn wore a T-shirt with the words "Rock the Vote" emblazoned on it to the awards ceremony.)

Tamblyn made the announcement at a February 4, 2004 Rock the Vote gathering of Hollywood heavyweights at the swanky home of producer Lawrence Bender (*Pulp Fiction, Good Will Hunting, Kill Bill*). Speaking about the influence young stars exert over youth, Tamblyn told the Bel Air powwow: "We [celebrities] need to do it [be politically active], and recognize our power. The greatest force behind that [persuading youth] is the celebrity," the would-be 21st century Joan of Arc asserted about Tinseltown star power.

Rock the Vote is a nonprofit, nonpartisan voter registration organization targeting youth that claims to have registered 3.5 million mostly young voters. It grew out of the music world, and previous celebrity endorsers included Madonna, sporting boxing gloves in clever TV commercials. The group's youthful African-American president, Jehmu Greene, said that Rock the Vote was currently focusing on support from the film and television community.

Other Hollywood notables at the event included Julia Ormond (*Sabrina*), "Sex in the City" co-star Willie Garson and Robert Greenwald. Civil libertarian and attorney-to-the-stars Gloria Allred also attended, while LAPD Chief Bill Bratton and California Attorney General Bill Lockyer both addressed the overflowing crowd at the get-out-the-vote soirée.

In a reference to the then-recent Superbowl *faux pas*, Virgin Records' Jeff Ayeroff, who founded Rock the Vote in 1990 as an anti-censorship organization, declared: "I don't give a shit about Janet Jackson's breast." Commenting on the substantive issues of the day, Ayeroff, who wears a long, gray ponytail, added: "The longer we remain silent, the stupider this country gets." He lauded legendary CBS broadcaster Edward R. Murrow for exposing Senator Joe McCarthy, who'd persecuted dissenters in the 1950s.

On February 7, Rock the Vote presented the RTV Awards to the Dixie Chicks, the Tom Joyner Morning Show and Rhino Records' Richard Foos at the Hollywood Palladium. Grammy nominees N*E*R*D, Fountains of Wayne and the Black Eyed Peas performed, while composer Michelle Branch (*American Pie 2, Just Married*), actors Jake Gyllenhaal (*Donnie Darko, Bubble Boy*) and Danny Masterson (who has worn Che Guevara T-shirts on "That '70s Show") made special appearances.

Despite the violence that fills the Quentin Tarantino flicks that Bender produced, he has a reputation as one of filmdom's liberal stalwarts, who supports a variety of causes. The soirée stretched from the living room to the backyard, where bartenders served drinks beside Rock the Voters soliciting signups and selling T-shirts, as well as thongs, bearing the voter registration group's logo.

Drew Barrymore has also gotten involved with voter registration, making a documentary about the importance of voting for MTV. Jay-Z, Eminem, P. Diddy and Russell Simmons also participated in get-out-the-vote efforts, such as MTV's "Choose or Lose Presents: Vote or Die" and the Hip-Hop Summit Action Network. Sundance Channel aired the pro-Kerry "National Anthem: Inside the Vote for Change Concert Tour," featuring Bonnie Raitt, Bruce Springsteen, Dave Matthews Band, Dixie Chicks, Jackson Browne, James Taylor, John Fogerty, John Mellencamp, Jurassic 5, Keb' Mo', Kenny "Babyface" Edmonds, Pearl Jam and R.E.M.

HAREBRAINED TODAY, GONE TOMORROW

As Greenwald has asserted about the awareness of politically engaged artists: "I defy anyone to be more knowledgeable than [Mike] Farrell, Janeane [Garofalo] or James Cromwell. We provide briefings... It's more effective to send material. Solomon's book [*Target Iraq*], Zinn's *Terrorism and War*. We urge people to hear Ritter's tapes. Certainly in the group I'm working with, the amount of time and attention many have given to educating themselves surpasses the talkshow hosts, who focus on anger, bombast and talking louder," insisted the director of *Outfoxed*.

Time has passed, and the findings are in from American and British (though not Iraqi resistance, Arab, Muslim, North Korean, Iranian,

Cuban, et al) authoritative sources. Now the Iraq invasion can be Monday morning quarterbacked. The chief postwar U.S. weapons inspector, David Kaye of the Iraq Survey Group; the testimony of Bush's anti-terrorism czar Richard Clarke to the 9/11 Commission; the 9/11 Commission's Final Report; the Senate Intelligence Committee; Lord Butler's Report in Britain; Charles Duelfer's report and others have shown the lie to the claims that Iraq posed an imminent threat to the U.S. (let alone to other members of the Coalition of the Killing, such as far-flung Palau in the Western Pacific Islands).

It has been conclusively proven that Bush and Blair's claims and justifications for war—which were parroted by the media's and the right's *idiot savants*—were completely false and are now totally discredited. These include the allegations that Iraq had a nuclear program on the verge of producing a bomb, stockpiles of other weapons of mass destruction, a capacity to attack Britain with WMDs within 45 minutes, collaborative ties to al Qaeda and that Saddam was somehow involved in 9/11.

In their December 15, 2002 manifesto, the antiwar actors predicted "a pre-emptive military invasion of Iraq will harm American national interests. Such a war will increase human suffering, arouse animosity toward our country, increase the likelihood of terrorist attacks, damage the economy and undermine our moral authority in the world. It will make us less, not more, secure." With more precision than a so-called smart bomb, the Hollywood progressives accurately predicted the actual course of events that has been borne out by history, as opposed to conservative wet dreams of our troops being welcomed with flowers as liberators—instead of attacked as occupiers—as Iraq is transformed into a Jeffersonian democracy.

Based on what we now know, who was more knowledgeable and who was more (to use Hirsen's word) "harebrained" about the geopolitical realities (not NeoCon, Project for the New American Century fairy tales) of Iraq? Those "Hollywood celebs" who "have no... training or expertise in the stuff they're promoting," as Hirsen's book put it? Or what *Outfoxed* director Greenwald called "the nutcases on Fox," including Hirsen and his reactionary ilk? Instead of getting their marching orders from White House and Republican National Committee talking point, maybe Sean Hannity, Bill O'Reilly, and their fellow ideologues should attend some of those Hollywood tutorials given by policy experts, authors, et al, in order to get—as Sergeant Friday put it—the facts, ma'am, just the facts.

FOLLOW THE GREEN ENERGY: ENTERTAINMENT INDUSTRY POLITICAL DONATIONS

"Money makes the world go round...
A mark, a yen, a buck or a pound
A buck or a pound, a buck or a pound
Is all that makes the world go round."

— "Money, Money, Money" in *Cabaret*

Celebrities influence causes and candidates because of their fame, talent and fortune. We consider the latter here, financial donations that are given to and raised for causes and candidates by artists and the entertainment industry. Like big oil, banking, arms manufacturing, etc., the fields of television, movies, music, theater and so forth are big business in America. While this book stresses the roles individual talents play in the political process, it is also revealing to examine industry-wide trends *vis-à-vis* contributions to politicians and parties.

Show business greatly favors the Democratic Party. According to Common Cause, in the 2001-02 election cycle (which includes congressional by-elections that saw Republicans score gains), Democrats received almost six times the amount of donations from motion picture, TV, music, etc., firms than Republicans did. The total amount of money raised for the Democrats from the 150 entertainment industry donors was $23,500,660.72. This compared to 100 show biz contributors who raised $4,242,283 for the GOP. The top single Democratic donor, L.A.-based Saban Entertainment Inc., gave $9,252,936.36, while the biggest single contributor to Republicans was Philip H. Geier, with $500,000. (Rupert Murdoch's News Corp gave $90,032 to the Democrats, but $255,600 to the Republicans.)

According to *The Buying of the President 2004* by Chuck Lewis and the Center for Public Integrity, from January 1, 1978 to June 30, 2003, Saban Entertainment was the Democratic Party's second largest donor, contributing $12,703,582. Saban (which does business with Fox) is a broad-based entertainment company that develops, produces, acquires, distributes and merchandises children's television programming, including the *Mighty Morphin Power Rangers* and the *X-Men*. With $7,438,000 donated, Stephen Bing/Shangri-La Entertainment placed eighth on the donor list. Vivendi Universal was 28th, with $3,150,335, while AOL Time

Warner placed 29th, with $3,150,335. News Corp was number 37, donating $2,609,537 to the Democrats. Microsoft was 46th, with $2,141,977 and DreamWorks SKG number 47, with $2,118,529.

While the Democrats' second biggest contributor is from the entertainment industry, on the GOP side of the aisle, its biggest entertainment company contributor—Vivendi Universal—ranked 31st, with $2,439,227. (This is about one sixth the size of Saban's donations.) AOL Time Warner was 41st, with $2,200,120—roughly a fourteenth of what the same firm donated to the Democrats. Unless the MGM Mirage is included (with $2,025,900), no other entertainment companies rank in the Republicans' top 50 donors for this period.

Senator John Kerry sits on Senate committees that have oversight on the communications industry. Through June 30, 2003, Kerry's top career patron and top contributor was Mintz, Levin, Cohn, Ferris, Glovsky and Popeo PC, Boston (71st among U.S. law firms in 2002, with $229 million in gross). Mintz, Levin ponied up $223,046 to the Bay State senator. The law firm represents AT&T Wireless Services and the Cellular Telecom and Internet Association, the industry's lobbying arm. Kerry's brother Cameron works in Mintz, Levin's litigation section and has represented clients before the FCC. David Leiter, Senator Kerry's ex-chief of staff, is a vice president of a Washington Mintz, Levin affiliate that consults and lobbies.

Kerry's third largest career patron, AOL Time Warner, contributed $172,387 to his coffers. (The AOL Time Warner media conglomerate has owned CNN, Warner Bros., *Time* magazine, HBO, Cinemax, New Line Cinema, TBS, TNT, America Online and more.) Kerry's seventh largest career patron is America's largest law firm, Skadden, Arps, Slate, Meagher & Flom LLP, New York. Skadden, which is a lobbyist for News Corp and AOL Time Warner, gave Kerry $105,150. Another law firm with telecom clients Hale and Dorr LLP, Boston, donated $123,258 to the senator from Massachusetts. Comcast and AT&T gave Kerry, respectively, $54,000 and $21,300. From 1984 to 2003, the telecommunications sector contributed more than $1 million to Kerry. Other Kerry corporate media donors included Disney (ABC's owner), Viacom (CBS' owner) and News Corp (Fox's owner). Jointly, they contributed $300,000-plus to Kerry. The senator sits on influential committees—Commerce, Finance and is also a ranking member on the Small Business and Entrepreneurship Committee—with oversight over the business interests of the above contributors (as well as his wife's).

CELEBRITY FUNDRAISERS FOR KERRY

"...you invite 100 of your closest friends and ask them to give
$1,000, suddenly you're throwing a $100,000 house party."

— Lara Bergthold, celebrity liaison for the Kerry campaign

In addition to movie, TV and music firms *per se*, individual Hollywood
artists such as *La* Streisand also have deep pockets for supporting causes
and candidates. But entertainers are not only fiscally valuable for the
money that they and their industries donate, as Lara Bergthold explained.

The Boston-born, Santa Cruz, California-raised Bergthold attended
UC Berkeley, and got a master's in public policy from the Kennedy School
at Harvard. During the 2004 primaries, she was the political director for
Kerry's rival, General Wesley Clark. "Madonna, famously, endorsed us,"
Bergthold said. "He was a sort of darling of the entertainment industry for
a couple months." Producer Norman Lear held a pricey fundraising dinner at his home for the former NATO Commander, who was also backed
by Michael Moore.

After Clark dropped out of the race, Kerry's campaign manager Mary
Beth Cahill asked Bergthold to play the Hollywood role in the
Kerry/Edwards race. Bergthold's official job title was the National Deputy
Political Director for Kerry/Edwards, and she acted as the L.A.-based
celebrity liaison for the Kerry campaign. According to an April 16, 2004
news release at johnkerry.com, Bergthold also held the title of Director of
Entertainment Community Outreach. The release went on to say: "Before
joining the Clark campaign, Bergthold was the co-chair of the Board of
People for the American Way [which is linked to Lear] and the former
executive director of the Hollywood Women's Political Committee." There
are also online references to Bergthold attending the White House coffees
hosted by President Clinton.

"Most of the big fundraisers had celebrities at them," Bergthold said.
"Especially in New York and Los Angeles, where you tend to raise your big
money... We've used celebrities and performers as draws for donors. Both
when John Kerry and John Edwards are in attendance, and as surrogates
when they're not. The Disney Hall [L.A.] and Radio City Music Hall [Man-
hattan] concerts, where we put together a number of acts, was on the big
end of the scale... It's very expensive to come to those concerts.

"In L.A., it was $2,000 a ticket, [and up to] $25,000 a couple. In New York, the lowest ticket price was $350—maybe $250—up to $25,000, which is the legal limit." Bergthold explained that $2,000 is the legal limit for a campaign contribution in a White House race "unless it's a joint fundraiser with the Democratic National Committee, which is what these were... It's a segregated fund that can only be used for the presidential [race]."

According to Bergthold, the June 7, 2004 Disney Hall event in downtown L.A. raised "$5 million. [Artists included] Barbra Streisand, Neil Diamond, Billy Crystal, Robert De Niro, Leonardo DiCaprio... [The July 8 'Change Is Going To Come'] Radio City [concert] was $7.5 million. That was a bigger rock 'n' roll lineup—Jon Bon Jovi, John Mellencamp, the Dave Matthews Band, Mary J. Blige, Wyclef Jean and John Fogerty. Various celebrities were introducers; Sarah Jessica Parker, Meryl Streep, John Leguizamo, Chevy Chase."

Unfortunately, Chase didn't do his "SNL" signature pratfall as President Ford—due, Bergthold explained, to back injuries. Other stars who attended the Radio City gala included Paul Newman, Joanne Woodward and Christie Brinkley, as well as the candidates, their wives and the Kerry daughters. But not all the stars stayed on script. Whoopi Goldberg reportedly made offcolor double entendres regarding the Bush name at this event, which Bergthold—who was present—would not specify. Goldberg reportedly played on the sexual implications of "Bush."

"It was an inappropriate remark," Bergthold said. "She was the only artist who refused [to clear her remarks with the Kerry/Edwards campaign in advance]. And she was the only artist who went completely off inappropriately. There were other artists who'd improvised and said some things that we hadn't approved. We did ask her, she declined very strongly and she mentioned that in her performance."

Talk about getting the "base" out—when concert organizers asked to see Whoopi's *shtick* beforehand, she sent them a xeroxed picture of her butt with a kiss mark on it instead. Onstage, the comedienne joked: "Keep bush where it belongs, and not in the White House." The *Boston Herald's* headline for the event read: "Dems down and dirty: Kerry laughs, GOP howls over obscene fund-raiser." The *New York Post's* conservative Deborah Orin wrote "Jerky Jokester Whoopi in Dirty Diss at Dubya."

The Academy Award-winning actress stated: "I wasn't sure I was going to get the phone call... This is what I try to explain to people. Why are you asking me to come if you don't want me to be me?" Whoopi asked.

The other "improvised" remarks presumably included those by Chase, who quipped that the last recent book the president read was *Leader of the Free World for Dummies*. Academy Award-winner Jessica Lange called Bush "our so-called president" and his administration "a self-serving regime of deceit, hypocrisy and belligerence... I'll do everything that I can possibly do, short of selling my children," to re-defeat Bush.

Streep stated: "I wondered to myself through the shock and awe, I wondered which of the mega-ton bombs Jesus, our president's personal savior, would have personally dropped on the sleeping families in Baghdad." One of Bon Jovi's songs included the lyrics: "He's just another cheap thug that sacrifices our young... You're going to get us killed with your little white lies." Oscar winner Paul Newman assailed Bush's tax cuts: "I am a traitor to my class. I think that tax cuts to wealthy thugs like me are borderline criminal—I live very high off the hog."

Nevertheless, at the end of the concert, Kerry told the star-studded audience of 6,000 that the artists had "conveyed the heart and soul of America." Bush later used this phrase against Kerry at the Republic National Convention, stating: "If you say the heart and soul of America is found in Hollywood, I'm afraid you are not the candidate of conservative values."

Bergthold added that singer Tony Bennett also performed for Kerry at a separate—presumably less controversial—concert. According to a conservative website, the $5,000 a plate fundraiser took place at the Fairmont Miramar Hotel in Santa Monica on August 26. Courtney Cox, Leonardo DiCaprio, Melanie Griffith, Angelica Huston, Michael Keaton, Viggo Mortensen, Rob Reiner, Mary Steenburgen, Ted Danson and Sharon Stone were reportedly among the celebrities who attended the event.

Bergthold went on to say, "On the small end of the scale were house parties in L.A. and New York and, frankly, around the country that celebrities agreed to attend. Which ups the amount of money, sometimes doubles the amount of money you can take in from one of those events. They could perform briefly."

The Kerry/Edwards celebrity liaison said that it was more likely for these soirées to be thrown by studio executives, rather than by artists. "That's more common—then the actors come to them. I don't know that we've had any actors host anything in their homes. Because there's privacy issues—then everybody knows where you live," Bergthold said. The stars, however, help draw crowds to the soirées. "Will Ferrell was the headlining performer at one event... It's Los Angeles or New York, where you can have your best friend perform in your backyard. It's a very special intimate evening, and it makes it a lot easier to raise that money."

As for the suits, "It's a long list," Bergthold continued. "Most studios, studio heads, have had fundraisers. If they didn't host them, they were on the host committee of them. Sherry Lansing [the *Hollywood Reporter* calls the Paramount Pictures bigwig "the grande dame of female executives, but more than that, she is one of the most respected executives—male or female—in this business. She has held her current post longer than any current studio head"], Peter Chernin [News Corp president and COO], Norman Lear... It tends to [raise] about $100,000 to $150,000 an event. They were pretty regular. We call them 'classically house' parties. But in Los Angeles and New York, where you invite 100 of your closest friends and ask them to give $1,000, suddenly you're throwing a $100,000 house party."

Political education events sometimes cross over with fundraisers. "We generally have a surrogate speaker," said Bergthold. "That can range from a senior official in the campaign to Antonio Villaraigosa, who was the co-chair of the campaign, but was also the City Councilman in L.A. who often appeared... before he was running for mayor."

Villaraigosa did indeed attend a July 18 Kerry/Edwards fundraiser at the Hirsch Ranch, a spacious, hilly, grassy estate near Laurel Canyon. Fellow city councilman and rival mayoral contender Bernie Parks—who presided over the police brutality during the 2000 DNC—was also there with his fellow Democrats. People mingled while live bands played cowboy-like music on a stage in the distance. Tables laden with babaganoush and non-meat foods, and a bar serving wine and soft drinks, were shaded by tall trees. Pacifica Radio's Lila Garrett, hostess of KPFK's "Connect the Dots" program, sat near the front of a phalanx of folding chairs facing a flag-bedecked stage. A baldheaded 50-ish singer who had appeared at Kucinich campaign events during the primary season crooned a song with the lyrics: "The Democrats are stupid when they don't vote / The Republicans are stupid when they do."

When the official part of the function began, Senator Dianne Feinstein and other Democratic politicians spoke. California State Treasurer Phil Angelides, who is believed to want to run for governor against Schwarzenegger, delivered a populist-sounding rebuke of the Bush White House. Onstage, the beautiful former Bond girl and *Charlie's Angel* Tanya Roberts kibbitzed with the audience. In contrast to the ditzy blonde she played on "That '70s Show," the former *Beastmaster* co-star revealed herself to be a serious, ardent anti-Busher. The ubiquitous Arianna Huffington delivered what many of the 200 or so attendees considered to be the occasion's best speech. According to sources close to the ranch and the campaign, the property was donated to Kerry/Edwards at no cost. As of that date, the event raised more money ($100,000-plus) than any other California campaign fundraiser where neither Kerry nor Edwards personally appeared.

FUNDRAISERS FOR THE PEOPLE

"[T]hey took the art of fundraising—whether it was for diabetes or polio or whatever it was over the years, and realized you could do this for progressive causes or organizations."

— Marge Tabankin, in an interview with the author

Fundraisers in L.A. draw heavily on the largesse and talent of the creative community. These functions are often the source of the lion's share of the annual budgets of the groups, et al, who throw them. These occasions also have the benefit of bringing people together so they can touch base and network. With the various awards given out, notables, as well as behind-the-scenes activists and volunteers whose names may not be household words, receive public recognition for their good works.

Marge Tabankin, consultant to Hollywood heavyhitters, explained the importance of, and what goes into the making of, a successful left coast fundraiser. "Fundraising in Hollywood is an old, old, old situation. But what's unique is that they took the art of fundraising—whether it was for diabetes or polio or whatever it was over the years, and realized you could do this for progressive causes or organizations," the veteran organizer said.

Tabankin said the recipe for a successful fundraiser is "sort of the whole nine yards. It's having a really competent person who knows how to do it, because you've got major talent involved. It is putting together the right host committee, that is really committed to selling tickets... there's a team of people who are taking responsibility for this event and are going to go through their what used to be rolodexes—now I'd say palm pilots or databases—and make all those phone calls and do those 'asks.' And people have a hard time in saying 'no' when they ask. Who are willing to go to all the vendors they use. Who are really willing to go down their books and call everybody they know and say 'please support this.'"

Yet in order to receiveth, the good host must giveth. "They have to give them something they think is worth that donation, so they usually put on a fun, good show. Whether it's the event with Billy Crystal and Barbra Streisand that happened June 7, or the event in New York that Kerry did... It's putting the right ingredients together, having the right production staff and having the right people who are willing to sell tickets."

Tabankin cited other successful left-tilting fundraisers. "When Nelson Mandela was released from prison, the Hollywood community put on an event that raised $1 million for him to set up his own foundation to work on programs and problems with children in South Africa... [In 2004] the National Resources Defense Council raised over $2 million at a Hollywood fundraiser with Bobby Kennedy, Jr., Willie Nelson and Sheryl Crow. It was really a time for Hollywood to come out and support this organization, that is one of the premier environmental organizations in the country, fighting to change our policies on global warming and trying to clean up the country," said Tabankin.

She went on to discuss the voluntary role of talent in fundraisers. "The performers are not paid in these kinds of situations. There was a scandal recently, evidently, with some guy who was—if he wasn't paying people to show up, he was actually getting them gifts, or something like that. The progressive events that I know about—really most of them don't even get paid to have a driver to pick them up at their house. They pay their own way. Nobody's [paying] for Barbra's dress or hair or make-up—she's gonna show up and sing, basically. They're gonna pay for the musicians, the working, regular musicians, who should get paid, they get paid union scale and that's what they do for a living. But the Willie Nelsons, the Barbra Streisands, the Billy Crystals don't get paid for anything. And it takes time, because it takes time to rehearse," Tabankin explained.

Celebs also turn their premises over for worthy causes. "Laurie David has lots of them at her home. Mike [Farrell] and Shelley Fabares have had some at their home. Barbra [Streisand] did one at her home for Madeleine Albright to talk about world politics. She lives out of town, so it's hard for people to get there. It's usually people who live on the west side of town. Robert Greenwald holds some at his house. [Lyricists] Marilyn and Alan Bergman often hold things at their house," stated Tabankin.

ACLU-SC

Novelist, muckraker, Utopian socialist and future gubernatorial candidate Upton Sinclair founded the American Civil Liberties Union of Southern California in 1923. It is an affiliate of the national organization, and ACLU-SC is composed of about 12 chapters. It has often been in the SoCal vanguard of championing the First Amendment and human rights. For example, leading up to Election 2004, it campaigned for Proposition 66, which would change California's notorious three strikes law so that offenders convicted a third time would not receive draconian sentences if their last offense was of a nonviolent, petty nature. Previously, ACLU-SC unsuccessfully tried to stop the California gubernatorial recall race, but did succeed in defeating Ward Connerly's Proposition 54, which would have prevented government entities from gathering or utilizing race-related information—including health data. On the federal front, ACLU-SC strongly opposes the PATRIOT Act and the proposed Federal Marriage Amendment to the U.S. Constitution, which would inject anti-gay discrimination into the nation's framed rules.

As such, the various branches of the ACLU-SC stage a number of fundraising activities per year, which make liberal use of left coast talent. The ACLU-SC's Bill of Rights dinner is an annual highlight, and on December 15, 2003, it was held at the posh Beverly Wilshire Hotel near Rodeo Drive celebrating the anniversary of the Ten Amendments. The Bill of Rights Awards were bestowed on the Dixie Chicks' music manager Simon Renshaw and writer/director/producer Jon Avnet, whose work includes two Greenwald pictures—the Farrah Fawcett anti-domestic violence TV movie "The Burning Bed" and the Abbie Hoffman biopic *Steal This Movie*. Columnist Molly Ivins, the co-author of *Shrub*, was honored with the Eason Monroe Courageous Advocate Award. The Chicks' brave outspokenness and their manager's steadfast defense of their rights earned Renshaw the Bill of Rights award.

Among the 500-ish guests at Beverly Wilshire's ballroom was Larry Flynt, who said that "the First Amendment is to protect not necessarily speech you love, but speech you hate the most. *L.A. Times* doesn't need the First Amendment—it's not going to offend anyone... The advancements we made in civil rights and individual liberties were always brought about by civil litigation by minorities." *Hustler*'s publisher called ACLU "the only organization defending the Bill of Rights. They should have lots more support than what they're getting."

Hustler publisher Larry Flynt, author of *Sex, Lies & Politics: The Naked Truth*, speaks at a 2004 Southern California Americans for Democratic Action book fair in the L.A. Convention Center.

Blacklisted actress Marsha Hunt at the November 24, 2003 performance of *The Waldorf Conference* at the Writers Guild of America Theater in Beverly Hills on the anniversary of the November 24, 1947 meeting of movie moguls at Manhattan's Waldorf Astoria in order to enforce the Hollywood blacklist.

Chris Trumbo, the son of Hollywood Ten screenwriter Dalton Trumbo, talks with actor Ed Asner at the same performance of *The Waldorf Conference*. Anser played L.B. Mayer.

Introducing the award-winners, Ramona Ripston, Executive Director of ACLU-SC, told the attendees, "Jon Avnet... entertained millions and wrestled with important issues. We need freedom of speech, so artists can speak their minds, and challenge our conscience... Molly Ivins [proves] some good things come out of Texas." Ripston also thanked to loud applause the union workers serving the banquet.

Tony Award winner Poetri, of HBO's "Def Poetry Jam" and L.A.'s Def Poetry Lounge, rocked the house. David Schwimmer presented the Bill of Rights award to Jon Avnet, who'd directed the "Friends" co-star in the Warsaw Ghetto drama "Uprising."

Populist/socialite Arianna Huffington presented the Eason Monroe Courageous Advocate Award to that other Dixie Chick—Texan Molly Ivins—who, Huffington said, "uses satire as a political weapon in the tradition of Mark Twain and Jonathan Swift." In her acceptance speech, Ivins ridiculed "sending out [Attorney General] John Ashcroft on a charm offensive for the PATRIOT Act."

In an interview, the *Bushwhacked* author said: "I love ACLU dearly, it does tremendous work. ACLU fights the good fight. The fact that they'll fight for anybody on behalf of principle makes it one of the country's most worthwhile organizations. ACLU doesn't care if you are some gonzo left-winger who's burned the American flag or Oliver North. If your rights are being jeopardized, they will defend you."

Ivins insisted: "Karl Rove and Bush are very good at politics. It's going to be a tough election. I think he's beatable... Only a nincompoop would call a political race this far out." Flynt said his New Year's resolution is: "Stop Bush! That's going to be my whole focus."

Producer/director Jon Avnet said progressive Hollywood's election role is "To get somebody in who could be president."

As noted above, among those Hollywood progressives who open their homes to various causes and groups are the Sheinbaums, whose Brentwood home includes ample front and back yards. ACLU-SC threw its 40th annual Garden Party there on September 7, 2003, emceed by Ed Asner. The organization's executive director, Ramona Ripston, made an introductory speech and presented Greenwald with a Garden Party Award. Steve Rohde, an ACLU-SC board member, presented Greenwald's comrade in non-arms, Farrell, with a Garden Party Award. Ed Asner presented *Boondocks* cartoonist Aaron McGruder with his award. The Chapter Activist Award went to longtime volunteer Selma Rubin of the

ACLU-SC Santa Barbara branch. In addition to ticket sales, an art auction of political cartoons by McGruder, Paul Conrad, Robbie Conal and others hosted by actor Bill Schallert (of the 1960s sitcom "The Patty Duke Show") raised money for the venerable civil liberties organization.

Various chapters of ACLU-SC present their own fundraisers. *The Waldorf Conference* was read at the Writers Guild of America Theater in Beverly Hills on November 24, 2003—the anniversary of the November 24, 1947 meeting of movie moguls at Manhattan's Waldorf Astoria in order to enforce the Hollywood blacklist. Ed Asner, Paul Mazursky and Harlan Ellison appeared in the play, which was co-written by ACLU-SC board member Nat Segaloff. At the one night only performance, blacklistees in the audience, including Bobby Lees, Norma Barzman and Marsha Hunt, were recognized and honored. Afterwards, a reception took place in the WGA lobby (where a silent auction with blacklist memorabilia was also held), and Asner (who had played L.B. Mayer) *kibbitzed* with Barzman. Tickets cost up to $55.50, and the show and auction were a joint benefit for the Writers Guild Foundation and the ACLU-SC Hollywood chapter.

The South Bay Chapter's Second Annual Upton Sinclair Freedom of Expression Awards (called the "Uppies") took place May 15, 2004 at the Warner Grand Theater in the port city of San Pedro. The event's theme was "Become the Media," and the evening included some lively guerrilla street theater and music. Journalist Norman Solomon, executive director of the Institute for Public Accuracy and former Uppie recipient, delivered the keynote address. Uppie winners included Air America and KALW host and author Laura Flanders; the veteran civil rights and peace organizer Reverend James Lawson; co-founder of the Yippies and *Realist* editor Paul Krassner (who had bestowed the Uppie on comic George Carlin a year earlier); and the San Pedro 9, for their "courage in civil disobedience." Greg Palast and "Democracy Now's" Amy Goodman were awarded Uppies *in abstentia*.

THE LIBERTY HILL FOUNDATION

"In the twilight, it was a vision of power."

— Upton Sinclair, in *The Jungle*

The May 13, 1923 arrest of Sinclair the socialist as he tried to read the U.S. Constitution to 3,000 striking longshoreman at San Pedro's Liberty

Hill and the ensuing brouhaha is credited with rekindling Southern California's labor movement. In addition to inspiring the ACLU-SC and its Uppies, this historic happening also stimulated the Liberty Hill Foundation. It was co-founded in 1976 by film producer Sarah Pillsbury (*And the Band Played On, Eight Men Out, Desperately Seeking Susan*). Liberty Hill has made grants to grass roots organizations in order to carry out its gospel of social change philanthropy in Los Angeles. Grantees have included the Bus Riders Union, L.A. Coalition to End Hunger and Homelessness, Transgender Resource Center of Southern California, Homies Unidos and many others. Liberty Hill is at the forefront in reminding the public of discomfiting facts, such as that nearly half of all Angelenos live below the poverty line and the 50 wealthiest people in L.A. have a net worth of $60 billion, which is more than the 2 million people on the bottom combined have. The Foundation's motto is "change, not charity."

In order to endow these environmental, social justice, pro-gay rights organizations, the Foundation holds its Annual Upton Sinclair Dinner, which Liberty Hill ballyhoos as "the best benefit dinner in town." The 21st annual affair was produced by Foundation board member and movie producer John Bard Manulis (*Tortilla Soup, The Basketball Diaries, V.I. Warshawski*) and took place at the Beverly Hilton Hotel on June 2, 2003. Another way celebs can support causes, candidates and groups is by lending their names to them: the dinner's co-chairs included producer Lawrence Bender, actress LisaGay Hamilton and comic Bill Maher. Individuals and companies can also contribute to fundraisers by becoming sponsors (Creative Artists Agency co-sponsored this function). Events also feature elaborate printed programs, which contain messages on pages which awardees' friends, business associates, relatives, etc., pay for. In the program for the Liberty Hill dinner, KCRW took out a full pager to congratulate Arianna Huffington—a commentator on the NPR station's *Left, Right & Center* program with Robert Scheer—for winning the Upton Sinclair Award. Creative Artists Agency saluted *Vagina Monologues* playwright Eve Ensler with another full-page ad for winning the Creative Vision Award. Rhino Records took out a two page psychedelic-looking ad to honor all the award recipients, including community activist Reverend Eugene Williams and Taco Bell philanthropist Rob McKay, who is on the board of *Mother Jones*. The program also listed donors and supporters.

The Beverly Hills dinner included readings of Ensler's work by writer and former Sandinista Gioconda Belli and actresses such as Julia

Ormond, who starred in 1995's *Sabrina* opposite Harrison Ford, and Lisa Gay Hamilton, who directed "Beah: A Black Woman Speaks." Ensler and the thespians highlighted "V-Day," which focuses on ending violence against women, and is supported by Jane Fonda and financial guru Suze Orman. Hamilton presented the award to Ensler. Clips of Arianna Huffington's TV appearances were screened, and Bill Maher—who has said that Arianna is his favorite guest—presented her award.

Liberty Hill's net assets at the beginning of 2002 were $5,176,989. The total amount it gave for 403 grants was $3.3 million, and 2,000 people attended Foundation events in 2002. Ticket prices for the 2003 dinner ranged from $275 to $500, and sponsorship packages of up to $25,000 were offered. 800 people attended the Annual Upton Sinclair Dinner, which netted $215,000.

According to Barbara Osborn, who handles media and research for the Foundation: "The Upton Sinclair dinner represents a significant and important portion of Liberty Hill's unrestricted dollars (nearly 20% this last year). Unrestricted money is money that hasn't been earmarked for specific programs which enables us to put it into one of the grants funds or into the new voter registration/mobilization campaign, LibertyVote!, wherever we think it's most needed. It's also—and not insignificantly—a way we introduce lots of new folks to Liberty Hill and build community for our supporters," said Osborn, who also hosts KPFK's *Deadline L.A.* program.

SCADA

"Do what you feel in your heart to be right—for you'll be criticized anyway. You'll be damned if you do, and damned if you don't."

— Eleanor Roosevelt

New Deal liberals such as Eleanor Roosevelt, Walter Reuther, John Kenneth Galbraith and Hubert Humphrey founded Americans for Democratic Action in 1947. My father belonged to this group that is dedicated to civil liberties and democratic principles, as enshrined in the U.S. Constitution and the U.N.'s Universal Declaration of Human Rights. The Washington-headquartered ADA claims to have 30,000 members and 20 chapters nationwide, of which its Southern California branch, or SCADA, claims to be the largest and most active. According to its website, SCADA's "main

Jane Fonda shares a table with Michael Moore at the March 20, 2003 Southern California Americans for Democratic Action's 20th Annual Eleanor Roosevelt Awards Dinner.

activities consist of participating in marches and rallies for liberal causes; interviewing, endorsing and contributing to progressive candidates for public office; holding educational forums on topical issues and hosting politically-relevant theater events."

SCADA's annual budget is $125,000, which is raised in part by annual membership dues ranging from $20 to $100. The other source of SCADA's funds is the annual Eleanor Roosevelt Awards Dinner. Warren Beatty made national news there in 2000 with his visionary speech; Huffington made much hay out of this and briefly ballyhooed Beatty as a left-leaning alternative to Al Gore during the presidential race. On March 20, 2003, as war broke out and the Oscar ceremony loomed, hundreds attended the annual dinner at the Beverly Hilton. Nearby, antiwar demonstrators tensely faced off against LAPD. Some, such as activist and KPFK producer Lisa Smithline, then joined the dinner already in progress, which was full of anti-Bush outrage.

After being presented with the Eleanor Roosevelt Civil Rights Award, civil rights attorney Connie Rice blasted the regime of her cousin, Condoleezza Rice. Michael Moore was awarded the Eleanor Roosevelt Freedom of Speech Award, and his fiery antiwar acceptance speech presaged the Oscar address he'd give on live TV just a few nights later. Rhino Records' Richard Foos won the Eleanor Roosevelt Humanitarian Award, while Tom Hayden accepted the Eleanor Roosevelt Peace Award. In his speech, Hayden kept invoking the spirit of the woman who was America's First Lady during the Great Depression, New Deal, World War II and is

SCADA's patron saint. Moore sat at the same table as Hayden and his ex-wife, buckskin jacket-clad Jane Fonda.

On October 1, 2004, SCADA sponsored a "Big Bad Bash Bush Bash" at a private home in Santa Monica. The cocktail party honored the authors of the following day's "Democracy & Truth, Regime Change 2004—Conference and Book Fair" at the L.A. Convention Center. Participating authors included Larry Flynt signing *Sex, Lies & Politics: The Naked Truth*, Kristina Borjesson, editor of *Into the Buzzsaw*, Nancy Snow, author of *Information War* and Jimmy Walter of the Walden Three environmental think tank, who demanded the reopening of the investigation into 9/11. The guerrilla theater troupe Billionaires for Bush performed, and moderators included actress Mimi Kennedy.

NLG-LA

"First thing we do, is kill all the lawyers."

— "Dick the Butcher" in *Henry VI, Part 2*, Act IV: Scene II

According to Hollywood agent provocateur Paul Alan Smith, "The National Lawyers Guild has been on the frontlines of the fight for justice ever since President Roosevelt called for its formation in 1937. It was the first racially integrated bar association; the first to defend FDR's 'New Deal' programs in the courts; the first and only bar association to defend people called before HUAC, including the 'Hollywood Ten'; the first bar group to send lawyers into the South in the '60s to defend the civil rights movement; and the first bar group to speak out against the war in Vietnam and set up military law counseling centers for G.I.s protesting the war," said Smith, who emceed the annual award dinner of the Guild's L.A. chapter.

The dinners have taken place at a downtown L.A. hotel, and in typical fashion, in 2004 speakers at the NLG event blasted the hotel for poor labor practices, and the head of the hotel workers' union addressed the hundreds of guests about contract negotiations and a possible strike and lockout. In 2003, Arianna Huffington (who, like Tom Joad, appears to be "all around in the dark" in L.A.'s left-leaning social circuit) presented Greenwald with his award. The Guild also honored Bonnie Garvin, who had written and produced Showtime's 2001 Attica prison

The Institute for Public Accuracy's Executive Director Norman Solomon, who accompanied Sean Penn to Baghdad in December 2002, at a 2002 Beverly Hills *soirée* presented by agent Paul Alan Smith.

rebellion drama "The Killing Yard," directed by Euzhan Palcy. In the TV movie, Alan Alda portrays one of the Guild's founders, Ernie Goodman, who defends one of the Attica uprising's black political prisoners, Shango (Morris Chestnut). "The Killing Yard" was the first progressive fiction film released after 9/11. In addition, the legal eagles Hugh Manes (who had defended victims of McCarthyism) and Carol Watson, an implacable foe of prison guard and police misconduct NLG, were honored at the awards dinner Smith emceed.

The directors' agent was also the master of ceremonies for the 2004 NLG awards dinner, where he delivered a withering attack on TV programming, noting how many of the new season's series were cop shows. Smith blasted the new programs for being completely out of touch with reality. Guerrilla artist *extraordinaire* Robbie Conal—who openly sold his work at the function, but is well known for surreptitiously (and illegally) plastering political posters on walls and lampposts around L.A.—was presented with his award by Dan Castellaneta, the actor who gives voice to Homer and other characters on "The Simpsons." Longtime activist Preston Wood, who is currently with the leading antiwar group International A.N.S.W.E.R. (Act Now to Stop War and End Racism) was presented with his award by A.N.S.W.E.R.'s and the International Action Center's Brian Becker (in lieu of an ailing Ramsey Clark, the former U.S. Attorney General who now heads the I.A.C.).

According to Smith, the annual budget of NLG's L.A. chapter is $100,000. Ticket prices for the yearly awards dinners range from $85 each up to tables for $1250 each. Ads in the dinner journal ranged from $35 to $1000 for a full page. The annual gatherings help fund the Guild and its activities, which includes providing legal watchdogs at demos to keep tabs on police abuse of power and to ensure protesters' constitutional rights. Jim Lafferty, who hosts KPFK's "The Lawyers Guild Show" and is the executive director and one-man staff of the NLG's L.A. chapter, also spoke at the awards dinner.

KPFK

"In radio broadcasting operations to engage in any activity that shall contribute to a lasting understanding between nations and between the individuals of all nations, races, creeds and colors; to gather and disseminate information on the causes of conflict between any and all of such groups; and through any and all means compatible with the purposes of this corporation to promote the study of political and economic problems and of the causes of religious, philosophical and racial antagonisms."

— From the Pacifica Radio Foundation's Mission Statement

KPFK 90.7 FM is the L.A. affiliate of Pacifica Radio, the nationwide listener-sponsored, community-oriented, left-leaning network that preceded Air America on the air by more than a half century. National Pacifica programs such as the Manhattan-based "Democracy Now" and local L.A. shows such as Ian Masters' *Background Briefing* present info and analysis one would be hard pressed to find elsewhere on the radio dial. Since it is listener sponsored, KPFK does not rely on government and corporate grants, but rather on direct public support.

Periodic pledge and membership drives, along with other fundraisers, keep the Pacifica stations on the air. These often involve collaborations between the affiliates and left-tilting talents, authors in particular. A case in point is Texas writer and populist Jim Hightower, whose homespun yet subversive commentaries are regularly broadcast by KPFK. According to general manager Eva Georgia, "When Jim's new book came out, we decided to ask him to do a fundraiser... This is actually three fundraisers we did with Jim in two days, which were very successful. We had him last year for his book [*Thieves in High Places: They've Stolen Our Country— And It's Time to Take It Back*]."

When Hightower's next book, *Let's Stop Beating Around the Bush*, came out, the Texan's book tour took him to events in areas reached by KPFK's signal—Long Beach, Santa Barbara and, of course, the City of the Angels. The former Texas agricultural commissioner spoke there on August 23, 2004, at the Immanuel Presbyterian Church, a gathering place for activists. All of the SoCal events were heavily promoted by KPFK.

"The great thing about Jim is, the bigger and more successful he gets, the more supportive he is of independent, progressive media," said Georgia. "He's part of the KPFK family, always available to do interviews and commentaries on what's happening... I think he's stronger in L.A. He's much more involved with KPFK, even though he does do events for the other Pacifica stations... People want to know if their votes will count. A lot of the questions on this tour have been about the elections. So he's speaking out a lot about the elections."

In addition to in-person events, authors appear on the air during fund drives as guests and their books are offered as premiums to entice listeners into making pledges to and becoming members of the listener sponsored station. "We get a publisher's discount," Georgia stated. "Sometimes we pay a third of the book. So we get a huge discount. We also get all the authors we work with, they give us free copies. And they'll do the interviews, events and tours for us. So we get a lot from independent authors, progressive people like Jim Hightower," the KPFK general manager said.

It's a symbiotic relationship that benefits both writers—who sell books and get free airtime—and KPFK, which receives prestigious content and products that assist with the fund drive. And this helps L.A.'s Pacifica affiliate to continue challenging the status quo with an alternative voice.

FREE LEONARD!

As has been mentioned, some of the fundraisers raised money by auctioning and selling art. From August 1-2, 2003, progressive Hollywood got behind an art exhibit of Leonard Peltier's painting, in order to generate cash for America's number one political prisoner. Following the 1973 "domestic insurrection" at Wounded Knee, South Dakota, a battle pitting traditionalists against Indian collaborators and the F.B.I. took place at the Pine Ridge Indian Reservation. Peltier was convicted in connection to the June 26, 1975 shooting of F.B.I. agents Jack Coler and Ron Williams during the shootout at Pine Ridge (a Native American, Joe Stuntz, also died). Three other Indians were acquitted.

The case is too complicated to go into here, but suffice it to say there are dubious irregularities in the government's case against Peltier. Myrtle Poor Bear's statement to the F.B.I. led to Peltier's extradition from Canada (where he'd fled to, presciently fearing he couldn't get a fair trial in America). But, despite her subsequent recantation, Poor Bear wasn't allowed to testify in court. Nor did the jury hear that a ballistics test proved the fatal shots were not fired from Leonard's rifle. The shootout, et al, took place during the height of the F.B.I.'s COINTELPRO dirty tricks campaign that targeted minority rights groups such as the American Indian Movement and Black Panthers.[14]

For the past 30 years, the Anishinabe and Lakota Peltier, whom Amnesty International calls "a political prisoner," have arguably been the F.B.I.'s enemy number one. Debra Peebles, of the Red Lake Band of Chippewa, is the coordinator of the Lawrence, Kansas-based Leonard Peltier Defense Committee, an international movement with a 10-person legal team. Growing up in North Dakota and Minneapolis, Peebles and Leonard had mutual friends, and in the early '90s her work as spiritual adviser to the 100 or so Indians incarcerated at Leavenworth Prison led her to Peltier. Peebles says that Peltier is forced to work in a prison factory for slave wages, and has had numerous health problems, including diabetes, brought on by an extremely poor penal diet.

Barring major new evidence, by 2003 Peltier's appellate process had been largely exhausted. Through the Freedom of Information Act, LPDC is seeking release of classified documents that could contain evidence leading to the reopening of the case. (One reason for the art exhibition was to raise money for software and experts to help wade through these voluminous records.)

Peebles said Clinton leaned towards granting Peltier clemency, but backed down after threats from the Justice Department. Except for an unlikely presidential pardon, parole is the next best bet for Leonard's liberty. "The parole board violated his due process," contended Peebles.

The fundraising exhibit at Santa Monica's Frumkin Gallery to support the free Leonard cause was the idea of Greenwald. The producer/director visited Leonard behind bars in May 2003, as he is interested in doing a docudrama about the case. Although Greenwald said the Frumkin volunteered its space for the show and waived commissions, the 6:00 p.m., August 1 invitational ceremony, at which Leonard's grandson Cyrus spoke, sought $100 contributions. But during the day on August 1 and

---

14. For details of Peltier's case, see *Incident at Oglala,* a 1992 documentary produced and narrated by Robert Redford. Its director, Michael Apted, likewise helmed the 1992 feature *Thunderheart,* a loose fictionalization suggested by some of these events that starred Val Kilmer and Graham Greene.

2, admission was free of charge. Peltier's oils and acrylics sold for up to $8,000; his lithographs went for $100 each. Guerrilla artist Robbie Conal collaborated with singer Graham Nash, who owns a high quality giclee printer, to render limited edition prints of an indigenous elder for sale at the exhibition.

"Painting is creatively and practically very important to him," said Greenwald, who collects Peltier's Indian-themed pictures. "They're very striking and soulful, with a very strong use of color and a really commanding presence. You see the talent, passion and dignity."

Other members of the exhibit's host committee include *Smoke Signals* director Chris Eyre, Robbie Robertson, Jackson Browne, Redford, Bonnie Raitt, DreamWorks' Andy Spahn and Alcatraz-occupation veteran Jane Fonda.

According to the largely self-taught Peltier, who received carving and drawing lessons from tribal elders during his childhood: "Painting is a way to examine the world in ways denied me by the U.S. Justice System, a way to travel beyond the walls and bars of the penitentiary. Through my paints I can be with my people, in touch with my culture, tradition and spirit. I can watch little children in regalia, dancing and smiling, see my elders in prayer, behold the intense glow of a warrior's eye. As I work the canvas I am a free man," related the man some call the American Nelson Mandela.

The exhibit was called "The Warrior's Eye—In the Spirit of Crazy Horse." According to Greenwald, the fundraiser was very successful, selling numerous works and raising money for Leonard's legal defense, healthcare and family. Hopefully Leonard Peltier won't have to bury his art at Leavenworth.

ACT 4

===

THE RETURN OF

PROGRESSIVE CONTENT

"Once more unto the breach, dear friends, once more...
In peace there's nothing so becomes a man
As modest stillness and humility;
But when the blast of war blows in our ears,
Then imitate the action of the tiger:
Stiffen the sinews, summon up the blood."

— *King Henry V*, Act III: Scene 1

INTO THE ABYSS

"Do you think that ABC and the other networks should apologize
for providing an uncritical forum for the administration to lay out
their unsubstantiated claims of weapons of mass destruction?"

— Amy Goodman to Ted Koppel, on "Democracy Now," July 29, 2004

Since 9/11, and especially since the invasion of Iraq, in that hallowed Tinseltown tradition of the sequel, progressive Hollywood has returned, off—and most importantly—onscreen.

This book's prologue showed how Hollywood progressives filled a vacuum in 2002 that was created when the opposition party failed to oppose—and in many cases actually supported—Bush's drive towards war in Iraq. Producer/director Robert Greenwald, actor Mike Farrell and other artists galvanized and spearheaded the resistance in the streets to Bush's invasion of Iraq and became the public face and voice of the anti-war movement. In a similar way, when the corporate-owned, mainstream media likewise abdicated its responsibility to report the facts, truth-telling fell upon the shoulders of progressive Hollywood.

For the Hollywood left, when it came to most TV, radio and print reportage on Iraq, it was another case of "Once more unto the breach, dear friends!" The second phase of the return of progressive Hollywood was to do the same exact thing it accomplished in the political arena in the arena the talents know best: skillful communication of stories, emotions and ideas. And they did so for the exact same reason that left-coasters had marched in the streets.

Whereas before artists had mainly appeared in front of the cameras to duke it out with the Sean Hannitys and Bill O'Reillys, now many talents got behind the cameras as directors, producers, writers, etc., to create the counter-narrative to the Bush Big Lie Machine and its corporate news collaborators. The creators of *Bush's Brain* stated on Pacifica's Blase Bonpane-hosted "World Focus" that they "filled a void" and probably would not have made their Karl Rove exposé if mainstream media reporters did their jobs.

With most journalists abdicating their roles as fourth estate watchdogs—and worse, even colluding with the Bush administration and their Iraq and 9/11 lies—including the venerable *Washington Post* and *New York Times*, once again Hollywood progressives had to step up to the plate abandoned by most newsmen, perform the roles and functions theoretically left to reporters. In doing so, it was "batter up!" for progressive Hollywood—and it came out swinging.

In *Fahrenheit 9/11*, Bush might commit one of his innumerable verbal gaffes and stumble over the homily, "Fool me once, shame on you. Fool me twice, shame on you." Similarly, the Great Emancipator was right: "You can fool some of the people all of the time, and all of the people some of the time, but you can't fool all of the people all of the time." This remains so in our own troubled time, as more people refuse to be fooled by Bush & Co. But unlike the '70s generation, today's Woodwards and Bernsteins are only rarely found in mainstream news media. The investigative reporting Woodward and Bernstein pioneered in the *Washington Post* that led to the so-called "gotcha journalism" and "adversarial relationship" between the press and government is no longer found in the pages of corporate-owned dailies or on broadcast/cable TV and radio.

For example, instead of the "liberal" *New York Times* carrying out the tough investigative reporting and asking the administration the hard questions about Iraq's alleged WMDs in the lead-up to war, the *Times* ballyhooed bald-faced lies as if they were the gospel truth. What's the source of this?

The *Times'* own confession (relatively brief—in comparison to the *Times'* preceding Jayson Blair and Rick Bragg *mea culpas*—buried inside the *Times* on page A10). According to the *Times'* May 26, 2004 "editorial note":

> [W]e have found a number of instances of coverage that was not as rigorous as it should have been. In some cases, information that was controversial then, and seems questionable now, was insufficiently qualified or allowed to stand unchallenged. Looking back, we wish we had been more aggressive in re-examining the claims...
>
> The problematic articles varied in authorship and subject matter, but many shared a common feature. They depended at least in part on information from a circle of Iraqi informants, defectors and exiles bent on 'regime change' in Iraq, people whose credibility has come under increasing public debate in recent weeks.
>
> Administration officials now acknowledge that they sometimes fell for misinformation from these exile sources. So did many news organizations—in particular, this one.
>
> Some critics of our coverage during that time have focused blame on individual reporters. Our examination, however, indicates that the problem was more complicated. Editors at several levels who should have been challenging reporters and pressing for more skepticism were perhaps too intent on rushing scoops into the paper.

And perhaps too anxious to push a pro-war agenda. As appears to be the case of Judith Miller, who wasn't fired (unlike CBS management fired January 10, 2005 due to the "60 Minutes II" brouhaha about Bush's avoidance of Vietnam service, which didn't cost any lives). The *Times* report went on to cite examples of its egregiously inaccurate misinformation and disinformation, such as the bogus aluminum tubes/nuclear bomb lie, that arguably caused massive loss of lives.

On August 8, 2004, the *Times* website published the following *AP* report about a source journalism's "Old Gray Lady" named in its *apologia*: "Iraq has issued arrest warrants for Ahmad Chalabi... on counterfeiting charges, and for his nephew Salem Chalabi—head of the tribunal trying Saddam..."

As Steve Martin used to say: "Well, excuuuuse me!" 1,500-plus dead Americans, 20,000-plus U.S. casualties, 100,000 estimated Iraqi civilians dead—and on January 12, 2005, the official hunt for WMDs end, without one found. Nor did a single head roll at the *Times* for helping mislead a nation into war. Unlike in the wake of the Blair and Bragg scandals—which involved the non-lethal offenses of plagiarism and improper attribution of credits, led to reporters being the fired, and the June 2003 resignations of the executive and managing editors.

On August 12, 2004, the *Washington Post* ran a similar recantation of its Iraq disinformation campaign. Bob Woodward, the onetime Tricky Dick toppler, confessed: "We did our job but we didn't do enough, and I blame myself mightily for not pushing harder. We should have warned readers we had information that the basis for this was shakier than widely believed. Those are exactly the kind of statements that should be published on the front page."

If the "liberal" *Times* and *Post* got it so wrong, then it comes as no surprise that a conservative cable news channel apparently set up to ballyhoo the official Republican Party line and Bush played cheerleader for warfare. According to Fairness and Accuracy In Reporting's May/June 2003 *Extra!* from March 20-April 9, 2003: "Eighty-one percent of Fox's ["Special Report With Brit Hume"] sources were pro-war... the highest of any network."

Much of the mainstream media didn't fare too well, either, as FAIR surveyed "ABC World News Tonight," "CBS Evening News," "NBC Nightly News," CNN "Wolf Blitzer Reports," PBS "NewsHour With Jim Lehrer," as well as Fox's "Special Report With Brit Hume" and found: "Nearly two thirds of all sources, 64 percent, were pro-war, while 71 percent of U.S. guests favored the war. Antiwar voices were 10 percent of all sources, but just 6 percent of non-Iraqi sources and 3 percent of U.S. sources. Thus viewers were more than six times as likely to see a pro-war source as one who was antiwar; with U.S. guests alone, the ratio increases to 25 to 1."

On July 29, 2004, "Democracy Now" broadcast an interview from the Democratic Convention with ABC's "Nightline" anchor Ted Koppel. Amy Goodman asked Koppel: "Do you think that ABC and the other networks should apologize for providing an uncritical forum for the administration to lay out their unsubstantiated claims of weapons of mass destruction?" Koppel laughed and replied: "I'm glad you phrased your question so nicely. No, I don't think an apology is due. If what you are saying is, could we all have been more critical, I think the answer is yes." Goodman added, "at a time when about half the population was opposed to the invasion, wanting more inspections and diplomacy... In a study of the two weeks around Colin Powell giving his address at the UN, for war, [FAIR] looked at the four major nightly newscasts, ABC, NBC, CBS and the PBS 'NewsHour with Jim Lehrer.' Of the 393 interviews done around war, only three were with anti-war representatives." In other words, during this period, according to the FAIR report, less than 1% of interviewees represented the peace perspective.

Today we're almost experiencing the reverse of the 1970s reportorial process. If Bob Woodward and Carl Bernstein were breaking the Watergate break-in and cover-up during the Bush era, it would first become a book or movie, and then be reported in a major daily.

BBC investigative reporter Greg Palast excoriates the corporate press. "In America, the media stopped reporting; it's just repeating... I do investigative reporting—something that is, I believe, against the PATRIOT Act... The market's been created by mainstream media's self-censorship. The *New York Times, Washington Post* and *L.A. Times* are becoming the new red, white and blue *Izvestia* and *Pravda*. It's the official word, repackaged. Therefore, people are really hungry for real information," the author of *The Best Democracy Money Can Buy* insisted.

In *Embedded: Weapons of Mass Deception, How the Media Failed to Cover the War on Iraq*, "news dissector" Danny Schechter commented on the reporters who were in bed with the Defense Department as part of "the campaign that involved co-opting and orchestrating the news media. The most visible center of this strategy was the effort to embed reporters whose work was subsidized by the Pentagon, overseen by 'public affairs' specialists and linked to TV news networks dominated by military experts approved by the Pentagon... The Project on Excellence in Journalism studied the early coverage and found that half the embedded journalists showed combat action but not a single story depicted people hit by weapons. There were no reporters embedded with Iraqi families. None stationed with humanitarian agencies or the antiwar groups... [T]he embedded reporters' work prompted former Pentagon press chief Kenneth Bacon to tell the *Wall Street Journal:* 'They couldn't hire actors to do as good a job as they have done for the military.'"

At a December 2, 2004 Writers Bloc event in L.A. with Michael Moore and John Dean, Dean complained that Woodward, who'd helped topple Nixon, had degenerated into a "stenographer" for Bush. "Where are the Woodwards and Bernsteins today?" Nixon's ex-White House counsel asked.

Moore said Katie Couric confessed off the air that "You're so right, we don't do our job. There was an administration memo [regarding Cheney on 'Today'] that they did not like Katie's tone of voice. There's Fox News, and Ann Coulter calling me 'Eva Braun.'" Moore didn't buy the multi-millionaire "journalist's" fears, contending: "The First Amendment [stipulates] democracy can not survive unless the people are informed. We've got 1300 American kids dead because you didn't ask the tough questions." If nothing else, *Fahrenheit 9/11* asks the tough questions that make administration apologists squirm.

Why is so much mainstream media so complacent? In his book *Big Lies: The Right-Wing Propaganda Machine and How It Distorts the Truth,* Joe Conason theorizes that the "docile press" doesn't expose Bush's patrician pedigree (among other things) because right-wing "Complaining constantly about [liberal media] bias serves to intimidate journalists, enforce demands for favorable coverage and privileged access and, ultimately, to maintain the overpowering influence conservatives now enjoy." Economist Paul Krugman notes in *The Great Unraveling: Losing Our Way in the New Century* that "Fox News, the *Washington Times*, the *New York Post*... harass other media outlets" that report scandals of a White House that "doesn't accept the right of others to criticize its actions... [T]hose who question... the administration are demonized, their ethics questioned, their careers destroyed..."

The Dan Rather drama is an example. On the BBC "Newsnight," the then-CBS news anchor said "journalists... asking the toughest of the tough questions" faced being "necklaced" with "a flaming tire of lack of patriotism." No rightist rage was aimed at the "CBS Evening News" managing editor when Rather emotionally declared his fealty shortly after 9/11 on CBS "Late Show With David Letterman": "George Bush is the president. He makes the decisions and... wherever he wants me to line up, just tell me where. And he'll make the call." On October 2, 2001, Rather told "Entertainment Tonight": "If he needs me in uniform, tell me when and where—I'm there." However, the necklacing began after a September 8, 2004 "60 Minutes II" segment criticizing Bush's Air National Guard service, that resulted in Rather leaving the anchor's chair and the departure of four CBS executives (see below).

On the July 30, 2004 "Real Time With Bill Maher," referring to previously unseen footage of Bush sitting in a classroom after being informed America was under attack that is revealed in *Fahrenheit 9/11*, Moore said: "The national media didn't air it that way... You never saw the seven minutes... Because they don't want our leader to look like a deer in the headlights." On December 2, 2004, Moore said a phone call to the school and $5 produced a home video of Bush cooling his heels in the schoolroom.

Greenwald echoed the sentiment: "The primary media is not giving us information to help us make those critical decisions. So people are searching for other ways to get the information: Internet, books and film are all viable ways to get points of view and perspectives in depth, that we don't get in the 30 second sound byte. Politics aside, right or left aside, just wanting the information, to try to be an informed citizen or somebody to make up their mind about how do you deal with this."

CRITICAL MASS AUDIENCES AWAKENED

Never before has America's news media been so omnipresent, possessed such whiz bang gadgetry or had such reach, including 24/7 cable news channels. It outstrips Goebbels' vision. And never has the so-called corporate-owned "news" media so abdicated its role and flagrantly violated the public trust aspect of journalism.

When the corporate-owned news media has bloodstained hands and not only fails to do its job, but actually *disinforms* the public, viewers/listeners/readers do not simply give up. The people search elsewhere for truth tellers. Inquiring minds *still* want to know. If the corporate press is the fourth estate, now that so much of it is in cahoots with the Bush administration (as networks and publishers have pressing business before Congress and Secretary of State Colin Powell's son Michael is Federal Communications Commission's Chairman), dissident filmmakers—along with progressive authors—have become the Fifth Estate.

The June 18, 2004 *St. Petersburg Times* article "Controversy is no longer box-office poison," noted that the controversial *The Last Temptation of Christ, Priest, Dogma* and the NC-17-rated *Showgirls* were all box office flops. However, Steve Persall adds: "In 2004, things are different. Perhaps a presidential election in wartime has whetted our appetite for contentious material... [M]oviegoers are seeking out films that somebody is warning them to avoid, films dealing with issues that historically have split opinions down the middle or into splinters. Religion, politics, nutrition and environmentalism sound like topics for Sunday morning television, not megaplexes. Moviegoers are proving that assumption wrong."

Robert Greenwald contends critical films have found critical mass audiences because this is a matter of the historical moment. "*Fahrenheit 9/11* is a terrific movie... The fact that it's a documentary, and the documentaries I have done have found an audience, are related to... that we're at a time of huge political import where politics are personal because it affects whether somebody's going to die, whether somebody's going to go to war. Friends, relatives... That takes it out of the abstract. That makes it deeply... jobs, healthcare, education. So politics are not really something you debate in an academic sense in the period of time we're living in now."

The producer/director adds, "Suddenly, we can say, with Michael's movie—I mean, Michael has walked the walk and talked the talk his whole life—so he's not suddenly getting religion, as it were. But certainly, with a $[2]00 million[-plus] documentary about the Bush administration and the war, you could have asked every expert in the world six months ago, and they would have said 'You were crazy.' So clearly, however you characterize it, it's a huge upset and an enormous surprise. I'd say that with the '*Un*' films and *Outfoxed*, had you asked me or any of the people connected with them six months ago, nine months and would you have said all of these sales would have happened, and all of these awards... I would have said, 'nice pipe dream.' So clearly, there's an audience. Clearly there are some films that have gotten made," Greenwald noted.

The most astonishing, hopeful thing about the new wave of progressive Hollywood isn't that the films are getting made. As remarkable as *Fahrenheit 9/11* is, the most incredible, mind blowing thing about it is that—not unlike 1969's sleeper *Easy Rider*—a $6 million dollar movie has earned back $200 million-plus more than its production costs. *Fahrenheit 9/11* was number one at the box office the weekend it opened, earning $23.9 million in 868 theaters, beating out the Wayan Brothers' comedy *White Chicks* with $19.7 million at 2,726 theaters. *9/11* became the first documentary ever to rank in the weekend top five, and it more than doubled the number of tickets sold for a Palme d'Or winner (*Pulp Fiction*). The doc averaged $27,558 per theater, the second highest receipts for a wide release, and the top per theater grosser of 2004, surpassing *The Passion of the Christ* (by $4) and *Shrek 2*.

Weeks later, instead of disappearing from the charts, it remained at number seven, continuing to make money. It held its own against the marketing onslaught of blockbusters such as *Spider-Man 2*. According to *Variety*, *Fahrenheit 9/11* was number ten during the weekend of August 6, earning back almost all of its original costs in just that weekend's take— $5,054,410—at 1,217 theaters across America. Its cumulative gross at that point—after less than six weeks on screens—was $111,388,019. Moore's audience even surpassed that of Rush Limbaugh. According to a University of Pennsylvania National Annenberg Election Survey, while 7% of those surveyed listened to Limbaugh, 8% had seen *Fahrenheit 9/11*.

In *Fahrenheit 9/11*, Moore brilliantly distills the essence of the criticisms of the Bush dynasty and regime that have flowered in the many Bush-bashing books and reportage by investigators like Palast and Hatfield. He does so with great wit, cinematic skill and a bigger budget than other docs. *Fahrenheit 9/11* is the pinnacle and crème de la crème of the tidal wave of dissident documentaries. Moore is the 21st century American equivalent of the 1920s' Soviet documentarian Dziga Vertov, director of *The Man With the Movie Camera*.

Moore's decision to remove *9/11* from consideration for the Best Documentary Oscar may have backfired—the Flynt filmmaker went for broke, and sought a Best Picture nod instead; in the end, the incendiary documentary didn't receive any Academy Award nominations. However, in January 2005 *Fahrenheit 9/11* won the People's Choice Awards (voted for by film fans, not members of the Academy) for Best Picture, with more than 23 million moviegoers casting ballots for the awards.

In his opening monologue of the 2005 Oscar ceremony, host Chris Rock said: "One of my favorite movies this year was *Fahrenheit 9/11*. [It] was beautiful. I think Bush is a genius. Could you imagine applying for a job, and while you're applying for that job there's a movie in every theater in the country that shows how much you suck at that job?"

Like Lindsay Anderson's 1969 *If...*, *9/11* won Cannes' prestigious top prize. This was the first time a documentary had taken this honor since Louis Malle and Jacques Cousteau's 1956 *The Silent World*.[15]

Greenwald's *Uncovered* and *Outfoxed* sold more than 100,000 DVDs and were highly ranked by Amazon.com, with *Outfoxed* quickly becoming that website's number one bestseller. Of course, the self-evident point is that what this all means is that today, there are mass audiences for progressive Hollywood's films.

As Joel Bakan, the author of *The Corporation: The Pathological Pursuit of Profit and Power*, and co-author of the film adaptation told *The Christian Science Monitor*: Bush "has done a service for political authors and nonfiction filmmakers... Popular culture is embracing politics in a way it

---

15. The last time an American left-wing film scored the Palme d'Or was in 1970—Robert Altman-Ring Lardner, Jr.'s *M*A*S*H*. In 2002, Moore's *Bowling for Columbine* won a 55th Anniversary of the Cannes Festival award.

hasn't since the 1960s... I remember that [a Marxist theoretician] used to talk about heightening the contradictions of capitalism. I think [Bush] has done a good job of that, and has created a market of critical people. They have a thirst for political stuff." Achbar added, "Dissident documentary-film culture... is kind of like Jell-O. The more you try to suppress it and push it down... the more it's gonna ooze out between your fingers. There's no stopping it. There's so little of this kind of analysis in the mainstream that when it does become available, people *pounce* on it!"

The Independent Film Channel's 2003 documentary *A Decade Under the Influence* emphasized the role American audiences played in 1970s cinema. Julie Christie said: "There was a different audience. There was a new audience, wasn't there? There was an audience that the studios didn't even know existed... politicized by Vietnam and Watergate. Whose consciousness had been changed with drugs—I think that's very important. And it was an open audience... It wanted to deal with difficult films, and to see difficult films and different films. And it didn't want the same old stuff—like nowadays. Where the same old stuff is repeated and repeated. And it wanted to be challenged and it wanted to be surprised."

As Paul Schrader, screenwriter of 1976's *Taxi Driver*, 1978's *Blue Collar* and 1988's *The Last Temptation of Christ* said about '70s audiences in the 2003 documentary: "If you're coming out of the drug revolution, and the sex revolution, and the civil rights revolution, you got a lot of attitude... And you've been taking on the military-industrial-complex [and] all kinds of religious structures... involved in all kinds of protests. And so you have those tools, and... self-confidence, just to be saying, 'I know what we should be doing. I know what we should be doing about Vietnam. I know what we should be doing about women's rights. I know what we should be doing about motion pictures'... The film business was... a decadent, decaying, emptied whorehouse. And it had to be assaulted, you know. So you had that film student mentality, that—you know—'let's pick up the banner of Godard and walk in there and take it over!'" As Schrader waves a fist, *Decade Under* cuts to a montage of protests intercut with shots of European directors, such as Godard, and their work, as the Stones' militant anthem "Street Fighting Man" is heard.

Just as Vietnam and Watergate triggered the collapse of the public's faith in the government, the nonstop dissembling and lies of the Bush cabinet have led to a similar crisis in credibility. From Bush's first cousin John Ellis calling the contested Florida election for him on Fox News to the fabrications of WMDs in Iraq to the absurd May Day 2003 aircraft carrier "Mission Accomplished" stunt to the Halliburton, etc., no-bid contracts to the July 2, 2003 "Bring 'em on" lunacy to an out-of-control Iraqi insurgency that brought on 1,500-plus American deaths, an increasing percentage of the audience no longer willingly suspends its disbelief. Unable, unwilling to take responsibility for any blunder, in April 2003 Bush repeatedly refused to admit any mistakes at a rare press conference. Unlike President Harry S. Truman, Bush's presidential slogan could be: "The buck stops—uh—there."

In addition to movies, audiences failed by the corporate news media are turning to other outlets, such as the Internet and books. According to "Air America" host Al Franken, Bush-bashing books have become national bestsellers "because of tremendous disillusionment with this guy, and anger. Because after 9/11... there was a united country. He had an opportunity to lead... in the spirit of mutual purpose and sacrifice and didn't. Instead, he used 9/11 for political purposes, and to do things... neocons wanted. They made the decision to go into Iraq long before they said they did... Because they acted so unilaterally, our soldiers and this country are paying the price... Bush has no ideas economically. He's not asked people at the top—we're at war!—to share the burdens at all. All he's done is given them bigger and bigger tax cuts every year. We're looking at gaping deficits out into the future... It's very frightening... he's... the first president since Hoover to create no new jobs... We have a president who doesn't care anything about... policy, and has no ideas. If he comes out to do a little dog and pony show about some new policy, you know it's doomed. 'No Child Left Behind' is the most ironically named legislation since the 1942 'Japanese Family Leave Act'... Single moms are losing... Medicaid coverage for their kids... states are growing broke. People are hurting because of him," the humorist lamented.

In an interview, Texas populist Jim Hightower described the demographics of the new public: "Estimate that the audience includes at least everyone who voted for Gore and Nader, plus a percentage of disgruntled former Bush supporters, plus a substantial percentage of alienated American voters (the 65% of Americans who didn't vote in the 2002 mid-term election), plus a percentage of international readers alarmed at the turn American foreign policy has taken—how do you put a number on that? 200 million people?" said the author of *Let's Stop Beating Around the Bush*.

Mass audiences thirst for the truth. When Franken appeared October 22, 2003 at a CalTech reading of *Lies and the Lying Liars Who Tell Them: A*

Al Franken at a mobbed reading at CalTech.

Fair and Balanced Look at the Right, he packed Beckman Auditorium's 1200 seats. Hundreds more listened outside as the satirist-in-chief skewered pompous pundits, politicians and plaintiffs with his scathing wit—and sold hundreds of copies of his latest book. Franken's *Lies* beat out his nemesis O'Reilly's tome (which Franken quipped is about herpes), and was number one on the *N.Y. Times* bestseller list. Asked if there's a big market for Bush-bashing books, Franken replied: "Yes, obviously. Michael Moore's *Dude, Where's My Country?* [was] number one."

Bush-bashing books are big business, as readers propel hardcovers and paperbacks criticizing the president onto bestseller lists—where they consistently outsell right-wing scribblers. At a January 12, 2004 reading of Kevin Phillips' *American Dynasty* at Vroman's Bookstore in Pasadena before a 200-plus standing room-only crowd, all 120 copies sold out. *Dynasty* debuted as number five on January 18's *N.Y. Times'* nonfiction hardcover besteller list, following O'Reilly's *Who's Looking Out for You?.* The Fox News/talk radio host trailed his gadfly, Franken, at number three, and Michael Moore's *Dude* at number two, and then found itself in the coveted number one spot.

N.Y. Times columnist Krugman decries the "world class mendacity [and] outrageous dishonesty of the Bush administration" in his bestseller. Dishonesty is a recurring theme in Bush trashing tomes. "George W. Bush is a liar" is the lead sentence in *The Lies of George W. Bush: Mastering the Politics of Deception,* by David Corn, the *Nation's* Washington editor. Kevin Phillips' *American Dynasty* is subtitled *Aristocracy, Fortune and the Politics of Deceit in the House of Bush.* Shrub appears on the cover of Al Franken's number one bestseller *Lies and the Lying Liars Who Tell Them*. *New York Observer*'s national correspondent Conason denounces Bush administration "lies and hypocrisy" in *Big Lies*. Danny Schechter alleges the administration manipulated war news in *Embedded: Weapons of Mass Deception, How the Media Failed To Cover the War on Iraq*. Christopher and Robert Scheer and Lakshmi Chaudhry question the rationales for war itself in *The Five Biggest Lies Bush Told Us About Iraq*, contending: "Lying was at the core of a deliberate method of marketing a war they must not have believed we'd support if they told us the truth." Paul Waldman's exposé is called *Fraud: The Strategy Behind the Bush Lies and Why the Media Didn't Tell You*. Eric Alterman and Mark Green's *The Book on Bush* is subtitled *How George W. (Mis)leads America*.

Stealing and other crimes form another leitmotif of anti-Bush books, such as Jim Hightower's *Thieves in High Places, They've Stolen Our Country—And It's Time To Take It Back* (which reached number nine on the *N.Y. Times* nonfiction bestseller list).

Also implying theft, Michael Moore's longtime number one bestseller, *Dude, Where's My Country?* refers to the missing car in a popular flick's title. A cartoon of Bush standing in front of a pile of money appears on the cover of Palast's *The Best Democracy Money Can Buy: The Truth About Corporate Cons, Globalization and High-Finance Fraudsters*.

WHAT'S UP, DOC?: A PERFECT DOCUMENTARY STORM AND THE NEW UNIVERSE

"You don't need to wait for the gatekeepers."

— Robert Greenwald, in an interview with the author

During progressive Hollywood's first two great periods, films falling through the cracks of the studio system managed to find their ways onto the silver screen. King Vidor's 1934 collective farm homage *Our Daily Bread*; Chaplin's 1936's class struggle classic *Modern Times* and 1940 antifascist masterpiece *The Great Dictator*; John Ford's 1940 dustbowl *piece de resistance*, *The Grapes of Wrath*; Orson Welles' 1941 *Citizen Kane*; Haskell Wexler's 1969 *Medium Cool*; and 1969's *Easy Rider*.

Today, some of the crucial elements and conditions that led to the creation of America's most humanitarian and politically committed movies have reemerged, generating the promise of a return of progressive Hollywood onscreen. New cracks have sprung up, and productions—particular-ly documentaries—are falling through these cracks in the studio system.

"Even Michael [Moore]'s didn't get made totally within the system, by the way," Greenwald said. "It was this kind of strange thing where Disney gave him the money, but the Weinsteins covered it... In my movies it was MoveOn, and the Center for American Progress, and the fact that I have editing equipment and offices I can throw in. So it's not like the studios, who are essentially the financiers of the system, are saying, 'Oh great, let's start making these.' That's not the case. But fortunately, these movies have been made, and to the degree that a few new movies are a trend or an opening, then sure"—progressive films are making a comeback.

I believe Sergei Eisenstein said "anyone can become a film director." Today, this democratic aesthetic ideal is closer to becoming a reality than ever.

Robert Greenwald, who spearheaded progressive Hollywood's peace movement offscreen, also pioneered its return onscreen. The co-founder of Artists United discovered a way of translating left-coasters' politics into films seen by mass audiences. As in his organizing, Greenwald went against the established grain of the MPAA, and its crusade against pira-cy. Having turned for the first time to full-length documentaries, Greenwald told audiences to feel free to make copies of his films and dis-tribute the docs themselves—without his receiving royalties, residuals, etc.—because he's passionate about getting anti-Bush messages out. (Ironically, Greenwald's 2000 biopic about Yippie Abbie Hoffman, starring Vincent D'Onofrio and Janeane Garofalo, is titled *Steal This Movie*.) Thus, it's consistent for Greenwald to reveal a new, 21st century way for mak-ing, financing and distributing productions—a process he's in the vanguard of, just as he is in progressive Hollywood's politics.

Today, documentarians are discovering new models of financing and distributing political nonfiction, the stuff that they usually had to suppli-cate studios, distributors and financiers for years in order to be allowed to make (if at all). And this new way of making documentaries is helping to usher in the new era of progressive Hollywood film culture.

In cinema's early days, filmmakers such as France's Lumiere Broth-ers, America's Thomas Edison, Robert Flaherty, Pare Lorentz, the U.S.S.R.'s Dziga Vertov, Britain's John Grierson, Holland's Joris Ivens, and others ushered in a golden age of nonfiction films. They depicted real peoples and places, as opposed to actors appearing in scripted dramas shot—more often than not—on studio sets and backlots, instead of in the city streets, the Great Plains, jungles and tundra. Over the years, there have been other great documentarians, from Edward R. Murrow to Emile de Antonio, etc. But today, documentaries are experiencing a second golden age and have arguably never had it better. According to an August 22, 2004 *Detroit Free Press* article: "Of the current Top 100 films, 19 are docs. According to the trade journal *Variety*, that's the highest number in history."

The headline of an October 3, 2004 *L.A. Times* article about Robert Altman and Garry Trudeau's Sundance Channel *Tanner on Tanner* series referred to "A docu-jungle out there," and referred to "The summer of political documentaries... [T]he world of documentary filmmaking... has become obsessed and entwined with politics as never before..." According to Altman, Moore "has breathed real life into the documentaries. They are no longer marginalized. For better or worse, he has made something people want to see."

A major reason for this documentary renaissance is the mushrooming of outlets for viewing nonfiction films, once confined to theaters and film society venues, and then network TV. In addition to a number of 24/7 all-news-oriented cable channels—CNN, MSNBC, CNBC, C-SPAN, Fox and their various variations (plus community-oriented cable access channels for live coverage of public affairs)—the expanded television universe offers many other avenues for airing docs. Nonfiction-based programming fills the History, Discovery, National Geographic, Travel, Animal Planet, Learning, A&E, Bravo, IFC and Sundance channels. The lattermost even offers "DocDay, documentaries all day, Mondays."

On PBS, "P.O.V.," "Frontline," "American Experience," "Wide Angle," "Independent Lens," "Nova" and sometimes the Bill Moyers-originated "Now" series, among others, have given filmmakers such as Ken Burns platforms for nonfiction films. On September 25, 2004, "P.O.V." aired Aaron Matthews' documentary "A Panther in Africa," about Pete O'Neal, who has lived in Tanzania for 33-plus years, after being charged with transporting a gun across state lines in 1969.

A crucial element in the resurgence of documentaries is the so-called reality TV craze sweeping network programming. Shows such as "Survivor," "Big Brother," "American Idol," "Queer Eye for the Straight Guy" and "Fear Factor" are ratings hits. These more cheaply-produced programs, usually minus (preexisting) stars and scriptwriters plus their high salaries, have to a large extent usurped the traditional role sitcoms and dramas played on network schedules. To be sure, much of this purportedly nonfiction programming has networks moving in *schlock*-step, producing *drek* and worse. However, their popularity has greatly broken down the resistance audiences have long had against nonfiction film in favor of scripted studio productions shot on sets with professional actors.

Reality TV is breaking down these prejudices and divides. Indeed, their formats owe something to Vertov's *Kino Pravda* ("Film Truth"—or "Candid Camera," as Allan Funt called his Peeping Tom series that was a precursor to the reality vogue) philosophy, as well as to Italian Neo-Realism. Most of these shows emphasize the common-man-in-the-street, the so-called *Average Joe*, as one series was called. Elitist snobbery should not discount the *vox pop* culture quality of these programs, and how they have lowered the barriers that kept most film fans away from documentaries with their educational and informational formats. Reality TV proved that reality could be as entertaining as sitcoms, dramas and features, and reminded audiences that truth really is stranger than fiction (especially in the case of the Bush White House).

The new wave of progressive documentaries is powered by a public whose appetite for reality has been whetted by the popularity of nonfiction TV/film, and is hungry for the truth denied the masses by the mainstream media. Especially during a crisis—with 1,500-plus Americans dead and thousands more wounded after being sent on a fool's errand—and election year, when the people's attention is more focused than usual on politics. Other factors contributed to the documentary wave, including technology and a new 21st century model for financing and distributing documentaries.

All of these elements combined to create what Greenwald called "a perfect storm," which he explained in a 2004 interview at his Culver City offices:

> But there's a way to make films inexpensively and get them out quickly. We're at this time where there's this perfect storm of the technology driving the [cost of] making the films way down, that is cheap, inexpensive, flexible, small cameras... and editing equipment. So on the making of it side, in the worst case scenario, you did a 35mm film and you cut it on a cam, now you can have literally almost a home movie camera, and you can cut it on your computer with Final Cut Pro [cost: circa $850]. It's a huge, huge difference on the making-of side. And also creatively, because you can get it into situations, you're unobtrusive, etc.

Producer Robert Greenwald, co-founder of Artists United, during a 2002 interview with the author at Greenwald's Culver City office.

And on the distribution side, the Internet allows you to reach an audience. You don't need to wait for the gatekeepers. Good gatekeepers, bad gatekeepers. They tend to be slow—whether they're a cable company or theatrical distributor. But now, with certain kinds of movies, and the ability of the Internet to reach [audiences], as we've done with *Uncovered*, and now with *Outfoxed*—which by Aug. 2, after a little over 10, 11 days sold over 100,000 DVDs. Now that's a combination—it's the Internet and Amazon.com, and a commercial distributor [Disinformation]. But it's an extraordinary number. So I think it's hopefully proving to people there are other ways than just making your film and waiting to see if it's been accepted to Sundance.

The big trick with the Internet is reaching the audience. In other words, it's a distribution system, but it's a distribution system with enormous information and material. The... films I did, I was fortunate enough to have the involvement of MoveOn.org, which is very active on the Internet. I produced the third of the 'Un' movies, *Unconstitutional*, and one of my significant partners is ACLU. The ACLU will use its mailing lists and ability to reach people around the country to let people know about the film.

In this particular case—and I fell into this; let me be clear. When I started *Uncovered*, my hope was maybe that 2,000, 3,000 people would buy the video. When I took on producing *Unprecedented*, I can remember specifically sitting right here on this couch, with the directors, Joan Sekler and Richard Perez, who came in with shopping bags of film they had shot. They had used their frequent flyer miles, slept on people's couches and they wanted a partner and some assistance. I remember thinking, 'Well, I think I can help get this done, and it'll sit on a shelf at Vidiots [an L.A. specialty video store], and five years from today some student will do a master's thesis, and they'll find it.' And I said, 'that's great, because we want a record of this. Because those who don't learn from history are forced to repeat it.'

So my expectations have never been—if you had said to me *Uncovered*'s going to sell 100,000 or it's going to be in theatres or it's going to go to Cannes, I would have told you you were out of your mind. So, understand where I started and where we are today is very, very different. Having said that, there is now evidence that certainly with some films of a political nature you can reach an audience.

MoveOn.org is not so much [selling the DVD/video on the] website as that they send e-mails to people. It's outgoing; it's not incoming. Website, you have to go to; e-mail goes out to people. With *Uncovered* what I did was, I said I don't have Paramount Studios, so I went to Alternet.org, Buzzflash.org and the Nation Institute [TheNation.org], and they, with MoveOn and the Center for American Progress [AmericanProgress.org] became my distributors. The Center did some e-mails around the country, MoveOn did e-mail to its members, and the *Nation*, Alternet and Buzzflash kept talking about it both in their e-mails and websites. And people could order from any of those entities [and from Amazon.com]. So that was the distribution mechanism.

With *Outfoxed*, there's been all this extraordinary publicity, so it's a bit easier in that anybody who could read has heard about the movie... They're talking about it on Fox News—they're trashing it, but that's fine. I never know how transferable the specific model is, but certainly the notion that you can reach people in other ways is now proven. It's nice to have your name up in lights at a movie theatre, but there are other ways to have your film seen.

Now, the DVDs are being sold at video stores. When we did *Uncovered*, again, nobody—truly, I have an e-mail from one of the MoveOn folks saying they thought we'd sell 2,000 of them, so nobody had expectations. What happened with *Uncovered*, we sold a lot of DVDs—it was the exact reverse of the traditional theatrical pattern. We started on the Internet, we sold a lot of copies, we got the attention of some innovative distributors—the first was Gary Baddeley, from the Disinformation Company Ltd., who called. I'm sure there were a few—there were three or four who pursued me quite aggressively. And I said, 'but hasn't everybody who bought the DVD bought it already?' They said: 'No, no, no, that's just Internet.'

So, we were first on the Internet, then it became available in the various stores around the country, then the Sundance Channel bought it, and now it's going into movie theatres. Because [film distributor] Cinema Libre, even with all of that exposure, a million people have seen it but there's still an audience for it.

Disinformation sold it through stores... what we did on each film, we set up our website and then drove people to it. And put clips up... people announced screenings on the website. So it became a good place for information about the films.

Greenwald also discussed new ways of opening wide distribution methods.

MoveOn—because they're so smart and technologically ahead of all the rest of us—with *Uncovered*—I think it was [MoveOn.org's] Eli Pariser who said—'let's do house parties.' I said, 'What's that?' He said, 'We'll go out to our members, we'll ask those who want to screen the movie at their home, and they'll post it on our website.' You go to the state, you go to the city, then you go to the part of the city by zip code. You go to your zip code and you'd see whatever it was—1, 2, 7, 10 house parties in your area. And it would list the address. And somebody would say [online], 'Okay, I've got room for 10 people on the couch. I've got the potato chips, you bring the beer.' Somebody else said, 'We've got a converted bowling alley in Jacksonville, we can seat 100. We're asking everybody to contribute 10 bucks.' Somebody else converted a yoga studio. It was every possible permutation.

But they all screened on the same night at approximately the same time. They would pay for a DVD that they would then have, and there was a conference call set up where I was on the call, both with *Uncovered*, and then we did it with *Outfoxed*, a couple thousand people on the phone. Then thousands more listening in. And that became another component in spreading the word and getting people to see it. So with *Uncovered* and *Outfoxed*, in that one night, somewhere between 20,000, 50,000, 75,000 people saw the film.

Unprecedented was the first one, and the one that I really started figuring this out. Again, with *Unprecedented*, as I said, I really thought we'd make one or two copies, they'd go to Vidiots [and] the library someplace. And then—and this is the wonderful thing about film—Marcos Barron, [California Director of] People for the American Way, called me up out of the blue, he'd seen it, and said: 'I want to help. I want People for the American Way to help. We want to get the word out.'

We met with him right here, we're saying, 'why?' And he said, 'I think it's important. I think it's important we spread the word.' And to their credit, Marcos and People said 'okay,' they set up some screenings. Marcos found some donors who arranged for a screening in L.A. at the Directors Guild. We did one at San Francisco, then the NAACP did some screenings. Then the Nation Institute did some screenings. And at each screening, the irrepressible Joan Sekler would go and was selling DVDs and spreading the word. Then Joan and Richard went down to Florida, toured the churches there. Suddenly, we were selling DVDs and getting the word out. I said: 'Hmm, this is interesting. Maybe this is more than one or two copies.' Clearly, it was.

When it came time to do *Uncovered*, I learned from that. And when it came time to do *Outfoxed*, I learned from *Uncovered*. So, in a short period of time, it's been an unbelievable amount of hard work. But it's also been an extraordinary concise education, where you learn about how to set up the website, how you set up a[n e-commerce] store, how people send in their orders. Do you use PayPal or Google, or—all these elements, what should be on the website. And how do you draw traffic there? You know, new things.

Instead of sitting in a meeting with 20th Century F—well," the director of *Outfoxed* stopped in mid word and corrected himself. "Instead of sitting in a meeting with Paramount Studios talking about the artwork for the poster, you're saying: 'Well, this artwork looks great, but how's it going to look on a website? Is it going to be too slow, it's too much detail, and people won't be able to download it? And how long should the clip be?' So it's a new universe, and an interesting one.

[By the end of July 2004,] *Uncovered* sold about 120,000. Due to the activity—it had been past 100,000, Gary [Baddeley] got involved and I think they sold another 10,000, 15,000. Now, with all of this new focus around *Outfoxed*, *Uncovered* was up to number nine or something on Amazon.com. *Outfoxed* has been number one for over a

week [since its debut] on Amazon.com. *Uncovered* went back up too—
so I think *Uncovered* sold 125,000 now? *Outfoxed* will be 100,000 by
August 2." [On September 17, 2004, Amazon.com ranked *Outfoxed* as
18, and *Uncovered* 30.]

    Unprecedented was the first documentary I got involved with. I was
the executive producer. Joan and Richard came to me with their shopping bags of videos, and I had just purchased Final Cut Pro, which is
an inexpensive editing system—relative to the Avid, which is $100,000.
Because I had wanted to make available the skills I have in terms of
filmmaking... I never thought I'd do documentaries, but I thought I
would be making little advocacy videos. I had done a 15-minute piece
for a gang prevention center called 'A Place Called Home.' I had done a
10-minute piece for a group called Venice Community Housing, that
does low income housing. And I had wanted to be able to do more of
those, because they're very helpful to the local organizations. I thought,
'Well, if I can get this inexpensive editing system, we can do even more.'
So I'd just purchased that system, and Joan and Richard came along,
and I said, 'Well, maybe we can do a film on it.' So I invited them to
move into the offices, set up the editing system, and was able to get—
we had no money, we really had zero money—get some friends and
colleagues to volunteer their services. And then Marcos Barron, Earl
Katz, [Public Interest Pictures'] Alison Friedman and Dan Raskof all got
involved in helping to raise some money. We were able to keep going.
And it was one of those—you raise $5,000, and you do a little bit
more... The Streisand Foundation, through Marge Tabankin, helped us
out early on. A lot of people, incredibly critical in making it happen."

Greenwald went on to discuss the screening of *Uncovered* at the 2004
Cannes Film Festival:

The great story with *Uncovered* was that I couldn't go, because I was
too busy working on *Outfoxed* at that point. But Ambassador Joe Wilson went, who represented the film, and who has been going around
the country speaking on behalf of the movie. They had a line around
the block [at Cannes]—it was an out of competition screening. Cinema Libre has been selling it around the world as a result of the
screening in Cannes [for theatrical distribution]. So good things continue to happen... You can't judge if they've all paid for themselves,

because I volunteer and lots of people work for a lot less money. And Joan and Richard didn't take money. So I don't know how you can evaluate if they've paid for themselves. Had everybody been charging their fees, and the editors who worked for less money, and the mixing houses that gave us deals—I don't think the financial accounting is the way to judge these films. Because that's not why anybody does them, anyway. I think it's impact, reaching audiences, getting into the culture and seeing them used as tools by organizing groups, *Unprecedented* playing in churches around the south. And *Uncovered* being all over the country at antiwar rallies, seeing it quoted. I'd be reading speeches of politicians, I'd say, 'Oh, they must have seen it, because I know that line! I know where it came from.' So that's really, to me, the impact. And *Outfoxed* now. You see articles about Fox News, and the frame has shifted. The frame is they gotta prove [something] now—we're not just going to let them get away with it. So you're seeing more and more articles from that perspective. So to me, that's the success.

Indeed, during the Republican National Convention in Manhattan, there were unprecedented protests in front of Fox News' national HQ.

THE '*UN*' SERIES AND *OUTFOXED*

"The Fox effect is an effect from Fox on other news organizations."

— Robert Greenwald, in an interview with the author

It took commitment and *chutzpah* for Joan Sekler (who'd never made a full-length film before) to co-create *Unprecedented: The 2000 Presidential Election* with Richard Ray Perez—and, in the process, help kick off the tidal wave of dissident documentaries. Even though the result is a fine film, it was more a matter of sheer political will and tenacity than of talent, because Joan hadn't even directed a movie before. As Greenwald put it, Sekler and Perez "had used their frequent flyer miles, slept on people's couches" to carry out what Greenwald called "guerrilla filmmaking." What she lacked in cinematic skills, Joan more than made up for with her outrage at the theft of the presidency and "The Undermining of Democracy in America," as the documentary's tagline puts it.

According to Sekler, who co-founded the L.A. Independent Media Center, "I have been an associate producer and/or publicist for numerous political documentaries in the past [such as Barbara Trent's 1992 Oscar-winning *The Panama Deception*], but *Unprecedented* was the first time I co-directed and co-produced a political documentary from scratch. "I conceived of the idea of making a documentary about what happened in Florida in November 2000 after Bush was inaugurated on January 20th, 2001, and recruited Richard Ray Perez, an independent filmmaker, to be co-director and co-producer with me, so it's our film, not my film, although it was my original idea."

Perez had previously co-directed *Crashing the Party: The Democratic National Convention 2000* (Sekler lists a producing credit for this doc), produced and directed projects for the AFL-CIO and Center for American Progress, KCET/PBS, ACLU, MoveOn.org, the multi-media campaign for Arianna Huffington's book *Pigs at the Trough*, and was a technical director for the Fox Broadcasting Network.

Sekler went on to say, "I took out $20,000 from my pension savings and within 6 months, by July 2002, we had enough footage from interviews and stock footage to put together an 8 minute trailer. I then mailed it to about 30-40 contacts—Hollywood liberals, foundations, etc., asking for money to help us make our film. Robert Greenwald and Earl Katz were two people in Hollywood who responded and each said they would help us. Robert gave us a free office and edit facility and Richard and I worked with our editor intermittently between August 2002 to August 2003 to make our film. Robert also lent us money for postproduction needs and was eventually paid back. Earl Katz is a fundraiser for progressive causes and raised $100,000 from Hollywood liberals to help us finish our film, which we did in August 2002. Through Earl's help, I got my $20,000 back. Both Robert and Earl became our Executive Producers.

"After Richard and I finished *Unprecedented,* it was launched in public screenings all over the country and I started applying to film festivals. By the summer of 2003, we had been in about 50 film festivals (we are now up to 65 film festivals) and had received wonderful newspaper reviews," Sekler stated.

Greenwald, who became *Unprecedented*'s executive producer, was unprepared for what happened next. The documentary made the film festival circuit (I first saw it at the 2003 Pan African Film Festival in L.A.'s Magic Johnson Theaters); the Sundance Channel aired it around election time in 2003 and 2004; Cinema Libre theatrically released it before 2004's presidential election; as of August 2004, 20,000 DVDs and videos had sold, and on September 17, 2004, its Amazon.com sales rank was 68.

It didn't hurt that *Unprecedented* had a stellar cast, including George W. Bush, Katherine Harris, several Supreme Court justices and Greg Palast with his investigative reporting about blacks purged from balloting and more. And it helped that they found a left-wing fairy godfather. In addition to providing editing facilities and fundraising, as *Unprecedented*'s executive producer Greenwald drew upon his experience as a feature film and TV movie director/producer. "The most critical part, and maybe the most demanding, is the storytelling. Because there's been lots of films done—good politics, bad politics—but there's lots of lousy films, frankly, that are just boring. Always part of the job on these movies is to go overboard in making sure there's a strong dramatic drive," said the man who has directed actors such as Russell Crowe, Salma Hayek and Vincent D'Onofrio.

"*Unprecedented* is a great story," Greenwald said. "It's a tragic story, if you will. But it's a strong story. And you see it years later and you still get knots in your stomach. There was a question really of the research. And that wonderful shot where we freeze frame, and put the names under all of the Republican operatives who are rioting in the halls as they're counting the votes. Or finding the people of color who went on camera and said, 'Yeah, I didn't get to vote.' Or explaining the felons list. There's complex stuff there, and Richard and Joan did an unbelievable amount of research, which is the demand on all of these pictures," the executive producer stated.

This low-budget 2002 picture is an excoriating electoral exposé, and was one of the first films to open the floodgates for post-9/11 progressive content. *Unprecedented* boldly showcases Palast's allegations of how Bush's brother, Florida Governor Jeb Bush, and Florida Secretary of State Katherine Harris, who also served as co-chair of Florida's Bush campaign, and DBT ChoicePoint (purportedly an identification and credential verification service) conspired to ethnically cleanse the Sunshine State's voter rolls. By scrubbing "felons" (many of them actually innocent victims of the scheme who'd never served prison time) from the list of eligible voters, thousands of blacks—who tend to vote Democratic—were disenfranchised. This resulted in an electoral squeaker wherein Bush was selected president over the winner of the popular vote by a Supreme

Court that included justices appointed by his own father, in the mother of all conflicts of interest.

Sekler added, "Richard and I hired an editor in the spring of 2004 and worked with him to edit a new segment at the end of *Unprecedented*, about touch screen voting machines and the potential for voter fraud in the November 2004 election because these machines don't generate a paper receipt and these machines are owned by manufacturers who are all contributors to the Republican Party and the Bush campaign. It was Earl Katz who got us Danny Glover to introduce the new updated version of *Unprecedented* on camera and who also narrates the new segment."

With *Unprecedented*, Sekler, Perez, Greenwald and Palast arguably played similar roles to those Woodward, Bernstein, Katharine Graham and Ben Bradlee had played during Watergate. With a crucial difference— by 2002 there no longer was an independent-minded *Washington Post* (let alone Washington press corps) to spread the word, with the *Post*, by its own post-Iraq invasion admission, complacently deferring to power. And Woodward had gone from a toppler of presidents to more of a cheerleader of one. Pursuing the *Unprecedented*/Watergate analogy, it's as if the investigative reporters this time around skipped the daily newspaper staff reporters and just went straight to video, with nonfiction film versions of Woodward and Bernstein.[16]

Sekler observed "in the summer of 2003 Robert Greenwald decided to direct and produce his own, and first, documentary, based on the success of *Unprecedented*." So, *Unprecedented*, directed and produced by Joan Sekler and Richard Ray Perez, jump-started the new career in documentary filmmaking of a producer/director who'd previously specialized in made-for-TV-movies—Robert Greenwald, Hollywood's "Un-cola." He went on to make *Uncovered: The Whole Truth About the Iraq War*. The film is a WMT—Weapon of Mass Truth—intended as an imminent threat to Bush's re-election. One would expect a progressive filmmaker to round

---

16. Michael Moore's *Fahrenheit 9/11* almost literally opens where the original version of *Unprecedented* ends, with Bush stealing the election. "To the degree that it continues on, I'm thrilled," Greenwald said. The opening sequence of *9/11* shows the protests during Bush's inauguration that forced him to change his motorcade's route and forsake the traditional inaugural stroll, as demonstrators pelt his limo. Vice President Al Gore, in his function as Senate President, presides over his own defeat, as members of the Congressional Black Caucus try in vain to protest Bush's selection— only to be overruled by Gore on the Senate Floor. Meanwhile, Moore eerily asks: "Was it all a dream?"

up the usual lefty subjects, such as Noam Chomsky or Howard Zinn, for a documentary revealing White House whoppers about Iraq.

Instead, in *Uncovered* there are interviews with around 25 intelligence/military/weapons inspector/foreign policy establishment sources intercut with news clips of Bush, Rumsfeld, Powell, Rice, Wolfowitz and Fleischer. When the officials aren't hanging themselves with their own words or hoisted by their own petards, the public service professionals debunk wild-eyed administration claims, from Saddam's alleged nuclear program to the war's actual monetary costs. With its cinematic Monday morning quarterbacking, *Uncovered* reminds us about Rice and Bush's false assertions regarding "smoking guns" and "mushroom clouds," and that the Bush-oisie told us rebuilding Iraq would cost from zero to a couple billion, thanks to Baghdad's supposed oil revenues. The film is also a record frozen in time of establishment dissent, of ruling circle factions vying for public opinion hegemony.

The shock and awe of this documentary's skillful editing demolishes Bush league lies, like a heat-seeking truth missile targeting the mendacity that manipulated a nation into a "preemptive" strike based mostly on fabrications. Interviewees presumably include onetime/current Republicans, such as Watergater John Dean and ex-Marine Scott Ritter, plus: Milt Bearden, CIA station chief during the Afghan *mujahadeen*'s anti-Soviet *jihad*; John Brady Kiesling, who resigned from Bush's foreign service to protest the Iraq War; and ex-Assistant Defense Secretary Philip Coyle (who participated in a panel discussion at *Uncovered*'s packed Veterans Day 2003 L.A. premiere in Santa Monica's Laemmle Theater). Feisty Ambassador Joe Wilson steals the show in this uncompromising exposé of the Bush administration's egregious lies about Iraq.

In *Outfoxed: Rupert Murdoch's War on Journalism*, Greenwald likewise exposes the deceit of the so-called "fair and balanced" Fox News Channel. Former Fox employees, and current staffers whose identities are concealed, join media experts such as Jeff Cohen (formerly of FAIR), Walter Cronkite, David Brock (*Blinded By the Right, The Conscience of an Ex-Conservative*) and Bob McChesney (the *Media Matters* radio program) in critiquing mogul Murdoch's media empire. They are counterpointed to extensive clips from Fox News itself, that serve to illustrate the film's main contention: That far from being either fair or balanced, Fox is a propaganda outlet that egregiously pushes a pro-Republican Party, pro-Bush agenda.

As in Moore's *9/11*, Greenwald got a hold of some choice outtakes never previously aired. They include correspondent Carl Cameron's chummy pre-interview schmoozing with then-candidate Bush, whom Cameron's sister was campaigning for (Bush calls her a "good soul"). The sequence exposing a personal relationship between a newsman and the newsmaker he is covering encapsulates the central thesis of *Outfoxed*, and is yet another blatant example of the Bush administration's never-ending conflicts of interest. It never seems to have crossed either of their minds that this backslapping buddy-buddy *entre nous* familiarity between a journalist and a politician (especially one running for president!) is entirely inappropriate—that is, until Cameron got caught with his pants down and mike on.

"Cameron originally accused me of trick editing in that section," Greenwald said. "We then released the full transcript and the full video. I think on some days I'm a pretty decent filmmaker, but I'm not clever enough to put words in his mouth in a close-up shot. There is no trick editing. I don't know what goes on in his mind, but I can say objectively and certainly, there is no trick editing, and he knows that."

Did Fox disqualify Cameron from covering the 2004 presidential race? No—he was assigned to cover his buddy Bush's opposition. And in October, Cameron's insulting comments about Kerry—supposedly written in jest—were somehow posted on Fox's site. Fox's "Newswatch" program reviewed the matter and failed to even mention the fact that he had previously been caught redhanded, videotaped sucking up to Shrub. The unfair and mentally unbalanced network continued to allow the obviously partial, twice-caught Cameron cover Kerry.

Greenwald went on to explain that "The Fox effect is an effect from Fox on other news organizations. It's a two-part effect, and it was explained to me by reporters and journalists. I didn't discover this or make this up myself. The first is the financial viability of this pseudo-patriotism, or as one of the people in the movie—I think it's in the film still—says: 'There's money in the flag.' They discovered they can make a profit by this totally false patriotism." Others complain that Fox acts as the patriot police.

Greenwald added, "The second part of it is less known but equally bad, which is that it's cheap to put two people in a room screaming at each other, and call it news. It's expensive to send reporters out to research, to go to foreign countries, to spend days or weeks or months really probing a story and then reporting. But Fox doesn't do that. They have people yelling at each other or they have somebody rewriting the *AP* press reports. Both those things are the Fox effect, and both those things one can track and show that they are having an impact on other news organizations."

The quintessential, single most destructive effect Fox had on its media counterparts was the outrageous conflict of interest of having John Ellis, Bush's first cousin, calling the election results in Florida. "In *Outfoxed*, John Nichols makes the point very well that in many ways, the premature calling of the election for Bush—without having evidence—was far more critical than the [missing] chads or the felon list," Greenwald insisted. "Because the frame then became: 'Bush won, Gore is taking it away from him.' Think how different it would be had all the networks said what they should have said, which is: 'It's too close to call.' Everybody would have been looking at it in a very different way in that period of time."

In the period before Bush invaded Iraq, as a mastermind of Artists United, Greenwald helped book antiwar actors on the air—including Fox—to debate pundits, talk show hosts, etc., about war and peace. Greenwald himself appeared on some of the cable programs. "[C]ertainly having firsthand experience, and being subjected to not just the pseudo-patriotism flag waving, but a news channel trying to silence people who had a difference of opinion" influenced Greenwald's decision to make *Outfoxed*. "I mean, that's pretty strong stuff. We have the quotes from the ever-quotable Bill O'Reilly saying, 'I'm watching you! You better be careful. I know what you're saying.' Which was the mood at the time. I came by my concerns about how Fox was affecting the culture honestly from those encounters during the buildup to war," Greenwald stated.

The next documentary Greenwald produced was *Unconstitutional: The War on Our Civil Liberties*, the third in the '*Un*' Series. It opened September 13, 2004. "The ACLU is one of the sponsors, and it deals with civil liberties after 9/11," Greenwald said. "The changes in the country, what we've gone through, the fear that we've had, how we've reacted, how we've overreacted, the toll it's taken on civil liberties. And I think, most importantly to me, it hasn't made us safer. In fact, there's a very, very strong argument to be made that it's made us less safe, in two ways."

Unconstitutional goes into the Jose Padilla so-called "dirty bomb" case and other experiences of Muslims' and dissenters' with the Ashcroft Justice Department and PATRIOT Act. One interviewee is the father of an internee at Gitmo. Sekler said, "*Unconstitutional* has a different production story

than *Unprecedented*. Robert and Earl [Katz] formed a new non-profit company, called Public Interest Pictures, which finally got a 501C3 status.
Robert and Earl got the ACLU to fund *Unconstitutional* and hired independent filmmaker Nonny de la Pena to make the film... Robert did have
editorial input, but she is still credited as the writer, director and producer."

Inspired by Sekler and Perez, Greenwald and his *kino* comrades pioneered an end run around the conventional Hollywood studio system and
gatekeepers, scoring touchdowns with new financing and distribution
methods. Others would take notice—and heart.

THE MEN/WOMEN WITH THE MOVIE CAMERAS: THE TIDAL WAVE OF DISSIDENT DOCS

*"Propaganda is any organized and systematic effort to dissemi-
nate a particular doctrine; it is mass persuasion with a purpose
that advantages the intentions of the sender; it's essentially a
neutral set of techniques that derives its positive/negative effects
from specific application of those techniques."*

— Dr. Nancy Snow, in an interview with the author

It is appropriate that working class hero Michael Moore helped launch the
post-9/11 tidal wave of dissident documentaries. But before 2002's *Bowling
for Columbine*, a biopic about an even more legendary leftist returned radical
politics to the screen in 2001. *Fidel* opened at New York's Urbanworld Film
Festival a month before the terrorist attacks, and played at the Toronto Film
Festival three days after September 11th. *Fidel* is an admiring look at Cuba's
el Jefe, directed by Estela Bravo, an American filmmaker living in Havana. It
won film festival awards and went on to a limited U.S. theatrical release.

Bowling for Columbine, which premiered at the Cannes Film Festival
on May 15, 2002, has the distinction of being the first major political documentary to be shot (at least in part) and released after 9/11. As the son
and nephew of Flint car factory workers and a college dropout, Moore
can't easily be dismissed as an elitist limousine liberal or egghead. Moore
undoubtedly has the common touch, enhanced by his bluejeans, girth
and disarming sense of humor. A cottage industry of would-be debunkers
has emerged, with documentaries, books and websites meant to shoot
down the big bad Moore. (On MichaelMoore.com, he refers to this phenomenon as "make-believe stories" and "humorous fiction.") With his

proletarian persona and, above all, massive following, Moore drives the right—well-heeled or hardhatted—to distraction.

A case in point is the Wednesday Morning Club, a forum co-founded by counterculture Quisling David Horowitz, which presents right-tilting speakers and perspectives to the Tinseltown community. In March 2003, while embedded at the culture war's frontlines, Christopher Hitchens was the featured speaker at a Club luncheon in the posh Beverly Hills Hotel. Most of the 150 diners appeared to be recipients of Bush's tax cut largesse. A befuddled woman asked Hitchens: "Why is Michael Moore so popular? [WMCers laughed.] Why is *Stupid White Men* on top of the *New York Times'* bestseller list? Why are his movies doing so well?"

Later, at the Southern California Americans for Democratic Action's Eleanor Roosevelt Annual Awards Dinner, where Moore sat at a table with Jane Fonda and Tom Hayden, I repeated the above WMC questions to him. Moore replied: "Don't pick on them... They're upset because they know they live in a very liberal, left-wing country. The majority of Americans support the environment, labor organizations and are pro-choice... When you're in a small group, sometimes you get a little angry. I understand their anger and feel their pain."

This, of course, was days before his Oscar speech, and more than a year before the release of *Fahrenheit 9/11*. At the time, the right was angry with Moore over the then-Oscar nominated *Bowling for Columbine*. The complex 2002 documentary is a scathing critique of violence and fear in a gun-obsessed USA, and how the use of force—to paraphrase Rap Brown—is as American as apple pie. What really riled reactionary wrath was Moore's interview with then-National Rifle Association President Charlton Heston.

While it's more or less true that Moore made a monkey out of the *Planet of the Apes*[17] star, Charlton Heston hanged himself with his own words. The then-NRA chief contended "having a more mixed ethnicity" was a major reason why there are so many more shooting deaths in America than in countries with more homogeneous populations. The remark by the aging movie Moses could be interpreted as callous, even racist. Moore also took the actor to task for appearing at NRA gun rallies near Columbine and Flint shortly after murderous school shootings there.

But it's untrue that this was a shotgun interview. Moore purchases one of those maps to the stars' homes and is shown on camera arriving

---

17. Written by blacklistee Michael Wilson, with Rod Serling.

unannounced at Heston's *chateau*, and is seen making an appointment Charlton Heston hanged with Heston, whose voice is heard over an intercom. Moore appears the following morning at the appointed time to conduct the interview in Heston's lair. At the time of the interview, Heston's Alzheimer's disease was not public knowledge, so it cannot be argued Moore knowingly took advantage of a sick old man.[18]

In *Bowling*, Moore pointed out that near Columbine High School, where the mass murder occurred, is a Lockheed Martin plant, which mass-produced WMDs for decades. A Lockheed official is taken aback when Moore asks if there could be a correlation between the two, and says: "We don't get irritated with somebody, and just 'cause we're mad at them drop a bomb, shoot at them or fire a missile at them." Moore cuts to a montage depicting numerous U.S. covert actions and foreign interventions, concluding with: "Bin Laden uses his expert CIA training to murder 3,000 Americans."

Moore masterfully connects the dots between domestic violence and a foreign policy that spreads mayhem around the globe. *Bowling for Columbine* paints a portrait of a post-9/11 America gripped by fear and paranoia, where banks give guns away to entice new clients. What disturbs neocons most about Moore is that his is no lone voice crying in the wilderness. He is a virtuoso communicator with a mass audience. Moore not only won the Best Documentary Oscar, but *Columbine* did boffo box office, earning $22 million at home and $36.5 million abroad. Up until that time, it was the most financially successful documentary ever. And this success helped pave the way for a tidal wave of dissident documentaries—and also, arguably, for politically-themed, left-leaning features.

I saw Michael Galinsky and Suki Hawley's *Horns and Halos* on July 11, 2002 at the American Cinematheque in the Egyptian Theatre, the Hollywood Boulevard movie palace that has been converted into one of the world's greatest repertory cinemas for specialty films. The 79-minute documentary is about Jim Hatfield, author of the suppressed 1999 *Fortunate Son: George W. Bush and the Making of an American President*, first of the Bush bashing books. Hatfield raised questions about Bush's military record, Bush family ties to Saudi oil interests and G.W.'s alleged cocaine bust.

---

18. The subsequent disclosure of Heston's unfortunate condition raised questions about the efficacy of a P.R.-seeking shooting star whose light in Tinseltown's constellation had faded long ago and whose mind was being ravaged by mental illness heading an organization fanatically devoted to gun rights.

Hatfield included allegations that Bush had been arrested for cocaine possession in 1972, and after his father pulled strings with the judge, W. performed community service mentoring black youth in exchange for having the coke bust expunged from his record. When St. Martin's Press published *Fortunate Son* in October 1999, the Bush administration counterattacked. Hatfield's own criminal record (which he lied about) was exposed; Hatfield was discredited; *Fortunate Son* was removed from distribution. Soft Skull Press acquired the book, and Hatfield and publisher Sander Hicks struggled to release it. In July 2001, Hatfield died—reportedly a suicide due to an overdose of prescription drugs.

I saw *The Revolution Will Not Be Televised* at the Egyptian's Alternative Screen, a cutting edge showcase for indie and experimental work. This doc is about the purportedly U.S.-backed April 12, 2002 coup that attempted to remove Hugo Chavez from the presidency of Venezuela. Irish filmmakers Kim Bartley and Donnacha O'Briain were inside the presidential palace both when Chavez was removed by force and returned to power there days later. This eyewitness-to-history report is the ultimate in reality TV. The 2003 documentary is a meditation on the power of the media, in particular the McLuhanesque "cool medium" of television. The filmmakers call the anti-Chavez putsch "the world's first media coup," and the documentary reveals the crucial role TV played in Venezuela's crisis, as state-owned Channel 8 competes with privately owned TV stations to spin the story. Key players in the real and reel-life political drama stress the importance of televising their version of events, as if whoever controls the airwaves will win the revolution.

The 145-minute *The Corporation* is an in-depth look at modern capitalism based on the book *The Corporation: The Pathological Pursuit of Profit and Power* by Joel Bakan, who co-wrote the film with Harold Crooks. It is directed by Jennifer Abbott and Mark Achbar, who previously directed documentaries on East Timor and 1992's *Manufacturing Consent: Noam Chomsky and the Media*. The M.I.T. professor returns in 2003's *The Corporation*, which manufactures dissent against corporate powers-that-be. Chomsky is joined by other leading dissidents, including Moore, author Naomi Klein and Howard Zinn, plus by corporate apologists, like *über*-free trader Milton Friedman.

The Corporation reveals how Fox News squelched its own investigation about genetically modified milk. A U.N. personality checklist recurs throughout the film, demonstrating that if corporations' disregard for

THE RETURN OF PROGRESSIVE CONTENT

safety, decency, society, etc., to maximize profit was displayed by an individual, he/she would be considered psychopathic. Chomsky grouses that corporations "have no moral conscience," and sweat shop exploitation is revealed as Kathie Lee Gifford gets hers. Advertising execs discuss manipulating consumers. Although the film portrays the faceless power and greed of today's leviathans, *The Corporation* also depicts successful anti-corporate struggles, such as the uprising by indigenous Bolivians against corporate attempts to privatize water.

HBO's "Beah: A Black Woman Speaks" is about actress Beah Richards, best known for playing Sidney Poitier's mother in *Guess Who's Coming to Dinner?* Beah was a poet, activist and teacher who told her fellow black actors that when it came to selecting parts, "You must not betray your people!" Ruby Dee and Ossie Davis also appear in director LisaGay Hamilton's documentary, which was featured at the 2004 Pan African Film Festival and was a 2003 AFI Film Festival Grand Jury prizewinner.

In *Fog of War: Eleven Lessons From the Life of Robert S. McNamara,* Errol Morris trains his camera and Interrotron on the Vietnam-era Secretary of Defense. In 1988's *The Thin Blue Line,* Morris proved inmate Randall Dale Adams was innocent of murdering Dallas policeman Robert Wood, and helped save Adams from execution. In *Fog,* Morris turns to war crimes—not only McNamara's Indochina escapades but his role, with Curtis LeMay, in WWII firebombings that killed 100,000-plus Japanese civilians.

Upon accepting the Best Documentary Oscar in 2004, Morris gave the evening's most political speech: "Forty years ago this country went down a rabbit hole in Vietnam and millions died. I fear we're going down a rabbit hole once again—and if people can stop and think and reflect on some of the ideas and issues in this movie, perhaps I've done some damn good here!"

Directed by Sam Green and Bill Siegel, and narrated by Lili Taylor, *The Weather Underground* documents the SDS terrorist offshoot. By the late '60s, hundreds of youth concluded that world revolution was imminent. Disenchanted by U.S. imperialism, radicalized white students were disabused by the Chicago '68 police riots, police shootings of Panthers, etc., of the notion that America could change peacefully through elections. Believing they were acting in solidarity with national liberation movements in Third World countries such as Vietnam, they opted for armed struggle, and the Weathermen were born. Weather Underground bombings targeted symbols of authority, such as the U.S. Senate's cloakroom and NYPD's HQ. This gripping documentary includes interviews with Bernardine Dohrn, Mark Rudd and Kathleen Cleaver.

Robert Stone's *Guerrilla: The Taking of Patty Hearst* is about another homegrown terrorist group, the Symbionese Liberation Army, which kidnapped *Citizen Kane*'s granddaughter in 1974. Stone skillfully uses archival footage to show the age's angst and intensity. He explores pop culture's impact on SLA commandos, incorporating shots of *Swamp Fox*, *Zorro*, Errol Flynn's *Robin Hood*, Omar Sharif's *Che!* and Costa-Gavras' 1973 *State of Siege*. One ex-SLAer says some of the extremists met at a screening of one of these freedom fighter-oriented pictures. The newspaper heiress' abduction became one of the first modern media events. The SLA sent "communiques" to the press, much as Osama would later do. Especially interesting is the food-for-the-poor program the SLA coerced the millionaire Hearsts to set up.

Another documentary that catches the temper of those turbulent times is *Chisholm '72—Unbought & Unbossed*, about the first presidential candidacy of an African American woman. Shola Lynch's 2004 documentary about the antiwar, feminist, pro-civil rights Democratic Congresswoman Shirley Chisholm is irresistibly upbeat. Her grass roots, Panthers-endorsed campaign for the presidency in 1972 expressed the era's idealism, as newly enfranchised 18-year-olds turned out *en masse* and 49% of 18-to-24-year-olds voted, the high-water mark for youth participation in a national election, as Democrats actually nominated a peace candidate, George McGovern.

Sandra Dickson and Churchill Roberts' *Negroes With Guns: Rob Williams and Black Power* tells the story of Robert Williams, a mythic man called the godfather of the Black Power movement. Williams was a NAACP chapter president and publisher of the *Crusader* newspaper. He turned the North Carolina arrest of 8- and 10-year-old black boys for kissing a white girl into an international *cause célèbre*. At a time when the civil rights movement advocated nonviolence, Williams favored armed self-defense, and organized the Black Guard to counter the Ku Klux Klan and Jim Crow. Following trumped-up kidnapping charges in 1961, this apostle of black liberation fled America and went into exile in Castro's Cuba, where he broadcast "Radio Free Dixie" on short wave radio, combining jazz and soul music with radical politics. Williams next moved on to Chairman Mao's China.

Edgy Lee's *The Hawaiians* represented Hawaii at the 2004 opening ceremonies of the Smithsonian's National Museum of the American Indian. A traditional celestial navigator, healer, salt maker, musician and scientist reveal what being Native Hawaiian means. The film recounts the U.S. role in the 1893 overthrow of the Polynesian kingdom and conquest of Hawaii. Sumptuous cinematography reveals the beauty of the *aina*—land—and the aboriginal people's mystic attachment to it. Directed by Hawaii's greatest local filmmaker, this is a film of transcendent splendor, from splendid scenery to an undiminished spirit in the face of U.S. colonialism, as the indigenous endure.

Directed by Nickolas Perry and Harry Thomason, 2004's *The Hunting of the President* is based on investigative reporters Joe Conason and Gene Lyons' book about the vast right-wing conspiracy and its witch-hunt against the Clintons. *Hunting* exhaustively exposes shady characters such as Pittsburgh tycoon Richard Mellon-Scaife, who bankrolled much of the anti-Clinton sleaze machine. Along with wife Linda Bloodworth-Thomason, Arkansas-born Thomason produced and directed the popular TV series "Designing Women."

Egyptian-American Jehane Noujaim's *Control Room* is a great inside look at the Aljazeera satellite TV news network and its Iraq War reportage. Noujaim's 2004 doc shows what drove U.S. officials mad: they couldn't control these Arab reporters and prevent them from airing a counter-narrative to the White House's spin, and the sanitized war broadcast by embedded American journalists. On March 23, 2003, the channel aired pictures of dead Americans and POWs. Aljazeera apparently disturbed the Bush crew so much that on April 8, 2003 its Baghdad HQ was hit by laser-guided missiles fired by U.S. F-16s, killing Aljazeera correspondent Tariq Ayoub. Six days earlier, the Basra Sheraton—whose only guests were Aljazeera reporters—was hit by U.S. artillery. (In 2001, the Arab network's Kabul HQ was similarly bombed by Americans.) In a telling postscript to *Control Room*, the sole Yankee mouthpiece who displays any sensitivity and intelligence—Marine media spokesman Lieutenant Josh Rushing—is "subsequently... reassigned and ordered not to comment on the film," as Roger Ebert wrote.

Veteran newsman and documentarian Danny Schechter's brilliant *WMD: Weapons of Mass Deception* also deals with Arab media. The "News Dissector" attends an Arab conference on reporting and this nice Jewish boy dares show the Arab side of the story. He contrasts U.S. coverage of warfare in Iraq with Aljazeera's. Whereas Americans stress the whiz-bang wizardry of high-tech bombers and the like, Arabs focus on their effects and human costs, revealing the death and destruction U.S.

viewers rarely, if ever, see. It's as if two different wars are being covered. After *9/11*, Schechter's *WMD* may be the tidal wave of dissident docs' most aesthetically rendered, conceptually cogent critique of the Bush administration.

Super Size Me's Michael Moore-like, anti-corporate, subversive sensibility packs a punch with panache, as it takes on what author Eric Schlosser called the *Fast Food Nation*. Onscreen, director Morgan Spurlock subjects himself to a radical body and mind change, exclusively eating McDonald's for breakfast, lunch and dinner for an entire month. Not only does Spurlock pick up 25 pounds, but a host of health problems as well in his culinary crusade against the junk food-ization of America. This powerful and witty documentary debuted at 2003's Sundance Festival and won its prestigious Best Director award. *Super* went on to become the first documentary to make America's weekly top ten box office list. The documentary's production budget was $65,000; by January 2005, *Super* had earned $28 million-plus since its May 7, 2004 release. According to BoxOfficeMojo.com, it is the fourth-highest grossing documentary made since 1982; *USA Today* listed it as the third highest ever.

Anti-globalization activists the Yes Men trick corporateers by posing as World Trade Organization spokesmen. Their travels and antics are recorded by Dan Ollman, Sarah Price and Chris Smith in their 2004 documentary of the same name, as the hoaxsters infiltrate an economics conference in Helsinki, extolling the virtues of slavery. The WTO "experts" tell State University of New York students the solution to Third World hunger is recycling human waste byproducts into McDonald's burgers. At a forum down under, gullible Aussie technocrats are told the WTO is disbanding due to its unsustainable development model and unethical nature.

"Hitler's Pawn: The Margaret Lambert Story" gives the lie to Leni Riefenstahl's 1938 *Olympia*, and is a perfect companion piece to Hitler's favorite filmmaker's sports *agitprop*, intended to showcase the new Germany and Hitler via the 1936 Berlin Olympics. The truth of the fatherland is unmasked in "Hitler's Pawn," by Erik Kester and Steven Hilliard—the story of the fascists' diabolical manipulation of a Jewish athlete to ensure FDR's America participated in the Olympics. By exploiting Lambert, who trained alongside Aryan athletes, the Nazis deceived the U.S. into believing a Jew would compete in the Berlin games. Once the Nazis succeeded in tricking the Yanks and the Jewish high-jumper was no longer useful to *der fuhrer*, Lambert was barred from competing.

Another documentary made for a cable television network sheds light on how Tinseltown depicted the Shoah. Daniel Anker's well-researched *Imaginary Witness: Hollywood and the Holocaust* was screened at AFI's 2004 filmfest and shot for Turner Classic Movies. *Imaginary Witness* uses clips dating back to 1930s movies, including Edward G. Robinson's *Confessions of a Nazi Spy*, Chaplin's *The Great Dictator*, Anne Frank adaptations, Kramer's *Judgment at Nuremburg*, the TV miniseries "Holocaust," *Sophie's Choice*, *Schindler's List*, etc. There's also archival footage plus interviews with Steven Spielberg, Neal Gabler, Rod Steiger, Sidney Lumet, etc., on how moviedom portrayed the final solution.

Reality TV combined with political documentary in Michael McNamara's "American Candidate," which premiered during the convention season in the summer of 2004 and stretched on to Election Day. Ten would-be politicians contended to become a "people's candidate," first prize being the opportunity to address the nation on the Showtime network and launch a possible career in politics. Instead of getting voted off the island, at each episode's end, the two lowest vote-getters at various campaign functions faced off in debates, with their contenders voting on the winner. Host Montel Williams announced who was voted off of the campaign trail. Liberal candidates did well, notably openly gay African American Keith Boykin and Honolulu's Malia Lazu, although they were ultimately defeated by conservatives on October 10.

Ragin' Cajun James Carville of CNN's "Crossfire" co-starred in "K Street," a short-lived but thought-provoking 2003 HBO series about political consultants in Washington. "K Street" innovatively combined elements of reality TV with fictional drama, with Carville and wife Mary Matalin playing versions of themselves as political lobbyists/consultants, alongside actors such as Roger Guenveur Smith (who wrote and starred in Spike Lee's *A Huey P. Newton Story*). The consulting firm becomes embroiled, amidst a lesbian love affair and other sexual subplots, in scandal in this Steven Soderbergh/George Clooney experiment.

Bush's Brain is based on the 2003 book *Bush's Brain: How Karl Rove Made George W. Bush Presidential* by Texas-based investigative reporters James C. Moore and Wayne Slater. Directed by Michael Paradies Shoob and Joseph Mealey, the documentary probes the inner recesses of Bush's rogue state. It reveals *über*-nerd Rove's Republican Party origins during Watergate, when Rove first encountered the Bush dynasty, namely then-RNC chairman George H.W. Bush. *Bush's Brain* documents Rove's

Machiavellian tactics, such as targeting opponents' strengths (say, being decorated war heroes), rather than weaknesses. Robert Edgeworth, an ex-friend and fellow Republican, recounts Rove's underhanded tactics to win a GOP leadership post in the 1970s (John Sayles reprises this in *Silver City*). Rove wreaks havoc on allies of Texas' then-Democratic Agriculture Commissioner, Jim Hightower, with devastating consequences.

The progressive biopics *Imelda*, *The Agronomist* and *Howard Zinn: You Can't Be Neutral on a Moving Train* were also theatrically released—although *Imelda* was almost canned. The Filipina ex-first lady sought a Philippines court injunction against what she regarded as an unflattering portrait of herself and late husband dictator Ferdinand Marcos. But Imelda lost, and *Imelda* was distributed in the Philippines and U.S. in 2004.

Jonathan Demme directed *The Agronomist*, another biopic set in a troubled tropical island. This 2003 documentary is about Haitian human rights activist and radio journalist Jean Dominique, whose quest to change Haiti ended in assassination. This documentary reveals the *Silence of the Lambs* director's more progressive side, and is in keeping with Demme's producing of *Beah* and 1996's *Mandela*, and directing the anti-AIDS features *Philadelphia* and 1976's *Fighting Mad*.

Musica Cubana depicts another Caribbean isle. Following Wim Wenders' popular 1999 *Buena Vista Social Club*, Wenders executive-produced this ebullient film, shot on location in Havana. Directed by Buenos Aires-born German Kral, 2004's *Musica Cubana* follows *Buena Vista*'s 85-year-old Pio Leiva, as he forms an all-star band of top young talents, who adapt classic Cuban songs.

Howard Zinn: You Can't Be Neutral on a Moving Train, about the *A People's History of the United States* author, was released late in 2004, and is a revealing look at one of the left's leading lights. It traces Zinn's WWII service and involvement at a southern university during the civil rights and antiwar movements. Zinn is seen traveling to northern Vietnam and helping to free U.S. P.O.W.s. He comes across as a thoughtful, all-around nice guy, who always has compassion for the little guy/gal. The biopic is co-narrated by Zinn's former neighbor Matt Damon, with music by Billy Bragg and Woody Guthrie. The documentary also discusses Zinn's play *Marx in Soho* and explains the meaning of the carbuncles on Marx's derriere: To get rid of those pains in your ass, one must get up and do something about them. A perfect metaphor for a life devoted to activism.

"Death in Gaza" is a compelling 2004 HBO documentary that sheds light on the Palestinian cause, from occupation to suicide bombers to targeted assassinations. It follows three Palestinian children growing up in the Gaza Strip, as boys battle tanks and bulldozers in an all-too-real game of cowboys and Indians—or, as Ahmed and his friends call it, Jews and Arabs. The occupation's cruelty and the fanaticism it unleashes are almost unbearable, as 14-year-olds such as Salem die almost in front of our very eyes. The heartbreaking documentary was co-directed by Saira Shah and James Miller (who co-made the 2001 Afghan-shot films *Beneath the Veil* and *Unholy War*), and shockingly ends with Miller's own death.

The Discovery Channel's "Off to War" is an inside look at ordinary Arkansas National Guardsmen unexpectedly called up and sent to Iraq. The Little Rock, Arkansas-born and bred documentarians Brent and Craig Renaud were embedded in the 239th Infantry of the Arkansas National Guard and recorded how the deployment affects families at home and Guardsmen once they are in the combat zone. This is a heartbreaking account of families torn asunder by a president who avoided combat by joining the Guard, and apparently failed to fulfill his duties there when it was highly unlikely Guardsmen would be sent to Vietnam. Unlike today, with 40% of servicemen in Iraq being reactivated reservists and would-be weekend warriors coerced into duty by backdoor drafts.

"Off to War" exposes how unprepared the Guardsmen really are. Their training is inadequate and trucks outdated—yet they are thrust into a war, with shattering consequences for both the soldiers and the families left behind. Some know they are cannon fodder, especially black Guardsmen. One points out that Bush's children aren't in Iraq, and that discrimination and fewer job opportunities pressure blacks to join up. The African Americans perform an impromptu version of "War," Edwin Starr's pacifist anthem. NPR reported that the 9/11 Commission's findings that Saddam was not connected to 9/11 angered unit members. "Off to War" reminds us that war is hell.

So does HBO's "Last Letters Home: Voices of American Troops From the Battlefields of Iraq," by Bill Couturie. Relatives of ten slain G.I.s read their final written messages to their families before their deaths in Iraq. The war's devastating effects are brought home as homefront survivors reveal how the loss of loved ones affect those left behind. Couturie's documentary also reveals the fallen soldiers' fears. This emotion-packed film really brings home what it must be like to die for Bush, Halliburton and

Oil Inc. in what U.N. General Secretary Kofi Annan called an "illegal war" based on outrageous lies.

In 2004's *Arlington West*, Veterans for Peace build *faux* burial sites on beaches such as Santa Monica as tributes to fallen soldiers in Iraq. The crosses evoke and provoke a range of responses from passersby in this moving documentary directed by Peter Dudar and Sally Marr. The Pentagon/Bush cowards may try banning coverage of flag draped caskets returning home, but "Off to War," "Last Letters Home" and "Arlington West" blow the lid off government suppression of the war's true impact.

Orwell Rolls in His Grave is a brilliant media critique presented within an Orwellian framework by director Robert Kane Pappas. Charles Lewis, Michael Moore, Robert McChesney, Mark Crispin Miller, Representative Bernie Sanders, Vincent Bugliosi, Jeff Cohen, Greg Palast and Danny Schechter dissect the news in this perceptive, troubling 2004 documentary about media manipulation. The documentary repeatedly refers to George Orwell's *1984*, raising disturbing questions about how Big Brother controls a media suffused with doublespeak. Washington's relations with Saddam are ideal examples of the shifting military alliances between the superpowers Oceania, Eastasia and Eurasia in *1984*. The state-run media Winston Smith worked for at the Ministry of Truth couldn't have been more effective at pounding the drums for invading Iraq as America's corporate media was.

In *Bush Family Fortunes*, America's great investigative reporter in exile, Greg Palast, returns to the scenes of the crimes previously revealed in his bestseller *The Best Democracy Money Can Buy* to rake more First Family muck. *Bush Family Fortunes* discloses damaging information regarding Bush's Guard service. Retired Texas Air National Guard Lieutenant Colonel Bill Burkett (subsequently implicated in the Dan Rather documents docu-drama) states on camera that shortly after G.W. became Texas' governor, Burkett witnessed a speakerphone call from Governor Bush's office to TANG, telling Guard officers: "clean [Bush's] records from his files." Palast said after the call, Burkett "asked the officers if they had carried out the questionable orders, and they said 'absolutely.' They pointed, and Burkett saw in the trashcan Bush's personnel, pay records."

But *Bush Family Fortunes* deals with much more than Bush's military record. It delves into the Bush family's murky finances and business dealings with assorted sordid weapons merchants and Arab oil tycoons. Palast sketches a truly chilling scenario tying backers of Bush's early oil ventures, as well as Bush Senior's post-presidency business activities, to the Bin Ladens and other unsavories. Palast raises disturbing questions about where Bush government policy begins, and family enterprise ends. He also revisits the Florida debacle that scrubbed thousands of blacks from the Sunshine State's voter rolls, setting the stage for the Jeb Bush/Katharine Harris orchestrated coup.

9/11 in Plane Site has a conspiracy-theory take on the September 11th terrorist attacks, and raises questions that many will dismiss as farfetched, but are nonetheless disturbing. One of the 2004 nonfiction film's most serious allegations is that the Twin Towers' collapse was due to explosives—not plane crashes. Even more jarring is the assertion that a plane did not hit the Pentagon, and no jet wreckage was found there. *Plane Site* is narrated on camera by Dave vonKleist, who hosts "The Power Hour" radio program with wife Joyce Riley, one of Showtime's "American Candidates." Narrated by Canadian journalist Barry Zwicker, 2004's *The Great Conspiracy* also raises blood-curdling questions about what really happened on September 11, and who was really behind it. The film brazenly points a finger at Bush's White House.

The Media Education Foundation's 2004 *Hijacking Catastrophe, 9/11, Fear & the Selling of American Empire* is a hard-hitting investigation into how neocons in the Bush regime manipulated fear to co-opt the September 11th catastrophe in order to pursue their Project for a New American Century global hegemony plans. Sut Jhally and Jeremy Earp's cogent film generally avoids wild-eyed conspiracy theorizing, although some interviewees claim Afghanistan was invaded because of a projected Afghan oil pipeline.

The well-put-together documentary interviews Tariq Ali, Benjamin Barber, Medea Benjamin, Noam Chomsky, Michael Eric Dyson, Stan Goff, Chalmers, Johnson, Norman Mailer, Mark Crispin Miller, Scott Ritter, Norman Solomon, Jody Williams, bell hooks, Susan Faludi, Todd Gitlin, Naomi Klein, John Stauber and Cornel West. Retired Air Force Lieutenant Colonel Karen Kwiatkowski exposes a Pentagon propaganda scheme to exploit 9/11-related anxieties to enable an attack on Iraq and more. *Hijacking* clarifies why no color signifies "all's clear" on the Homeland Security's color-coded terror alert system, as the administration terrifies people with endless scenarios of terror and perpetual war.

It also reveals the fetishization and glamorization of war, including media infatuation with the razzmatazz military hardware. *Hijacking* shows what these weapons do to humans, particularly unarmed civilians. *Hijacking* also exposes the military records of Bush and Wolfowitz, who avoided combat.

Other 2004 documentaries of interest include *Persons of Interest* and *The Art & Crimes of Ron English*. The former consists of interviews with a dozen post-9/11 Islamic detainees and their relatives, who were denied legal representation and held indefinitely and incommunicado by Ashcroft's America. Directed by Alison MacLean and Tobias Perse, *Persons* played at human rights filmfests, winning Amnesty International's 2004 Humanitarian Award. Pedro Carvajal's *The Art & Crimes of Ron English* documents a guerilla artist and "billboard bandit" who spoofs and mocks advertising brands with politically astute jabs displayed via outdoor art.

Fahrenheit 9/11 is the culmination of the renaissance of progressive documentaries. *Bowling* opened the path to political documentaries' resurgence by becoming the most financially successful nonfiction film ever, plus an Oscar winner. His speech at the Academy Awards ceremony as Bush launched war was the second greatest moment in Oscar's political history:

"...I'd like to thank the Academy for this. I have invited my fellow documentary nominees on the stage with us... they're here in solidarity with me because we like nonfiction. We like nonfiction and we live in fictitious times. We live in the time where we have fictitious election results that elects a fictitious president. We live in a time where we have a man sending us to war for fictitious reasons. Whether it's the fiction of duct tape or fiction of orange alerts we are against this war, Mr. Bush.

"Shame on you, Mr. Bush, shame on you!

"And any time you got the Pope and the Dixie Chicks against you, your time is up. Thank you very much."

Amidst all of the attacks on Moore and his film, few GOP or Bush dynasty spinners have attempted to refute *Fahrenheit 9/11*'s damning accusations. Have the Bushes denied their business dealings with Saudi royals, oilmen and, in particular, with the Bin Ladens? Or the Bushes' ties to the Carlyle Group, a multi-billion dollar defense contractor, which the Bin Ladens invested in? That almost no Congress members have children serving in Iraq, or are willing to send them to the frontlines?

One Republican who tried defending Bush is former Contract on America Congressman Joe Scarborough. At a September 18, 2004 Wednesday Morning Club breakfast in the Beverly Hills Hotel, a resentful Scarborough disputed Moore's contentions in his "cynical piece of garbage" about the Afghan oil pipeline and 2000 election outcome. However, Scarborough didn't mention, let alone refute, most of Moore's "lies"—such as Bush Senior attending a Carlyle meeting in Washington with Shafiq Bin Laden, Osama's half-brother, on 9/11.

In comparison to networks and major publications, Moore had a puny operation, yet it was he who showed what most mainstream media didn't—civil disturbances at Bush's inauguration; wounded and dead U.S. soldiers in Iraq; a funeral service for a slain serviceman; Bush cooling his heels for seven minutes in a school after learning of the terrorist attacks, and then scurrying about on Air Force One.

One attempt to defame and defuse Moore is to deny 9/11 is even a documentary (this tactic parallels efforts to deny Kerry's combat record). Some call it "propaganda" instead. However, the difference between propaganda and documentary is not necessarily the difference between deception and truth (although sometimes it is).

Dr. Nancy Snow worked as a government propagandist for the U.S. Information Agency and as an Assistant Professor of Communications at Cal State Fullerton and Adjunct Assistant Professor of Communication at USC Annenberg. She has written *Propaganda, Inc., Information War* and is co-editor of *War, Media and Propaganda: A Global Perspective.* According to Snow, "Propaganda is any organized and systematic effort to disseminate a particular doctrine; it is mass persuasion with a purpose that advantages the intentions of the sender; it's essentially a neutral set of techniques that derives its positive/negative effects from specific application of those techniques.

"Three important characteristics of prop[aganda] are: 1) It is intentional or purposeful, designed to incite a particular reaction or action in the target audience. 2) It is advantageous to the propagandist or sender (advertising, P.R. and political campaigns are considered forms of propaganda). 3) It is usually one-way and informational as opposed to two-way and interactive communication."

The fact is that *Fahrenheit 9/11* is both a documentary *and* a work of propaganda. Indeed, it is a piece of agitprop, meant to agitate an audience through propaganda in order to take action (in this case, resist Bush). Propaganda always aims at persuading, but that doesn't mean it always lies. It is, more accurately, the difference between advocacy and objective journalism. Moore's film was vigorously fact checked, and many of his controversial contentions have been upheld by the 9/11 Commission, or not even disputed.

All documentaries have a point of view. There is no pure *cinema verite*—even bankcams have points of view. Certainly all of the previously mentioned documentaries in this book have strong political perspectives.

Moore certainly has enemies—but they're far outnumbered by fans. On July 30, 2004 Moore appeared on the season premiere of Bill Maher's *Real Time* HBO show and faced off against Representative David Drier, an important figure in Bush's campaign. I was in the studio audience that night, and before the show began, a producer told us not to boo and hiss speakers we disagreed with. Ovations for Moore were so overwhelming that Maher quipped that Moore, and not another guest, rapper Andre 3000, was getting the "rock star" treatment. Even though Dreier admitted he hadn't seen *9/11*, the GOP hack attacked Moore; virtually the entire audience booed and laughed so hard at the Pasadena congressman on live TV that Maher had to stop the show and admonish the audience.

Michael Eisner dumped *Fahrenheit 9/11*, and financially-troubled Disney backed another documentary instead, the supposedly patriotic *America's Heart and Soul.* According to BoxOfficeMojo.com, Disney has not released the documentary's production costs. However, *Heart* had a three-week run in July 2004 and played at 98 theaters during its widest release, grossing $314,939. *Fahrenheit 9/11* opened in theaters on June 23, playing until October 28; 2,011 theaters screened it during its widest release. Its production budget was $6 million, and *9/11* has earned $220,694,771-plus. This means *Fahrenheit 9/11* out-grossed *America's Heart and Soul* by $220,379,832—or by more than a fifth of a billion dollars. Eisner had his dubious reasons for dumping the most profitable documentary ever. But by the logic of capitalism he should not only be immediately fired, but forced to pay Disney shareholders and the struggling company back for the $220 million loss his business decision cost the firm.

THE NEW WAVE OF PROGRESSIVE FICTION FILMS

> "[A]t a time where the issues are so profound, and the people—left or right—are struggling with them at such a deep level, artists, communicators, filmmakers, musicians, writers, directors are going to find a way to go into some of those questions. I mean, we'd be deaf, dumb and blind if we weren't, right?"

— Robert Greenwald, in an interview with the author

The documentary has long been Hollywood's poor relation (although the post-9/11 upsurge may change this). Tinseltown's *metier*, what it's best known for are movies with actors, scripts, production values, etc. And never before have special effects played such a key role in filmmaking.

Asked if the progressive trend of contemporary documentaries is bleeding over into features, Robert Greenwald states: "*The Manchurian Candidate*... I think at a time where the issues are so profound, and the people—left or right—are struggling with them at such a deep level, artists, communicators, filmmakers, musicians, writers, directors are going to find a way to go into some of those questions. I mean, we'd be deaf, dumb and blind if we weren't, right? If we're living in this period of time, and you don't make a film that touches on any of these things, then you're in an insane asylum someplace, because you're pretending this reality isn't happening. I think we will see more of it, some will be lousy, some will be good, some will do business, some won't do business. It'll never be an avalanche, because the system essentially is not designed to do that. Not from a conspiracy point of view, but from an economic point of view."

Greenwald points out: "The big issue is when the financing kicked in. Because right after 9/11, all financing for anything critical came to an immediate halt. Until people realized, oh wait a minute, you're not unpatriotic [for] looking at the world differently."

To its credit, on September 23, 2001, Showtime aired a film directed by a niece of Franz Fanon. Euzhan Palcy, the first black female director of a major Hollywood feature (1987's South Africa drama *A Dry White Season*, which scored Brando an Oscar nomination), helmed "The Killing Yard," about the 1971 Attica prison uprising in upstate New York. Governor Nelson Rockefeller brutally suppressed the rebellion, and inmates were blamed for the bloodshed. Shango (Morris Chestnut) is charged with murdering guards (probably killed by authorities during the raid), and is defended by National Lawyers Guild co-founder Ernie Goodman (Alan Alda). In 2003, the Guild's L.A. chapter honored "The Killing Yard's" writer/producer at its annual awards dinner. The made-for-TV-movie directed by Martinique's Palcy (*Sugar Cane Alley*) packs a wallop. Opening September 10, 2001 at the Toronto Film Festival, *Yard* then played for U.S. audiences on Showtime less than two weeks later. This radical picture, completely sympathizing with the black militant and his leftist lawyer, was the first progressive fiction film released in 9/11's wake.

The first theatrically released post-9/11 feature was an anti-Hollywood blacklist drama, the big budget *The Majestic*, released December 21, 2001. With its anti-McCarthyism and pro-civil liberties message, this Jim

Carrey vehicle was a huge flop. Carrey plays Peter Appleton, an innocent Hollywood screenwriter subpoenaed by HUAC, who mistakes him for a Communist or Party sympathizer during the Red Scare. (At least the 2000 biopic *One of the Hollywood Ten* featured an actual card-carrying Communist, Jeff Goldblum as Herbert Biberman.) After a car crash, Appleton winds up at a California all-American town named Lawson (as in John Howard Lawson), where he is mistaken for a missing WWII hometown hero. After a bout with amnesia, like Woody Allen before him, Appleton ultimately resolves to confront the Tinseltown witch-hunters, and to make socially meaningful movies.

The Majestic's message about domestic repression failed to resonant with terrified ticket buyers in the America of the PATRIOT Act, Homeland Security and the Afghan War, losing about $60 million.

Michael Mann's *Ali*, which opened on December 25, 2001, suffered a similar fate. Although it won Will Smith a Best Actor Oscar nomination for playing the Black Muslim boxer, as Americans smarted from September 11th and invaded Afghanistan, audiences were in no mood to see a film that accurately portrayed history's most famous draft resistor. The feature showed Ali's refusal to go to Vietnam. "No Viet Cong ever called me 'nigger,'" Ali famously said, and onscreen Smith urges blacks not to serve in whitey's army to fight other non-whites. Still-traumatized audiences weren't ready for something so "unpatriotic," even if it depicted the most famous, popular man on Earth. Three years after its release, the $130 million-plus feature had earned back only $87,713,825.

Just as the first progressive documentary to screen after September 11th was a Castro biopic, the fourth American dramatic production to deal with left-wing politics after 9/11 and second on TV was a biopic about the Cuban revolutionary. (Castro also "starred" in two Oliver Stone-helmed HBO docs, 2003's "Comandante" and 2004's "Looking for Fidel.") In January 2002, Showtime premiered its Cuban Revolution miniseries about Castro, starring Victor Huggin Martin. *The Motorcycle Diaries*' Gael Garcia Bernal alternates between ruthlessness and starry-eyed idealism as Che. When he informs Castro of his impending departure for Bolivia, Che dreamily reveals his plan to ignite world revolution.

The producer who co-led Hollywood's antiwar movement and helped usher in the tidal wave of dissident docs also brought one of the first progressive fiction productions made after 9/11 to the little screen. Greenwald's "The Redeemer" aired March 18, 2002 on the USA Network.

Matthew Modine plays a prison teacher convinced that one of his pupils is a framed-up political prisoner, and campaigns to free him. Obba Babatunde co-stars as a Black Panther set up by the F.B.I. in a COIN-TELPRO sting operation. Apparently loosely based on an actual case, the film is a powerful condemnation of COINTELPRO and the F.B.I. The TV movie was directed by Aussie Graeme Clifford, who helmed 1982's *Frances*, wherein Jessica Lange won an Oscar nomination for portraying leftist actress Frances Farmer.

The third post-9/11 progressive feature that was theatrically released was also (like *Fidel*) about Latin American revolutionaries. *Frida* was co-produced by a Mexican actress who dreamt of making a biopic about her homeland's great painters. The determined Salma Hayek reportedly beat out Jennifer Lopez and Madonna to play Frida Kahlo, a woman who was a revolutionary in and out of bed. Of course the emphasis of this 2002 drama is on Kahlo's tempestuous love life and her crippling accident. She and muralist Diego Rivera (Alfred Molina) were not only not married, but were also members of the Mexican Communist Party (PCM). Indeed, they moved further left as acolytes of Leon Trotsky (Geoffrey Rush). Although separated, Frida and Diego set aside their differences to offer Trotsky refuge, as Stalin's KGB hunts him down. The scene where the aging Trotsky and injured Frida climb an Aztec pyramid is quite moving. Frida was supposely hot-to-Trotsky, and the biopic portrays her rumored love affair with the married Bolshevik.

Julie Taymor's imaginative direction brings Kahlo's art alive. According to boxofficemojo.com, *Frida*'s production budget was $12 million, and its marketing costs $10 million. Since its October 2002 release, the feature's worldwide gross has been more than $56 million, proving a well-made, spicy film about Communists can find audiences, critical acclaim and Academy Awards—Best Makeup and Original Score—and was nominated for Best Actress, Art Direction, Original Song and Costume.

A month after *Frida* premiered, Australian Phillip Noyce's version of Graham Greene's novel *The Quiet American* was theatrically released—after a long delay. Productions with contrarian stances got caught in the post-9/11 crossfire, and perhaps foremost among them was *The Quiet American*. Michael Caine—a two-time Oscar winner and recipient of a British knighthood—campaigned like a first-time indie filmmaker for *Quiet*'s release while it languished on the shelf. According to the *Toronto Sun*, Miramax "abandoned it because... Harvey Weinstein did not like the politics... Only the success of the film in the 2002 Toronto film festival saved it..." Shot in Vietnam, Caine plays a British foreign correspondent. Brendan Fraser co-stars as an intelligence agent masquerading as an American aid worker stationed at the U.S. embassy in Saigon during the 1950s. Their competition for the Vietnamese beauty Phuong (Do Thi Hai Yen) symbolizes Washington's campaign to win hearts and minds in Indochina. More faithful to Greene's 1955 novel than Joseph Mankiewicz's 1958 cold war version, the remake restored the novel's anti-Americanism, delaying its release until about a year after 9/11. Moviegoers were not in the mood to see Washington's Machiavellian machinations overseas excoriated, and *Quiet* lost money.

The Greenwald-produced "The Crooked E: The Unshredded Truth About Enron" aired December 30, 2002 on CBS, starring Mike Farrell as Enron CEO Kenneth Lay, in the only major screen production Greenwald and Farrell collaborated on. Farrell turned in a solid performance as "Kenny Boy," in what Greenwald jokingly referred to as "the role Mike was born to play." (Lay threatened to sue, but the filmmakers were undeterred.) Brian Dennehy co-starred in this adaptation of Brian Cruver's autobiographical exposé, directed by Penelope Spheeris and scripted by Stephen Mazus. From 2001 to 2002, Enron's shares plummeted from $62 to 20 cents each. Greenwald's saga of corporate greed and treachery run amok, and the Texas corporation's downfall, eschews the "few bad apples" theory and envisions Enron's rise and fall as a systemic problem of capitalism itself.

The 2002 CBS TV movie "Salem Witch Trials" starred Shirley MacLaine, Peter Ustinov and Alan Bates. Like Arthur Miller's *The Crucible*, this miniseries used the 1692 Salem witch-hunt to comment on contemporary politics. Whereas Miller condemned the blacklist and McCarthyism, *Salem* tackles the USA PATRIOT Act, mass detentions, mass deportations, Gitmo, etc. The miniseries depicted extremist Puritans as counterparts to 21st century Christian rightists, revealing them as hypocrites hiding behind doctrine to pursue their own greedy, power-mad agendas. Of course, one of the few nonwhites is scapegoated—"witch" Tituba Indian (Gloria Reuben), an African slave. But nobody's safe from being executed— MacLaine as the devout Rebecca Nurse is finally accused of sorcery, and her speech denouncing the witch-hunters for attempting to stifle "dissent" could just as easily have been hurled at latter-day puritan John Ashcroft. *Salem* was produced by Ed Gernon, later fired by CBS after producing the 2003 miniseries "Hitler: The Rise of Evil," as conservatives accused him of attacking Bush through Nazi analogies.

Martin Scorsese's 2002 *Gangs of New York*, set in 19th century Manhattan, had a sharp commentary on prejudice against Irish immigrants, gang violence, war and the draft. I asked what Scorsese thought when he heard people with names like O'Reilly—who likely would have been reviled in the 19th century—rail against modern day immigrants, and the director said, "That's my point." *Gangs* ends with the bloody anti-draft riots in Manhattan—as the Iraq War loomed—and has a nod towards class warfare.

2003's "And Starring Pancho Villa As Himself" starred Antonio Banderas as the mustachioed Mexican. Villa has been portrayed in *Yanqui* movies primarily as a *bandito*, but in this HBO TV movie, he's depicted as a serious revolutionary out to right social wrongs. (However, some objected to the Mexican being played by a Spaniard.) The made-for-TV-movie fictionalizes Villa's efforts to use motion pictures to capture his guerrilla heroics and spread his radical cause. With "Villa," Larry Gelbart—best known for writing the "M*A*S*H" sitcom and 1982's *Tootsie*—probably penned his most complex script. "Villa" contains thoughtful ruminations on propaganda, film, politics and revolution. D.W. Griffith, Raoul Walsh and John Reed are depicted in this period piece directed by Australian Bruce Beresford, co-starring Alan Arkin and Jim Broadbent.

Showtime made a cycle of black-themed productions in 2003. "Jasper, Texas" is based on the true story of the dragging death of African American James Byrd by white supremacists in June 1998. "Jasper, Texas" reveals how Governor Bush deserted the east Texas town (population 8,247) in its hour of need, and how a proposed hate law is defeated in the Texas State legislature. When the armed New Black Panther Party converges on Jasper at the same time as the Ku Klux Klan, and a race riot appears imminent, the state does little to assist the besieged town. Bokeem Woodbine plays New BPP leader Khalid X, based on Minister Khallid Abdul Muhammad, formerly spokesman for Nation of Islam's Minister Louis Farrakhan. The film's sympathy is with the Byrd family, and it sensitively portrays the friendship between the town's first black mayor, R.C. Horn (Lou Gossett Jr.) and Jon Voight as the white sheriff Billy Rowles.

Showtime's "Deacons for Defense" is based on the true story of an armed African American self-defense group in Bogalusa, Louisiana. During 1964's "Freedom Summer," the Deacons fight back against the KKK with force. Forest Whitaker and Ossie Davis co-star in this fictionalized account of the heroic group that emerged shortly before the Panthers did

"Pentagon Papers" hero Daniel Ellsberg with his book *Secrets: A Memoir of Vietnam and the Pentagon Papers*, shows solidarity with a contemporary whistleblower, Ambassador Joe Wilson, at a 2003 forum in the Armand Hammer Museum at UCLA. The FX biopic "The Pentagon Papers" starred James Spader as Ellsberg.

in Oakland in 1966. Black actor/director Bill Duke helmed the TV movie, which was based on a story by Michael D'Antonio, who also wrote the story Showtime's "Crown Heights" was based on. Directed by Jeremy Kagan, it is based on 1991 race riots that erupted in Brooklyn between blacks and Hasidic Jews. "Crown Heights" starred Howie Mandel as a rapping rabbi and Mario Van Peebles as a youth counselor. The two form an anti-violence, pro-tolerance group called Project Cure that seeks to bridge the gap between the two ethnic groups. The film premiered February 2003 (Black History Month).

As the Bush regime plunged America into another military quagmire, the Daniel Ellsberg biopic "The Pentagon Papers" aired March 9, 2003 on the basic cable FX Network—owned by none other than Fox's Rupert Murdoch. The made-for-TV-movie unambiguously portrays Ellsberg as an antiwar hero, taking his side as he liberated the classified Pentagon Papers and the *New York Times* and *Washington Post* published the 7,000-page hidden history of the Vietnam catastrophe. James Spader plays Ellsberg in this tale of sex, lies and Xeroxing, which co-starred Alan Arkin and Damir Andre as Ellsberg's attorney Leonard Boudin. I asked Ellsberg what he thought of the FX pic, and Ellsberg said that while he enjoyed the TV movie, it bore little resemblance to what really happened. I also asked the *über*-leaker if someone had leaked a copy of the script to him, and Ellsberg laughed, answering "yes."

T for Terrorist is a witty Arab-American-made short that spoofs Tinseltown stereotypes and won awards on the film festival circuit. It stars Egyptian-born actor Sayed Badreya as an Arab actor tired of playing terrorists. (In 1999, Badreya—who produced *T*—played a Hezbollah gunman in *The Insider* and an Iraqi tank officer in *Three Kings*.) In a plot twist, Badreya turns the tables on a racist movie set. Hollywood's leading Arab actor, Tony Shaloub, who co-starred in movies like *The Siege*, appears in *T* as the man in white. (In the USA Network series "Monk," starring Shaloub, the detective deduces that a suspect is preparing to become a U.S. citizen when he spies a copy of the Constitution—which, Monk joked, no American reads.)

Directed, co-written by and starring Chris Rock, 2003's *Head of State* alternates between slapstick and satire, as a black activist runs for, and wins, the presidency. Along the way, community activist turned candidate Mays Gilliam makes trenchant observations on race and politics in the USA. His conservative white opponent, Senator Bill Arnot (James Reb-horn) ends his speeches saying: "God bless America—and nobody else."

What was all that *sturm und drang* regarding "The Reagans" about? Was it the fact that the conservatives' beloved icon was portrayed by Bar-bra Streisand's husband James Brolin? That Nancy Reagan was played by non-American actress Judy Davis, who previously depicted a Red in 1996's *Children of the Revolution* and a left-wing terrorist in 1982's *The Final Option*? That someone filmed a Reagans biopic that wasn't a hagiog-raphy—especially as the Gipper lay dying of Alzheimer's?

The vast right-wing conspiracy knocked the miniseries off its originally scheduled November 2003 CBS broadcast. Without having seen it, radio jock Michael Reagan whined: "I fully expect this mini-series will be largely unfavorable to my dad... Hollywood has been hijacked by the liberal left."[19]

"The Reagans" was rescheduled for screening on Showtime, which—like CBS—is owned by Viacom, but has a far smaller viewership. As seen in late 2004, the Emmy-nominated miniseries committed the cardinal sin of criticizing the Reagans. Ronnie is depicted as being a blacklist informer while Screen Actors Guild president. From McCarthyism to *glasnost*, Reagan's anti-communism is a recurring theme in this made-for-TV-movie. Watching Ronnie collaborate with HUAC conjured up unhappy memories for right-wingers who preferred to forget Reagan's sordid past, including his offscreen role as F.B.I. informant T-10, finking on talents (some in the union he led) to J. Edgar Hoover.

While still in the Oval Office, Reagan's Alzheimer's is alluded to, and he is depicted as being pretty dimwitted overall. However, the October Surprise allegations are never mentioned. (Indeed, Reagan is shown peeved that the *mullahs* released the hostages during his inauguration, upstaging the actor.) Ronnie is criticized for the Iran-Contra affair, and the Cold Warrior's enthusiasm for Star Wars is attributed to his appear-ance as Secret Service agent Brass Bancroft in the 1940 sci-fi pic *Murder in the Air*, which depicted a space-based missile defense system.

---

19. Perhaps not coincidentally, the relationship between the ex-president and his adopted son is not always presented in a glowing light in the TV movie.

Reagan's silent indifference as the AIDS epidemic mounted is prominently shown. Nancy, on the other hand, is heroic in this regard. After her beloved hairdresser dies, she tries to get the president to use his bully pulpit to speak out against the disease.[20] But in most other regards, Nancy does not fare well. The couple meet because Nancy is confused with a commie of the same name during Tinseltown's witch-hunt, and the SAG president/washed-up actor playing opposite Bonzo the chimp clears her. Judy Davis portrays Nancy Davis as a scheming harridan, who conspires to persuade Ronnie to marry her, and consults the stars for advice. The overly ambitious Nancy pushes her has-been husband into politics. Both Reagans came from dysfunctional families, and then created one. The "family values" icons are depicted as having premarital sex, which leads to Nancy's out-of-wedlock pregnancy (with Patti Davis). But despite it all, the couple's genuine affection and enduring devotion to one another (even if it is often at the expense of their offspring) comes through in this biopic that dared to give the former first family mixed reviews.

Directed by the German filmmaker Katja von Garnier, 2004's "Iron Jawed Angels," about the Suffragette movement, reveals just how violent government repression of the women's voting rights movement was. Oscar winner Hilary Swank, Anjelica Huston and Julia Ormond portray Alice Paul, Carrie Chapman Catt and Inez Milholland in this excellent TV movie about the struggle for women's suffrage.

Hidalgo stars Viggo Mortenson as a half-Indian equestrian grappling with his indigenous heritage. In the beginning of this 2004 feature, the Wounded Knee slaughter of Native Americans is depicted—one of the rare times it's dramatized onscreen. Most of the action also takes place in Arab lands, where the film's big horserace occurs. This depiction of U.S. war crimes and of Arabs was screened as Americans remained embroiled in Iraq, and the Palestinian struggle intensified. Just as the genocidal Sand Creek massacre of Indians in 1970's *Soldier Blue* symbolized the My Lai massacre, Wounded Knee is a stand-in for the horrors Washington perpetrated in Iraq. It's no accident that *Lord of the Rings* co-star Mortenson has spoken at antiwar rallies.

Disney's big budget *The Alamo* premiered in San Antonio on March 27, 2004 and is a premonition of the March 31, 2004 bushwhacking of four civilian contractors in Fallujah. The burned corpses of the Americans were

---

20. In any event, Brolin/Reagan's most controversial comments regarding AIDS seemed to have been redacted from the version I saw on Showtime.

desecrated, dragged through the streets, beaten with sticks and hung from a bridge over the Euphrates. That same day, five U.S. soldiers were killed in a roadside bombing near Habbaniya. White House press secretary Scott McClellan called on the media to report on the Fallujah massacre "responsibly."

Hollywood's three most filmed American battles are the Alamo, Custer's Last Stand and Pearl Harbor—all clashes of civilizations, with surprise attacks by nonwhite, non-Protestants against predominantly WASP Americans, resulting in slaughters of the Yankees engaged in the expansion and defense of empire. John Lee Hancock's *The Alamo* reminds us of this. The San Antonio mission is an architectural archetype that has come to symbolize the Twin Towers and the Pentagon. The film is a meditation on empire-building and race relations, and is full of Iraq references. During a squabble between the whites that precedes the siege, a man who appears to be Tejano calls the Caucasians "lowlifes" and "disgraces who want the whole world." There's actually an explicit Arab reference—to bloodthirsty battle music Santa Anna's troops play.

Along with a handful of other features directors, notably Oliver Stone and John Sayles, Spike Lee almost single-handedly perpetuated American cinema's left-leaning tradition during the Thermidorian decades between the second and current age of progressive pictures. 1989's *Do the Right Thing* and 1992's *Malcolm X* are among the most powerful black consciousness films ever made. Lee's 2004 *She Hate Me*, starring Ellen Barkin, Monica Belluci, Jim Brown, Ossie Davis, Brian Dennehy, Woody Harrelson and John Turturro, satirizes corporate scandals and flashes back to Watergate. Various figures connected to the bungled Democratic Party headquarters break-in are depicted, including John Dean, G. Gordon Liddy, Nixon—and Frank Wills (Chiwetel Ejiofor), the black security guard who caught the third rate burglars and set the stage for the only U.S. presidential resignation. Lee told the *L.A. Times*: "Wills is a great American hero. He changed history, but he died penniless, while the bad guys went on to make plenty of money"—unlike *She Hate Me*, which tanked.

What may be 2004's most politically sophisticated U.S. feature is, appropriately, written and directed by John Sayles, who has created numerous left-leaning indies, such as the 1987 class struggle drama *Matewan*. Haskell Wexler also lensed 2004's *Silver City*, co-starring Chris Cooper as Dickie Pilager, tongue-tied stumbling scion of a Colorado political dynasty. This son of Senator Judson Pilager (Michael Murphy) and

A bumper sticker created to publicize John Sayles' 2004 *Silver City*.

gubernatorial candidate is an obvious reference to Bush. Richard Dreyfuss is Machiavellian consultant Chuck Raven, clearly based on Karl Rove. Kris Kristofferson plays a rugged individualist/industrialist, who—in a *quid pro quo*—backs Pilager's campaign. Darryl Hannah is Pilager's hippie-ish sister. David Clennon plays a wannabe real estate developer supported by his attorney wife, Mary Kay Place.

Danny Huston portrays Danny O'Brien, an investigator for Place's law firm and ex-writer for an alternative newspaper that went bust after O'Brien was set up with a false tip (presaging the Dan Rather/"60 Minutes II" debacle). Danny tries to unravel the mysterious death of an undocumented Latino farmworker, whose corpse makes an unplanned appearance at a Pilager photo op Raven wants to cover up. Investigating the migrant worker's death, Danny recovers his integrity, dignity and ex-lover (Maria Bello). Tim Roth plays Danny's ex-partner in the newsweekly, who remains true to his crusading credo by operating a website for investigative reporting. The finale—with innumerable fish floating dead on the surface of a pristine-looking, yet contaminated Colorado lake—is an apocalyptically portentous metaphor for Bush's America.

The feature blockbuster equivalent to *Fahrenheit 9/11* is Fox's *The Day After Tomorrow*, which played wide in 3,444 theaters and earned $542 million-plus by November 2004. Writer/director Roland Emmerich successfully wed the 1970s disaster genre to a global warming epic that conjured up many of the moviemakers' state-of-the-art special effects. The title is a reference to the 1983 TV movie "The Day After," which warned against nuclear war at the peak of the Reagan vs. the evil empire madness. *The Day After Tomorrow* is a riveting, slambang critique of the Bush administration's destructive environmental policies, as another ice age is unleashed. In one breathtaking sequence, a tidal wave washes over Manhattan. The Statue of Liberty freezes over. Tropical Mexico turns Norte Americanos back from its border and safety. An eco-Armageddon ensues—a premonition of the hurricanes that lashed the South and Caribbean and Indian Ocean tsunami in 2004, plus California's January 2005 torrential rains. Amidst the eye-popping special effects, willing suspension of disbelief was hardest when Kenneth Welsh as Vice President Becker (a dead ringer for Dick Cheney) broadcasts an apology's for Washington's disastrous eco-policies.

The Day After Tomorrow inspired the mid-November 2004 CBS miniseries "Category 6: Day of Destruction." As super-storms converge on Chicago, and a feisty Secretary of Energy (Dianne Wiest) contends with a nonresponsive administration, a computer hacker cracks the energy grid and an Enron-like company pulls a power scam. Daredevil stormchaser Tornado Tommy (scene-stealing Randy Quaid) is literally blown away, and a TV reporter (Nancy McKeon) tries blowing the whistle on the corrupt energy company, over the objections of her bottom line, ratings conscious producer.

HBO's 2003 "Angels in America" won more Emmys than any other miniseries in TV history. Al Pacino won for his unflattering portrait of Joe McCarthy's closeted sidekick Roy Cohn. Meryl Streep won the Emmy for Best Actress in a Miniseries for her sympathetic, poignant portrayal of Ethel Rosenberg, the Jewish Communist electrocuted for allegedly participating in a Red atomic spy ring. Upon accepting her award, Streep said: "The bravest thing in the world is that writer who sits alone in a room and works out his grief, his rage, his imagination and his deep desire to make people laugh. And he makes a work of art that then transforms the world with the truth, because that's all we want, you know. It's all we need."

The writer in question, Tony Kushner, also snagged an Emmy, as did director Mike Nichols. In addition to the pariah subjects of drugs and communism (not to mention Mormonism!), "Angels" also deals, of course, with AIDS and homosexuality. TV has been playing an important role in demystifying and de-stigmatizing gays, with a more open presentation of homosexuality. HBO's groundbreaking "Six Feet Under"—created by gay screenwriter Alan Ball—has a very human, empathetic depiction of gays. So do the Showtime series "Queer as Folk" and "The L Word"; the latter focuses on lesbians with an ensemble cast that includes Pam Grier. Basic cable and network TV are getting into the act, depicting positive gay characters on programs such as the reality show "Queer Eye for the Straight Guy" and NBC's sitcom "Will and Grace."

It would stretch a point to claim the *Spider-Man* movies have progressive politics, although the films repeat a line that could be the mantra for Bush critics. In both films, Uncle Ben tells nephew Peter Parker (Spidey's secret identity): "With great power comes great responsibility."

Likewise, it's probably an overstatement to say that the inspirational underdog saga *Seabiscuit* is a progressive movie. After all, once the scene is set for the Depression, the cure for hard times' hardships isn't the New Deal or socialism, but a racehorse. On the other hand, director/screenwriter Gary Ross created 1998's anti-McCarthyite *Pleasantville*, and wrote 1993's mild presidential satire *Dave*. *Seabiscuit* is a celebration of the little guy (and horse), as *Spider-Man*'s Tobey Maguire plays a down-and-out lad who gets a second chance, and—like his steed—competes his heart out despite his disabilities. The real life horse also represents the regular Joe, who out-races the ultra-capitalist stallion, War Admiral, owned by an elitist snob.

In 2004's sequel to *Meet the Parents*, Barbra Streisand triumphantly returns to the screen after eight years in *Meet the Fockers*, which earned almost a quarter billion dollars in three weeks. La Streisand plays the sex therapist wife of house husband Dustin "The Graduate" Hoffman, the '60s-style Jewish parents of Ben Stiller, who is marrying a blonde *shiksa*. Her parents, the Byrnes, are uptight WASPs—retired CIA agent Robert De Niro and Blythe Danner. Culture wars ensue in this sly comedy of manners. At one point, citing his civil rights past, Hoffman stages a sit-in, blocking De Niro's RV with the civil disobedience tactic. Ultimately, blue state America converts red state America, as the Byrnes learn to loosen up in this liberal fantasy.

La Streisand and Hoffman presented 2005's Best Picture Oscar to Clint Eastwood for *Million Dollar Baby*, which prevailed at the Academy Awards, despite right wing attacks claiming that the boxing picture endorsed euthanasia. Morgan Freeman and Hillary Swank also won gold statuettes in the Best Supporting Actor and Best Actress categories, while Eastwood picked another one up for Best Director, snubbing conservatives (and, by the way, Mel Gibson's *The Passion of the Christ*, which didn't win a single Academy Award). What may have added fuel to the reactionary fire was that in the previous year, Eastwood had directed Tim Robbins and Sean Penn to Best Supporting Actor and Best Actor Oscars for their work in *Mystic River*. Thus, the man who had incarnated "Dirty

Harry" and been the Republican Mayor of Carmel helped the careers of the Tinseltown *bête noire* of the right, and made them more "bulletproof" from attacks by pro-Bush forces.

What theatrical genre would best serve to express the Mesopotamia mess? Gilbert and Sullivan comic opera? Theater of the Absurd? Artaud's Theatre of Cruelty? Shakespearian tragedy? In *Embedded*, Tim Robbins opts for the consciousness-raising *agitprop* of Brecht's Theatre of Alienation. This Actors' Gang play demolishes the Bushies' laughable buffoonery in ignoring world opinion and weapons inspectors, launching "preventive" war on a nation enfeebled by sanctions and disarmament— only to find out, uh, there were no WMDs. *Embedded* is one of the first fictional works about the Iraq War—the Sundance Channel reportedly will air a filmed version of it, directed by Robbins.

During the election, the Sundance Channel aired "The Al Franken Show," a version of Franken's "Air America" radio program, with liberal contributors and guests, such as Paul Krugman and Joe Conason.

Comedy Central's *faux* nightly news program, "The Daily Show," won Emmys in 2004 for Outstanding Variety, Music and Comedy series, and Outstanding Writing for Variety, Music and Comedy series. During the 2000 campaign, Larry King interviewed "anchorman" Jon Stewart, who described himself as a "socialist." Stewart and company's satirical jibing at newsmakers and newscasters alike is in the tradition of Chaplin's *The Great Dictator*. Unrestrained by "objectivity" or the need to suck up to high level sources to ensure access (which they know they're not going to get anyway), "The Daily Show" captures a story's essence better than its corporate "real" news counterparts do, and remembers Freud's dictum: "Humor is rebellious."

During the 2004 season of HBO's "The Sopranos," the gangsters refer to no-bid contracts awarded by the Bush administration or Defense Department, joking that they know all about no-bid contracts. John Calley, who was Warners' production head in the 1970s and released confrontational classics such as *Hearts and Minds* and *All the President's Men* has bought former counter-terrorism chief Richard Clarke's *Against All Enemies* in order to film it as a thriller. And so it goes.

When the opposition political party refused to oppose, progressive Hollywood stepped into the breach. And when the news media refused to report, progressive artists once again filled the vacuum. The powers-that-be couldn't make dissent vanish, it only reappeared in different forms and outlets. And thus a new oppositional culture was born.

CHE RIDES AGAIN!

"Let me say, at the risk of sounding ridiculous, that the true revolutionary is guided by great feelings of love."

— Che Guevara

Nothing is so indicative of the mood of the times than the return to the screen of Che Guevara, the *über*-world revolutionary. Just as Guevara, the slave rebel Spartacus and Che's fellow world revolutionary Trotsky appeared in '60s/'70s pictures, they are making comebacks today. Trotsky in *Frida*; Spartacus in an excellent 2004 miniseries adaptation of Howard Fast's novel for the USA Channel, starring Goran Visnjic and Alan Bates. Comic and '60s free speech icon Lenny Bruce is back too— Shout Factory released the six CD boxed set *Let the Buyer Beware*, and Showtime is reportedly producing a movie about Bruce, whom Bernie Travis and Dustin Hoffman depicted in 1965's *Dirtymouth* and 1974's *Lenny*. The boxer depicted in 1970's *The Great White Hope* made a comeback in *Unforgivable Blackness: The Rise and Fall of Jack Johnson*, a two-part Ken Burns documentary that aired on PBS in January 2005. Castro and Malcolm X were likewise highlighted in early 2005 documentaries aired on PBS.

But there's a bumper crop of Guevaras—to paraphrase Ernesto's famous Vietnam slogan: "Create one, two, three, many Ches!" Irishman Gabriel Byrne's 2003 *Meeting Che Guevara & the Man From Maybury Hill* is a sci-fi short co-starring John Hurt and inspired by an actual event— Guevara's brief stopover at Ireland en route from Cuba to the East Bloc. In addition to the miniseries *Fidel*, Gael Garcia Bernal reprises his role as a youthful Ernesto in 2004's *The Motorcycle Diaries*, which premiered at Sundance and was executive produced by Robert Redford, who screened it in Havana for Che's widow.

Motorcycle's screenwriter Jose Rivera (who was nominated for an Oscar for Best Adapted Screenplay) says Che is returning because: "There's certain figures that recur, there's something about Che—every generation, every group, every particular time has its own Che. Some people look to Che to be a symbol of resistance. Others look to him as a romantic ideal... the symbol of the united South America... a martyr to idealism. He's one of those figures that the Rorschach test [applies to]. Right

The Motorcycle Diaries costars Rodrigo de la Serna (a distant relative of Che Guevara) and Gael Garcia Bernal and director Walter Salles at a 2004 pre-release screening of the Che biopic.

now, given the world political situation, some people may be looking at him and saying, 'Oh, he's a symbol of anti-imperialism or resistance'... I do think that he's one of these historical characters that warp through time, and that each culture, each people bring their own needs..."

Bernal adds: "I think that this experiment, this film is an approach, like a Brazilian journalist wrote, it's an important way of approaching Che. Why? Because it develops, it's a kind of film... Does it matter that it was Ernesto Guevara, who became Che?... I think what you get in this film, in this approach, which I think is very needed in this time, the politics are somewhat separate. This film offers a reminder, you know, of politics... the real politics... you go out and walk in the streets... and the real politics you live is a day-by-day struggle. And Ernesto Guevara is said to be someone who brought that back into that school."

"It's an interesting thing," notes John Sayles. "Because *The Motorcycle Diaries* is the portrait of a young man, but it's also especially the portrait of a young man's consciousness and political consciousness being formed, which is a rare thing to see on film." The feature's tagline is: "Let the world change you... and you can change the world."

Whether riding a hog from his native Argentina to Central America, or fighting in Bolivia's mountains, Ernesto was quite the diarist. (In 1994, Swiss filmmaker Richard Dindo made a documentary based on Che's Bolivian diary.) Brazilian director Walter Salles' adaptation is based on the journal Guevara kept as the uneasy rider and Alberto Granado (played by Rodrigo de la Serna, a distant Che relative) choppered their way across South America. They politically came of age as eyewitnesses to the *campesinos'* hardships. *En route*, there's spellbinding scenery at places like Machu Picchu, and a Neorealist use of indigenous people.

Che's asthma gives the middle class youth insight into human suffering. He wants to become a doctor to alleviate human misery, and is serious, honest to a fault and compassionate. The medical student's experience at a so-called leper colony on the Amazon is transcendental. A Christ-like Che refuses to wear latex gloves and befriends the Hansen's disease sufferers. Che swims across the river full of deadly creatures that symbolically separates those with and without the disease, becoming the first person to ever swim across it. Joining the afflicted, Che casts his lot with the wretched of the Earth. The "lepers" are overjoyed by his act of solidarity, inspired by his compassion and courage—a wonderful metaphor for who Che would become.

At 2003's Oscar ceremony, Bernal presented the Original Song award *Frida* was nominated in and presented one of the telecast's most political moments. To an ovation, Bernal quoted Frida: "I don't paint my dreams; I paint my reality," adding: "The necessity for peace in the world is not a dream; it is a reality. And we are not alone. If Frida was alive, she would be on our side, against war."

In fair-turn-around, at the 2005 Academy Awards, Frida's Salma Hayek introduced "Al Otro Lado Del Rio," which was nominated for (and won) in the Original Song category. Hayek told millions of viewers that the song is from "the extraordinary film *The Motorcycle Diaries*, about the lives of the two passionate, young idealists Alberto Granado and Ernesto Guevara." Thus, the actress who played the lover and acolyte of Leon Trotsky introduced a song from a biopic about another champion of world revolution.

Steven Soderbergh is reportedly making a Che biopic in 2005, written by Terrence Malick and starring Benicio del Toro and Benjamin Bratt. Che has been depicted as the incorruptible revolutionary—in Alan Parker's 1996 *Evita*, Antonio Banderas' Guevara is counterpointed to Madonna's manipulative, material *chica* Evita Peron as the steadfast friend of the people. Che is generally portrayed as a hardline, even merciless foe of imperialism, a selfless socialist savior. Even Omar Sharif portrayed Guevara as misguided, yet devoted, fearlessly facing death. Bernal gives us the compassionate Che.

ON THE TRAIL OF THE POP CULTURE ASSASSINS

"I think we have to lance the fucking boil."

— Jay in *Checkpoint*, Nicholson Baker

Along with the reappearance of the *über*-revolutionary is another trend: The return of the assassin as a pop culture figure. Movies have long dramatized assassins, going back to Raoul Walsh as John Wilkes Booth in Griffith's 1915 *The Birth of a Nation*. Why are assassins (an Arabic-derived word) re-emerging as such hot characters?

Attempted and successful assassinations and political violence have swept Iraq, Georgia, Russia, Chechnya, Pakistan, Holland, Palestine, Israel, Turkey, etc. On September 15, 2004, as parliament debated outlawing foxhunting, London police clashed with 10,000 demonstrators. Five protesters entered the House of Commons, disrupting the debate— the first time since 1642 (when King Charles I entered parliament with soldiers to arrest opponents) the House of Commons was invaded. Two days earlier, a Batman-clad fathers' rights activist breached Buckingham Palace, standing for five hours on a ledge outside of Queen Elizabeth's main London residence. His group, Fathers 4 Justice, pelted Blair and other politicians in the House of Commons with condoms filled with flour dyed purple on May 19, 2004. Blair told *Time Out*: "If they are going to get you, they are going to get you."

The May 4, 2004 *N.Y. Post* declared: "Bush Bomb Plot—Qaeda Cell Smashed By Cops; Turks Foil Thugs' Plot to Kill Bush." On September 20, 2004, Derek Potts purportedly shot and killed security guard William Wozniak at the Illinois State Capitol Building, which was locked down afterwards. On September 23, 2004, "Democracy Now" reported the Secret Service was investigating New Jersey mother Sue Niederer, whose son died in Iraq. Niederer was arrested after interrupting a speech by Laura Bush while wearing a T-shirt declaring "President Bush, You Killed My Son." On Counterpunch.com, Niederer wrote she wanted to "rip the president's head off" and "shoot him in the groined area." Shots were fired into the Bearden, Tennessee office of the Bush campaign on October 5, 2004. That day the Republicans' Wisconsin Chairman complained that 50-plus pro-Kerry demonstrators stormed a West Allis GOP campaign office. Leftists reportedly plotted to assassinate Bush during his November 2004 Cartagena, Colombia visit. On December 1, 2004, shots were fired outside of Haiti's presidential palace as Secretary of State Colin Powell attended meetings inside. That month, men suspected of conspiring to kill Iraqi interim-Prime Minister Iyad Allawi were arrested in Germany shortly before Allawi met Chancellor Shroeder in Berlin. An alleged al Qaeda plot to assassinate President Bush—reputedly involving U.S. citizen Ahmed Omar Abu Ali, who claimed to be detained for 20 months by Saudis and tortured by them—was reported in February 2005.

Jonathan Demme's big budget *The Manchurian Candidate*, starring Denzel Washington, Meryl Streep, Liev Schreiber and Jon Voight, is the most prominent work in the assassin cycle. Demme's remake is as political a thriller as John Frankenheimer's 1962 original—the mind control and presidential assassination plot remains. 2004's *Manchurian* has been updated to Gulf War I. The Manchurian Global corporation is a clear reference to both the Cheney-linked Halliburton and the Bushes-linked Carlyle Group. Voight's liberal senator tells Schreiber: "Raymond, you're about to become the first fully-owned and operated Vice President of the United States," a reference to Cheney and the war profiteering Halliburton. The line also suggests Nader's critique of Bush as "a wholly-owned subsidiary" and "giant corporation in the White House masquerading as a human being." Nader also denounced Bush as a "messianic militarist" and "a selected dictator"—similar to what Streep's Senator Eleanor Shaw plots for Schreiber's Raymond.

Sean Penn stars as Samuel Bicke in Niels Mueller's 2004 *The Assassination of Richard Nixon*. It's suspected the 9/11 skyjackers planned to smash the jet that went down in Pennsylvania into 1600 Pennsylvania Avenue. In 1974, Bicke also attempted to hijack a jet and fly it into the White House. In Mueller's movie, news footage shows a military helicopter commandeered by a disaffected soldier landing near the Nixon White House. (A small plane violated White House airspace during Clinton's presidency, crashing onto Executive Mansion grounds.)

In *The Assassination of Richard Nixon*, Penn portrays Bicke as an increasingly desperate man, whose marriage and career collapse. Initially a successful salesman, Bicke can't bear the lies of American business. His honesty and integrity cause the onetime salesman of the month to get fired. Bicke then fails to receive a federal SBA loan for a business he's trying to launch with Don Cheadle (Bicke cries "racism").

Impressed by a TV report about the Panthers, Bicke goes to the local BPP headquarters, offering his services, cash and an interracial alliance. After pointing out to the black militants that he's Caucasian, the salesman tries to sell the Panthers on a surefire scheme to double membership: Admit whites to the party and change their name to the "Zebras."

Nixon is generally glimpsed in the background on TV as subtext. If one is unfamiliar with that era, the impact of why a malcontent tried assassinating Tricky Dick (the only president who resigned) as Watergate unfolded is diminished. Bicke is reduced to the stereotypical lone gunman, a loony loser seeking his 15 minutes of fame, thus depoliticizing the political subject matter. Mueller adds: "We're lucky there aren't more incidents like this in this country, given the availability of firearms."

Penn stars in the third installment of his assassin trilogy in 2005's remake of *All the King's Men*. Penn goes from would-be assassin to a governor who gets assassinated, portraying Willie Stark, *alter ego* of Louisiana's Depression-era governor Huey Long in Robert Penn Warren's Pulitzer Prize-winning novel and its 1949 film adaptation directed by ex-Red Robert Rossen. *King's* won the Best Picture Oscar, and Broderick Crawford earned the Academy Award portraying the Kingfish.

The fixation on political assassins has spilled over into other art forms. Stephen Sondheim's 2004 Tony-nominated Broadway musical *Assassins* portrays actual and would-be presidential assassins, including Booth, Oswald, Squeaky, Hinckley, etc. "Sex in the City's" Mario Cantone stole the show as Samuel Byck. Cantone says he suspects Byck's assassination attempt was covered-up because of the national anti-Nixon climate.

The Imagination Liberation Front's off-Broadway *"I'm Gonna Kill the President!" A Federal Offense*, by "Hieronymous Bang," is about confused revolutionaries trying to overthrow the government. Ticket holders must report to a Manhattan street before showtime, where the play's "agents" direct them to the secretive venue. Theatergoers are asked to volunteer their cells to make prank calls to the White House, as the audience shouts death threats.

Nicholson Baker's 2004 novel *Checkpoint* is about two old college buddies, Jay and Ben, who meet in a Washington hotel room, where Jay declares: "I'm going to assassinate the president... I haven't felt this way about any of the other ones. Not Nixon, not Bonzo, even. For the good of humankind... I think we have to lance the fucking boil."

Byck/Bicke was largely forgotten to history, yet here he is again after a 30 year hiatus, back in productions created by Broadway's foremost musical genius, and depicted by 2004's Best Actor Oscar winner. He was also the subject of a January 27, 2005 History Channel documentary, "The Plot to Kill Nixon." I asked Niels Mueller, director/co-writer of *The Assassination of Richard Nixon*, why Bicke was back. Mueller replied, "[producer] Kevin Kennedy and I finished the script in 1999, after Sean Penn got involved with the script, so it was well before 9/11... We wrote it during the Clinton years, so it wasn't a response to the Bush administration or anything like that... For me... I was interested in what takes a person from point A to point B, with point B being where somebody loses all empathy for the human beings right in front of him and lashes out in indiscriminate violence. That was my initial interest."

Mueller noted that financing repeatedly fell through, although Penn maintained involvement: "He had a very rare depth of commitment. He's a man of his word," Mueller said. The movie didn't get greenlighted until Bush's presidency. "The script got to the right producers who didn't shy away from the material... It got to the right people at the right time... When Sean Penn went to Iraq, and producer Jorge Vergara saw him on Larry King and yet was further impressed by him," Vergara agreed to back the politically-charged picture.

ACT 5

DIXIE CHICKED

"Go fuck yourself."

— Vice President Dick Cheney to Senator Patrick Leahy on the
Senate Floor, June 22, 2004

"You differ, you get destroyed."

— Senator Ted Kennedy on the Bush administration, *Hardball With
Chris Matthews*, September 27, 2004

NECKLACING DISSENT

We Americans have always prided ourselves on living in a free country,
where we can say and do whatever we want. This has been our calling
card to the world for centuries. But under the Bush administration, the
moment Americans publicly exercise their rights to freedom of speech and
dissent is precisely when they lose them. If you openly oppose the Bush
regime, you must be punished for doing so and made an example of. If
you speak freely and dissent in public, you lose your constitutionally
guaranteed rights. This intimidation has been true for ordinary citizens
and residents and world famous celebrities alike.

If you stand up and speak out, you must be vilified as "unpatriotic" and
painted with the scarlet "T" for traitor, treason, treachery and/or terrorist.
The chapter "Traitor Baiters" in *Banana Republicans* quotes the February 26,
2003 *diktat* from Fox's resident *grupenfuhrer*, Bill O'Reilly, that Americans
who didn't support the then-imminent war in Iraq should "just shut up" or
"be considered enemies of the state." According to John Stauber, co-author
of *Banana Republicans*, Tennessee State Senator Tim Burchett (R-Knoxville)
drew cheers in April 2003 when he said of war critics: "That's treason, not
patriotism. They ought to be run out of our country and not allowed back."

In contrast, the titles of left-leaning books that criticize Bush, such as Joe Conason's *Big Lies*, question the chief executive's candor, not his patriotism *per se*. On the other hand, political hit men have discovered that traitor baiting is a highly lucrative enterprise often underwritten by conservative publishers, think tanks, etc. Stauber cited a number of right-wing books that are reminiscent of the 1964 reactionary screed *None Dare Call It Treason* with intimidating titles and text aimed at silencing opposition.

They include: Mona Charen's *Useful Idiots: How Liberals Got It Wrong in the Cold War and Still Blame America First*; Fox News commentator and hooker toe sucker Dick Morris' *Off With Their Heads: Traitors, Crooks & Obstructionists in American Politics, Media & Business*; Fox's Sean Hannity's *Deliver Us From Evil: Defeating Terrorism, Despotism and Liberalism*; Daniel Flynn's *Why the Left Hates America: Exposing the Lies That Have Obscured Our Nation's Greatness*; Michael Savage's *The Enemy Within: Saving America From the Liberal Assault on Our Schools, Faith and Military* and *The Savage Nation: Saving America From the Liberal Assault on Our Borders, Language and Culture*; Laura Ingraham's *Shut Up and Sing: How Elites in Hollywood, Politics and the UN are Subverting America*; and that all-time favorite, *Treason: Liberal Treachery From the Cold War to the War on Terrorism* by Ann Coulter. The latest tome by the right's pin-up girl is quaintly entitled *How to Talk to a Liberal (If You Must): The World According to Ann Coulter*. (Larry Elder's *The Ten Things You Can't Say in America* may also deserve a dishonorable mention.)

Stauber pointed out: "Treason is a very specific crime punishable by death. There's a very high standard for ever convicting anyone of treason. Very few people have been convicted of it [in the U.S.]. So just to throw around words like this creates a really nasty, dangerous, un-American environment for politics, debate and civil discussion... Any books that impugn the motives of people who are saying things that frankly we now know to be true, like the war on Iraq was... unjustified by the evidence is anti-American." But where does this surly viciousness come from?

According to *The Godfather*. "The fish stinks from the head down." As investigative reporter Seymour Hersh documented, the "you're-with-us-or-against-us" mentality of the White House clearly set the tone. The chain of command flowed downwards from the Executive Mansion, where, as Truman said, the buck stops. Cavalierly ruling that the inmates of Camp X-Ray at Guantanamo are not entitled to the rights prescribed under the U.S. Constitution and the "quaint" Geneva Convention (as Bush's replacement for Attorney General Ashcroft, Alberto Gonzales, charmingly/alarmingly described the international rules for treating prisoners of war when he was White House counsel), the Bush regime set the stage for civil and human rights abuses, from Abu Ghraib prison to the Dixie Chicks backlash.

In Bush's America, nothing is sacred—no, not even our elections. Not content with stealing the 2000 race, it was disclosed in July 2004 that the chairman of the new Election Assistance Commission, DeForest Soaries, wrote a letter to Homeland Security head honcho Tom Ridge. It urged Ridge to seek emergency legislation from Congress that would allow Soaries' agency to reschedule the vote in the event of a terrorist attack.

Given the climate of repression in Bush's America, the questions are: How free is freedom in Bushworld? How free is free speech in America? Is the First Amendment still number one? How free is America?

At the Southern California American Civil Liberties Union's Bill of Rights dinner in December 2003, Executive Director Ramona Ripston addressed Bush's assault on constitutional rights in an impassioned speech. "The past two years would shock and shame those who wrote the Bill of Rights... The executive branch cynically used... September 11th to grab power, and take repressive measures that make us less free without making us more safe.

"We've seen Attorney General John Ashcroft use the PATRIOT Act to give the government more power to obtain your... records without court orders. We've seen the government take the power to seize the library records of Americans not charged with any crime, and to forbid librarians to inform patrons... Ashcroft authorized government spying on religious and political organizations without any evidence of wrongdoing... We've seen people who disagree with U.S. policy intimidated, investigated, prosecuted and called 'unpatriotic' in an effort to shut them up... 8,000 immigrants, mostly Arab and South Asian, detained and interrogated. Not because they're suspect of a crime—but simply because of their race, religion, ethnicity...

"What will happen tomorrow if we do not stop the government's disregard of the Bill of Rights and our freedoms? We cannot accept more intimidation of people expressing their political beliefs. No more Americans spirited away in the dark of night under the cloak of secrecy and denied access to friends, family and legal help. No more government eavesdropping on our conversations. No more extreme right-wing judges appointed to the courts... ACLU fights day and night to defend the dream of what America should be, and to prevent the nightmare of what John Ashcroft would do to it... We certainly hope Ashcroft will be out of a job next November," Ripston thundered.

HEY, MR. WILSON!

The list of the punishment wreaked on dissenters is long (indeed, it is a whole book unto itself). The government and right-wing's dossier on dissent details diplomats, teachers, gallery owners, soldiers, journalists, legislators and many ordinary people, as well as singers, movie stars and other show business personalities. A key chronicler of this account book of those held accountable by a vengeful administration and its conservative cronies and co-conspirators is John Stauber, founder and executive director of the Center for Media and Democracy. This Madison-based non-profit has investigated, exposed and countered organized government and corporate propaganda campaigns since 1993. The Center publishes the quarterly *PR Watch*; Stauber and CMD staffer Sheldon Rampton have published five books, including *Banana Republicans: How the Right Wing is Turning America Into a One-Party State* and *Weapons of Mass Deception: The Uses of Propaganda in Bush's War on Iraq.*

In 2003 Ramona Ripston may have hoped that Ashcroft would "be out of a job next November," but in the meantime, a woman that did lose her position was Valerie Plame. After Joseph Wilson, IV became the ambassador who came in from the cold, his wife was tossed out into the cold, exposed by Bush administration officials as a CIA operative. "Wilsongate" proved that no good deed goes unpunished: In February 2002, the CIA— under the direction of Vice President Dick Cheney—dispatched the ex-diplomat with African expertise to Niger to examine allegations that Iraq was trying to buy yellowcake uranium for a nuclear program. Wilson reported back that the charges were bogus—but this didn't stop Bush from repeating similar claims in his January 28, 2003 State of the Union address. On July 6, 2003 Wilson published in the *New York Times* his side of what Condoleezza Rice derided as just "16 words."

On July 14, 2003, reactionary columnist Robert Novak blew the cover of Wilson's wife, calling Plame "an Agency operative on weapons of mass destruction. Two senior administration officials told me Wilson's wife suggested sending him to Niger to investigate." Novak played the role of Dennis the Menace to society to the ambassador's Mr. Wilson. According to 1982's Intelligence Identities Protection Act, those outing covert agents can be fined $50,000 and/or imprisoned for up to 10 years. Attorney General Ashcroft excused himself from the ensuing official investigation.

In an interview, Ambassador Wilson told me: "I've always assumed that what they intended to achieve by outing my wife's name was to discourage others from coming forward. There was not really very much they could do to me. After all, I had said my piece. The rational conclusion is by outing my wife they were basically telling anybody else who might come forward that should you decide to, we will do to your family what we've done to Wilson's. We'll embarrass or compromise them, or drag them out into the public square and administer a beating to them."

Wilson went on to say, "I mean, these are really nasty guys. Rove, whether or not he leaked the name of my wife or authorized the leak, nonetheless pushed the story for a week after the leak came out. Even in a tough town like Washington, the idea of dragging somebody's family member into the debate, because you have a dispute with the husband, is just unprecedented. I frankly think Rove ought to be fired for having violated the president's own campaign promise of restoring dignity and honor to the White House and changing the tone in Washington."

The ambassador added: "The argument before Congress today is whether or not the U.S. government went to war on false pretenses. That's what they're trying to prevent from coming out. Trying to discredit me, by saying they basically lied on this subject, they're trying to keep others from coming forward and pointing out other places where they misstated the facts."[21]

---

21. The Wilson matter bears remarkable parallels to the Dreyfus case, wherein Jewish army captain Alfred Dreyfus was falsely accused of treason. Just as Emile Zola's written words about the Dreyfus Affair printed in the Paris newspaper *L'Aurore* threatened France's government, Wilson's *New York Times* op-ed challenged the Bush administration. Zola's 1898 letter to France's president about that infamous anti-Semitic miscarriage of justice was published in newspapers and called: *"J'accuse!"* ("I accuse!") Attorney General Ashcroft's decision to remove himself from the Department of Justice's probe into *"L'affaire* Wilson" could be headlined: "Je recuse!" The chief investigator in Dreyfus' secret court martial was Du Pati Du Plame—who, ironically, has the same uncommon last name as Wilson's wife, Valerie Plame. Zola's letter to France's president about the anti-Semitic Dreyfus case resulted in Zola's being convicted for libel, the journalist's fleeing into exile and, eventually, the exoneration of both Dreyfus and Zola, and the fall of France's conservative government, which advanced the cause of its progressive republican wing. As of this writing, the political outcome of Wilson's words and the probe into the disclosure of Plame's name, including whether anyone will serve time at a contemporary Devil's Island, remain to be seen.

LIONS AND TIGERS AND BEARS, OH MY!

"There was always the potential the Bush administration would use its new repressive apparatus to go after domestic political foes."

— Matthew Rothschild, in *The Progressive*

Ambassadors and CIA agents aren't the only ones stung by the Bush administration's repressive climate. *The Banana Republicans* chapter entitled "Traitor Baiters" contains "a long litany—although it's not exhaustive" of people high and low who have been investigated and intimidated by the government and corporations for expressing or even allowing dissenting viewpoints to be aired.

According to Stauber, the owner of a Houston art gallery was visited by F.B.I. agents, who'd received an anonymous tip that the exhibit "Secret Wars"—which displayed paintings inspired by U.S. covert actions and government secrets—was anti-American. Secret Servicemen interrogated a North Carolina college student about a poster in her apartment that criticized Bush's support of capital punishment. New Mexico high school teacher Bill Nevins was suspended and told his contract would not be renewed after a student in his poetry club read an antiwar poem over the school's closed circuit TV system. The club was also disbanded. Other disenchanted teachers in the so-called Land of Enchantment were similarly disciplined, including Albuquerque high school instructor Geoff Barrett, who was suspended for refusing to remove displayed student art expressing pro and con views of the war. Barrett said he was told that the posters in favor of the Iraq invasion weren't "pro-war enough."

"Democracy Now" reported on October 8, 2004 that a public university in Florida cancelled a speech by activist and academic Terry Tempest Williams because they feared she would criticize Bush for his environmental policies. Williams is a University of Utah professor of Environmental Studies and author of *The Open Space of Democracy* (which was apparently closed at Jeb's state).

Even legislators are not safe from Republican wrath and reprisals. On October 6, 2004, the House Ethics Committee scolded House Majority Leader Tom "The Hammer" DeLay for ethical transgressions, including behavior that suggested political donations might influence legislative action. The Ethics Committee, which consists of five Republicans and five Democrats, voted unanimously on its findings, and informed DeLay in writing that: "In view of the number of instances to date in which the committee has found it necessary to comment on conduct in which you have engaged, it is clearly necessary for you to temper your future actions to assure that you are in full compliance at all times with the applicable House rules and standards of conduct." According to *AP*, in the previous week, "In a separate case, the ethics committee admonished DeLay for offering to support the House candidacy of a Michigan lawmaker's son in return for the lawmaker's vote for a Medicare prescription drug benefit."

Even worse, "DeLay also raised 'serious concerns,'" the panel said, by contacting the Federal Aviation Administration to help locate Texas Democratic lawmakers fleeing the state in an effort to prevent the GOP-controlled legislature from passing a redistricting plan." They fled Texas to avoid voting on a reapportionment plan favoring Republicans, which Eleanor Clift alleged DeLay concocted with Bush adviser Karl Rove. In May 2003, the Majority Leader allegedly contacted the section of the Homeland Security Department that searches for terrorists to track a plane carrying state legislators.

Matthew Rothschild wrote in the *Progressive*: "There was always the potential the Bush Administration would use its new repressive apparatus to go after domestic political foes. Bush, Ridge and Ashcroft assured us no such thing would ever happen. Well, it has already," Rothschild asserted. CBSNews.com quoted Texas Democratic Congressman Martin Frost: "Not since Nixon and Watergate 30 years ago has anyone tried to use law enforcement for domestic political purposes." Texas ACLU executive director Will Harrell told CBSNews.com: "Getting Homeland Security surveillance assets involved in the political hunt for the missing state lawmakers demonstrates the extreme likelihood that unchecked surveillance powers will eventually be abused for political reasons."

Nobody's safe, not even relatives of the 9/11 catastrophe. On February 5, 2003, during the lead-up to war, Bill O'Reilly screamed at young Jeremy Glick, an anti-imperialist whose father had died in the World Trade Center, to "shut up—[he] wouldn't let him respond and told his producer to cut his mike," stated Stauber. Glick said in *Outfoxed* that once they were off air, a staffer warned him to leave the premises immediately to avoid an encounter with the enraged (and 6' 4") O'Reilly.

Those on the front lines supposedly defending democracy aren't allowed to use their democratic rights. Stauber said that *Stars and Stripes* reported "Soldiers are smacking head-on into public limits on their free speech." The military publication quoted a G.I. complaining that: "I find it absurd that these same people we put our lives on the line for can punish us for having our own opinions."

These opinions include seeking conscientious objector status. According to Amnesty International: "On 21 May 2004, a U.S. military court sentenced Staff Sergeant Camilo Mejía Castillo of the Florida National Guard to the maximum penalty of one year's imprisonment for desertion. He had refused to return to his unit in Iraq, citing moral reasons, the legality of the war and the conduct of U.S. troops towards Iraqi civilians and prisoners. Amnesty International considers him to be a prisoner of conscience, imprisoned for his conscientious opposition to participating in war."

After members of the Third Infantry Division criticized Bush and Rumsfeld, their families on the home front received e-mails from a commander warning against contacting the press "in a negative manner." Reporters embedded with the infantrymen were expelled, and troops were forbidden to talk with newsmen without prior approval.

"RATHER-GATE"

Journalists who don't toe the party line pay a high price. In 2002, CBS News anchorman Dan Rather told BBC's "Newsnight": "It's that fear that keeps journalists from asking the toughest of the tough questions... [T]here was a time in South Africa when people would put flaming tires around people's necks if they dissented. In some ways, the fear is that you will be necklaced here. You will have a flaming tire of lack of patriotism put around your neck." According to Greg Palast, who reports for "Newsnight," Rather went on to say that no U.S. reporter who values his neck or career will "bore in on the tough questions."

When the putative heir to Edward R. Murrow's legacy finally dared stick his neck out on September 8, 2004, like Rather predicted, his neck was expeditiously chopped off. In the "60 Minutes II" report, Ben Barnes confessed that when he was the Texas speaker of the House in 1968 he had helped pull strings behind the scenes to get George W. Bush out of going to Vietnam and into the Texas Air National Guard. (Shortly afterwards Barnes became Texas' lieutenant governor.) Rather also produced documents purportedly from Bush's late squad office, Lieutenant Colonel Jerry Killian, criticizing the young lieutenant for not fulfilling his Guard obligations, including disobeying a direct order to take his mandatory annual physical, which led to Bush's grounding.

The authenticity and provenance of the alleged documents were immediately questioned, and the veracity of the "60 Minutes" investigative report was greatly undermined. The story unleashed a furor that led to calls for Rather's head, the anchor's televised apology, and the postponement until after the election of another "60 Minutes" exposé that was potentially even more damaging to Bush. House Majority Whip Roy Blunt (R-Mo.) led 40 members of Congress in sending a letter addressed to CBS' president to demand that CBS retract the story and reveal its sources. Texas Republican Representative Joe Barton, chairman of the House Commerce Committee, called for a congressional investigation into the accuracy and fairness of news reporting. What was almost completely lost in the ensuing *sturm und drang* was Barnes' on-the-air confession, and the subsequent interview with Killian's secretary, Marian Carr Knox. While she, too, disputed the authenticity of the purported records in question, Knox insisted their content and contentions were essentially correct.

But from conservative bloggers to frothing-at-the-mouth hard right TV/radio jocks, Bush's Big Lie Machine was in high gear and dudgeon. The story was spun so that the "60 Minutes" allegations about G.W.'s sweetheart deal to get into the Guard and then not performing his duty were discredited. Instead of discussing whether or not Bush pulled strings and shirked military obligations, the subject was changed to those "forged" documents (a charge that the independent report on CBS contended was unproven) and Rather himself. I heard only one journalist dare ask if Bush had not taken his required annual physical because the exam tested for substances. (Ian Williams, author of *Deserter: Bush's War on Military Families, Veterans and His Past*, asked this on Pacifica's "Democracy Now.") The entire question as to whether or not Bush had gone AWOL and even deserted in time of war was deflected.

In addition, the Bush Guard story had bumped a reportedly half hour "60 Minutes" report on the phony Niger documents that tied into Bush's false assertion of those 16 words in his State of the Union address that claimed Saddam was seeking yellowcake uranium in Africa. This was the un-truth that had triggered the whole Ambassador Wilson/Valerie Plame brouhaha. It is important to note that CBS said that it went ahead with its "60 Minutes II" Bush Guard story after it had showed the Killian documents to the White House, which then did not contest their validity. How interesting that the Executive Branch, with all of the resources at its disposal (including the planet's biggest intelligence agencies) wouldn't pick up on supposed discrepancies in the documents, such as fonts, but mom and pop bloggers supposedly would.

During the 2000 race, author Jim Hatfield claimed that Karl Rove told him Bush Senior cut a deal with a Texas judge after his son was allegedly busted for cocaine. In exchange for expunging his record, W. would have to do community service at an inner city center for black youth. Once Hatfield revealed this charge in *Fortunate Son*, his criminal past was exposed, and by discrediting the messenger, the message itself was discredited.[22]

Hatfield was discredited, but his story itself was not disproven. One can only wonder if a September surprise was afoot vis-à-vis the "60 Minutes II" Guard story. It succeeded in not only tainting the Guard story, which chipped away at Bush's credibility as a war leader and truth-teller, but knocked another possibly even more harmful and recent story about another Bush lie off the air until after the election. Bear in mind that CBS had taken the lack of protest by the White House against the purported documents as further proof of their veracity, which had encouraged the Tiffany Network to run with what turned out to be a disastrous story for it. Was this yet another covert action of the Rove State?

According to Palast: "This is not a story about Dan Rather... This is really a story about fear, the fear that stops other reporters in the U.S. from following the evidence about this Administration to where it leads. American news guys and news gals, practicing their smiles, adjusting their hairspray levels, bleaching their teeth and performing all the other activities that are at the heart of U.S. TV journalism, will look to the treatment of Dan Rather and say, 'Not me, babe.' No questions will be asked, as Dan predicted, lest they risk necklacing and their careers as news actors [being] burnt to death."

Rather eventually resigned. Following an independent report, four CBS executives were axed on January 10, 2005.

---

22. By the way, the timeline of Hatfield's accusations matches the period when Bush was ducking taking physicals that could have revealed if he was using coke and other substances.

SCREWED, BLUED AND DONAHUED

For John Stauber, "Exhibit A" at the top of the roll call of rolled-back Bush critics is longtime TV host-no-more Phil Donahue. Jeff Cohen, formerly of Fairness and Accuracy In Reporting and a communications director for Dennis Kucinich's presidential campaign, was the senior producer of the short-lived MSNBC show *Donahue*, which aired weeknights. "Donahue was actually fired by MSNBC [February 28] 2003 just before the U.S. launched its attack on Iraq... There's a myth in the U.S., carefully planted and cultivated by the right-wing think tanks and media, that the mainstream corporate media has a liberal bias... If this was true, the media would be filled with people like Donahue... who supported the 2000 Ralph Nader campaign.

"The network said that 'Donahue' was cancelled because it didn't have a decent audience," Stauber continued. "That actually wasn't true... Although the network claimed poor ratings, 'Donahue' was actually pulling more viewers than any other program on MSNBC, including its signature program, 'Hardball With Chris Matthews.' The program was doing very well... by MSNBC standards." According to CNN, "Donahue" had 446,000 viewers, about one sixth of Phil's Fox competitor, "The O'Reilly Factor."

Stauber went on to say: "A leaked MSNBC memo was posted on the Internet [which] recommended getting rid of Donahue because he presented 'a difficult public face for NBC in a time of war. He seems to delight in presenting guests who are antiwar, anti-Bush and skeptical of the administration's motives... ["Donahue" could become] a home for the liberal antiwar agenda at the same time that our competitors are waving the flag at every opportunity'... General Electric is a major military contractor, so you could make the argument that while war's a horrible thing, it's not so bad for the owner of MSNBC," Stauber jabbed.

The cancellation of "Donahue" marked MSNBC's sharp turn to the right. A week after Phil got the axe, arch-reactionary radio host Michael Savage went on MSNBC with his vicious Saturday show "The Savage Nation." His TV tenure was shorter than Donahue's, as Savage was pulled by July, after telling a gay caller to "get AIDS and die" on live television. Former "Contract on America" GOP Congressman Joe Scarborough's weeknight program in a time slot later than "Donahue's" premiered April 14, 2003 on MSNBC. "Scarborough Country" producer George Uribe would not reveal the program's ratings, but as of this writing it remains on the air.

AN ATTEMPTED PALACE COUP AGAINST THE KING OF ALL MEDIA

The twilight of the gods has cast a long shadow on Howard Stern too. On April 9, 2004 the Center for Public Integrity reported: "The Federal Communications Commission has proposed $4.5 million in fines for broadcast indecency since 1990, with more than half the total assessed to stations that aired shock-radio pioneer Howard Stern. Yesterday, the FCC proposed a $495,000 fine against six Clear Channel Communications Corp. stations that aired Stern's show, prompting the giant radio broadcaster to drop the show from its broadcast lineup permanently. On March 18, the FCC proposed a $27,500 fine against Stern for a broadcast that aired in Detroit on July 26, 2001. Before that action, Stern had not been cited since June 1998. The FCC has sought $2.5 million in fines from stations that carried the controversial New York-based disc jockey's show since 1990."

Stern responded to the FCC in his usual inimitable way: "This is not a surprise. This is a follow up to the McCarthy type 'witch hunt' of the administration and the activities of this group of presidential appointees in the FCC, led by 'Colin Powell Jr.' [FCC Chairman Michael Powell] and his band of players. They and others... are expressing and imposing their opinions and rights to tell us all who and what we may listen to and watch and how we should think about our lives. So this is not a surprise. It is pretty shocking that governmental interference into our rights and free speech takes place in the U.S. It's hard to reconcile this with the 'land of the free' and the 'home of the brave.' I'm sure what's next is the removal of 'dirty pictures' like the 20th century German exhibit in a New York City Museum and the erotic literature in our libraries; they too will fall into their category of 'evil' as well."

Was it Stern's famed bawdy banter alone that incurred the wrath of the FCC? The shock jock insisted that it wasn't his raunchy repartee that got him kicked off of six Clear Channel stations. CNN quoted Stern as saying that the San Antonio, Texas-based "'Clear Channel is very tied to the Bush administration. Clear Channel for years has been defending me... I criticize Bush and then I'm fired... They acted out of politics."

Salon.com reported on the fact that "the content of Stern's crude show hadn't suddenly changed, but his stance on Bush had, [and that] gave the theory more heft. That, plus his being pulled off the air in key electoral swing states such as Florida and Pennsylvania... Stern himself went on the warpath... accus[ing] Texas-based Clear Channel—whose Republican CEO, Lowry Mays, is extremely close to both George W. Bush and Bush's father—canned him because he deviated from the company's pro-Bush line. 'I gotta tell you something,' Stern told his listeners. 'There's a lot of people saying that the second that I started saying, I think we gotta get Bush out of the presidency, that's when Clear Channel banged my ass outta here.'"

Salon.com also reported that the King of All Media was "Declaring a 'radio *jihad*' against President Bush... his burgeoning crusade to drive Republicans from the White House is shaping up as a colossal media headache for the GOP, and one they never saw coming." CNN quoted Howard as saying, "John Kerry will receive more votes because of this... My audience will vote in a bloc... We're also in a lot of key states... If we can affect that state that's big news'... The pioneering shock jock... has emerged almost overnight as the most influential Bush critic in all of American broadcasting, as he rails against the president hour after hour, day after day to a weekly audience of 8 [*AP* claims 12] million listeners. Never before has a Republican president come under such withering attack from a radio talk show host with the influence and national reach Stern has."

Stern is highly rated in the coveted 18-49 year old male demographic and his millions of listeners have been described as "schwing" voters. According to BoycottLiberalism.com, some of the shock jock's *bon mots* on Bush include: "George Bush has got to go and I'll do everything I can," February 24, 2004. "I think this guy has flipped his lid... When he is not doing this, he is on vacation. Rat fink... Our president, little monkey, time for him to go," February 25. "Get him out of office. I'm tellin' you, man, he's in dangerous territory [with] a religious agenda and you gotta vote him out. Anyone but Bush," February 29.

CPI noted: "So far in 2004, the FCC has proposed more fines for broadcast indecency than the previous 10 years combined... In terms of total fines, no broadcast compares to the long-running Stern show. Second behind Stern for the largest amount of proposed fines is Clem, with $753,000; third is the Opie and Anthony Show, now off the air, with $378,500; fourth is "Elliot in the Morning" which broadcasts in the Washington, D.C. area, with $302,500; fifth is long-time Chicago disc jockey Erich 'Mancow' Muller with $42,000 in proposed fines... when U2 lead vocalist Bono shouted 'this is really, really f***ing brilliant' at the Golden

Globe Awards, it still did not rise to the level of indecency, at least not initially. The FCC recently decided that it was indecent, but opted not to issue a fine."

According to *AP*: "In July, Clear Channel sued Infinity for more than $3 million, claiming Stern broke their contract by violating federal indecency regulations. The lawsuit came after Stern filed a $10 million suit against Clear Channel, the nation's top radio station owner, which had $8.9 billion in revenues last year."

In any case, as of this writing the King of All Media had not been dethroned. After losing the six Clear Channel stations, Stern announced that he had been picked up by nine new markets, some of them in the cities where he had been yanked off the air. In October 2004 Stern proclaimed that he was leaving broadcast radio at the end of 2005 when his contract expired and would go on to air his show on Sirius Satellite Radio. (The Opie and Anthony Show returned to the airwaves via satellite broadcaster XM Radio in October 2004.) Appearing on subscriber-based satellite radio would unshackle the shock jock from federal regulators. "My dream is going to satellite, and making Clear Channel's $85 million radio properties worth 50 cents," Stern said. "I hope it comes true."

PRIME TIME AND PUNISHMENT

Many other governmentally incorrect celebrities have felt the sling and arrows of outrageous fortune hurled at them since September 11th by the Bush administration. Responding to "Politically Incorrect" host Bill Maher's 9/11-related comments, Bush's ex-press secretary Ari Fleischer set the tone by warning: "Watch what you say."

Open season on left-leaning talents was declared September 17, 2002, when the mockumentary "Darkness at High Noon: The Carl Foreman Documents" was nationally broadcast. This hit piece was written and directed by Hollywood's über-right-winger Lionel Chetwynd. To be fair, Chetwynd has written some good films, such as 1974's *The Apprenticeship of Duddy Kravitz*, which arguably made Richard Dreyfuss an actor of renown, and the 2001 antifascist drama *Varian's War*, starring William Hurt as a Schindler-like rescuer of Jews. But Chetwynd, like all ideologues, is undone by trying to insert ideology in entertainment to the point where the propaganda takes precedence over the art form and drowns out the drama—especially when you're dead wrong.

Stanley Kramer defied the Hollywood blacklist in the opening credits of 1958's *The Defiant Ones*. Kramer gave blacklisted screenwriters Nedrick Young and Harold Jacob Smith bit parts and their credits were printed under their faces. (Courtesy of Karen Kramer)

For example, critic Leonard Maltin wrote that the 1987 American POW pic written and directed by Chetwynd, *The Hanoi Hilton*, was "unbearably dull, impossibly overlong and embarrassingly clichéd... does a real disservice to its subject matter... and throws in right-wing polemics and potshots at Jane Fonda to boot." Chetwynd even managed to render D-Day boring in the talky 2004 cable TV movie he wrote starring an uninspired Tom Selleck as General Eisenhower in "Ike: Countdown to D-Day."

In *Darkness at High Noon*, Chetwynd blames Hollywood's social message *maestro* Stanley Kramer for the blacklist woes of screenwriter and former Communist Carl Foreman, who wrote *High Noon* and other classics that Kramer produced. Kramer is accused of kicking Foreman while he was down, and exploiting Foreman's summons to appear before HUAC by stealing his producer-related credit on *High Noon* and kicking him out of their company.

Kramer was aged and ailing when the production started, and died before it was broadcast, so he was unable to defend himself. His widow, Karen Sharpe Kramer—who had married Stanley in the 1960s—insisted on appearing onscreen to present Stanley's side of the story. But Chetwynd used the artificial device of declining to interview sources on camera who weren't eyewitnesses to the early 1950s events in question to peremptorily exclude any sort of pro-Kramer viewpoint. This convenient ruse enabled Chetwynd to present an egregiously one-sided picture under the guise of "journalistic ethics," even though Chetwynd repeatedly violated his own witness formula when it suited his purposes.

In the process, Chetwynd managed to exonerate friendly witnessses and perpetrators of the Hollywood inquisition, such as Ronald "Agent T-10" Reagan, Gary Cooper and John Wayne. But Kramer's role in breaking the Hollywood blacklist is never mentioned. In addition to employing ex-Reds like Foreman, he hired Edward Dmytryk, and not only hired blacklisted screenwriters Ned Young (AKA Nathan E. Douglas) and Harold Jacob Smith to write 1958's anti-racist *The Defiant Ones* starring Sydney Poitier and Tony Curtis, but used them as actors in the title sequence. Indeed, their credits roll when the blacklistees are seen on screen. They also wrote *Inherit the Wind* for Kramer.

And where did this hit job on the producer/director of Hollywood's great classics of conscience, such as *On the Beach* and *Guess Who's Coming to Dinner* air? On that bastion of "liberal" media: PBS. The message was clear: If the creator of message movie masterpieces like *Judgment at Nuremburg* could be slimed, no talent and voice of principle was safe.[23]

In the filmmaking community, Chetwynd's mockumentary set the tone for silencing dissent. Everyone had to march in lockstep or be subject to character assassination. As the Iraq War loomed, the peace sign Amanda Bynes flashed was removed from ads for 2003's *What a Girl Wants*. Madonna self-censored her "American Life" music video.

In February 2003, Sean Penn sued producer Steve Bing for $10 million for allegedly firing the actor from a film. Penn alleged he was sacked because of his 2002 *Washington Post* antiwar ad and Baghdad trip. Bing counter-sued.[24]

Setting a bad precedent, CBS dropped Ed Gernon prior to "Rather-gate." Gernon, producer of the 2002 CBS miniseries "Salem Witch Trials" and of the Tiffany Network's "Hitler: The Rise of Evil." CBS had discussed the docudrama with *TV Guide* shortly before it was broadcast. Gernon said the story "basically boils down to an entire nation gripped by fear who ultimately chose to give up their civil rights and plunge the whole world into war. I can't think of a better time to examine this history than now."

---

23. David Horowitz and Chetwynd co-founded the Hollycon Wednesday Morning Club and worked together on PBS' "National Desk," until they had a business dispute. Horowitz sued Chetwynd in 2002 and told this writer that Chetwynd had done to him what Chetwynd alleged Kramer had done to Foreman. The matter was settled out of court.

Rupert Murdoch's *N.Y. Post* attack dogs assailed Gernon's comment as "a sign of Hollywood's anti-Americanism." Columnist and Fox News talking head John Podhoretz, the author of *Bush Country*, also wrote in his *Post* column that the miniseries was "an act of slander against the President of the United States." CBS fired Gernon two days later.

There's no better way to prove how freedom-loving we are than by acting in authoritarian ways! That'll teach those evildoers a lesson! In any case, the Tiffany Network's display of backbone malfunction opened the floodgates of intimidation that followed in its wake: the rescheduling of "The Reagans" biopic on another channel, the FC fines for Janet Jackson's Super Bowl wardrobe fiasco and "Rather-gate."

Nevertheless, some entertainment community big mouths, such as Whoopi Goldberg, still had to be taught a lesson. After the comic compared the Bush name to female genitalia at a major Kerry/Edwards fundraiser at Radio City Music Hall, *Associated Press* reported on July 16 that Slim-Fast Foods Co. had dropped Whoopi as its celebrity spokesperson. *AP* quoted the comedienne's response: "While I can appreciate what the Slim-Fast people need to do in order to protect their business, I must also do what I need to do as an artist, as a writer and as an American—not to mention as a comic. It's unfortunate that, in this country, the two cannot mesh." The wire service noted that while Slim-Fast is operated by S. Daniel Abraham, a major donor to the Democratic Party, the firm "is based in West Palm Beach, Florida, where the president's brother, Jeb Bush, is governor."

Reprisals against outspoken stars had become so commonplace that *AP* called the Whoopi-Slim-Fast flap "the latest case of celebrity censure over political remarks." Another example *AP* cited took place in 2003, when "the Baseball Hall of Fame in Cooperstown, N.Y., scrapped an event for the 15th anniversary of the popular baseball movie *Bull Durham* because of the antiwar stance of stars Tim Robbins and Susan Sarandon." Previously, reactionaries had tried impeaching "acting president" Sheen from "The West Wing" and his American Express endorsements. Conservative groups also lobbied MCI to drop Danny Glover as its spokesman.

---

24. According to Yahoo.com, Sean's father Leo Penn's "film career had just begun when Penn was blacklisted after attending a pro-union meeting with other actors. That the group was actively supporting the first blacklistees, the Hollywood Ten, only worsened matters. Unable to work in film, he turned to Broadway," and eventually became a TV director in the 1960s.

UNDAUNTED: THE DIXIE CHICKS

"[S]ometimes you've got to be the one... We still want to stand up for what we believe is right."

— Emily Robison of the Dixie Chicks

Punishment meted out to other singers was so egregious that it produced a new term for the English language: to be "Dixie Chicked." The Grammy-winning, ticket-selling Dixie Chicks' name was turned into a verb after singer Natalie Maines told a London concert audience on March 10, 2003: "Just so you know, we're ashamed the President of the United States is from Texas." The response to the Chicks' remark was more panicky than the one Chicken Little received when he announced that the sky was falling. "The Clear Channel radio network [which owns more than 1,200 commercial radio stations in the U.S.] pulled the Dixie Chicks from their playlist," Stauber said. "In Colorado Springs, two DJs were suspended from Clear Channel affiliate KKCS for defying the ban."

Losing much of their airtime, weekly sales of the album *Home* plunged. As Emily Robison admitted: "Radio directly has an impact on sales. Country radio still doesn't play us that much. We're still dealing with that. Sales continue to lag... because of all this... Country radio's really leading a lot of it by the boycott." Chicks CDs were demolished during "Dixie Chicks Destruction" days, and rallies denounced them.

On December 15, 2003 Maines and co-Chick Robison attended the Southern California chapter of the American Civil Liberties Union's annual Bill of Rights Dinner at the Beverly Wilshire Hotel. The event celebrated the 212th birthday of the Ten Amendments and presented awards to Chicks' manager Simon Renshaw, author Molly Ivins and director Jon Avnet for sticking up for freedom of speech.

Asked which of the Ten Amendments is their favorite, Maines, Robison and manager Simon Renshaw all proclaimed the First. Renshaw added: "You know! The big one! The whole like speech thing one!... The right to bare big mouths." If they had to choose between ten platinum albums or the First Amendment, Robison preferred: "Freedom of speech. That's... really easy to answer. It was hard for us to be made an example of this year—but sometimes you've got to be the one... We still want to stand up for what we believe is right." However, the Chicks' outspoken manager stated, "I'd rather have them both. It appears we're rapidly approaching a condition where very shortly, everyone's going to have to make the decision as to which they'd rather have."

How is it that while Americans pride themselves on being free to speak their minds they're punished if they publicly express dissent? "That's the new system here," responded Renshaw. "Certain people in the country have figured out that the best way of actually curtailing freedom of speech is to make sure people understand freedom of speech is no longer free, and there's consequences to exercising free speech. What we saw in 2003, when people spoke out, there was a very well organized, vociferous group that immediately went after them and attempted to harm their well-being. Certainly, the Dixie Chicks saw death threats as a result of what they said," asserted the Englishman.

Maines added: "After September 11th, we felt lots of vulnerability, and wanted somebody to lead and save us. The country's been in a strange state... so try not to get too discouraged about everything that occurred. Things like that should always be a reminder, that we haven't necessarily come as far as we think we have, and we have to constantly be checking ourselves. A mother of a military guy wrote us saying, 'Freedom's not something you can write on a wall. It's something you live.' So I feel proud that I use my freedoms, and don't just claim on a daily basis to have freedom," said Maines.

The country singer also expressed admiration for ACLU: "Standing up for the underdog sometimes is not politically correct." Renshaw also mocked Bill O'Reilly for blasting Renshaw's management company, The Firm, on "The Factor" for using porn stars in Pony footware commercials. "Fantastic human being. I'd certainly be grateful if Mr. O'Reilly cares to mention it a little bit more. It did wonders for sales."

Laughing and saying she was at the awards dinner for "moral support," Robison said that because "Natalie had her foot in her mouth, she gets to present" ACLU-SC's Bill of Rights Award to Renshaw. When the tongue-in-cheeky Maines presented the honor, she poked fun at those questioning her patriotism: "Lots of people will be surprised to hear I was here tonight—because they were waiting for me to get out of that hole with Saddam." She went on to say, "Another power the federal government refuses to limit—the power of the corporate media. Not the media's right to speak, but the media's obligation to let other people speak. I don't want to mention any names, but freedom of speech requires a *clear channel* to communications," Maines quipped.

Praising her courageous manager, Maines concluded: "We can't leave it to the Simon Renshaws of the world. We have to all get active and challenge our government, or... the Bill of Rights will just be something from history we learn about in school. So Simon, tonight I promise I'll do my part. You can count on me—the same way I've been able to count on you." Renshaw took the stage, mocking Bush's response to the Dixie Chicks' comments: "Aw shucks. They shouldn't have their feelings hurt because people don't want to buy their records when they speak out. Freedom is a two-way street..."

"Certainly, 2003... [was] the year America was deceived into a war, and part of that deception was putting on notice any dissenting voice to ensure they understood freedom of speech is not free. The concept of 'shut up and sing' was born... It's now possible to be 'Dixie Chicked'... There are many well-organized groups of right thinking citizens who will work selflessly to make sure that those who dare to speak up and dissent are suitably 'Dixie Chicked.' They make their views known from the safety and anonymity of the Internet and radio talk shows," railed Renshaw.

"They're determined to ensure that we understand freedom of speech is not free. Especially you—Hollywood. You music and movie celebrities... are all on notice: Shut up and sing—or act or whatever. But shut up! I also learned we can count on America's liberal media—yeah, right! Instead of asking the questions and encouraging debate, our new media conglomerates issue corporate *fatwas* on those to be Dixie Chicked. Music networks can ban your music, talkshows can vilify your personality, what remains of this country's so-called news media trivializes it all into neat 30 second sound bytes... You may have freedom of speech, but our media now seems to be designed so we'll never be heard... A well-known German TV personality... told us: 'In my country, our media would never allow this to happen again.'"

Renshaw concluded: "I'd like to thank the Dixie Chicks, I'm immensely proud of them for the stand they took, and the way they handled themselves through a lousy time... and for having the strength to say 'no,' and for their insistence on always doing the right thing... Freedom of speech is only important if it's exercised. Celebrities should not shut up and sing: they should stand up and shout, and we must support them."

On October 1, 2004, the country singers stated on that forum of free speech, "Real Time With Bill Maher," that many country-western stations were still Dixie Chicking them, and that the loss of airtime was still affecting their ticket sales. But the undaunted Texans continued to stand tall, as they joined Bruce Springsteen, R.E.M., John Fogerty, Pearl Jam, the Dave Matthews Band, Jackson Browne, Bonnie Raitt, Keb' Mo' and John Mellencamp as part of the musician mobilization Vote for Change tour. (Can Clear Channel ban this many groups at once?) Their live October 11 concert in Washington, D.C. was aired on the Sundance Channel.

THE PASSION OF THE MOORE

"Didn't they used to have those poll tests where you had to take tests before you could vote? Maybe we could just ask them questions about Fahrenheit 9/11*?"*

— Joe Scarborough, MSNBC talk show host, at the Wednesday
        Morning Club

"For me the real Oscar would be Bush's defeat on November 2."

— Michael Moore, September 26, 2004

John Stauber's long litany of lament in *Banana Republicans* also cited the example of 60-year-old retired phone worker Barry Reingold, who was questioned by the F.B.I. after criticizing Bush at his gym as "a servant of the big oil companies." This was one of the cases regarding the infringement of our liberties that's also depicted in *Fahrenheit 9/11*. For this and other reasons, like Sir Thomas More before him, Michael Moore has been branded Public Dissident #1, and as such has, but of course, been targeted for special punishment. As was noted December 2, 2004 at a Writers Bloc-presented forum featuring Moore in conversation with John Dean, while there was only one anti-Kerry documentary during the campaign (*Stolen Honor: Wounds That Never Heal*) there were six anti-Moore mockumentaries.

There have been so many attempts to silence and threaten Moore that it's hard to know where to begin. Certainly Michael Eisner's decision to drop the distribution of *Fahrenheit 9/11* and Moore's scrambling for a distribution deal—even after the documentary won Cannes' coveted Palme d'Or!—is the most obvious and prominent case of intimidation.

However, "Tonight Show" host Jay Leno told the *L.A. Weekly* about what might have been the most serious act taken against the controversial filmmaker. "After he had done his speech to the Academy, the next day I said

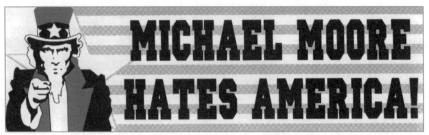

A bumper sticker created by Right Stuff Comedy impresario Eric Peterkofsky. (Courtesy of Eric Peterkofsky)

[in the "Tonight Show" monologue], 'You think President Bush is keeping an eye on Moore? Can we go to Moore's house?' You saw a shack in the desert. And then a missile blew it up. Which to me was a joke about Bush. And then I said, 'Gee, I think the president's angry at Moore.' And it got a big laugh." However, Moore was unamused, for as Leno went on to say, 'then he said he'd had some problems. His house had been vandalized.'"

At the December 2 Writers Bloc event in L.A., Moore groused that a right-wing "pro-family" group "published the home address of my house in rural Michigan. They published a photo of it. My home was vandalized. There have been attempts to do various things. Harvey and Bob [Weinstein] have to pay for 24/7 security for me. It's a rotten way to live," Moore complained onstage to Watergate's John Dean at the Wadsworth Theatre— flanked by at least two bodyguards in the wings.

Moore raises reactionary hackles even when he's not in the house. According to the *Las Vegas Sun*, Linda "Ronstadt was booted from the property after she dedicated a song ["Desperado"] to Moore and praised his movie *Fahrenheit 9/11* at her [July 17, 2004] concert at the Aladdin, prompting some audience members to walk out and ask for their money back... Ronstadt's dedication drew some boos and some of the audience walked out and marred posters for the concert as they left... [Aladdin president Bill] Timmins, who was among the almost 5,000 fans at the concert, had security guards escort Ronstadt to her tour bus and had her belongings brought down from her hotel room after the concert. The hotel president also sent word that Ronstadt was no longer welcome at the hotel for future performances.

"Timmins said he was concerned about customer satisfaction and safety. 'A situation like that can easily turn ugly and I didn't want anything more to come out of it,' Timmins said the day after the event. 'There were a lot of angry people there after she started talking. If she wants to talk about her views to a newspaper or in a magazine article, she is free to do so. But on a stage in front of four and a half thousand people is not the place for it.'"

The *Sun* article went on to say: "Moore criticized... Timmins in a letter posted on Moore's website Monday. Moore said throwing out Ronstadt was 'simply stupid and un-American. Invite her back and I'll join her in singing 'America the Beautiful' on your stage,' Moore wrote. 'Then I will show *Fahrenheit 9/11* free of charge to all your guests and anyone else in Las Vegas who wants to see it.'"

By the time the DVD and video of *9/11* were released, on October 5, Moore's documentary had earned around $213 million, meaning that a huge audience had seen his outspoken film. The powers that be pulled out all the stops to try everything in their power to suppress Moore's follow-up to *Columbine*. The Flint, Michigan filmmaker could not be allowed another platform for his dangerous (to the status quo) ideas either onscreen or onstage, receiving another Oscar before the eyes—and ears—of the world.

In addition to Disney's disavowal of the documentary's distribution deal with Miramax and Moore, the *New York Times* reported in June that "Citizens United, a conservative group in Washington... asked the Federal Elections Commission to stop Mr. Moore from running advertisements for his film during the period before the election when political commercials by outside groups are restricted. That complaint was dismissed after Mr. Moore said he would not run the commercials in question." Wikipedia.org added: "On August 5, the FEC unanimously dismissed the complaint finding no evidence that the movie's ads had broken the law." In any case, Moore did run some TV and other ads in October when the DVD debuted.

There was also a right-wing attempt to disqualify *9/11* from Oscar contention because of an unauthorized TV broadcast in Cuba. But the Academy responded by stating: "If it was pirated or stolen or unauthorized we would not blame the producer or distributor for that." According to Wikipedia.org, "On September 26, Moore announced that, because he was seeking a television airing of *Fahrenheit 9/11* prior to the November presidential election, the film would not be submitted for consideration for a Best Documentary Oscar (a television broadcast within nine months of the release would disqualify the film in the documentary category under Oscar rules). Moore instead planned to submit and promote his film for the Best Picture Oscar, but noted: 'For me the real Oscar would be Bush's defeat on November 2.' Moore... noted that in the current situation, the above priorities take precedence to winning a second

Oscar and as such, he would prefer his compatriot documentarians have a fair chance to win the Oscar themselves."

Wikipedia.org also stated: "Move America Forward, which has ties to Sacramento, California PR firm Russo, Marsh and Rogers, the campaign to prevent CBS from showing "The Reagans," and the campaign to unseat California Governor Gray Davis, mounted a letter-writing campaign to ask theaters not to show the film, which it compared to 'an al Qaeda training video'... 'We've been causing them [the cinemas] an enormous amount of aggravation,' said talk radio host Melanie Morgan. However, no theaters reported canceling their showings."

Sci-fi scribe Ray Bradbury demanded an apology from Moore because of his "theft" of the title of his novel *Fahrenheit 451*. *9/11*'s tagline is "The temperature where freedom burns," while the tagline for the Francois Truffaut-directed *Fahrenheit 451*'s was "The temperature at which books burn." In any case, Bradbury had reportedly not trademarked his title, and had himself used quotations for titles, such as *Something Wicked This Way Comes*, which is derived from Shakespeare.

The would-be censors cut their collective noses to spite their faces. Much like the brouhaha over that other 2004 indie flick, Mel Gibson's *Passion of the Christ*, the film's detractors provided Michael Moore with a massive advertising campaign, free of charge.

As Moore noted in the *Nation* after Senator McCain dissed him at the Republican National Convention: "To bring up the film in the speech tonight, it's not good for the Republican Party. It's just going to make more people say: 'I'd better go see this movie.' And when people see it, they don't feel much like voting Republican." The autoworker's son added that a Republican pollster had told him "They couldn't find anyone who sees the film and then says they are definitely voting for Bush."

The controversy over the contested documentary generated such a groundswell of support that the Cannes Film Festival summoned him to return to the south of France (after premiering *9/11* there, Moore had flown back to America to attend his daughter's college graduation). Safely back on liberated France's soil, on May 22 the filmmaker from Flint was awarded the Palme d'Or. In his acceptance speech at the French Riviera, the overwhelmed Moore declared: "I want to make sure if I do nothing else for this year that those who have died in Iraq have not died in vain."

On May 31, 2004, *N.Y. Daily News* reported: "The 41st President of the United States has stepped up to defend his son, the 43rd President of the

United States, against 'slimeball' filmmaker Michael Moore. 'I have total dis-dain for Moore,' George H.W. Bush told us when we saw him at the T.J. Martell Foundation Awards gala, where he was honored along with Stevie Wonder and Dr. Daniel Vasella the other night. '41' has heard enough about *Fahrenheit 9/11*, Moore's documentary indictment of President Bush, to know 'it's a vicious attack on our son. It's a free country, so he's free to say whatever he wants,' the former Oval Officer went on. 'But I don't appreciate it. I don't like it. [My son] served with honor, and to get knocked down by this guy,' he huffed. 'But you got to put up with it. That's what I'd say to [my son].'

"We asked what he thought of Moore's use of the comment Barbara Bush made at the start of the Iraq War: 'Why should we hear about body bags, and deaths?... [It's not relevant, so] why should I waste my beauti-ful mind on something like that? And watch [my son] suffer.' Said her furious husband: 'For him to take on Barbara is just beyond the pale. She's a decent, wonderful person, and to have to answer anything about what that slimeball says is just too much.'"[25]

The *Daily News* went on to write: "Informed of Bush's tirade, Moore told us he had 'fond memories' of '41' asking for a print of his movie *Roger & Me* to show at Camp David in the winter of 1990. Moore, whose film explores the financial ties between the Bush family and the Saudis, said, 'I appreciate all reviews of my films from the Bush family. And if they love the film this much, without having seen it, I can't wait for the reviews when they actually see it. I'd be more than happy to set up a White House screening.' Recalling the Bushes' nickname for Saudi Ambassador to the U.S., Prince Bandar, he added, 'I hope they invite Bandar Bush!'"

When *USA Today* assigned Moore to cover the Republican National Convention, security guards and NYPD harassed the smartass documen-tarian and blocked his entry to Madison Square Garden. According to *Editor & Publisher*, "Jerry Gallegos, superintendent of the U.S. House Daily Press Gallery, which oversees press credentials for the convention, said this about Moore's mistreatment: 'Not since 1968 in Chicago did police get this involved in media access. When you have the police force telling individuals what access they are going to have, and it is not based

---

25. Barbara Pierce Bush's ancestor, Franklin Pierce, was the 14th President of the United States—future President of the Confederacy Jefferson Davis was his Secretary of War—and she begins her Memoir gushing that hers "is a story of a life of privilege—privilege of every kind. If I didn't know it before, I certainly do now. No man, woman, or child ever had a better life."

---

on a safety issue, that is scary.' The *Nation* reported that cowboy hat-wearing Texas Republican Diane Francis said, 'I hope he's got security. He could get killed in here.'"

Once Moore was finally able to get inside the convention hall, Senator John McCain delivered an apologia and endorsement speech of the politician whose campaign had slimed him (as psychologically unbalanced), his wife (as a drug addict) and their adopted Bangladeshi daughter (as his out-of-wedlock black love child). Then the reputedly "moderate" Arizona senator attacked not his 2000 tormentor in South Carolina, but Moore, decrying him as "a disingenuous filmmaker who would have us believe that Saddam's Iraq was an oasis of peace."

A smiling Moore took it in his stride and was seen replying with gestures on live TV. He pumped his fist in the air, tipped his flag-emblazoned baseball cap to McCain, and made a peace sign-like symbol with two fingers that actually meant "two more months" for the Bush-Cheney regime as the Republican ruck chanted "four more years." Moore later invited McCain to attend a screening of his movie with him.

As John Nichols observed in the *Nation*: "Everyone in the hall, including McCain and Moore, realized that a rare moment in American politics was playing out. It's not often, outside the context of a debate, that such charges and countercharges fly in close proximity. Nor is it all that often that a film achieves the level of public awareness that leads a prominent politician to attack its maker in a primetime convention speech. And it is certainly not common for the filmmaker to be in a position to respond in real time."

McCain, Bush and Moore's other detractors (who—judging by the fact that *9/11* was the first documentary to ever open as the weekend box office champ, and earned $115 million in two months—are grossly outnumbered by Michael's fans) may name call, but in general they don't even try to refute most of the documentary's charges. There has been some dispute over the post-September 11th flights that allowed 142 Saudis—including 24 Bin Laden relatives—to hightail it out of the USA, although the filmmaker sticks by his guns on his website michaelmoore.com and elsewhere, insisting that the 9/11 Commission's Report confirms the allegations made in the film. (Moore's website devotes lots of space to refuting his attackers' allegations.) I also recall one critic contending that while Bush was governor, representatives of the Taliban visited Texas, and were wined and dined there, but Bush *per se* had nothing to do with this.

Why did the public have to wait two years for the up to seven minute tape of Bush remaining seated at that photo op in the Sarasota school on that fateful Tuesday morning? Maybe part of the answer can be found in this *Washington Post* dispatch: "The *New York Times* reports that a columnist for the *Texas City Sun* was fired after writing that Mr. Bush, instead of returning to Washington on the day of attacks, was 'flying around the country like a scared child, seeking refuge in his mother's bed after having a nightmare.'"

The same happened to a columnist in Oregon, who accused Mr. Bush of having "'skedaddled' in the wake of the attacks." The corporate media's lack of courage and coverage could also account for its post-9/11 failure to expose, among other things, Bush's month off. After only six months on the job, the people's servant gave himself four weeks off at his Crawford ranch, just about the longest presidential holiday ever. (The average American is lucky to get two weeks off after a full year's labor.) During his extended August holiday, Bush was briefed and read a closely held intelligence report for senior government officials entitled "Bin Laden Determined to Strike U.S." The presidential Daily Briefing included references to al Qaeda preparations for skyjackings—but the *New York Times* reported that Bush went fishing earlier that day. By the end of his month-long jaunt, Bush had spent 42% of his presidency at vacation destinations or en route to them.

Just as the press had failed to expose the Warren Commission's report on the Kennedy assassination, had participated in the assassination cover-ups and attacked Oliver Stone when he released *JFK*, with its counter-narrative to the official line, Michael Moore had to undergo character assassination for daring to try to tell the truth—or, at least, another version of it. But again, all of these attempts to libel and slander Moore by politicians and newsmen who have lost their credibility with much of the public have backfired, providing his film with the equivalent of a free publicity *blitzkrieg*.

One of the most virulent Moore critics is a TV talk show host and ex-Congressman who was a charter member of the Contract on America hitmen. "[H]ow anybody could sit there with a straight face and say *Fahrenheit 9/11* is an important piece of work tells me that they are either liars or extraordinarily naïve," Joe Scarborough said on September 18 at David Horowitz's ultra-right Wednesday Morning Club. "They should have the right to vote stripped from them immediately." The Wednesday Morning Clubbers burst out applauding and laughing in the posh Beverly Hills Hotel's Sunset Room.

The host of MSNBC's *Scarborough Country* was also enraged by sug-
gestions that Bush had stolen the 2000 election and went on to ask:
"Maybe we can have—what did they use to have? Didn't they use to have
those poll tests where you had to take tests before you could vote? Maybe
we could just ask them questions about *Fahrenheit 9/11*?"[26]

The remark angered John Stauber. "You know, Joe Scarborough loves
to wrap himself in the flag and declare his true blue patriotic American values. That statement is as un-American as any statement that could
possibly be made. It's an outrage, it's worse than an insult. What he's saying is that somebody who views media critical of this administration
doesn't have a right to cast a ballot. And it's a great example of the bel-
ligerent, extreme, fundamentally anti-American statements that
commentators on the right feel free to make and are able to get away with
in the current media environment. It's a really frightening statement if he's
saying it in any sense other than tongue-in-cheek. And if he's saying it
tongue-in-cheek, it's just a bad off-color joke," Stauber groused.

Scarborough, of course, represented Florida in the House. Let's take a
look at the history of poll tests and the like in the Sunshine State, where voting discrepancies led to Bush's selection as president by the Supreme Court
in 2000. According to a September 26, 2004 *L.A. Times* op-ed by Ann Louise
Bardach, author of *Cuba Confidential: Love and Vengeance in Miami and
Havana*—troubled by the 1866 14th Amendment, which guaranteed black
men the right to vote, "the Democratic-controlled Florida Legislature crafted
a raft of statutes to keep blacks out of the polling booths." These included
literacy tests, a grandfather clause that granted voting rights only to those
whose grandfathers had voted, a confusing requirement for voters to put
eight different ballots in eight separate boxes, and a poll tax. (One wonders
if the anti-tax and spend Scarborough would endorse the last measure
aimed at keeping African-Americans away from the polls.) Uppity "darkies"
who insisted on voting rights faced lynching. The worst remaining vestige of
these anti-suffrage maneuvers is Florida's denial of voting rights to ex-
felons, and abuses associated with this which Greg Palast revealed led to the
appointment of Jeb's big brother George as president. (Bardach appeared on
the "varsity panel" of Dennis Miller's CNBC show with Horowitz and Palast.
The latter gave a copy of his book *The Best Democracy Money Can Buy*,
which appears to have suggested Bardach's subsequent op-ed.)

---

26. I taped this tirade—I can't make this stuff up, folks.

Given the historical context of Donahue's putative successor, Scarborough's ill-chosen words would mean the disenfranchisement of the more than 12 million ticket buyers who'd seen *9/11* in theaters, plus additional more viewers who'd see it on DVD, video and TV once it was aired. Just as scrubbing ex-felons and purported former criminals from Florida's voter rolls gave the presidency to Bush, if carried out Scarbourough's modest proposal would probably deliver the White House to the Republicans again. He could even assign Katherine Harris and Jeb to count the box office receipts.

Controversy followed Moore as he launched his 60-city "Slacker Uprising Tour" in 20 battleground states in order to get the vote out. Moore began September 26 at Elk Rapids, Michigan, and ended on Election Day at Tallahassee, Florida in the belly of Jeb's beast. Moore appeared at college campuses and in sports arenas, but shortly after he announced the voter registration drive, two California colleges cancelled his appearances. Republicans requested the prosecution of Moore for offering free underwear and food such as Ramen noodles to students in exchange for their vow to vote. *AP* reported: "The Michigan GOP on Tuesday asked four county prosecutors to file charges against Moore, citing an election law provision that prohibits a person from contracting with another for something of value in exchange for agreeing to vote."

Agence France-Presse quoted Moore: "'The state of Michigan (where we spent most of last week) reported that over 100,000 young people recently registered to vote, a record that no one saw coming'... That, Moore says, has led the Michigan Republican Party to call for his arrest, having 'filed a criminal complaint with prosecutors in each of the counties where I spoke last week'... On his website the documentarian ridiculed the Ramen/undie flap as "Noodle-gate."

AP also quoted Moore: "It's ironic that Republicans have no problem with allowing assault weapons out on our streets, yet they don't want to put clean underwear in the hands of our slacker youth... The Republicans seem more interested in locking me up for trying to encourage people to participate in our democracy than locking up bin 'Darkness at High Noon' Laden for his attacks on our democracy."

In addition to distribution dust-ups, legal challenges and the like, a handful of right-wingers have tried to exploit Moore's fame with productions of their own that play off of his persona and the themes of his documentaries. Three of these mockumentaries were screened at the Pacific Design Center's theater as part of the October 1-3, 2004 Liberty

Film Festival in L.A., which billed itself as the first conservative filmfest in Hollywood. The first to screen was *Celsius 41.11*, which viewers are led to believe is "the temperature at which the brain begins to die." The project was ballyhooed as "The Truth Behind the Lies of *Fahrenheit 9/11*."

According to the *N.Y. Times*, *Celsius* was financed and produced by Citizens United—the same group that had unsuccessfully sought the FEC to stop Moore from running ads for *9/11* during the time when outside groups' political commercials are banned. Ironically, the *Times* noted: "In a separate ruling this month, the commission refused to allow Citizens United to advertise *Celsius 41.11* or pay to run it on television. David N. Bossie, the group's president, said this week that several distributors were interested in *Celsius 41.11* and that he hoped it would appear in theaters within two weeks.

Celsius' writer, Lionel Chetwynd, introduced the film to the Liberty Film Festival audience in his typical disingenuous way, claiming that it wasn't a "red meat" attack on Moore, but an "evenhanded" response to the charges made in *Fahrenheit 9/11*. The *Hollywood Reporter* quoted Chetwynd as saying: "We hang 'em with their own words. We don't need tricks." Now Chetwynd has as much right to make a propaganda picture as Michael Moore has, and *Celsius* may be many things, but "evenhanded" is not one of them. In fact, just like Chetwynd's one-sided frontal assault on another Hollywood leftist, Stanley Kramer, *Celsius* is a hit job that is careful to present only one side of the story in a cogent, articulate way.

Chetwynd told the Liberty Filmfest audience that he made the pic in only seven weeks, so given that time span, it's highly unlikely that *Celsius*' co-conspirators actually shot any of the footage screened of antiwar demonstrators. This probably means that the filmmakers carefully culled archival material and edited short shots of protesters looking and sounding at their most unflattering (to put it mildly). On the other hand, the hallowed experts who are interviewed at some length in august settings, are all—with no exception—the usual pro-war suspects who were paraded on Fox News and the like before the war, like Charles Krauthammer, Fred Barnes, Michael Medved and Michael Ledeen.[27]

The only difference is that now the NeoCon commentators continue spewing the same lunacy about WMDs, et al, after it has been completely discredited in the aftermath of the war. In Chetwynd's "evenhanded" one-

---

27. The film never mentions the fact that Ledeen's inexperienced Heritage Foundation-linked daughter Simone had a high-ranking position in Iraq's Coalition Provisional Authority.

sided world, the antiwar side gets quick goofy-sounding sound bytes by rank and fil-ers on the streets, while polished pro-Bush spinmeisters get relatively in-depth inter-views in controlled indoor environments. There is not one single solitary in-depth interview with any eloquent antiwar spokesman, such as, say, Professor Howard Zinn. So once again, Lionel Chetwynd stacks the deck—even as he deceptively pleads jour-nalistic standards.

While the film poses as a conservative response to Moore's *j'accuses* in *9/11*, his accusations that the Bushes did business

Talk show host Larry Elder at the West Coast premiere of his anti-Moore, pro-gun screed *Michael & Me* during 2004's right wing Liberty Film Festival.

with the Bin Ladens is never mentioned, let alone answered or debunked. Nor are the charges of Bush dynasty ties to and cronyism with the Saudi royal family considered in *Celsius*. And so on. Talking heads can be com-pelling, as they are in Greenwald's *Uncovered: The Whole Truth About the Iraq War* or Moore's *9/11*, because there's something inherently dramatic about hearing a previously suppressed counter-narrative that goes against the grain. But when the talking heads repeat the same old tired pro-war canards viewers have already heard a million times (which, according to a F.A.I.R. study, outnumbered antiwar spokesman 100 to 1 on television), the result is sheer boredom.

The same problem besets *Michael & Me*, a pro-gun screed that also had its West Coast premiere at the Liberty Film Festival. It features talk show host Larry Elder, who is widely disdained as a race traitor and black Bene-dict Arnold. Like *Celsius*, *Michael & Me* is supposedly a riposte to a Moore documentary (this time, *Bowling at Columbine*), but actually has little to do with Moore and merely trades on his world famous name in order to draw attention to its paltry self. But like clockwork, Moore is a recurring *leitmo-tif* in the pic who is briefly hauled out of the closet every 15 minutes or so.

Unlike *Celsius*, Elder does have some short original footage (which he stretches *ad infinitum* throughout the picture, adding a cartoon sequence that mocks Moore). He did a brief shotgun interview (if you can call it that) with Moore on what appears to be the Third Street Promenade in Santa Monica. Fair enough—unexpected, unannounced interviews are part of Moore's stock-in-trade. But note that Elder never answers Moore's repeated questions as to whether or not Elder owns guns. The repetitive mockumentary has none of Moore's wit or visual style, and is generally dull as it extols the virtues of gun ownership. The third pic that attacked the documentarian at the Liberty Film Festival was *Michael Moore Hates America*—the name says it all. As if endorsing sending more of your countrymen to die for a lie is a sign of loving your country.

On October 10, Fox News announced that while Sinclair Broadcasting (a conservative network that had yanked an ABC News "Nightline" program that aired the names and pictures of Americans killed in Iraq) planned to run an anti-Kerry production shortly before the election, Moore scheduled an election eve extravaganza. The three hour special would include anti-Bush celebrities and a screening of *Fahrenheit 9/11*. But on November 2 it did not air in the land of the free—although *9/11* was broadcast in Europe.

Controversy dogged Moore even after the election—and the GOP won. On December 8, the son of the industrial proletariat wrote on his website: "A group of top Republicans took out a full page ad in *USA Today* (and placed a similar one in the Hollywood trade magazine, *Variety*) proclaiming that 'An election is over, but a war of ideas continues.' The point of the ad was to say that while they, as right wing conservatives, were proud of getting rid of Kerry, there was still one more nuisance running around loose they had to deal with—me! They also issued a not-so-subtle threat to the Academy Awards voters that, in essence, said don't even THINK about nominating *Fahrenheit 9/11* for Best Picture. And Bill O'Reilly recently bellowed that if the Oscars recognize my work this year, Middle America will boycott Hollywood."

Talk about sore winners! That same day, conservative maverick Pat Buchanan hosted MSNBC's *Scarborough Country*, sitting in for Congressman Joe. The veteran culture warrior declared that if the Motion Picture Academy nominated both Mel Gibson's *The Passion of the Christ* and Moore's *Fahrenheit 9/11*, it would be a classic red state versus blue state confrontation, as Oscar fought for the soul of America (or visa versa). Indeed, should *The Passion of the Moore* beat out *The Passion of the Mel*, Buchanan intimated that it would be nothing less than blasphemy, as the Oscar race became the sequel to the presidential election.

One religious fanatic/panelist denounced "Hollywood's secular Jews," whom the Liberty Film Festival's Govindini Murty—a Hindu—defended. (However, Murty falsely asserted that Hollywood was "Republican" during WWII, which wasn't even true for at least some of the moguls, such as the Warner Brothers, let alone for many screenwriters, trade unionists, etc.)

But in a typical display of media "democracy," of the five speakers, not one was pro-Moore or *9/11*, which 10 million-plus Americans have seen, and was nominated in December by the People's Choice Awards as the American public's Favorite Film of the Year. And although it was noted that Moore is not Jewish, nobody pointed out that he is a Catholic, and one who practices what he believes about those quaint notions like "thou shalt not kill."[28]

On HBO's October 8, 2004 *Real Time With Bill Maher*, Moore was interviewed at one of the venues of his Slacker Uprising Tour, and the filmmaker declared: "People like me create the anti-propaganda." On December 2, Moore summed up what could be his credo: "I get upset about something—and I make a movie about it." And it drives reactionaries bonkers. So what's a right-winger to do?

RETURN OF THE HOLLYWOOD BLACKLIST?

Conservative commentators are seeking to rehabilitate Senator Joe McCarthy as Neo-McCarthyites are trying to revive a 21st century Hollywood blacklist during another period of government crackdowns on civil liberties and human rights. As a press release for the play *The Waldorf Conference* put it: "The Blacklist remains a hot topic six decades [later]... When... Tim Robbins, Susan Sarandon, Sean Penn, the Dixie Chicks, Martin Sheen, Bill Maher, Janeane Garofalo and Phil Donahue have had their patriotism questioned or their shows cancelled... for challenging White House policy, the subject remains very much alive. The political climate... today is frighteningly close to that of... McCarthyism."

In May 2003, WGA presented "We're Fighting For Freedom of Speech, So Kindly Shut Up! The First Amendment in Times of Crisis and War." The then-WGA West president Victoria Riskin said the symposium was inspired by "a worry blacklisting might recur... pressures we heard about... on networks not to hire people who spoke out against the war. I really don't think it resulted in people not getting work—I could be wrong."

At a September 2003 fundraiser for presidential candidate Dennis Kucinich, actor Ed Begley, Jr. ("Six Feet Under") told me: "There's a boycott list on the Internet for all the people who spoke out against the war, to write

---

28. Perhaps adding fuel to the Mel vs. Michael melee, at his December 2 Writers Bloc event at a veterans' center in L.A., Moore said that Gibson's Icon Pictures originally contracted to make *9/11*—until Gibson himself got wind of the deal and backed out of it.

letters to studios telling them you don't want to see shows featuring Jamie Cromwell, [myself], Asner, Robbins... Janeane Garofalo [took] a big hit. They've suffered financially, can't get work now. They've been blackballed. People don't want to hire them... Janeane gets so much hate mail... I didn't work from when that boycott list happened until just a few weeks ago... I worked three days in nine months—perhaps it's a coincidence... but I'll tell you this: I've never only worked three days in nine months since [joining] SAG in 1967... I don't know if this is why I haven't worked, but... it's why Janeane suffered... Draw your own conclusions," Begley said.

Brian Becker, a member of the steering committee of the Act Now to Stop War and End Racism coalition, which helped organize many of the antiwar demos, said: "The thing that we were most grateful for was that people took a stand. And you notice that many, many celebrities were punished actually for taking a stand. As the war began... there was an attempt to demonize those in Hollywood or anywhere who took a principled stand against the war and... acted as if they were naïve stooges of a devious antiwar movement or appeasers of Saddam... Or other categorizations that are really designed not to provoke and stimulate an honest political debate but to slander and marginalize people. Anyone in the public eye recognizes that there's such a vicious right-wing counterattack... from the media establishment in particular... from Fox News... against anyone who stands up as a matter of conscience. Those in Hollywood who stood up did it under really very difficult circumstances... Not just so much to limit the influence of those individuals, but to tell every other entertainer... that should you take a stand—which is your constitutional right, guaranteed by the First Amendment—you may not go to prison as the Hollywood Ten did... but you may, like those in the '50s who were punished for having 'unpopular' views, you may have your career short-circuited."

The following looks at some of the online attempts to drive outspoken stars out of show business.

BOYCOTT-HOLLYWOOD.NET

"Restraint of trade—Illegally interfering with free marketplace participation. Regulated by the Federal Trade Commission."

— Investorwords.com

Boycott-Hollywood.net went online February 12, 2003, proclaiming: "We... support the boycott of the following list of Hollywood Actors... 'Hollywood/Celebrity Pundits' need to realize... they do NOT speak for America... We support President George W. Bush [and] the liberation of Iraq... [C]elebrities who speak out against our president and against this war... need to understand that, in exercising their freedom of speech—they run the risk of... opposition... We have chosen to vote with our wallets..."

An icon marked "Citizens Against Hollywood Pundits" hyperlinks to a petition denouncing Hollywood dissenters. Underneath it says: "Will we go see... ONE... project by these people? HELL NO—WE WON'T GO!!"

In alphabetical order at the bottom of Boycott-Hollywood.net's home page are links to sites regarding dissident stars, which include their "unpatriotic" quotes, and links to the Internet Movie Database (imdb.com), listing films, DVD, video and TV shows to boycott. Some sites, such as Garofalo's, urge surfers: "Call her agent."

Garofalo's representatives didn't respond to an interview request, but Ed Asner jauntily retorted: "I'm glad I don't speak for them. I'm not out to limit their freedom of speech; evidently, they're out to limit [mine]... [and] my ability to earn a living." Asner added that his 1980s dramatic series "Lou Grant" "was cancelled because of my controversiality at the time." Asner was SAG president when ex-SAG prez Reagan was U.S. president, and their clash over Washington's Central America comedy led to "Lou Grant's" demise.

Mike Farrell, co-founder of Artists United to Win Without War, said attempts to blackball talent online is "a silly tactic... [that's] simply not going to have any impact. There are people I suppose who simply don't watch anything I'm in because they disagree with me, but I think they're a small minority. Most understand actors are also citizens," insisted "M*A*S*H's" co-star.

Boycott-Hollywood.net names names—but its operators won't name theirs. "I don't use my last name, publicly, on the website for... personal privacy and safety," "LisaS" replied to my October 2003 e-mailed request for her identity. Declining a telephone interview, LisaS agreed to answer "simple questions... via e-mail."

"The website, itself, was started, and is maintained, by three individuals," LisaS e-mailed. "The Boycott Hollywood website is run by me. I'm the owner... I live in Wisconsin... [M]y friends who help... are from Wisconsin and California. Boycott Hollywood has no office. It's just me, my computer and cable modem... I created the website, myself... designed... it on my own time with my own resources... I dabble in web site design and development... Occasionally, we receive donations... and sell merchandise that helps contribute to... hosting the website."

LisaS added: "In terms of how successful we['ve] been... causing the general public... to boycott movies, TV shows, albums, etc—I have no idea... Have we put anyone out of work? I highly doubt it." (Asner returned to prime time in September 2004 with a supporting role in the CBS sitcom "Center of the Universe.")

CELIBERAL.COM

"[W]e present... Hollywood celebrity liberals... that have nothing better to do than complain about America, our president, and the brave men and women defending our way of life. We do this to expose these celiberals for what we feel they really are—uninformed, misleading, money-hungry, two-faced, elitists who take unfair advantage of their popularity, and... media access... to express their controversial viewpoint. We know what you're thinking, 'This is just another right-wing, conservative, liberal-bashing website.' Technically yes..."

— Celiberal.com's front page

In October 2004, the Celiberal.com site offered a roster of: "The Righties: Although they are not given as much media coverage as the celiberals, the conservative celebrities (or those that lean slightly to the right), we call them 'The Righties', should be identified. These celebrities have the courage to speak out in an industry primarily flooded with liberals. We encourage all of you to take extra effort to patronize these patriotic celebrities." Surfers can click on links beside names such as Arnold Schwarzenegger, Kurt Russell, Robert Duvall, Larry Gatlin, et al, for a TV clip or newspaper clipping regarding the celebs' conservative cred.

On the other hand, Celiberal.com also features a "Celebrity Whine Rack," wherein dissenting talents are put on the rack. Click there on offending artists' names—alphabetically listed from Ben Affleck to Robin Williams—and his/her anti-Bush/antiwar quotes appear, with links to imdb.com.

Riskin remarked: "The sites sound like *Red Channels*. It's an exact parallel... an effort to make them public pariahs...." Blacklistee Bobby Lees added, "The sites are exactly a modernization of *Red Channels*, only vaster, because it's online."

Besides an e-mail address, Celiberal.com doesn't list names and contact info. A perfunctory non-response to an e-mailed interview in October 2003 request was signed "Celiberal.com." "Of course, that's the typically cowardly act of a zealot frightened by free speech and dialogue," Farrell said.

"They lack intelligence and don't lack cowardice," Asner mocked. Riskin added, "I don't think it's right... to point fingers, hide in the shadows, be secretive." "We're really talking about 'toads,' as Trumbo described people who'd take potshots at others, and not even stand up for what they believe," Segaloff fumed. "Any 12-year-old with a keyboard can put up a website... All they want is to collect money from visitors."

Celiberal.com links to James Hirsen's dissident-bashing "Left Coast Report" at conservative NewsMax.com. Hirsen's book, *Tales From the Left Coast: True Stories of Hollywood Stars and Their Outrageous Politics*, seems mostly derivative of others' material, with little original reportage. He attempts to restore tyrannical Senator McCarthy's tarnished reputation, as does *Treason*, by Ann Coulter. Both screeds are published by right-wing Crown Forum, which subsidizes reactionaries. Boycott-Hollywood.net quotes Coulter's *Treason*: "Honorable though it was, the Hollywood blacklisting had nothing to do with McCarthy... McCarthy never participated in any investigation of Hollywood."

This, of course, is yet another of Coulter's many inaccuracies. According to *Naming Names* author Victor Navasky, McCarthy called "Millen Brand, who co-wrote 1948's *The Snake Pit*, starring Olivia de Havilland." *Radical Hollywood*'s Dave Wagner added that screenwriter Arnaud d'Usseau was called before McCarthy. "Tailgunner Joe" is also seen facing off against Howard Fast in the documentary *Seeing Red*. Ex-Communist Fast belonged to the Joint Anti-Fascist Refugee Committee, was jailed during the Red Scare and wrote the novels that the 1960 and 2004 *Spartacus*, 1964's pro-Indian *Cheyenne Autumn* and 1979's *Freedom Road* were based on. In the latter, Muhammad Ali plays a Reconstruction Era senator who fights for the rights of the newly liberated slaves.

MUDSLINGING ON THE HUDSON

Celiberal.com links to a "very scary [site]... pretty horrifying. My god!" exclaimed Lees, who co-wrote *Abbott and Costello Meet Frankenstein*. Using cartoon and photographic imagery, the site savages *Le Divorce*'s Kate Hudson, depicting Goldie Hawn's daughter being defecated and urinated on by humans and dogs, ejaculated on by four penises, guillotined, apparently raped, mocked by an obscenity-spewing "comic" and also links to a cyberporn pay site.

Hudson and SAG's president didn't reply to interview requests. Farrell groused, "It's almost unworthy of comment... the kind of disgusting demonstration of cretinous behavior that's beneath contempt... just disgusting, vile, garbage... It should be condemned, ignored," urged Farrell.

Asner added: "It's a reflection upon the people who did it, showing them to be as vile as the acts they're committing." Wagner observed: "It makes David Horowitz's [online newsletter] look like the *N.Y. Times*." Riskin called it "profoundly disturbing... This depth of hate is very troubling."

What did Hudson do to merit such hatred? The 24-year-old ridiculed Americans' manners.

ONE-WAY TICKETS TO PALOOKAVILLE

"We will persistently clarify the choice before every ruler and every nation: the moral choice between oppression, which is always wrong, and freedom, which is eternally right. America will not pretend that jailed dissidents prefer their chains, or that any human being aspires to live at the mercy of bullies."

— George W. Bush, inaugural speech, January 20, 2005

"[O]ne does not judge an individual by what he thinks about himself."

— Karl Marx, *A Contribution to the Critique of Political Economy*, 1859

In 1954's *On the Waterfront*, while taking a ride in the backseat of a taxi shyster, Charlie (Rod Steiger) pulls a gun on his brother, Terry Malloy (Marlon Brando), to stop his testifying against mobsters. Brando reminds Charlie that his order to throw a fight ruined Terry's boxing career:

"...What do I get? A one-way ticket to Palookaville. You was my brother, Charlie... You should have taken care of me better... I could have had class. I could have been a contender. I could have been somebody, instead of a bum, which is what I am, let's face it. It was you, Charlie..."

Waterfront swept the Oscars, including: Best Picture, Actor (Brando), Supporting Actress (Eva Marie Saint), Cinematography (Boris Kaufman), Original Screenplay (Budd Schulberg) and Director (Elia Kazan).[29] In the 1940s, Kazan directed the Broadway debut of Arthur Miller's *Death of a Salesman* and Brando in *A Streetcar Named Desire* (as well as 1951's screen version), James Dean in 1955's *East of Eden* and Warren Beatty in 1961's *Splendor in the Grass*. Yet, despite his stellar work, Kazan's probably best remembered as "notorious, an 'informer,' a 'squealer,' a 'rat,'" as Kazan's own memoir put it.

When the Motion Picture Academy awarded Kazan a Lifetime Achievement Oscar in 1999, critics protested. Abe Polonsky declared, "I'll be watching, hoping someone shoots him... When he goes to Dante's last circle in hell, he'll sit right next to Judas." Upon hearing that 94-year-old Kazan had died on September 28, 2003, Ed Asner thought, "Snitching must be good for longevity." Nat Segaloff, vice president of the American Civil Liberties Union's Hollywood chapter, said, "I'm ashamed to say I sang, 'Ding Dong, the Witch is Dead.'" Just weeks before his death, PBS broadcast a documentary on Kazan and Miller. In 1988's *A Life*, Kazan wrote he "was the bone of contention." He remains so, even in death. If there was an Oscar for the Most Hated, it would have been awarded to Kazan. Why was Kazan arguably Hollywood's most detested man?

In 1952, he informed on Communists to the House Un-American Activities Committee (HUAC). Rubbing salt in the wound, he justified his squealing with a self-serving ad in the *New York Times*. Half a century later, Kazan's naming of names remains resonant, amidst repression targeting artists opposing the Iraq War/occupation and Bush. Against the USA PATRIOT Act/Homeland Security backdrop, attempts to rehabilitate Senator Joe McCarthy are especially chilling.

---

29. In late 2004, to commemorate the film's 50th anniversary, Sony Pictures Classics re-released *Waterfront* with a new 35mm print restored from the original negative and digitally re-mastered sound, featuring Leonard Bernstein's Oscar-nominated score.

Bernie Gordon's letter to the *L.A. Times* initiated the protests against Kazan's 1999 special Oscar, spurring the formation of the Committee Against Silence, which Gordon co-chaired. CAS launched a media offensive; hundreds demonstrated outside the awards ceremony. When Kazan received his statuette, "Only about a third of the audience stood and applauded," Norma Barzman quoted Sophia Loren as saying. Nick Nolte, Ed Harris, Steven Spielberg, Tom Hanks, David Geffen, Sherry Lansing and Roberto Benigni sat—some on their hands—protesting. "It was okay to give him an award for his work as a director—nobody objected to that," stated Gordon, author of *The Gordon Files*, about the F.B.I.'s 20-year surveillance of him. "But to give him an award for Lifetime Achievement on the Academy's [broadcast], was to say: 'America approved of what this stool pigeon did.'"

"Kazan's' 'Lifetime Achievement' was destruction of wonderful people," insisted Barzman. "The Carnovskys, Brombergs and other Group actors, those beautiful people... They'd been so good to Kazan... Blacklistees really felt destruction of health—not just careers—marriages, children... Kazan did a very evil thing... I found Kenneth Turan's *L.A. Times* piece [after Kazan's death] so objectionable, really awful. He said blacklisted critics of Kazan have 'mindless vindictiveness' and 'simplistic blame,'" complained Barzman.

"On one hand, we have to be vigilant not to allow any kind of blacklisting to ever happen again," WGA's Riskin cautioned. "On the other, we can't be alarmist and claim blacklisting's happening, unless we know it is." Artists aren't being hauled before congressional committees. Garofalo appeared in *Wonderland* and as of this writing is an Air America talk show host. Asner played Santa in *Elf*; Penn and Robbins co-starred in Republican Clint Eastwood's *Mystic River*. Their performances won each artist an Oscar that—in addition to honoring their bravura acting—were, perhaps, also designed to make the outspoken stars more reprisal-proof. It's harder to not cast an actor who has won that cherished golden statuette, moviedom's ultimate seal of approval and box office mojo.

However, Barzman warned: "What's happening today is worse, much more dangerous and frightening than McCarthyism. Corporate America's taken over the administration and media. There's few places where you can say what you believe... The Bill of Rights is under fire." Barzman added there were no mass detentions/deportations during the McCarthy era, nor holding prisoners incommunicado without charges. "McCarthyism never got so extreme," Lees also noted.

Betrayal is the theme of *On the Waterfront*. Like Kazan, screenwriter Schulberg was an ex-Communist who informed. According to the 2002 documentary *Dziga and His Brothers*, cameraman Kaufman first had to deny he still had living relatives in Russia before he was allowed to shoot *Waterfront*—even though his brothers, the great Soviet filmmakers Dziga Vertov and Mikhail Kaufman, were still alive in the U.S.S.R. In *Waterfront* Brando/Terry testifies against mobster "Johnny Friendly"—played by friendly witness Lee J. Cobb—and raises pigeons (an explicit reference to "stool pigeons").

Kazan tried projecting himself into Terry. But unfriendly witness Bobby Lees pointed out, "A whistleblower sacrifices the good of himself for others. Brando was a whistleblower—at great risk, for the union's benefit, he exposed gangsters." Lees added, "Kazan thought of himself as a whistleblower… But an informer sacrifices everybody for personal gain. Kazan profited by snitching."

Kazan denied career/money motives, but continued working openly in Hollywood—unlike many others refusing to name names. Kazan fancied himself to be Terry, but in reality, he was closer to Charlie, who sold his brother out. To paraphrase Terry: "It was you, Kazan…"

Kazan's informing cost more than his reputation—it psychologically plagued him throughout his life. When he was pressed about informing in Jeff Young's 1999 *Kazan: The Master Director Discusses His Films*, Kazan blacked out.

When congressional grand inquisitors asked Ring Lardner: "Are you now or have you ever been a member of the Communist Party?" he wittily replied: "I could answer it, but if I did, I would hate myself in the morning." Kazan arguably spent the rest of his life hating himself in the morning, afternoon and night. Despite his aesthetic achievements, instead of having "class" and being "a contender," Kazan took a dive, becoming "a bum." Like all of today's would-be blacklisters, censors, muzzlers, prosecutors and persecutors, Kazan bought a one-way ticket to Palookaville.

Green Party presidential candidate Ralph Nader during a press conference in the Long Beach Arena at one of Nader's last presidential campaign rallies in 2000.

Actor Ed Asner. (Courtesy of Ed Asner)

Comic Bill Maher and Playboy publisher Hugh Hefner check out an exhibit at the 2004 induction of Hef into the Hall of Fame of the Erotic Museum on Hollywood Boulevard.

EPILOGUE

"The fault, dear Brutus, is not in our stars,
But in ourselves, that we are underlings."

— William Shakespeare, *Julius Caesar*, Act I Scene II

THE POPULAR FRONT AND "ANYBODY BUT BUSH"

"This is the most important election of our lives."

— Senator John Kerry at a Wisconsin campaign rally, November 1, 2004

"We need an anti-Bush united front."

— Professor Cornel West on "Hardball," September 15, 2004

During WWII, the Big Three—Roosevelt, Stalin, Churchill—were the public face of the war against fascism. "It's easy to imagine FDR and Stalin as being part of the Popular Front," Professor Howard Zinn said. "It's harder to imagine Churchill, who's the most conservative of the three, and a long-time British imperialist. And a person, in fact, who—unlike FDR—was deeply suspicious of and hostile to Stalin and the Soviet Union... Only can imagine him being drawn closer to the Popular Front of FDR and Stalin by the exigencies of the war, and the need to win the war."

Regarding the "anybody but Bush" movement, the people's historian went on to say, "I think there is a parallel with the Popular Front. The desperate need to build a coalition against the right-wing in the United States and against fascism abroad created the urgency for this Popular Front. And what's happened today is that the coming to power of George Bush, and his immediately plunging the country into two wars in three years and his actions in beginning to curtail civil liberties and create an atmosphere of fear in the U.S.—the urgency created by Bush's policies I think has led to what you might call a Popular Front," Zinn said.

When the Iraq War began, and shortly before his *Bowling for Columbine* Oscar win, Michael Moore expressed this sense of urgency at the Americans for Democratic Action's annual Eleanor Roosevelt awards dinner at the Beverly Hilton: "My fellow Americans cannot survive... Bush, Ashcroft, Cheney, Rumsfeld for another four years."

At the National Lawyers Guild's June 2004 awards dinner in Los Angeles, Brian Becker, a member of the steering committee of A.N.S.W.E.R. (Act Now to Stop War and End Racism) said: "There's a real fear regarding Bush... so it's natural that people will have the idea that anybody but Bush would be better than Bush, because he seems so bad. And that's a natural and understandable reaction..."

As the 2004 election came to an end, Hollywood pulled out all the stops with an entertainment blitz. Bruce Springsteen performed along with other musicians at a series of "Vote for Change" concerts and events, drawing crowds of up to 80,000 people to Kerry rallies. Michael Moore's "Slacker Tour" stumped for Kerry/Edwards on college campuses. Danny DeVito and Rhea Perlman volunteered to chauffeur Florida voters to the polls in a minivan. Leonardo DiCaprio, Alfre Woodard and Larry David also went to the Sunshine State to uncurb voters' enthusiasm. The Buckeye State's get-out-the-vote organization Bring Ohio Back sponsored bus tours of actors such as Fisher Stevens and former *Melrose Place* co-star Chad Lowe, plus the Oscar-winning producer of *American Beauty*, Bruce Cohen, in that swing state. Martin Sheen, Brad Pitt, Josh Hartnett and "The O.C.'s" Ben McKenzie rallied college students for Kerry at Ohio, Missouri, Iowa and Oregon. Screenwriter Ed Solomon, who wrote *Charlie's Angels*, *The In-Laws* and *Men In Black*, gambled on Kerry in Las Vegas. Jeremy Kagan, who directed two classics about the '60s/'70s, "Katherine" and "Conspiracy: The Trial of the Chicago 8," campaigned in Arizona and Wisconsin, where he manned the phones for ACT. On October 18, Sally Field and Mimi Kennedy staged Tony Kushner's work-in-progress *Only We Who Guard the Mystery Shall Be Unhappy* at the Ricardo Montalban Theatre in Hollywood, as a benefit for Progressive Democrats of America and Progressive Majority. The night before the vote and on Election Day, Robert Redford's Sundance Channel aired a Robert Greenwald-palooza: *Unprecedented*, *Uncovered* and *Unconstitutional*, as well as *Bush's Brain*. On MTV, and on the "Saturday Night Live" broadcast the Saturday before the election, Eminem rocked the vote. So did Russell Simmons and P. Diddy, who told young people "vote or die." And so on.

But on November 3, cable TV's Mystery Channel appropriately played the 1983 adaptation of Ray Bradbury's *Something Wicked This Way Comes.* In the end, the entertainment emissaries' campaigning was in vain. Not even the Boston Red Sox's exorcising of the curse of the Bambino could save this doomed candidacy. There would be no Hollywood happy ending.

The discrepancy between the early exit polls that buoyed the hopes of Democrats and depressed Republicans (Karen Hughes reportedly told Bush he'd lose) with the officially announced tallies remains unexplained. Three Democratic congressmen demanded a GAO investigation into the disparity. Susan Sarandon appeared on the season finale of "Real Time With Bill Maher" (Noam Chomsky was also on the November 5 show) and raised the specter of voter irregularities. Barbra Streisand gave $10,000 to filmmakers working on a feature-length documentary called *Votergate,* which is, among other things, investigating allegations of electronic voter fraud and irregularities. According to Ilene Proctor, a publicist for the Hollywood left, another documentary, *Electile Dysfunction,* directed by Penny Little, also explores whether the 2004 election was tampered with.

But assuming that the Rove State had not put in the big fix and stolen the election again via touch screen computers that left no paper trail, etc., the Democrats had nominated two miserable excuses for candidates. And left-coasters eager to dump Bush had dutifully gotten behind the Kerry/Edwards ticket with their fame, fortune and talent. But even the performers' star power couldn't compensate for the two losers selected as the Democrats' standard bearers.

Which son of privilege and private schools should the masses vote for? Which Skull and Bonesman? Which professional politician? Which multi-millionaire? As *Rolling Stone* observed: "Kerry's background doesn't seem all that different from... Bush's."

The Republicans had a point when they criticized Kerry for trying to be all things to all people, for striving to be on all sides of an issue (although, of course, Bush, too, changed positions). After serving two tours of duty in Vietnam, Kerry became a leader in the antiwar movement. He and Edwards both voted to authorize Bush to use force in Iraq to remove those mythical WMDs, and then—when Howard Dean gained steam and seemed like he could win the Democratic primaries—Kerry out-Deaned Dean. He suddenly got religion and returned to his third-of-a-century old antiwar roots. Then, upon winning the nomination, Kerry moved rightward again. Towards the end he went hunting for gun votes in full daffy duck hunting regalia.

During the campaign Kerry vowed that—unlike the 2000 electoral debacle—every vote would be counted this time around. On election eve, he even sent Edwards scurrying out in the wee hours while Ohio hung in the balance to promise to ensure that every vote would count and be counted. But within 12 hours, while Ohio's provisional and absentee votes lay uncounted, and two other states had not reported their results, Kerry threw in the towel.

Kerry lost the presidential race the second he started his acceptance speech by declaring at the Democratic National Convention that he was "reporting for duty," and saluted. He went on to extol his militaristic service, and based his campaign on being a "war hero." The DNC based much of the presidential race on Kerry's Vietnam record, compared to Bush's (or lack of). Kerry said: "Bring it on!", presuming that his "heroism" in combat would outshine Bush's fearful fleeing into the National Guard in order to avoid going to 'Nam.

What was Kerry's point? That because he had actually fought in an imperialist war and possibly committed war crimes, while Bush cowered on the home front in the Guard, that he was more likely to win another war of aggression in Iraq? That he was more of a militarist and macho man than Bush or the oft-deferred Cheney? Kerry went on to call for expanding the Army by 40,000 soldiers, and for actually widening the war in Iraq by suckering our allies to joining us in the Big Muddy. (Mothers in Germany, France, etc., may have breathed a sigh of relief when go-it-alone Bush was reelected.) When asked if—knowing everything that we now know about WMDs, Saddam's nonexistent ties to 9/11 and al Qaeda, etc.—if he would have voted the same way, Kerry said he still would have authorized Bush's use of force. What's wrong with this picture?

The junior senator from Massachusetts then went on to stubbornly defend his vote by saying that Bush did not act in accord with the letter of the resolution authorizing Bush's use of force. What's Kerry's point? That he was gullible enough to not only believe Bush's remarkable lies (minus a shred of a little something prosecutors like to call "evidence"), but that he actually trusted the man in the White House who many believe had stolen 2000's election to abide by Senate stipulations? Was Kerry so naïve that he didn't know anything about the Bush family's murky record? As a senator who'd investigated the Iran-Contra scandal and Bush Sr.'s role in it, this is highly unlikely. What is probable is that the candidate did what was merely politically expedient at the time.

Basing his campaign on the Vietnam War proved, like that imperialist invasion itself, to be yet another lost cause. Kerry was slimed by the so-called Swift Boat Veterans for Truth (even though Ed Asner tried to defend Kerry's lost honor by narrating a MoveOn.org campaign commercial that sought to set the record straight). Kerry's service was probably defamed and misrepresented, but his heroics were successfully questioned, particularly in the battleground states targeted by the ads. Although the book *Unfit for Command* was almost certainly begun prior to Kerry's running largely on his combat record, Kerry committed the cardinal sin of people who are way too pleased with themselves when he boasted: "Bring it on." Like Bush's retort aimed at the Iraqi insurgents attacking American troops—"bring 'em on"—there was hell to pay. In Bush's case, the subsequent deaths of U.S. soldiers. In Kerry's case, a costly advertising blitz that diminished his stature as a warrior. (The important lesson to be learned: Never taunt powerful enemies.)

During the presidential debates, there was arguably more time wasted on debating not the merits of the Iraq War itself, but whether or not Kerry supported the war and Bush's policies of aggression. Once again, the American people were distracted from debating the real issue—war vs. peace—by squabbling over what Kerry's actual position was. Masters at changing the subject, Kerry handed the Republicans a monumental distraction on a silver platter. Another wasted opportunity.

Why didn't Kerry have the courage to run not on his warrior record, but on his antiwar record? Why didn't he argue, in unambiguous language, that unlike Bush, he firsthand knew the hardships and horrors of combat? That war is, at best, a last resort for self-defense when all other recourses have been completely exhausted? That it was his love of country as a true patriot that led him to oppose not only the Vietnam War, but the one in Iraq, too? That the government had lied regarding WMDs, Saddam's ties to 9/11 and Osama, and that in order to save more American lives, we had to immediately pull out of this deceptive, brutal war?

In an interview at the National Lawyers Guild's June 2004 annual awards dinner, A.N.S.W.E.R.'s Becker insisted, "Kerry is certainly not an antiwar candidate. He's made that clear. It's not conjecture on my part... that's his position. You can't really support Kerry and assert that's an antiwar position." James Lafferty, who's also in A.N.S.W.E.R.'s steering committee and is executive director of the Guild in L.A., added: "There's a very big danger [in the anybody but Bush mentality]... If you feel you must vote for Kerry, do so. But get your tennis shoes out, because you're going to be marching after he's sworn in as president against the war in Iraq and perhaps elsewhere too, because he's not a man of peace."

Because Kerry stood for nothing—except that he was not Bush—he and Edwards failed to rouse and inspire the citizenry. Almost half of all Americans eligible to vote—around 100 million!—didn't even bother to register and/or cast their ballots. As Nader complained shortly before Election Day, Kerry and Edwards should have been tearing that "corporation disguised as an individual" apart, mercilessly flaying Darth "Halliburton" Cheney with his flagrant conflicts of interest. The GOP contenders were such easy targets, the Democrats should have been handily picking them off.

Another of Bush's endlessly repeated lies was that Kerry was the most liberal senator. In fact, Kerry and Edwards not only both voted to authorize Bush to go to war, but voted for the PATRIOT Act. So did their fellow senator, Hillary Clinton. Much was made of the Democrats' hauling of her husband away from his heart surgery recovery for some last minute politicking, as if he was some sort of magic bullet, but, according to John Pilger in *The New Rulers of the World*:

"In academic literature and the media, Bill Clinton was described as 'center left,' a denial of the historical record. During the Clinton years, the principal welfare safety nets were taken away and poverty in America increased, an aggressive missile 'defense' system known as 'Star Wars 2' was instigated, the biggest war and arms budget in history was approved, biological weapons verification was rejected, along with a comprehensive nuclear test ban treaty, the establishment of an international criminal court, a worldwide ban on landmines and proposals to curb money laundering. Contrary to myth, which blames his successor, the Clinton administration effectively destroyed the movement to combat global warming. In addition, Haiti was invaded; the blockade of Cuba was reinforced; Iraq, Yugoslavia and Sudan were attacked."

As Ed Asner told me, "Clinton didn't give us healthcare. He didn't reduce our militarism." With liberals like this, who needs reactionaries?

And so, to use GOP—and Fox News—parlance, the flip-flopper flopped. The 21st century version of the Popular Front failed. Hollywood progressives rallied behind candidates (installed, by the way, as nominees with the votes of a small number of Americans) who proved to be losers. But as Cassius said in *Julius Caesar:* "The fault, dear Brutus, is not in our stars, but in ourselves..."

The fault is in profoundly flawed electoral systems designed not to express, but rather to thwart, what Rousseau called the popular will of the people. In the final round of France's 2002 election, millions of French *gauchistes* rallied and campaigned not for a fellow leftist, but for conservative Chirac against far right Le Pen. In 2003, although large majorities of their populations opposed attacking Iraq, putative democracies such as the UK, Spain, Australia, etc., opposed the will of their people and supported the war. What kind of democracies are these, where the masses march to the left but the governments march rightwards?

INCITATUS: BUSH UNBOUND

"I fear for this country if George Bush is reelected."

— Ed Asner, in a 2004 interview with the author

"This is going to be a bad time for civil rights and liberties."

— NAACP Chairman Julian Bond on "Democracy Now's"
post-election broadcast, November 3, 2004

After the contested 2000 election, Bush took office promising in his inaugural speech to "reap the whirlwind" (perhaps the only promise he ever kept). The loser of the popular vote, who'd been installed by Supreme Court justices (including Clarence Thomas, appointed by Bush's daddy), went on to rule as if he'd received a mandate. By the end of his first term, in addition to the executive branch, the Republicans controlled both houses of Congress, and held sway over the judiciary, as well as much of the media. Purportedly winning both the popular and electoral vote in an election which the typically spineless Democrats challenged for only about ten hours or so, Bush crowed at his first post-election press conference: "I earned capital in the campaign, political capital, and now I intend to spend it."

But does Bush really have a "mandate" in a country where about 100 million people eligible to vote didn't go to the polls? If you combine nonvoters with those who voted for Kerry and other candidates, even if you believe the announced tabulations, Bush (like Reagan before him, but minus the landslide) received the votes of about one in every four or five citizens eligible to vote. Bush supposedly won the popular vote by 3.5 million—which is precisely the number of votes he lost the 2000 popular vote by, if you combine the Nader and Gore voters. Precious little was made of this margin then. And in Ohio, assuming that the tallies were kosher, if only 67,000 voters had cast their ballots for Kerry, Bush would have lost the Buckeye State's electoral votes and the election. In reality, a sitting president during wartime barely squeaked through—with the help of who knows what dirty tricks. Bush "won" with the smallest margin of victory of an incumbent president since Woodrow Wilson in 1916.

In any case, with the apparent imprimatur of the first presidential majority since his father's election in 1988, the legitimization of winning minus Supreme Court installation, increased majorities in both houses of the legislative branch, plus the prospect of reshaping the Supreme Court and judiciary, America and the world are now faced with Bush unbound. (Chief Justice Rehnquist ailed as he swore Bush in for a second term, and the retirement of other aging judges looms.) Perhaps the only thing that kept the Bush/Cheney empire from totally striking back had been the need to win a second term. Now that they have it, for the next two to four years, Bush may be able to operate without the usual checks and balances that limit chief executive power. Without the countervailing force of the Soviet bloc, Bush is also largely unchecked on the international stage. To be sure, Iraqi insurgents challenge the limits of U.S. power and hegemony, as do al Qaeda and other likeminded terrorist challengers. But the Arab and Muslim countries are not formally arrayed in an anti-Washington alliance, as the Warsaw Pact nations were before the end of the Cold War.

What does Bush unchecked mean? Domestically, the complete liquidation of New Deal and welfare state reforms. Massive deficits will deliberately bankrupt the hard-fought-for gains of the past, such as Social Security, pensions, the 40 hour week and so on. The only essential service the government will offer is so-called security. The militarism that is bankrupting America at home also promises ever-expanding imperial adventures and empire abroad, as U.S. Incorporated hunts down the newest terrorist *du jour*, just the latest of our endless, eternal enemies. (Note that the Homeland Security color coded alert system has no color for "all's clear.") All this will incite more attacks on America, and the ever expanding limiting of our civil liberties and rights in the name of "national security."

What is the real Bush project? With their pedigree of princes, Puritans and pilgrims, F. Scott Fitzgerald could have been describing the Bushes in *The Rich Boy* when he wrote: "Let me tell you about the very rich. They are different from you and me." The Bushes' regal genes go back to England's Henry III and Charles II, and France's Robert I, according to *Burke's Peerage* publishing director Harold Brooks-Baker. George W. Bush "is closely related to every European Monarch both on and off the throne," including Queen Elizabeth II, Dutchess Sarah "Fergy" Ferguson, plus the late Queen Mother and Princess Diana, Brooks-Baker asserted.

According to the Mayflower descendants' newsletter *Scuttlebutt*, Bush is descended from Mayflower pilgrims on both his maternal and paternal lines. Puritan Robert R. Livingston, who came to America in 1673, is also an ancestor of the Bushes, whose "heritage intertwined with some of the great landowning families of colonial New York and New England." While everybody knows the 43rd president is son of the 41st president, Queen Elizabeth's 14th cousin, George W. Bush, is also related to the 14th U.S. president—Franklin Pierce, who served 1853-1857—on the side of mother Barbara (born a Pierce).

As Bush told Bob Woodward in his 2002 *Bush at War.* "I'm the commander—see, I don't need to explain—I do not need to explain why I say things. That's the interesting thing about being the president. Maybe somebody needs to explain to me why they say something, but I don't feel like I owe anybody an explanation."

If there is such a thing as genetic memory (or maybe he was just raised with what Professor Mark Crispin Miller called "a metaphysical conception of the nation as picked specially by History, or Providence, to dominate the world"), the Bush project is a restoration of divine right monarchy. Bush's bizarre alliance with fanatical "Christian" right zealots and extremist Likud-niks is evidence of his regime's theocratic aspirations. Their conundrum, however, is how to implement a medieval theocracy under the guise of a constitutional republic in the 21st century. Be that as it may, the Bushes, of course, will be the dynastic rulers of this empire.

History will liken the ascension of the *idiot savante* Bush to the throne to that of Rome's lunatic emperors like Nero and Caligula. Or, more precisely, to Caligula appointing his favorite horse, Incitatus, as a Roman senator, complete with golden stall and senatorial robes.

Even before returning to power, the Bush Justice Department fired the opening salvo a few weeks before the election, announcing an investigation of the NAACP and its tax exempt status. The venerable civil rights organization was being investigated because of comments its Chairman Julian Bond had made about the Bush White House in a highly critical speech. The message—and endgame—couldn't be clearer. And on the foreign front, Bush signaled his intentions by immediately escalating the Iraq War with Operaton Phantom Fury, the invasion of Fallujah—the biggest Marine-led urban combat since Vietnam.

Poor old Karl Marx. In *The Communist Manifesto* he wrote: "[T]he bourgeoisie has at last, since the establishment of Modern Industry and of the world market, conquered for itself, in the modern representative state, exclusive political sway. The executive of the modern state is but a committee for managing the common affairs of the whole bourgeoisie." But Marx and his 1848 treatise are oh-so-*passé* in the 21st century.

To be sure, the re-election of Bush is a disaster. But to use the old Marxist parlance, it sharpens the contradictions, and presents certain prospects and opportunities.

OF STARS AND MASS MOVEMENTS

"If you say the heart and soul of America is found in Hollywood, I'm afraid you are not the candidate of conservative values."

— George W. Bush, Republican National Convention speech, 2004

Moving forward, the Hollywood progressives and the left in general must ask what the role of the former in people's struggles is? According to the National Lawyers Guild's Jim Lafferty: "The celebrities will show up at the demonstrations. They don't help build it... They helped us get... TV time and notice that perhaps we otherwise would not have gotten from the corporate press. When 110,000 people marched down Hollywood Boulevard [on February 15, 2003], yes, there were some stars there, but those people were brought there by the 'grunts' [who] passed out flyers, going to union halls [and] classrooms [and] churches... That's what brought people there. The fact that the message may have been heard by more Americans is certainly in part owing in those early stages to the Hollywood personalities or elected officials who showed up." Lafferty cited former "Sopranos" co-star John Heard, whose latest film, *My Tiny*

Universe, premiered at 2004's AFI Film Festival, as one of the unsung but most committed of the politically engaged actors.

At NLG's 2004 awards dinner in Los Angeles, I interviewed Brian Becker, who'd replaced a then-ailing Ramsey Clark as a presenter. Becker belongs to the steering committee of A.N.S.W.E.R., which played a key role in organizing antiwar demos in New York, Washington, L.A. and elsewhere. Becker cited Susan Sarandon, Jessica Lange, Ossie Davis, Danny Glover and Martin Sheen as "being involved like other voices throughout the U.S. who are taking a stand of conscience against the war. I think it's important to, in some ways, not differentiate the voices of Hollywood personalities... from the voices of other people, because they are people. They represented the voice of public opinion, but certainly there's a great number of people in the Hollywood community who have stepped forward to say that they, like so many millions of Americans, don't allow the Bush administration to speak in their name. They were conscious of the fact that their recognition in the public eye would help bring an antiwar message to a larger part of the audience, of the people... Certainly, the media does focus on the celebrities...

"My point is that the celebrities have to be seen as part of a larger tapestry, they're part of the fabric of the U.S.," Becker continued. "They're not a separate class unto themselves. And while they're using their, perhaps, authority or recognition in order to parlay a message... they're joined in that effort by millions of other Americans. You find doctors, lawyers, trade union leaders and clergy who are famous to a smaller community... and as they themselves come into political activity, they become a voice for the antiwar movement. They bring that community with them and become a voice for that community... There are many activists and leaders in the grass roots who have a smaller stage—the celebrities have a larger stage... and for that, we're very grateful.

"The antiwar movement was conscious that those who are in the entertainment business have a particular role to play... We as organizers were reaching out to people who had that sort of stature... in order to bring that message to a larger part of the population. There's a certain kind of familiarity that the people have with celebrities... Part of the organizing strategy has been to reach out to all of those who could strengthen and enhance the movement. Certainly, those in the Hollywood play a major role," stated Becker, who added that he was "not aware" of left-coasters donating money *per se* to the cause.

As for what Hollywood's progressives should do, Howard Zinn stated: "They should play a role that their conscience suggests to them. They should not be inhibited by the fact that they are in Hollywood and people will point to them and say, 'oh, famous people shouldn't participate in politics.' No, they should behave like citizens and be absolutely bold about using their fame and the fact that they're well known to speak honestly about what they believe and there's nothing wrong with them participating. In fact, I think they have a responsibility to participate in the public debate around the war and other issues. Some of them are showing the way. When Tim Robbins and Susan Sarandon and Sean Penn—going to Iraq, coming back and writing about it. All of that. Hollywood people are citizens, and they should speak their minds."

WHAT DOES "PROGRESSIVE" MEAN IN THE 21ST CENTURY?

"We all want progress, but if you're on the wrong road, progress means doing an about-turn and walking back to the right road; in that case, the man who turns back soonest is the most progressive."

— C.S. Lewis

Left-coasters and the left-at-large also need to define and understand what "progressive" *means* in the 21st century.

America's level of political discourse is now so low that it's common for words and terms to be thrown around with imprecise definitions and meanings. For instance, in 2004 Bill O'Reilly took Arianna Huffington to task on "The Factor" for associating with "bomb throwers of the left" such as Molly Ivins and others of her ilk, whom he lumped in the same category as Fidel Castro, likening columnists to communists and satirists to guerrillas. This is an Orwellian exercise in language, that seeks to use words in order to obscure—rather than express—meaning.

In our degraded philosophical lexicon, foremost among these vaguely used words is "progressive." Its root, of course, is "progress." There is, perhaps, only one negative use of this word, as in "you can't stop progress." This usually refers to over-development of diminishing and overwhelming nature. Joni Mitchell expressed this concept well when she sang, "They paved paradise and put up a parking lot." But as a general rule, "progress" is a word that expresses a positive and forward-looking outlook that contains the notion that things will improve and get better. That workers will get more and more benefits, higher and higher wages, work less and less hours, and so on.

However, the term is often used interchangeably with "liberal." Since the Reagan era, the "L" word has been denigrated and almost relegated to the status of the "C" word (for "communist"). Hence, in this usage, a progressive attempts to be a liberal without all of the negative connotations and heavy baggage that the right has heaped upon the word. I asked the *Nation*'s editor Katrina vanden Heuvel what the difference is between the two:

"The difference between liberals and progressives—there's long traditions of progressivism and liberalism. On some core issues there's terrific overlap. What's sad about our current culture is that too many liberals don't take their own side in arguments, and don't lay out some of the great triumphs of 20th century liberalism, from the Voting Rights Act to… women's suffrage. The main difference is too often liberals construct a political system which involves top down organization. Whereas progressives, more often, believe ordinary people have the right, wisdom and good sense to organize their own politics, and build movements from the bottom up. It's more inclusive," Katrina said.

The author of *A People's History of the United States* put progressivism's progression into historical context. "The word progressive doesn't enter the political vocabulary very much until the 20th century," Zinn related. "The Socialist Party was very powerful. The Populists were the big left, anti-corporate power in the late 19th century. The Socialist Party was the big anti-capitalist party in the early 20th century. And the word progressive really wasn't used until… 1912, when Theodore Roosevelt ran as a third party candidate under the label of the Progressive Party. But the Progressive Party as led by Theodore Roosevelt was not as radical as later versions of the Progressive Party.

"In other words, the word progressive meant different things at different times. Theodore Roosevelt himself was an imperialist, a lover of war, a supporter of the Spanish-American War, the war in the Philippines and [gunboat] diplomacy in the Caribbean. But he had kind of liberal, reformist policies domestically… portraying himself as a trustbuster, anti-big business. The word progressive was attached to the party that he ran on. It wasn't very far left, it wasn't too far to the left of the Democratic Party.

"In 1924, however, when Robert LaFollette ran under the Progressive Party, it was somewhat different. Because LaFollette—unlike Theodore

Roosevelt—had not supported war. In fact, he had been one of the out-spoken opponents of American entrance into World War I. And LaFollette on domestic issues was pro-labor and pro-workingman. So the 1924 Progressive Party was much closer to the contemporary idea of progressive than it had been in 1912.

"And the LaFollette idea of progressivism was carried even a little further to the left in 1949 when Henry Wallace ran as a Progressive Party candidate against Truman and Dewey, and Wallace represented a kind of anti-Cold War position. Calling for peace and friendship with the Soviet Union, and better, more regulation of corporations at home and more rights for working people. That is the history of the Progressive Party and progressivism," Zinn said, noting that the 1912, 1920 and 1948 parties bearing that name were actually different political entities.

Zinn went on to say, "What a progressive with a small 'p' is, is a little different... Naturally, somebody like Bill O'Reilly will take anybody who is slightly liberal or progressive and try to attach them to anarchists and communists and socialists and all of that. But there is no Progressive Party today, there is no progressive movement today. The word progressive, of course, is used. And many people use the word progressive to describe their own views. It's very close, very close to the idea of a liberal but probably a little stronger, a little farther to the left. There are liberals who are like Democrats... and have fairly welfare state, New Deal ideas about domestic policy, but who are still hawks on foreign policy. In fact, the Democratic Party itself has been very much like that. To the left of the Republican Party on domestic issues, but actually going along, joining the Republican Party on foreign policy. So that kind of liberal is so different than I think people who call themselves progressive today are, people who are critical of American foreign policy. And who also have strong views about militarism, and the military budget, and the way American resources are being used, and the way the environment is being depleted. It's a very loose term. There is no actual group of people who belong to a Progressive Party or movement. That's what the word means in the year 2004," asserted Zinn.[30]

---

30. While we're at it, the terms left and right originate in the French Revolution. In 1789, the representatives of the third estate—comprising workers and merchants—sat on the left, while representatives of the nobility sat on the right. In essence, the left stands for the rights of the many, the right-wing for the privilege—from the French, for "private law"—of the few.

The role progressive Hollywood played in the antiwar and anti-Bush struggles provides a clue as to what it means to be "progressive" in 21st century America. When Robert Greenwald and Mike Farrell created Artists United to Win Without War, they did so because the Democrats failed to lead and oppose as an opposition party is supposed to. Even though Farrell was a longtime Kerry backer (who regretted the senator's pro-war vote), he and Greenwald found that they had to go beyond the two-party system, to transcend the Democratic Party, in order to spark resistance to the Iraq War.

The tidal wave of dissident documentaries, plus the new wave of progressive features, proceeded in a similar way. John Sayles told me, "*Silver City* was something that we decided to make pretty much in a political vacuum. We just did not see anything in the conversation, and a lot of what the movie is about, quite honestly is, what I see as the failure of the mainstream media to deal with what's been going on in the country." Michael Moore often said that after viewing *Fahrenheit 9/11* (which was, by the way, screened on broadcast TV in Europe on election eve, although it was banned on pay-per-view in the land of the free), audiences always remark that they never saw on television news much of what's in the documentary. When the corporate, mainstream media failed to inform the public with the facts, and gave Bush a pass, with cameras in hand, progressive filmmakers rose to the task.

Both off- and onscreen, progressive Hollywood advanced in the same way. Liberals believe social problems and war and peace issues can be solved by putting the liberal—or what Governor Dean humorously called the "democratic"—wing of the Democratic Party into power. However, Hollywood progressives found that to pursue a people's, pro-peace agenda, they had to go beyond the powers-that-be, in both government and media circles. Whether mobilizing antiwar resistance through marches in the streets or via informative films, left-coasters had to do so separately from, and independent of, the extant political and news machinery. Including acting outside of the Democratic Party—even its liberal faction.[31]

Bush said, "you're either with us or against us," and progressive Hollywood opposed the man who would be monarch. Just as Bush's war policies spurred the largest political demonstrations in human history in

---

31. It was a telling moment in the presidential debates when Kerry stated that the only ones in the room who benefited from Bush's tax cuts for the rich were both candidates—and the media moderator.

2003, the following year about 500,000 demonstrators—the largest number of people to ever protest a U.S. political convention—marched against
the Republican National Convention in Manhattan. At the peak of the
biggest demo organized by United for Peace and Justice, it was so crowd-
ed that it took marchers an hour to walk a city block. More than 1,700
protesters were arrested (and held under dubious conditions) during the
RNC convention—around triple the 589 protesters who were arrested during the Democratic Convention in Chicago in 1968.

Inspired by a desperate desire to depose the tinhorn Texan tyrant, left-
coasters joined forces with the "anybody but Bush" movement and got
behind the Democrats, and its putative (not-so-) liberal wing. But whether
or not the election was a preordained Rovian fix, the 21st century version
of the Popular Front was a losing strategy. And as we prepare for the
inevitable sequel, Hollywood progressives must learn the lesson of their
failures, as well as their success, in the antiwar and anti-Bush causes.

The lunacy of the American electoral system was quintessentially
revealed by the Nader/Camejo independent campaign. On the one hand,
you had candidates who appeared "presidential" but had voted for the war
and PATRIOT Act, and did not support rapid withdrawal from Iraq. On the
other hand, you had a consumer advocate who'd spent his life fighting the
good fight, opposed the Iraq War and PATRIOT Act, and supported a rapid
end to America's occupation of Iraq. His running mate had actually run for
president on the Trotskyist Socialist Workers Party ticket in the 1970s. Yet
true-blue, dyed-in-the-wool progressives not only backed and voted for the
party to the right of the independent candidates, but in some cases vigorously, even vehemently, opposed Nader/Camejo—almost to the point of
demanding that they be denied their constitutional rights to run. (However, on the "Real Time With Bill Maher" that aired on October 29, 2004,
Kevin Costner effusively praised Nader, and said that if he had "the balls,"
he'd vote for Ralph.)

But the fault is not in the stars—rather it is in a deformed winner-
takes-all (how American!) "electoral dictatorship" (as Nader called it) that
coerced honest people who were eager, anxious, to oust Machiavelli's monkey to support the lesser of two evils—instead of a champion of the people
whose life was devoted to fighting for their well-being. And whom most progressives, by the way, actually *agreed* with—unlike Kerry/Edwards.

To be progressive in 21st century America means to change this system so that it becomes a more popular, participatory, people's direct

democracy. And to do so means organizing and acting independently of the corporate-owned and financed lesser evil of the two-party duopoly. The left begins where the liberal wing of the Democratic Party ends. Progressive Hollywood had succeeded in tapping into masses of protesters and viewers by acting autonomously of the Democrats.

Historically, leftists rarely miss an opportunity for infighting—whether Trotskyists vs. Stalinists, or Nader and Camejo vs. Cobb and the Green Party. But progressives need to unite around their common interests with a pro-people's agenda, and aside from occasionally pressuring its liberal wing or trying to split it off, to avoid the Democratic Party, where—as the Greens' presidential candidate David Cobb said—"progressive ideas go to die."

As the Iraq War began, Michael Moore told the SCADA's annual Eleanor Roosevelt awards dinner: "We need Bush removal... I don't think we can leave it up to the Democratic Party."

During the campaign, celiberals listened to Democrats like Stanley Greenberg, and representatives of ACT and the Media Fund, who basically proselytized that the path to victory was via strategizing how to win for the Democratic Party a few swing voters here and there in the battleground states. But instead of tinkering around the edges, progressives need a bold new program that eschews the failed two party system. Greenberg is precisely wrong when he contends that there are two Americas—there are at least three Americas, if you include the approximately 50% of all Americans who are eligible to vote but don't exercise their franchise—circa 100 million-plus citizens. (This doesn't even include the non-citizens, underaged, felons, ex-felons, etc., who live in America and don't have the right to vote.)

Do the Democrats really feel that they can rally non-voters so estranged from the political system and candidates that they won't spend a few hours once every four years to register and vote by ballyhooing the 2.2% income growth of 1995-2000, as Clinton apologist Greenberg documented? Does John Kerry think he'll get the youth vote out by promising that 40,000 more Americans will serve in the Army—and possibly die in Iraq and God knows where else? Who do the Democrats think will make up those 40,000 soldiers—senior citizens or combat age youth? If Kerry hadn't turned his back so much on his long ago antiwar activism, he might've remembered that the high watermark for the youth vote was in 1972—when newly enfranchised 18-year-olds, *et al*, helped win peace candidate George McGovern the Democrats' presidential nomination.

James Lafferty, the former national National Lawyers Guild (which had represented the Hollywood Ten) director and current NLG executive director in L.A. and host of KPFK's *The Lawyers Guild Show*, said: "Between now and the '30s, the differences between the two parties are not what they once were... Clinton got more money from Wall Street than Dole did... Money plays such a role in politics today that both parties are beholden to the same corporate interests, on whose behalf the quest for oil in Iraq or a greater U.S. empire is being fought. That's why you have the Kerrys along with the Bushes only differing really on how to do it."

On November 6, 2004, MichaelMoore.com printed a report about a mini-spree of post-election student protests. At Syracuse University, film major Jason Tschantre said: "Forget the Democratic Party. Kerry failed me." The college's Democrats had nothing to do with the campus protest. Freshman Ryan O'Leary stated, "They're just standing by and doing nothing."

A.N.S.W.E.R. organizer Becker added: "If you look through American history... the thing that really has stopped wars, led to social change and caused progressive reforms... has very little to do with who's in power... and everything to do with how many people are in the streets... The composition of the Congress that passed the '64 Civil Rights Act... was identical to the congress that existed in 1954 that maintained Jim Crow... The politicians didn't change... the thing that changed from 1954 to 1964 was that people came into the streets. And that fire that started at the grass roots made it so irresistible that even the same reactionary politicians had to give. So my perspective for the peace movement is along the same lines—not so much who's in the White House, but how many people are outside the White House, organizing, demonstrating."

Instead of Clintonites, the left needs kryptonite to fight the right. And as far as all the post-election babble about sending the Dems back to bible school to get in tune with red state middle America's so-called "values," here's a few scriptural values that are not based on the end times, Book of Revelations and Armageddon:

"Thou shalt not kill"; "Blessed are the peacemakers"; "Peace on Earth"; "Love thy neighbor"; "Love thy enemy as thyself"; "Thou shalt not lie"; "It shall be easier for a camel to pass through the eye of a needle than for a rich man to enter heaven"; "The meek shall inherit the Earth," etc.

When Jesus preached about "the salt of the Earth," he wasn't referring to CEOs. Would the Christ who healed the lepers favor universal healthcare? Would the Prince of Peace who advocated turning the other cheek pursue an arrogant, aggressive foreign policy or the beating of missiles into plowshares? Would the messiah who healed the disabled and preached about caring for the least of those among us advocate tax cuts for the rich or for universal healthcare? Yes, what would Jesus *really* do? Will the real Prince of Peace please stand up? And so on. As Liberation Theology practitioners have pointed out, today the social agenda and program of the Gospel would be a radically pro-poor, pro-peace politics.

Whether publishing Lenny Bruce's autobiography, a *Playboy* interview with the Black Panthers, bailing American Indian Movement leader Russell Means out of jail or writing his longtime monthly column in *Playboy*, Hugh Hefner has long championed free expression and liberal causes. Shortly before the election, at his induction into the hall of fame of Hollywood's Erotic Museum, I asked the Playboy philosopher-king what he thought of the Bush administration, Ashcroft, the PATRIOT Act and the Iraq War. Hef said he wouldn't vote for Bush and gave a somewhat visionary response:

"Terrorism is a very real problem and 9/11 changed the nature of the world. Why our response to that was attacking Iraq was a little unclear to me. I think it probably fuelled the problem, more than solved it. We live in one very small planet. And most people have very similar dreams. They have to do with family, and hopefully staying in harmony with one another, harmony with the planet itself.

"The things that separate us—nationalism, ethnicity, religion—the things that keep us apart are the hurtful part. What we need to find— because we have come to a place on this planet in which we have the science and the technology to make this to some extent a heaven on Earth, or to destroy one another, and to destroy the planet. In a very real sense, we have the technology and science, but we still are superstitious, savages in the jungle. I think that's very, very sad. We need to be dealing with the world in a much more rational, humane and loving way," Hefner stated.

As Bin Laden warned in his chilling pre-election video: "No-one except a dumb thief plays with the security of others and then makes himself believe he will be secure. Whereas thinking people, when disaster strikes, make it their priority to look for its causes, in order to prevent it happening again... As has been said, 'An ounce of prevention is better than a pound of cure'... I tell you in truth, that your security is not in the hands of Kerry, nor Bush, nor al Qaeda. No. Your security is in your own hands. And every state that doesn't play with our security has automatically guaranteed its own security." Those who ignore the threats of a mad mass murderer who has successfully eluded them and continued to wreak mayhem do so at their own peril.

COMPASSIONATE CREATIVITY

> *"Why do writers write? If you have empathy for people, if you're a humanist, you won't write something anti-black or anti-Semitic, you'll write something good for society. As a human being and writer, you're going to be progressive."*

— Robert Lees, blacklisted screenwriter, in an interview with the author

"The general public ought to ask themselves why so many fine artists... tend to be... humanists," James Lafferty stated. "One cannot be a fine artist without understanding the human condition. If you [do], then you're going to oppose wars... be in favor of freedom of speech and artistic expression, against PATRIOT Acts and for working people, because after all, most actors themselves, even those who are now rich, spent lots of time waiting tables and were unemployed."

Ed Asner has long been one of the Hollywood left's most consistent and courageous champions of the oppressed, and has at times even bravely described himself as a socialist. In the 1980s, his stance as S.A.G. president opposing the Central America policies of Reagan—a former S.A.G. president himself—precipitated the demise of Asner's CBS series "Lou Grant," which had emerged out of one of television's most wildly successful sitcoms, "The Mary Tyler Moore Show." In a candid interview with the thoughtful actor, Asner said that while he's sometimes paid to appear on TV programs to promote various entertainment projects, he was unpaid for his appearances on political subjects such as the Iraq War on news-related shows like "Hannity and Colmes."

"It always costs you when you take a stand on something controversial, because as an actor you're appearing on TV or radio taking a position that some of those listeners will totally be opposed to," Asner said. "So that automatically begins to cut down those people who may— for instance, when I did [2003's] *Elf*, I got two letters... saying they wouldn't take their kids to see me as Santa Claus, because of what I represented. It saddened me... I feel sorry for the kids, because it's a lovely movie... You can witness the disinformation that goes on, with the right-wing control of the media, the discrediting of any progressive performer, the smarmy comments about Streisand... because they automatically degrade, defame and, I suppose, cause those performers and their viewpoints to be discounted. People across the political rainbow probably resent performers getting out there and talking about issues or politics. Feeling 'what gives them the right? Where did they get the knowledge that they can stand there and talk to us?'... In many cases, they're certainly better equipped to carry the battle flag for these causes than most of the politicians, because they at least have the passion for it," Asner asserted.

Where does this "passion" come from? Given the beating talents receive for taking controversial stands, why do they subject themselves to running the gauntlet? What is it about the artistic temperament that causes so many creative people to identify with the downtrodden? Why do disproportionate numbers of artists try to help the underdog?

"Well, the underdog is generally he who suffers from lack of freedom of speech, lack of ability to congregate, as he should be able to," replied Asner. And in a witty reference to the hammy side of the acting profession, Asner pointed out that his fellow thespians love drama and conflict and to be the center of attention.

But on a more serious note, playwright, professor and historian Howard Zinn said, "I think artists in general are better able than the ordinary citizen who is kind of trapped within the boundaries set by the culture... to sort of step outside of the given culture, outside the traditional wisdom and to transcend the orthodox and to think independently. They're not part of the business world. Of course, the arts are inevitably connected to the business world and dependent on the business world. But they're not as tied into the business world and dependent on it as other people are. Very often, because of their talent and fame, they have a certain independence, which emboldens them to speak out.

"And I think there's a special sensitivity among artists. The very fact that artists very often have to play roles in which they empathize with other people, and have to put themselves in other people's positions, that also enables them to think outside the box. Also, art is an international phenomenon. Artists travel overseas, and make movies overseas... they're

Actress Rena Owen. (Courtesy of Rena Owen)

not as nation-bound, they're not as nationalistic. They communicate more often and better with people in other countries. That enables them to see American policy with a more critical eye," Zinn said.

Mimi Kennedy, a co-star of the "Dharma & Greg" sitcom, said: "We've been happy. Somewhere along the line our needs have been met. And we decided the world was a safe place for us—[in] early childhood. Consequently, it was safe to look around. Concurrent with that were other things that weren't so good. Maybe not enough attention. Maybe something that made us project outwards into other people's minds and bodies, and we learned what they felt like on the inside. I really believe it might be hardwired...

"Artists have empathy. We came into the world and enough of our needs were met, and we moved to the next level. Which is, it's safe to think about this place and safe to imagine in this place. We're not watching our backs, we're not being hit upside the head, we're not [having] our wits knocked out of us. We are intact and allowed to imagine. After that things weren't perfect. [Laughs.] Obviously, because many of the distorted personalities of artists... from the despair of a Vincent Van Gogh to the machinations of some of our celebrities today. We're not perfect, but we do have empathy," insisted Kennedy, who played Dharma's mom Abby, a quintessential '60s protester perhaps named after Abbie Hoffman, who is not unlike the offscreen Kennedy herself, one of progressive Hollywood's most stalwart activists.

According to Rena Owen, who played the abused wife who triumphed over adversity in the acclaimed *Once Were Warriors*: "It has a very empowering ending. I wasn't surprised by *Warrior*'s international success... because it dared to deal with these social issues that had been in our closets for too long. And everyone was dying to go: Waaah! And it opened that door... in a very confrontational scene. Many people said to [director] Lee [Tamahori], 'Don't shoot that domestic violence scene.' He stuck to his guns. He said, 'If I just shoot the sound, and then you see the bruises, you don't get the point. I want to show the horror of what domestic violence looks like.'"

Owen went on to say: "It's always been the way and the responsibility of the artist. I've always seen writers as recorders of history. We have the ability, because it's within the creative confines to push boundaries, to question. It's always been the function of the artist. I've always felt that. To me it's nothing new, it's been happening century after century, where people have dared to question the establishment. It is the place for it—music, literature, film. Always has been. We have kind of a license and the obligation to come from it—because most artists will tend to be driven by humanity as a whole."

Artists have compassion for ordinary people and their suffering because "Art is the heart," Owen said. "We tend as human beings to operate more out of our hearts than the theory of the intellect. That's my summation." Owen discussed the connection between acting and empathy: "You've got to be that person. I don't like the word, 'pretending.' What makes a good performance is you... absolutely being that character... You've absolutely got to have empathy, because you've gotta love this character. As bad as they are, your job is not to judge them, your job is to justify them. As an actor, if you start to judge your character, you're in trouble. You have to justify their existence... At the end of the day, most artists have a passion for people, for humans, for the evolution of the human spirit, of the human species, of human behavior. Most artists are fascinated by human behavior. That's where you get your inspiration from. So you've gotta be a lover of the species. Empathy also comes out of the fact that most artists are very hypersensitive. So you have to have a sensitivity towards whom you're portraying."

Owen went on to say: "Am I gonna support and try to raise up the 97% of our population that are down and out?... I don't know, it's always been a part of who I am, I go for the underdog, as opposed to propping up a façade that serves nobody."

IN THE BEGINNING: THE BIRTH OF EXPRESSION

"The task I am trying to achieve is above all to make you see."

— D. W. Griffith

In Hollywood's beginning was D.W. Griffith. Griffith said let there be light, and there was light.

More than any other American filmmaker, Griffith created the visual language, lexicon and art of moving pictures, and established Hollywood as the West Coast movie colony. Griffith is credited with the artistic development of the close up, intercutting, fades and other cinematic techniques. After years of shooting shorts, in 1915 Griffith directed a full-length film that did boffo box office. After a special White House screening of it, President Woodrow Wilson supposedly said it was "like history written in lightning." But *The Birth of a Nation* sparked protests then and remains so controversial that in 1999 the Directors Guild of America stripped Griffith's name from its highest honor, now called its Lifetime Achievement Award. And in 2004, outrage and threats forced the Silent Movie Theater near Hollywood to cancel an August 9 screening.

At a subsequent *L.A. Times* private screening of the film and a contentious roundtable discussion about it, *Boondocks* cartoonist Aaron McGruder, who co-authored with filmmaker Reg Hudlin a graphic novel also called *Birth of a Nation*, stated: "People died because of this film... If this was 1915, and I had some position of authority, I would have stopped the movie from being seen. I'd have dragged all the filmmakers out in the street and shot them."

Much has been written about Griffith's egregiously racist views of the antebellum South, the Civil War and Reconstruction. The Kentuckian's epic fixed racial stereotypes of "darkies"—from the "Mammy" to the "buck" to the "tragic mulatto" and so on—in the collective psyche of audiences. Furthermore, based on *The Klansmen*, Thomas Dixon's work of historical fiction (emphasis on the latter), *The Birth of a Nation* glorified the Ku Klux Klan. The night riders are depicted as heroic hooded defenders of lily-white womanhood and a white civilization that faced becoming gone with the wind, as Margaret Mitchell would later put it in another popular racist masterpiece. Chillingly, *The Birth of a Nation* was reputedly used as a recruitment tool for the KKK, which experienced a remarkable rebirth during the 1920s.

Griffith and his film would be easy to dismiss, and relics long forgotten to history, except for two facts. In terms of strictly aesthetics, *The Birth of a Nation* is undeniably an artistic masterpiece of storytelling (certainly for 1915!)—no matter how deeply harmful, deceitful and flawed that story admittedly is. *Birth* holds a unique place in the motion picture pantheon because of the powerful role it played in galvanizing film as an art form, more than any other single movie of its day. Its form is as accountable for its sheer power as its content is. If it wasn't so well made, *The Birth of a Nation* might have been just another silent movie shot on nitrate stock that dissolved and vanished. Indeed, *Birth* set the high-water mark for silent picture propaganda until Sergei Eisenstein's *Potemkin* was released a full decade later in the Soviet Union.

The other reason why Griffith is remembered is because, surprisingly, he also directed some of the silent screen's most progressive classics. In 1909, he lensed the short *A Corner in Wheat,* a decidedly anti-capitalist allegory about farmers and speculators. Although the U.S. cinema strangely has a dearth of pictures about the American Revolution, Griffith directed many shorts set during the War of Independence, culminating with a full-length patriotic classic, 1924's *America.* But his most progressive picture was released in 1916 as a response to and sort of *mea culpa* for the criticism Griffith rightfully received for the despicable racist content of *The Birth of a Nation.*

In answering his critics, *Intolerance* sought to tell the story of man's inhumanity to man, "love's struggle throughout the ages." This theme was told in four unfolding stories from different epochs, intercut with each other. The four unfolding stories told in parallel time are: the fall of Babylon, the passion of the Christ, the St. Bartholomew's Day Massacre of the Huguenots in France and a modern day story about an industrial strike and unjustly imprisoned worker who faces execution. The U.S. military shoots down striking proletarians in the latter story, also known as "The Mother and the Law."

Pouring all his vast profits from the *Birth* blockbuster into *Intolerance,* in the Babylonian sequences, Griffith reconstructed a full-scale replica of parts of Babylon.[32]

---

32. Kenneth Anger and others derived the nickname "Hollywood Babylon" from this classic's gigantic sets reproducing the Mesopotamian city, which live on in the gigantic elephants and Babylonian *leitmotifs* constructed at the new Highlands mall in contemporary Hollywood, where the Oscar ceremony is held. Ironically, Babylon was located in what is now Iraq.

In addition to decrying religious persecution and class warfare, *Intolerance* has an idealistic ending, with soldiers on a battlefield dropping their rifles. As World War I raged, this pacifist message was a bold plea for peace, and to keep America out of the barbarism engulfing Europe.

But the lengthy film—the director's cut was reputedly eight hours long—and *avant garde* technique of weaving together four separate stories from different countries and eras unified by a single theme kept the audiences who flocked to *The Birth of a Nation* away. The picture's progressive perspective as America neared entering WWI probably also depressed box office. The film was only a smash hit in one country—the newly formed Soviet Union. But the Bolsheviks didn't believe in copyrights and royalties, so Griffith lost his shirt on *Intolerance*. If shot today on the same epic scale of Griffith's original *piece de resistance*, an *Intolerance* remake would probably be the most expensive production in cinema history.[33]

The politics of Griffith's output varied for the rest of his career, veering from the reactionary viewpoint of *Birth* to the progressivism of *Intolerance*. In a letter, Lillian Gish once tried to explain to me that Griffith's political inconsistency was primarily due to his being an entertainer who worked in a popular mass medium. In any case, in 1918, almost certainly in collaboration with the U.S. military, he made the WWI propaganda flick *Hearts of the World* starring the Gish sisters. But the following year, he directed the exquisite London-set *Broken Blossoms*, about the doomed friendship of a Chinese Buddhist (Richard Bathelmess in yellowface), and a frail blind woman (Lillian Gish). Perhaps still striving to make amends for the harm he'd caused with *Birth*, *Broken Blossoms* is an explicit plea for religious and racial tolerance and understanding. 1920's *Way Down East* re-teamed Miss Gish and Barthelmess in a melodrama critical of puritanical religious fundamentalism. And so on.

Today, 90 years after the release of Griffith's Civil War epoch, Hollywood filmmakers have a choice. They can follow the Griffith who made *The Birth of a Nation*. Or they can pursue the path of the D.W. Griffith who directed *Intolerance*. As the old song goes, artists have to decide: "Which side are you on?" Hollywood talents must decide. They can't do both.

---

33. It was surely poetic justice that Griffith did not get to keep his ill-gotten gains from the racist *Birth*, and that his fortune was spent on a progressive movie about class struggle, social injustice, religious fanaticism, etc.

Part of *Birth*'s enduring legacy is racism, and the celluloid stereotypes that Griffith pioneered continue to bedevil modern movies. After her stunning success in *Once Were Warriors*, Maori actress Rena Owen moved from New Zealand to L.A. but found it hard "to cross the cultural barriers here in Hollywood... I've often missed out on roles because I am mixed blood, because I am part-Polynesian, and they don't know quite where to place me... There is a need in this town to come in boxes, and I don't come in a box... Robert DeNiro and Al Pacino don't always play Italians, they just play characters... Even when you look at black actors, the only ones who have been able to achieve that are Morgan Freeman and Denzel Washington... Sci-fi is a good genre for me, because I have an unusual look and voice. I fit in this world of futuristic aliens." Tinseltown has cast Owen as the demi-goddess Dinza in the WB series *Angel* and in two *Star Wars* movies. (*Whale Rider*'s Keisha Castle-Hughes also appears in *Episode III— Revenge of the Sith*.)

Cynda Williams' screen career was launched by Spike Lee when she played Denzel Washington's lover in Lee's 1990 *Mo' Bettah Blues*. "Spike was very important. In the '60s/'70s, films were being made with and by black people, and then it dried up for a while. So him coming back, and opening up the doors to a wider audience... was very important," Williams asserted in an interview with the author.

The NYU film school grad not only helped revive African American filmmaking, but during the moribund Bush Sr. years also injected an essential element of black militancy and nationalism into the national debate. 1989's pull-no-punches *Do the Right Thing* powerfully reflected the then racial tensions in New York after the modern day lynchings of African American youths in Bensonhurst, Brooklyn and Queens, as well as the contentious Tawana Brawley rape allegations. In *Do the Right Thing*, Lee's character—Mookie—triggers the riot by throwing a garbage can through the window of Sal's (Danny Aiello) pizza parlor, which he delivers pizzas for.

Lee's near-masterpiece *Malcolm X*, starring Washington in an uncanny, Oscar-nominated portrayal of the charismatic nationalist leader, appeared on the screen during the same year as the Rodney King-related L.A. riot in 1992—the biggest civil disturbance in 20th century American history. The 2000 *Bamboozled* was Lee's scathing attack on the Jim Crow caricatures that have endured onscreen since the racist *The Birth of a Nation*.

As would be expected, Lee spoke out against invading Iraq. In a front page story featuring separate photos of fellow NYU film school graduate

Martin Scorsese and Lee, *Variety* reported that Lee joined the co-stars of his *25th Hour*, Ed Norton and Rosario Dawson, in openly condemning an attack on Iraq. The February 12, 2003 comments were made at the premiere of Lee's feature at the Berlin Film Festival—days before the massive antiwar rallies that produced the largest protests in human history. The same article said Martin Sheen, Sean Penn, Dustin Hoffman and New Zealand director Jane Campion also publicly opposed the war.

Lee's opposition to and disdain of U.S. policy in Iraq continued. According to the right-wing website WorldNetDaily.com, at a May 8, 2004 lecture in Seattle, Lee reportedly called Secretary of Defense Donald Rumsfeld a "gangster." Regarding the Abu Ghraib prison abuse scandal, Lee sarcastically said: "So we liberate people so we can torture them. I like that." On the subject of those missing WMDs, Lee reportedly quipped, "They will find Jimmy Hoffa first." Lee also expressed surprise that the Bush administration hadn't killed Michael Moore yet, and asserted that Disney's decision to not distribute *Fahrenheit 9/11* was due to outside pressures from above. Lee went on to tell the Seattle audience: "We live in very serious times now. We're living with the ramifications of the last presidential election. We all got hornswoggled. Run amok. Led astray. Bamboozled."

These critical comments are all to be expected from one of America's most controversial filmmakers—but his 1999 filming of recruitment ads for the U.S. military at Hawaii are *not*. According to a Native Hawaiian crewmember who spoke to me on conditions of anonymity, Lee's 40 Acres & A Mule production company was one of three bidders for the Navy commercials. The ads consist of scenic shots and pseudo-documentary footage of Lee interviewing U.S. Naval personnel. Lee's questions are along the lines of "the same old theme—join the Navy and see the world," said the crew member.

The *LA Weekly* reported in a July 1999 cover story that Lee's U.S. Navy spots are "A bit of an eyebrow raiser: Lee has said more than once that he would refuse to endorse whatever he considers morally reprehensible in the context of black folks, like malt liquor and cigarettes. The armed forces seems like a possible offender—blacks are certainly over-represented, and not entirely in a good way." (And—one might add—like alcohol and tobacco, war kills.)

Defending his Defense Department agitprop, Lee told the *Weekly*: "The Navy provides people with the money to get an education... People who are floundering, who have no direction, no discipline... I'm not saying join for life, but when they get out they're in a much better spot than they were before."

At a 2003 screening of *25th Hour* at the Directors Guild of America on Sunset Strip, I respectfully took Lee to task for being a Pentagon propagandist. He rationalized his production company's active seeking of the DOD contract and outbidding of competitors on the grounds that blacks had made an enormous contribution to the armed services over the years.

Lee countered that since the Civil War, the military presented African Americans with civil service opportunities for job and educational advancements. I asked him: "What would Malcolm do?" I implored Lee to not put his undeniable talent up for sale to and at the service of U.S. militarism. We'll never know how many impressionable and educationally/economically-limited blacks were influenced by Lee's recruitment propaganda to join the military, nor how many of them went on to be wounded or even die in a war that Lee later opposed.

Dave Robb, who reported for the Hollywood trade publications for 20 years, asserted in his 2004 book *Operation Hollywood: How the Pentagon Shapes and Censors the Movies*, that the DOD provides free or low cost access to military hardware and personnel to filmmakers in exchange for script control. In order to get freebies, screenplays must serve the military's purposes of recruiting and retaining personnel, and projecting a positive image so that the Defense Department can continue to get vast congressional appropriations.

Robb declared, "Hollywood has two roles to play." Noting that "It's a big economic advantage for producers to make a pro-war, pro-military movie," Robb added: "Half of Hollywood are pro-war cheerleaders. Jerry Bruckheimer, John Woo for caving in on *Windtalkers*; John Wayne." I asked Robb if any of them had served in the armed services. He replied: "I know John Wayne did not... I never heard Bruckheimer and Woo did..." Nor did Sylvester "Rambo" Stallone or Spike Lee, despite the fact that all of them profited by ballyhooing the military.

For Robb, Tinseltown's "villains include Pentagon film office head [Phil] Strub [who has overseen screenwriting and production in order to ensure recipients of DOD largesse are pro-military]. Bruckheimer, who caved into military demands more than any other Hollywood producer... Walt Disney, who allowed the Pentagon to shape "The Mickey Mouse Club." [Jack] Valenti, who allowed the military to pre-screen films at his offices... Wayne, who

[made] a propaganda film for the military, [1968's] *The Green Berets*... Pro-war movies seem to be gaining more box office appeal. After 50 years of being saturated with movies and TV shows with military propaganda... the movies have conditioned Americans to be more warlike," lamented Robb.

The longtime *Hollywood Reporter* and *Variety* staffer went on to describe the other role Hollywood filmmakers can play "as antiwar pro-testers. There have been many antiwar movies made... Hollywood can be an antiwar conscience of America, as in *Fail-Safe, Dr. Strangelove, Paths of Glory, Born on the Fourth of July*... There would be lots more antiwar movies and fewer pro-war movies if the producers weren't given economic incentives to create pro-war movies...

"[Vietnam veteran] Oliver Stone has received no assistance I know of... He requested assistance on *Platoon* and was turned down... and says they actually tried to stop his movie... Stone is a hero for refusing to change his scripts to get military assistance... Other heroes are Kevin Costner for refus-ing to tone down General Curtis LeMay in *Thirteen Days*, Clint Eastwood for *Heartbreak Ridge*, Robert Aldrich who fought the military in the 1950s over *Attack*... Victor Millan [the Latino co-star of 1955's *Battle Cry*, whose best performance ended up on the cutting room floor, due to the Red Scare and Pentagon pressure] is the actor most hurt by all this," insisted Robb, who added that an antiwar film has never received Pentagon support.

Stone has pursued the progressive path of the Griffith of *Intolerance*. Indeed, in what appears to be a nod to that masterpiece, he, like Griffith, reproduces Babylon in all its glory, hanging gardens and all, in 2004's *Alexander*, a timely rumination on empire and expansionism in the ancient world with strong parallels to the Bush imperial agenda. Like Alexander the Great, Bush the minor invaded Asia Minor, that is, Iraq, as well as Afghanistan, on a "civilizing" crusade to impose a Western political system.

At a December 9, 2004 event featuring Oliver Stone at the L.A. Coun-ty Museum of Art, I asked Stone what Hollywood progressives should do during a second Bush administration. Intriguingly, the *JFK* and *Born on the Fourth of July* director seemed to invoke Griffith's language in his reply: "Make entertaining movies, and include your *tolerance* and humanitarian-ism. Keep reminding the world that Hollywood is a big place that tolerates all breeds and all kinds. And to make great ideas that everybody in the world wants to see," Stone declared to an ovation from the audience. He also lamented that given the current warfare in Iraq, Americans had not learned the lessons of that long ago war he'd fought in in Indochina.

A.N.S.W.E.R.'s Becker added: "I believe a majority of people... have complete opposition to or deep skepticism about Bush's foreign policy. If there wasn't so much pressure applied on cultural workers as they tried to express the problems that average people face, or the feelings and sentiments of average people, there would be even greater production of antiwar materials in the culture."

As Malcolm X's one-time disciple, boxer Muhammed Ali, said when Uncle Sam tried to draft him: "No Viet Cong ever called me 'nigger.'" Spike Lee and all Hollywood filmmakers have to make a choice. As the old song goes: "Which side are you on?" They can take the Pentagon's money and be the new Leni Riefenstahls, propagandizing for the militarists and corporatists. Or they can take an independent path, like talents such as Charlie Chaplin and Stanley Kramer. They can make the films that glorify the Nazis' Nuremburg rallies, or those that mock fascist demonstrations and extol the Nuremburg trials that tried mass murderers for crimes against humanity. They can either follow the David Wark Griffith of *The Birth of a Nation* or of *Intolerance*—but they can't do both.

THE OPPOSITIONAL CULTURE: UNACKNOWLEDGED LEGISLATORS

"The cinema is truth 24 frames per second."

— Jean-Luc Godard

Two other "branches" of governance can limit, and even defeat, the Bush attempt to reestablish a modern day version of empire and divine right monarchy. In 1821, Percy Bysshe Shelley wrote about the first:

"Poets are the hierophants [i.e., the interpreters of sacred mysteries; ones who explain or make commentary] of an unapprehended inspiration; the mirrors of the gigantic shadows which futurity casts upon the present; the words which express what they understand not; the trumpets which sing to battle, and feel not what they inspire; the influence which is moved not, but moves. Poets are the unacknowledged legislators of the world."

Hollywood progressives put their bodies on the line during antiwar protest marches. Left-coasters provided a public face and badly need voice to the forces of peace. They attracted attention to candidates and causes, and donated generously to them, as individuals and as a collective industry. But their greatest gift and contribution to society is their ability to skillfully express and communicate to mass audiences. This is both their greatest promise to the people, and their direst threat to the powers that be.

Whether Kerry or Bush won, the left-leaning John Sayles had "the same message: keep the fire burning... Politicians are only as good as we can force them to be. [Laughs.] And it doesn't matter whether they're Democrats or Republicans. They're not really gonna serve the people, unless the people force them to do that... If there's a way that you can get a bigger platform by using whatever your art is, do it. Just try and tell the truth. Even that is pretty revolutionary sometimes."

"Art is the spearpoint of the progressive world," said Ed Asner in an interview with this author. "It helps achieve the advances that hopefully we'll all accept and march around with. Art opens doors... Who did the dictators work against first? Art, communications, the newspapers. Censorship is the first evil for fascism... I don't think our people are well-informed. I don't think our newspapers... and TV do sufficient jobs. So if we wish to further the ideal of information, art is certainly one of the last bastions of truth."

Asner went on to say, "We need an enormous amount of progressivism to get this country weaned away from its militarism, to attack its corporate greed... to give its people adequate healthcare, education. We are creating a bottom mass in our pyramid which is less educated, less cared for medically, less employed beneficially and we need some of the greatest progressivism in the world to pull us out of this quagmire that we sink further and further into."

A.N.S.W.E.R.'s Brian Becker said, "A culture that reaches people—not simply as a packaged, slick, commercial entity—is culture that really reflects the aspirations of people and the problems they're having. And takes the problems of everyday life and gives some deeper understanding or context for problems... The cultural workers... who do that best are the ones who reach people and touch them most... Artists have always had a key role. People are moved frequently by music or a poem or painting more than they are by a political speech... Any vibrant people's movement that reflects the grass roots has political leaders, cultural leaders, those who use every medium to express the will of the people."

Popular culture is one of the last spheres not completely under the thumb of the Bush administration, and as long as the First Amendment remains the law of the land, may it ever be so. Progressive Hollywood has already embarked on its most important work: resurrecting progressive content onscreen. Sometimes it appears in unlikely places—even on a Rupert Murdoch-owned network and TV show.

Dan Castellaneta, the voice of Homer Simpson, was interviewed at the National Lawyers Guild's 2004 dinner in L.A., where he presented guerrilla artist Robbie Conal with an award. The actor, who got his start in the Second City comedy troupe, said that according to "Matt Groening, one of the underlying messages of 'The Simpsons' is that authority figures don't always have people's best interests at heart. Even George Bush. These are people we hired to do a particular kind of a job and they sometimes get the impression that it was there to take—it was given to them—and if they abuse it, it should be taken away."

The critical and commercial success of *Fahrenheit 9/11*, *The Day After Tomorrow* and *The Motorcycle Diaries* (a low budget foreign film that had earned $55 million by this February 2005) prove beyond dispute that receptive audiences are there for left-leaning documentaries and features alike. At the screening of *The Assassination of Richard Nixon* during the American Film Institute's annual film festival, director Niels Mueller asserted that "*Fahrenheit 9/11*'s an important film because it shows that there's an audience for films that tackle difficult subject matter... There's an audience for films that are relevant, there's probably a longing for it... People want to see films that talk about their lives and the world they're living in."

The steadfast Ed Asner proclaimed, "Artists should try to stimulate progressive ideas, either when they produce, or by accepting the roles in casting... I've often said that the best Nazis in Hollywood were often played by Communists or extreme progressives... and Jews, certainly. So that by doing the best job, either in projecting the villain or the hero, or the values of that particular person or non-values, they execute the job."

In this book, I have focused on pro-people's pictures. To be sure, although this is a significant and growing segment of Hollywood's output, it is a minority. Much of what comes out of the studios is escapist fare, primarily aimed at making a buck at multiplexes in malls and—all too often—at a 14-year-old male demographic and mindset. Many movies have, as previously noted, pro-war and right-wing messages. It is therefore the role of progressive Hollywood to be a countervailing force to these types of flicks, as well as to the Bush regime's second term.

The election post-mortems stress that pro-Bush voters supposedly cast their ballots largely on the basis of so-called "moral values." Filmmakers need to be sensitive to this sensibility, and to not fill their work with gratuitous violence, vulgar language and sex. This does not mean that there should be absolutely no violence, etc.—my favorite propaganda film of all time, *Potemkin*, contains one of cinema's most riveting violent scenes, the famous Odessa Steps sequence. But Eisenstein contrived these images not for titillating kicks, but to convey the brutality of czarist oppression. Producers, directors, screenwriters, actors, *et al*, need to focus on making films that combine substance with entertainment values, instead of mere escapism and even degrading drek.

And those artists fortunate enough to have resources at their disposal should share with and invest in up-and-coming visionaries who have something valuable to say about society. I'm not his accountant, but given *Fahrenheit*'s enormous success, I'd imagine that Michael Moore alone could finance a documentary and indie mini-studio specializing in progressive productions. (He already made a point of giving away his Bush boondoggle tax cut.) However, when I asked Moore about supporting striving filmmakers, he replied: "I still haven't seen a dime from *Bowling for Columbine*."

Citing the corporate ownership of Hollywood *per se* studios and their concern over profits and not offending those who might regulate their various business interests, John Sayles doubts that many progressive features will emerge out of the studio system. Sayles said that "it's more likely" that indie filmmakers will shoot political pictures than the corporate-entrenched studios, but quickly added that they're obviously far more hard-pressed when it comes to the financing, production, distribution and release of movies. He sees documentaries as being the main sphere for politics onscreen.

During the election, producer/director Robert Greenwald said, "There are varied roles to be played. Writers, directors, producers can find—I hope—over time different ways to use their expertise. Because we do have an expertise at telling stories. As you said. There's an expertise at communicating. And I think that that's underutilized and unharnessed. MoveOn is doing this series of ads [and] I've been working with them just a little bit on "Bush in 30 Seconds II." Rob Reiner has directed one, John Sayles is doing one. It's a way to use some of the expertise in this community. But I think that's just the tip of the iceberg. There's lots of very strong creative talent here that can be harnessed and marshaled in a variety of ways, as I'm doing in a variety of different ways, to help progressive causes and progressive candidates."

Can movies change the world? Jean Renoir directed one of the all-time greatest antiwar classics, *La Grande Illusion*, which was banned by Goebbels, who prevailed upon Mussolini to likewise censor it. Nevertheless, *Illusion* won the Venice Film Festival's Best Artistic Ensemble award. Subsequently, when Renoir was asked how much effect pacifist pictures had, Renoir reportedly replied: "In 1936 I made a picture named *La Grande Illusion* in which I tried to express all my deep feelings for the cause of peace. This film was very successful. Three years later the war broke out. That is the only answer I can find..."

Nevertheless, it can be argued that the cinema can have an impact on the real world. Rena Owen, who starred in *Once Were Warriors*, has a more optimistic take. The 1994 New Zealand-made international hit about a dysfunctional Maori family and domestic violence was one of *Time* magazine's top ten films.

Asked if movies can change the world, Owen replied: "Absolutely. I don't even have to ponder upon that question, only because I've had the experience of being in a film that made an enormous difference... The themes of the film were incredibly universal. Domestic violence. Sexual violence. Alcohol abuse does not know cultural or class boundaries. It happens all around the world. Jakes [Temuera Morrison's violent character] also comes in three-piece suits or priests' costumes. So these things are very human. Hence the reason I always thought... that the film had the potential to be incredibly successful... Within a week of the film opening, it knocked *Jurassic Park* off the number one box office [spot in New Zealand and] you had lifelines, anger management groups, women's refuge groups, men against violence... you had men and women calling up all of these community support groups saying, 'I've got a *Warriors* problem'... Anybody can change themselves. There's a power to change for ourselves... You can overcome."

The Polynesian actress went on to say, "What this film did is it gave them permission to talk about some of the problems in their own lives. It gave them the password. So much so that as a result of the film a lot of companies made anti-domestic violence television commercials. It went all the way to... where the New Zealand government made domestic violence against the law. So yes, celluloid definitely has the power to change a consciousness and to make a difference. I have no doubts about that... I know that Sean Penn is a great advocate of that too, that you should go to a strip bar for entertainment, but film is about educating. I think celluloid has the ability to educate... enlighten and change," asserted Owen.

Movies such as *Born Free, To Sir With Love* and *Battle of Algiers* influenced Owen, who went on to become a public spokeswoman against domestic violence and abuse.

According to the documentary *Imaginary Witness: Hollywood and the Holocaust*, which was screened at the 2004 AFI Film Festival, after the release of the 1978 mini-series "Holocaust" starring Meryl Streep, the West German government voted to extend the laws that permitted prosecution of Nazi war criminals. And Oliver Stone's *JFK* resulted in the release of massive amounts of hitherto classified information pertaining to Kennedy's assassination.

There is no magic cure. At the most, artists can entertain, enlighten, educate and inspire audiences. As left-coasters continue the work of creating progressive pictures, hopefully they can motivate the final arbiter of our democracy to become politically active, that ultimate branch of government: the People. Progressive Hollywood can give the masses movie metaphors, visions and dreams of a better world to fight for. Films that bestow hope upon the despairing, promise to the downtrodden, solidarity to the solitary, meaning to the alienated and optimism to the pessimistic. A sense that you're not in it alone, that many others share your predicament, and somehow, by coming together to solve our common problems, we can change the world for the better. Artists can uplift the brokenhearted. Through the power and dignity of art, filmmakers can continue to generate a culture in opposition to the Bush White House, and in doing so, help ignite and spread mass resistance. For an aroused People are the world's other superpower.

The anti-corporate Asner insisted that, as far as what Warren Beatty referred to as "the 'S' word" in the witty *Bulworth*—socialism—was concerned, "I think this country can use more of it. I think it's a crime that 40 million [-plus] people in this country are not covered medically. I think it's a crime that our people—can you imagine what the $500 billion, at least, used in war and armaments would have done for the people of this country? Of course, with the Congress and president we have, that money would never have gravitated to educating, clothing, employing, housing people. It could have done it so easily—and there would have been plenty left over to feed the world when it got hungry. Had we been more socialistic, I think that would have been achieved... I do know that when more numbers of people are taken care of, it's because of socialistic methods, not capitalistic methods," stated Asner, whose favorite films include *The Best Years of Our Lives* and *Spartacus*. Regarding Santa Claus, the *Elf* co-star added: "I think he's a great idea. I think we have to create one, a real one."

In IFC's *Decade Under the Influence*, Francis Ford Coppola proclaimed: "It was the blossoming of the counterculture movement... now picked up through the dissent over Vietnam, the honest difference of opinion and questioning of our government's motives, to the civil rights movement, questioning this injustice. Then the woman's movement grew out of the political movements... Of course we thought that movies could make the world better and could illuminate contemporary life. And that artists didn't have to be employees. That artists could stand with the other leaders of society and contribute," the godfather of '70s pictures stated.

Reflecting on '70s films, in the same documentary Jon Voight waxed poetic: "No one's saying anything. Let's say something! Let's make stories about what is. There's so much going on. That's what I was going through. I was feeling... artistic," Voight said, laughing.

"Everything is linked in these discussions... The generation of the '70s, as always, was standing on the shoulders of giants," Coppola added in *Decade Under the Influence*, specifically referring to the '60s directors—like Arthur Penn, Sydney Lumet and John Frankenheimer—who emerged out of the Golden Age of television.

In the same way, the Hollywood progressives of today stand on the shoulders of their antiwar, Black Power, sexual revolutionary '60s/'70s forebears, who in turn stood on the shoulders of the Popular Front and New Deal filmmakers of the '30s/'40s generation, who won the war against fascism. In a cinematic continuum, all fought the good fights of their eras. And now, what may be progressive Hollywood's good fight looms before it.

In the aftermath of the '04 electoral debacle, the new conventional wisdom contended that the "Hollywood elite's" support for the Democrats turned red state voters off. But Moore disagrees. "O'Reilly and Hannity said: 'Get away from Hollywood.' Think O'Reilly will give you helpful advice?" Moore pointedly asked on December 2, in a Writers Bloc event at L.A.'s Wadsworth Theatre wherein the filmmaker was in conversation with *Worse Than Watergate* author John Dean.

"Bush got his sequel, now we'll have to do ours," Moore told the sold-out crowd. "The Republicans understand pop culture. It's very scary to

them. They don't know how to do it [make movies]. It drives them crazy."
In response to my question about what Hollywood progressives should do
during the second Bush administration, Moore offered a recipe for effective pro-people's filmmaking:

"There's so much talent in this town. Get busy doing what we do.
Make work that inspires. Don't make polemics. Make a good film first—
don't put the politics first. There's nothing wrong with giving great
entertainment."

Moore proceeded to cite examples from the first and second great eras
when progressive Hollywood held sway, and beyond: "Under FDR, John
Steinbeck helped get support for [New Deal] programs. Harriett Beecher
Stowe primed the pump for Lincoln. There's *The China Syndrome*. Use
comedy and humor. We need our Preston Sturges and Groucho Marxes."

The documentarian went on to say: "We have to create our own media.
When Dylan came along, radio was not playing him. It was word of mouth,
clubs, FM radio—when it was worse than UPN—[that helped make Dylan
successful]. Today there's the Internet, Air America, Gore will have a liberal [TV] network. There's always Pacifica."

Commenting on the '04 campaign, Moore said: "The Republicans out-
Hollywooded Hollywood in image creation and branding... We can't let the
Democratic Leadership Council run the Democratic National Committee.
Bob Shrum has got to go. We should not be embarrassed to run a star [for
office]... When will we run our Arnolds? Who wouldn't vote for Tom Hanks,
Robert Redford, Paul Newman? People like celebrities, they'll vote for
celebrities, no matter how many nude photos of them at drugged-out par-
ties there are. Bush equalled Gilligan."

For those daunted by the harrowing prospects of *Gilligan's Island*
reruns or a Bush second term, remember Shelley's *Ode to the West Wind*:

"...by the incantation of this verse,
Scatter, as from an unextinguish'd hearth
Ashes and sparks, my words among mankind!
Be through my lips to unawaken'd earth
The trumpet of a prophecy! O Wind,
If Winter comes, can Spring be far behind?"

The last word belongs to—who else?—the silent screen's greatest comic.
Hitler and Stalin were momentarily aligned, and anti-fascist films were

frowned down upon in Tinseltown. But during the nadir of mankind's existence, Charlie Chaplin somehow created the pinnacle of Popular Front pictures. At the end of 1940's *The Great Dictator*, Paulette Goddard plays the despairing Jewish refugee Hannah, who is terrified that the Nazis will capture her and her fellow Jews. But then, over the radio, she is stirred by Chaplin's immortal speech of hope:

"...Look up! Look up! The clouds are lifting—the sun is breaking through. We are coming out of the darkness into the light. We are coming into a new world. A kind new world where men will rise above their hate and brutality.

"The soul of man has been given wings—and at last he is beginning to fly. He is flying into the rainbow—into the light of hope—into the future, that glorious future that belongs to you, to me and to all of us. Look up, Hannah. Look up."

To quote "Chairman Mao-cluhan":

The media is the messiah.

Political power grows out of the barrel of a camera lens.

The revolution will be televised—and broadbanded, videostreamed, uplinked, downloaded, digitalized and theatrically released—and is coming soon, to a theater near you.

Note: An index for this book is available at **books.disinfo.com**

Photo credit: Harris Fogel

ABOUT THE AUTHOR

Ed Rampell has co-authored four books, including two film histories. He has reported for various media outlets worldwide, including ABC News' "20/20," The Australian Broadcasting Corporation, Radio New Zealand, *Newsweek*, AP, Reuters, *Honolulu Weekly*, *Mother Jones*, *In These Times*, *L.A. Times*, *Boston Globe*, *Toronto Globe & Mail*, *Variety* and many others. He lives in Los Angeles.